C++ High Performance

Second Edition

Master the art of optimizing the functioning of your
C++ code

Björn Andrist

Viktor Sehr

BIRMINGHAM - MUMBAI

C++ High Performance
Second Edition

Producer: Tushar Gupta

Acquisition Editor – Peer Reviews: Divya Mudaliar

Content Development Editor: Joanne Lovell

Technical Editor: Gaurav Gavas

Project Editor: Mrunal Dave

Proofreader: Safis Editing

Indexer: Priyanka Dhadke

Presentation Designer: Sandip Tadge

First published: January 2018

Second Edition: December 2020

Production reference: 1181220

Published by Packt Publishing Ltd.
Livery Place
35 Livery Street
Birmingham B3 2PB, UK.

ISBN 978-1-83921-654-1

www.packt.com

packt.com

Subscribe to our online digital library for full access to over 7,000 books and videos, as well as industry leading tools to help you plan your personal development and advance your career. For more information, please visit our website.

Why subscribe?

- Spend less time learning and more time coding with practical eBooks and Videos from over 4,000 industry professionals
- Learn better with Skill Plans built especially for you
- Get a free eBook or video every month
- Fully searchable for easy access to vital information
- Copy and paste, print, and bookmark content

Did you know that Packt offers eBook versions of every book published, with PDF and ePub files available? You can upgrade to the eBook version at www.Packt.com and as a print book customer, you are entitled to a discount on the eBook copy. Get in touch with us at customercare@packtpub.com for more details.

At www.Packt.com, you can also read a collection of free technical articles, sign up for a range of free newsletters, and receive exclusive discounts and offers on Packt books and eBooks.

Foreword

Two years ago, the first edition of *C++ High Performance* was published, and I had the privilege of writing its foreword. Then, C++17 was state of the art and C++20 was in the early stages of development. Now, C++20 is widely available for development and specification work on C++23 is underway.

C++ stepped onto the stage in 1983, and hasn't stopped reinventing itself for a single year since. It has gone from a single frontend language on top of C to a first-class citizen of the compiler world. The continued wide use, as it nears its 40th anniversary, is a testament to both its incredible depth and diverse features. Each new C++ standard has added substantial functionality—sometimes to excess. In the words of Stroustrup, "Within C++, there is a much smaller and cleaner language struggling to get out."

The problem, of course, is that the "smaller and cleaner language" to be found within C++ changes with each and every situation. Mastering C++ is akin to mastering a multitude of domain-specific languages, each tailored to a specific use. The dialect that makes sense for an embedded system is nonsensical for large enterprise applications, and the phrasing that powers a game engine is unbearable when applied to a word processor.

C++ High Performance teaches you a C++ dialect for rapidly developing high-performance code. From C++11 onward, there has been a vast array of new features in both the C++ language and the C++ STL. When applied with care, they let you spend more time writing your application and less time handling implementation details. This is the focus of the book and where it shines.

One of the biggest topics that separates professionals from journeymen in C++ is understanding, from top to bottom, what is really happening in their code. Ultimately, a programmer is responsible for driving hardware in service of their goals, and the concepts in this book will help you develop an intuitive understanding of what your code is doing under the hood. Each topic is framed in the larger context of application development and computer science. For the reader who needs to get up to speed with the latest C++ techniques on short notice, this information provides the necessary landmarks for you to stay oriented. Specific examples, recipes, and logical progressions take you from a basic use of auto and <algorithm> all the way up to using asynchronous coroutines and parallel algorithms.

Fundamental issues around modern C++, such as memory management and ownership, considerations of time and space, advanced template usage and others, are explained step by step; by the later chapters, the reader can proceed into advanced territory with confidence. Since the first edition, every topic has been revisited and expanded to be up to date with the latest standards.

I have worked on a wide variety of projects—large and small, low level and managed, and some even in custom languages I designed and built—but C++ holds a special place in my heart. My first full-time job was writing C++ code for a game technology company in the early 2000s. I loved it, not least of all because a big part of the technology revolved around the reflection of the C++ code base into the editor and scripting language. Someone once described C++ as an octopus made by nailing extra legs onto a dog, and I spent a lot of time with a hammer making our code base do things that C++ was never intended to do. Yet the octopus we ended up with was, in its own way, beautiful and very effective.

C++ has evolved tremendously since those days, and it is my privilege to open the door for you as you walk into an exciting new world of possibilities. Viktor and Björn are brilliant and experienced developers with a remarkable pedigree, and they have a lot of great things in store for you.

Ben Garney

CEO, The Engine Company

Contributors

About the authors

Björn Andrist is a freelance software consultant currently focusing on audio applications. For more than 15 years, he has been working professionally with C++ in projects ranging from UNIX server applications to real-time audio applications on desktop and mobile. In the past, he has also taught courses on algorithms and data structures, concurrent programming, and programming methodologies. Björn holds a BS in computer engineering and an MS in computer science from KTH Royal Institute of Technology.

I'm overwhelmed by the positive responses the first edition of this book has generated. The feedback has been a true source of inspiration and the major reason for me taking the time to write a second edition. Thank you to all readers and reviewers!

Without the team at Packt Publishing you wouldn't have this book in your hands. Writing a book for the Expert Insight series has been a true pleasure. Special thanks goes to Joanne Lovell, Gaurav Gavas, and Tushar Gupta.

The technical reviewers of this book have been extraordinary. Timur Doumler, the main technical reviewer, has been nothing but outstanding throughout the project. Thank you so much! Thank you Lewis Baker, Arthur O'Dwyer, and Marius Bancila also.

Last, and most of all, I must thank my family for their support and their patience, again. Thank you Aleida, Agnes, and Clarence.

Viktor Sehr is the founder and main developer of the small game studio Toppluva AB. At Toppluva, he develops a custom graphics engine that powers the open-world skiing game *Grand Mountain Adventure*. He has 13 years of professional experience using C++, with real-time graphics, audio, and architectural design as his focus areas. Across his career, he has developed medical visualization software at Mentice and Raysearch Laboratories, as well as real-time audio applications at Propellerhead Software. Viktor holds an MS in media science from Linköping University.

About the reviewers

Timur Doumler is a C++ developer specializing in audio and music technology, a conference speaker, and an active member of the ISO C++ standard committee. He is passionate about clean code, good tools, building inclusive communities, and evolving the C++ language.

Lewis Baker is a C++ programmer specializing in concurrency and asynchronous programming. He is the author of the cppcoro open-source library for C++ coroutines and has also been a major contributor to Facebook's `folly::coro` coroutine library and `libunifex` async programming libraries. He is also a member of the C++ Standards Committee and was actively involved in the standardization of the C++20 coroutines language feature.

Arthur O'Dwyer is a professional C++ instructor who maintains a blog mostly about the language. He is the author of *Mastering the C++17 STL*, also published by Packt, and is occasionally active on the C++ Standards Committee.

Marius Bancila is a software engineer with almost two decades of experience in developing solutions for the industrial and financial sectors. He is the author of *The Modern C++ Challenge* and co-author of *Learn C# Programming*. He works as a software architect and is focused on Microsoft technologies, mainly developing desktop applications with C++ and C#. He is passionate about sharing his technical expertise with others and, for that reason, he has been recognized as a Microsoft MVP for C++ and later developer technologies since 2006. Marius lives in Romania and is active in various online communities.

Table of Contents

Preface	**xiii**
Chapter 1: A Brief Introduction to C++	**1**
Why C++?	**1**
Zero-cost abstractions	2
Programming languages and machine code abstractions	2
Abstractions in other languages	4
The zero-overhead principle	4
Portability	5
Robustness	5
C++ of today	5
C++ compared with other languages	**5**
Competing languages and performance	6
Non-performance-related C++ language features	8
Value semantics	9
Const correctness	11
Object ownership	12
Deterministic destruction in C++	13
Avoiding null objects using C++ references	13
Drawbacks of C++	15
Libraries and compilers used in this book	**15**
Summary	**16**
Chapter 2: Essential C++ Techniques	**17**
Automatic type deduction with the auto keyword	**17**
Using auto in function signatures	18
Forwarding the return type using decltype(auto)	19
Using auto for variables	19
A const reference	20
A mutable reference	21

A forwarding reference 21
Practices for ease of use 22
Const propagation for pointers 22
Move semantics explained **24**
Copy-construction, swap, and move 24
Copy-constructing an object 24
Resource acquisition and the rule of five 26
Named variables and rvalues 29
Default move semantics and the rule of zero 31
Rule of zero in a real code base 33
A common pitfall – moving non-resources 34
Applying the && modifier to class member functions 36
Don't move when copies are elided anyway 36
Pass by value when applicable 37
Cases where pass-by-value is not applicable 38
Moving constructor parameters 39
Designing interfaces with error handling **40**
Contracts 41
Class invariants 42
Maintaining contracts 43
Error handling 44
Programming error or runtime error? 45
Programming errors (bugs) 45
Recoverable runtime errors 47
Function objects and lambda expressions **52**
The basic syntax of a C++ lambda 52
The capture clause 53
Capture by reference versus capture by value 54
Similarities between a lambda and a class 54
Initializing variables in capture 55
Mutating lambda member variables 57
Capture all 58
Assigning C function pointers to lambdas 60
Lambda types 60
Lambdas and std::function 61
Implementing a simple Button class with std::function 62
Performance consideration of std::function 63
Generic lambdas 65
Summary **66**
Chapter 3: Analyzing and Measuring Performance **67**
Asymptotic complexity and big O notation **68**
Growth rates 73
Amortized time complexity 74

What to measure and how?   **76**
Performance properties   78
Speedup of execution time   79
Performance counters   80
Performance testing — best practices   81
Knowing your code and hot spots   **82**
Instrumentation profilers   83
Sampling profilers   85
Microbenchmarking   **87**
Amdahl's law   89
Pitfalls of microbenchmarking   90
A microbenchmark example   91
Summary   **97**

Chapter 4: Data Structures   **99**
The properties of computer memory   **99**
The standard library containers   **104**
Sequence containers   104
Vectors and arrays   105
Deque   107
List and forward_list   108
The basic_string   109
Associative containers   109
Ordered sets and maps   110
Unordered sets and maps   111
Container adaptors   114
Priority queues   115
Using views   **117**
Avoiding copies with string_view   117
Eliminating array decay with std::span   119
Some performance considerations   **120**
Balancing between complexity guarantees and overhead   120
Knowing and using the appropriate API functions   121
Parallel arrays   **123**
Summary   **130**

Chapter 5: Algorithms   **133**
Introducing the standard library algorithms   **134**
Evolution of the standard library algorithms   134
Solving everyday problems   135
Iterating over a sequence   135
Generating elements   136
Sorting elements   137
Finding elements   137

Finding using binary search   138
Testing for certain conditions   139
Counting elements   140
Minimum, maximum, and clamping   141
Iterators and ranges   **142**
Introducing iterators   142
Sentinel values and past-the-end iterators   143
Ranges   144
Iterator categories   145
Features of the standard algorithms   **148**
Algorithms do not change the size of the container   148
Algorithms with output require allocated data   150
Algorithms use operator==() and operator<() by default   151
Custom comparator functions   152
Constrained algorithms use projections   152
Algorithms require move operators not to throw   153
Algorithms have complexity guarantees   154
Algorithms perform just as well as C library function equivalents   155
Writing and using generic algorithms   **156**
Non-generic algorithms   156
Generic algorithms   156
Data structures that can be used by generic algorithms   157
Best practices   **159**
Using the constrained algorithms   160
Sorting only for the data you need to retrieve   160
Use cases   162
Performance evaluation   162
Use standard algorithms over raw for-loops   163
Example 1: Readability issues and mutable variables   164
Example 2: Unfortunate exceptions and performance problems   165
Example 3: Exploiting the standard library optimizations   168
Avoiding container copies   170
Summary   **171**

Chapter 6: Ranges and Views   **173**
The motivation for the Ranges library   **173**
Limitations of the Algorithm library   174
Understanding views from the Ranges library   **176**
Views are composable   178
Range views come with range adaptors   179
Views are non-owning ranges with complexity guarantees   180
Views don't mutate the underlying container   181
Views can be materialized into containers   181

Views are lazy evaluated 183
Views in the standard library **184**
Range views 184
Generating views 185
Transforming views 185
Sampling views 186
Utility views 186
Revisiting std::string_view and std::span 187
The future of the Ranges library **189**
Summary **189**
Chapter 7: Memory Management **191**
Computer memory **192**
The virtual address space 192
Memory pages 192
Thrashing 194
Process memory **194**
Stack memory 195
Heap memory 198
Objects in memory **199**
Creating and deleting objects 199
Placement new 200
The new and delete operators 201
Memory alignment 203
Padding 208
Memory ownership **210**
Handling resources implicitly 211
Containers 213
Smart pointers 213
Unique pointer 214
Shared pointer 214
Weak pointer 216
Small object optimization **217**
Custom memory management **220**
Building an arena 221
A custom memory allocator 225
Using polymorphic memory allocators 230
Implementing a custom memory resource 234
Summary **236**
Chapter 8: Compile-Time Programming **237**
Introduction to template metaprogramming **238**
Creating templates 239
Using integers as template parameters 241

Providing specializations of a template   242
How the compiler handles a template function   242
Abbreviated function templates   243
Receiving the type of a variable with decltype   244
Type traits   **245**
Type trait categories   245
Using type traits   246
Programming with constant expressions   **247**
Constexpr functions in a runtime context   248
Declaring immediate functions using consteval   249
The if constexpr statement   249
Comparison with runtime polymorphism   251
Example of the generic modulus function using if constexpr   252
Checking programming errors at compile time   253
Using assert to trigger errors at runtime   254
Using static_assert to trigger errors at compile time   254
Constraints and concepts   **255**
An unconstrained version of a Point2D template   256
Generic interfaces and bad error messages   257
A syntactic overview of constraints and concepts   259
Defining new concepts   259
Constraining types with concepts   260
Function overloading   261
A constrained version of the Point2D template   261
Adding constraints to your code   263
Concepts in the standard library   264
Real-world examples of metaprogramming   **264**
Example 1: creating a generic safe cast function   265
Example 2: hash strings at compile time   268
The advantages of the compile-time hash sum calculation   269
Implementing and verifying a compile-time hash function   270
Constructing a PrehashedString class   270
Evaluating PrehashedString   272
Evaluating get_bitmap_resource() with PrehashedString   273
Summary   **274**

Chapter 9: Essential Utilities   **275**
Representing optional values with std::optional   **276**
Optional return values   276
Optional member variables   277
Avoiding empty states in enums   278
Sorting and comparing std::optional   279

Fixed size heterogenous collections   **279**
Using std::pair   280
The std::tuple   281
Accessing the members of a tuple   282
Iterating std::tuple members   283
Unrolling the tuple   283
Accessing tuple elements   286
The variadic template parameter pack   288
Dynamically sized heterogenous collections   **291**
The std::variant   292
Exception safety of std::variant   293
Visiting variants   294
Heterogenous collections using variant   296
Accessing the values in our variant container   297
Global function std::get()   298
Some real-world examples   **299**
Example 1: projections and comparison operators   299
Example 2: reflection   300
Making a class reflect its members   301
C++ libraries that simplify reflection   301
Using reflection   302
Conditionally overloading global functions   302
Testing reflection capabilities   303
Summary   **304**
Chapter 10: Proxy Objects and Lazy Evaluation   **305**
Introducing lazy evaluation and proxy objects   **305**
Lazy versus eager evaluation   306
Proxy objects   307
Avoiding constructing objects using proxy objects   **307**
Comparing concatenated strings using a proxy   307
Implementing the proxy   309
The rvalue modifier   310
Assigning a concatenated proxy   310
Performance evaluation   311
Postponing sqrt computations   **312**
A simple two-dimensional vector class   312
The underlying mathematics   313
Implementing the LengthProxy object   315
Comparing lengths with LengthProxy   317
Calculating length with LengthProxy   318
Preventing the misuse of LengthProxy   318
Performance evaluation   319

Creative operator overloading and proxy objects — **321**

The pipe operator as an extension method — 321

The pipe operator — 322

Summary — **323**

Chapter 11: Concurrency — **325**

Understanding the basics of concurrency — **326**

What makes concurrent programming hard? — **326**

Concurrency and parallelism — **327**

Time slicing — 328

Shared memory — 329

Data races — 331

Example: A data race — 331

Avoiding data races — 333

Mutex — 333

Deadlock — 334

Synchronous and asynchronous tasks — 335

Concurrent programming in C++ — **336**

The thread support library — 337

Threads — 337

Thread states — 339

Joinable thread — 341

Protecting critical sections — 343

Avoiding deadlocks — 345

Condition variables — 346

Returning data and handling errors — 348

Tasks — 350

Additional synchronization primitives in C++20 — 352

Using latches — 352

Using barriers — 354

Signalling and resource counting using semaphores — 358

Atomic support in C++ — 363

The lock-free property — 364

Atomic flags — 365

Atomic wait and notify — 366

Using shared_ptr in a multithreaded environment — 367

Atomic references — 370

The C++ memory model — 373

Instruction reordering — 373

Atomics and memory orders — 375

Lock-free programming — **377**

Example: A lock-free queue — 377

Performance guidelines — **380**

Avoid contention — 380

Avoid blocking operations — 380

Number of threads/CPU cores	381
Thread priorities	381
Thread affinity	382
False sharing	383
Summary	**383**
Chapter 12: Coroutines and Lazy Generators	**385**
A few motivating examples	**386**
The coroutine abstraction	**388**
Subroutines and coroutines	388
Executing subroutines and coroutines on the CPU	391
CPU registers, instructions, and the stack	391
Call and return	393
Suspend and resume	395
Stackless versus stackful coroutines	399
Performance cost	400
Memory footprint	400
Context switching	401
What you have learned so far	401
Coroutines in C++	**402**
What's included in standard C++ (and what's not)?	403
What makes a C++ function a coroutine?	404
A minimal but complete example	406
The coroutine return object	408
The promise type	409
Awaitable types	410
Passing our coroutine around	411
Allocating the coroutine state	411
Avoiding dangling references	413
Passing parameters to coroutines	413
Member functions that are coroutines	415
Lambdas that are coroutines	416
Guidelines to prevent dangling references	418
Handling errors	418
Customization points	418
Generators	**419**
Implementing a generator	419
Using the Generator class	423
Solving generator problems	425
An iterator implementation	428
A solution using the Ranges library	429
Conclusion	430
A real-world example using generators	431
The problem	431
Delta encoding	432

Performance   **438**
Summary   **438**

Chapter 13: Asynchronous Programming with Coroutines   **439**
  Awaitable types revisited   **440**
    The implicit suspend points   442
  Implementing a rudimentary task type   **442**
    Handling return values and exceptions   445
    Resuming an awaiting coroutine   446
    Supporting void tasks   448
    Synchronously waiting for a task to complete   450
      Implementing sync_wait()   451
      Implementing SyncWaitTask   452
    Testing asynchronous tasks with sync_wait()   454
  Wrapping a callback-based API   **455**
  A concurrent server using Boost.Asio   **459**
    Implementing the server   460
    Running and connecting to the server   462
    What we have achieved with the server (and what we haven't)   463
  Summary   **464**

Chapter 14: Parallel Algorithms   **465**
  The importance of parallelism   **466**
  Parallel algorithms   **466**
    Evaluating parallel algorithms   466
    Amdahl's law revisited   467
    Implementing parallel std::transform()   468
      Naive implementation   469
      Divide and conquer   474
    Implementing parallel std::count_if()   479
    Implementing parallel std::copy_if()   480
      Approach 1: Use a synchronized write position   481
      Approach 2: Split the algorithm into two parts   482
      Performance evaluation   485
  Parallel standard library algorithms   **486**
    Execution policies   487
      Sequenced policy   488
      Parallel policy   488
      Unsequenced policy   489
      Parallel unsequenced policy   491
    Exception handling   491
    Additions and changes to parallel algorithms   492
      std::accumulate() and std::reduce()   492
      std::for_each()   494

Parallelizing an index-based for-loop   494
   Combining std::for_each() with std::views::iota()   495
   Simplifying construction via a wrapper   495
Executing algorithms on the GPU   **496**
  Summary   497

Other Books You May Enjoy   **499**

Index   **503**

Preface

The C++ of today provides programmers with the ability to write expressive and robust code, while still making it possible to target almost any hardware platform, and at the same time meet performance-critical requirements. This makes C++ a unique language. Over the last few years, C++ has turned into a modern language that is more fun to use and has better defaults.

This book aims to give you a solid foundation to write efficient applications, as well as an insight into strategies for implementing libraries in modern C++. I have tried to take a practical approach to explaining how C++ works today, where features from C++17 and C++20 are a natural part of the language, rather than looking at C++ historically.

This second edition was written to cover new features added in C++20. I have included features that I think fit well with the rest of the content and the focus of this book. Naturally, chapters that discuss new features serve more as an introduction and contain fewer best practices and well-proven solutions.

At the time of publishing this book, the compiler support for some C++20 features presented is still experimental. If you read this book near to the publication date, the chances are that you will have to wait for some features to become fully supported by your compiler.

Many chapters span a wide range of difficulty. They start with the absolute basics and end with advanced topics such as custom memory allocators. If a section is not relevant to you, feel free to skip it or come back to it later. Apart from the first three chapters, most chapters can be read independently.

Our main technical reviewer, Timur Doumler, has had a big impact on this new edition. His enthusiasm and brilliant feedback have led to some chapters from the first edition being reworked to explain topics more thoroughly and in more depth. Timur has also been a vital contributor when it comes to incorporating new C++20 features into the chapters where they fit naturally. Select parts of the book have also been reviewed by Arthur O'Dwyer, Marius Bancila, and Lewis Baker. It has been a true pleasure to have had such excellent reviewers on this project. I hope you enjoy reading this new edition as much as I have enjoyed writing it.

Who this book is for

This book expects you to have a basic knowledge of C++ and computer architecture, and a genuine interest in evolving your skills. Hopefully, by the time you finish this book, you will have gained a few insights into how you can improve your C++ applications, both performance-wise and syntactically. On top of that, I also hope that you will have a few "aha" moments.

What this book covers

Chapter 1, A Brief Introduction to C++, introduces some important properties of C++, such as zero-cost abstractions, value semantics, const correctness, explicit ownership, and error handling. It also discusses the drawbacks of C++.

Chapter 2, Essential C++ Techniques, outlines automatic type deduction using auto, lambda functions, move semantics, and error handling.

Chapter 3, Analyzing and Measuring Performance, will teach you how to analyze algorithmic complexity using big O notation. The chapter also discusses how to profile your code to find hotspots and how to set up performance tests using Google Benchmark.

Chapter 4, Data Structures, takes you through the importance of structuring data so that it can be accessed quickly. Containers from the standard library, such as `std::vector`, `std::list`, `std::unordered_map`, and `std::priority_queue`, are introduced. Finally, this chapter demonstrates how to use parallel arrays.

Chapter 5, Algorithms, introduces the most important algorithms from the standard library. You will also learn how to use iterators and ranges, and how to implement your own generic algorithms.

Chapter 6, Ranges and Views, will teach you how to compose algorithms using the Ranges library introduced in C++20. You will learn why views from the Ranges library are useful and some benefits of lazy evaluation.

Chapter 7, Memory Management, focuses on safe and efficient memory management. This includes memory ownership, RAII, smart pointers, stack memory, dynamic memory, and custom memory allocators.

Chapter 8, Compile-Time Programming, explains metaprogramming techniques using `constexpr`, `consteval`, and type traits. You will also learn how to use C++20 concepts and the new Concepts library. Finally, it provides practical examples of metaprogramming use cases, such as reflection.

Chapter 9, Essential Utilities, will guide you through the Utilities library and how to benefit from types such as `std::optional`, `std::any`, and `std::variant` using compile-time programming techniques.

Chapter 10, Proxy Objects and Lazy Evaluation, explores how proxy objects can be used to perform under-the-hood optimizations while preserving clean syntax. Additionally, some creative uses of operator-overloading are demonstrated.

Chapter 11, Concurrency, covers the fundamentals of concurrent programming, including parallel execution, shared memory, data races, and deadlocks. It also includes an introduction to the C++ Thread support library, the Atomic library, and the C++ memory model.

Chapter 12, Coroutines and Lazy Generators, contains a general introduction to the coroutine abstraction. You will learn how ordinary functions and coroutines are executed on the CPU using the stack and the heap. C++20 stackless coroutines are introduced and you will discover how to solve problems using generators.

Chapter 13, Asynchronous Programming with Coroutines, introduces concurrent programming using stackless coroutines from C++20 and touches on the subject of asynchronous network programming using Boost.Asio.

Chapter 14, Parallel Algorithms, starts by showing the complexity of writing parallel algorithms and how to measure their performance. It then demonstrates how to utilize standard library algorithms in a parallel context using execution policies.

Get the most out of this book

To get the most out of this book, you need to have a basic knowledge of C++. It's preferable that you have already faced problems related to performance and are now looking for new tools and practices to have ready for the next time you need to work with performance and C++.

There are a lot of code examples in this book. Some are taken from the real world, but most of them are artificial or vastly simplified examples to prove a concept, rather than provide you with production-ready code.

I have put all the code examples in source files divided by chapter so that it is fairly easy to find the examples you want to experiment with. If you open up the source code files, you will note that I have replaced most of the main() functions from the examples with test cases written with the Google Test framework. I hope that this will help you rather than confuse you. It allowed me to write helpful descriptions for each example, and it also makes it easier to run all the examples from one chapter at once.

In order to compile and run the examples, you will need the following:

- A computer
- An operating system (the examples have been verified on Windows, Linux, and macOS)
- A compiler (I used Clang, GCC, and Microsoft Visual C++)
- CMake

The CMake script provided with the example code will download and install further dependencies, such as Boost, Google Benchmark, and Google Test.

During the writing of this book, I found it helpful to use **Compiler Explorer**, which is available at https://godbolt.org/. Compiler Explorer is an online compiler service that lets you try various compilers and versions. Try it out if you haven't already!

Download the example code files

The code bundle for the book is hosted on GitHub at https://github.com/ PacktPublishing/Cpp-High-Performance-Second-Edition. If there's an update to the code, it will be updated on the existing GitHub repository.

There are other code bundles from Packt's rich catalog of books and videos available at https://github.com/PacktPublishing/. Check them out!

Download the color images

Packt also provides a PDF file that has color images of the screenshots/diagrams used in this book. You can download it here: https://static.packt-cdn.com/ downloads/9781839216541_ColorImages.pdf.

Conventions used

There are a number of text conventions used throughout this book.

CodeInText: Indicates code words in text, folder names, filenames, file extensions, dummy URLs, and user input. Here is an example: "The keyword constexpr was introduced in C++11."

A block of code is set as follows:

```
#include <iostream>

int main() {
  std::cout << "High Performance C++\n";
}
```

When I wish to draw your attention to a particular part of a code block, the relevant lines or items are set in bold:

```
#include <iostream>

int main() {
  std::cout << "High Performance C++\n";
}
```

Any command-line input or output is written as follows:

```
$ clang++ -std=c++20 high_performance.cpp
$ ./a.out
$ High Performance C++
```

Bold: Indicates a new term, an important word, or words that you see on the screen. For example: "Fill in the form and click on the **Save** button."

 Warnings or important notes appear like this.

Get in touch

Feedback from readers is always welcome.

General feedback: If you have questions about any aspect of this book, mention the book title in the subject of your message and email Packt at customercare@packtpub.com.

Errata: Although we have taken every care to ensure the accuracy of our content, mistakes do happen. If you have found a mistake in this book, we would be grateful if you could report this to us. Please visit www.packtpub.com/support/errata, select your book, click on the **Errata Submission Form** link, and enter the details.

Piracy: If you come across any illegal copies of our works in any form on the Internet, we would be grateful if you could provide us with the location address or website name. Please contact us at copyright@packt.com with a link to the material.

If you are interested in becoming an author: If there is a topic that you have expertise in and you are interested in either writing or contributing to a book, please visit authors.packtpub.com.

Reviews

Please leave a review. Once you have read and used this book, why not leave a review on the site that you purchased it from? Potential readers can then see and use your unbiased opinion to make a purchase decision, we at Packt can understand what you think about our product, and our author can see your feedback on their book. Thank you!

For more information about Packt, please visit packt.com.

1

A Brief Introduction to C++

This book aims to provide you with a solid foundation to write efficient applications, as well as an insight into strategies for implementing libraries in modern C++. I have tried to take a practical approach to explain how C++ works today, where modern features from C++11 up to C++20 are a natural part of the language, rather than looking at C++ historically.

In this chapter, we will:

- Cover some of the features of C++ that are important for writing robust, high-performance applications
- Discuss the advantages and disadvantages of C++ over competing languages
- Go over the libraries and compilers used in this book

Why C++?

Let's begin by exploring some of the reasons for using C++ today. In short, C++ is a highly portable language that offers zero-cost abstractions. Furthermore, C++ provides programmers with the ability to write and manage large, expressive, and robust code bases. In this section, we'll look at what we mean by *zero-cost abstractions*, compare C++ abstraction with abstraction in other languages, and discuss portability and robustness, and why such features are important.

Let's begin by getting into zero-cost abstractions.

Zero-cost abstractions

Active code bases grow. The more developers working on a code base, the larger the code base becomes. In order to manage the growing complexity of a code base, we need language features such as variables, functions, and classes to be able to create our own abstractions with custom names and interfaces that suppress details of the implementation.

C++ allows us to define our own abstractions but it also comes with built-in abstractions. The concept of a C++ function, for example, is in itself an abstraction for controlling program flow. The range-based for-loop is another example of a built-in abstraction that makes it possible to iterate over a range of values more directly. As programmers, we add new abstraction continuously while developing programs. Similarly, new versions of C++ introduce new abstractions to the language and the standard library. But constantly adding abstractions and new levels of indirection comes at a price – efficiency. This is where zero-cost abstractions play its role. A lot of the abstractions offered by C++ come at a very low runtime cost with respect to space and time.

With C++, you are free to talk about memory addresses and other computer-related low-level terms when needed. However, in a large-scale software project, it is desirable to express code in terms that deal with whatever the application is doing, and let the libraries handle the computer-related terminology. The source code of a graphics application may deal with pencils, colors, and filters, whereas a game may deal with mascots, castles, and mushrooms. Low-level computer-related terms, such as memory addresses, can stay hidden in C++ library code where performance is critical.

Programming languages and machine code abstractions

In order to relieve programmers from the need to deal with computer-related terms, modern programming languages use abstractions so that a list of strings, for example, can be handled and thought of as a list of strings rather than a list of addresses that we may easily lose track of if we make the slightest typo. Not only do the abstractions relieve the programmers from bugs, they also make the code more expressive by using concepts from the domain of the application. In other words, the code is expressed in terms that are closer to a spoken language than if expressed with abstract programming keywords.

C++ and C are two completely different languages nowadays. Still, C++ is highly compatible with C and has inherited a lot of its syntax and idioms from C. To give you some examples of C++ abstractions, I will show how a problem can be solved in both C and C++.

Take a look at the following C/C++ code snippets, which correspond to the question: "How many copies of Hamlet are in this list of books?"

We will begin with the C version:

```
// C version
struct string_elem_t { const char* str_; string_elem_t* next_; };
int num_hamlet(string_elem_t* books) {
  const char* hamlet = "Hamlet";
  int n = 0;
  string_elem_t* b;
  for (b = books; b != 0; b = b->next_)
    if (strcmp(b->str_, hamlet) == 0)
      ++n;
  return n;
}
```

The equivalent version using C++ would look something like this:

```
// C++ version
int num_hamlet(const std::forward_list<std::string>& books) {
  return std::count(books.begin(), books.end(), "Hamlet");
}
```

Although the C++ version is still more of a robot language than a human language, a lot of programming lingo is gone thanks to the higher levels of abstraction. Here are some of the noticeable differences between the preceding two code snippets:

- The pointers to raw memory addresses are not visible at all
- The std::forward_list<std::string> container replaces the hand crafted linked list using string_elem_t
- The std::count() function replaces both the for-loop and the if-statement
- The std::string class provides a higher-level abstraction over char* and strcmp()

Basically, both versions of num_hamlet() translate to roughly the same machine code, but the language features of C++ makes it possible to let the libraries hide computer-related terminology such as pointers. Many of the modern C++ language features can be seen as abstractions on top of basic C functionality.

Abstractions in other languages

Most programming languages are based on abstractions, which are transformed into machine code to be executed by the CPU. C++ has evolved into a highly expressive language, just like many of the other popular programming languages of today. What distinguishes C++ from most other languages is that while the other languages have implemented these abstractions at the cost of runtime performance, C++ has always strived to implement its abstractions at zero cost at runtime. This doesn't mean that an application written in C++ is by default faster than the equivalent in, say, C#. Rather, it means that by using C++, you'll have fine-grained control of the emitted machine code instructions and memory footprint if needed.

To be fair, optimal performance is very rarely required today, and compromising performance for lower compilation times, garbage collection, or safety, like other languages do, is in many cases more reasonable.

The zero-overhead principle

"Zero-cost abstractions" is a commonly used term, but it is afflicted with a problem – most abstractions usually do cost. If not while running the program, it almost always cost somewhere down the line, such as long compilation times, compilation error messages that are hard to interpret and so forth. What is usually more interesting to talk about is the zero-overhead principle. Bjarne Stroustrup, the inventor of C++, defines the zero-overhead principle like this:

- What you don't use, you don't pay for
- What you do use, you couldn't hand code any better

This a core principle in C++ and a very important aspect of the evolution of the language. Why, you may ask? Abstractions built on this principle will be accepted and used broadly by performance-aware programmers and in a context where performance is highly critical. Finding abstractions that many people agree on and use extensively, makes our code bases easier to read and maintain.

On the contrary, features in the C++ language that don't fully follow the zero-overhead principle tend to be abandoned by programmers, projects, and companies. Two of the most notable features in this category are **exceptions** (unfortunately) and **Run-time Type Information (RTTI)**. Both these features can have an impact on the performance even when they are not being used. I strongly recommend using exceptions though, unless you have a very good reason not to. The performance overhead is in most cases negligible compared to using some other mechanism for handling errors.

Portability

C++ has been a popular and comprehensive language for a long time. It's highly compatible with C, and very little has been deprecated in the language, for better or worse. The history and design of C++ has made it into a highly portable language, and the evolution of modern C++ has ensured that it will stay that way for a long time to come. C++ is a living language, and compiler vendors are currently doing a remarkable job to implement new language features rapidly.

Robustness

In addition to performance, expressiveness, and portability, C++ offers a set of language features that gives the programmer the ability to write robust code.

In the experience of the authors, robustness does not refer to strength in the programming language itself – it's possible to write robust code in any language. Rather, strict ownership of resources, const correctness, value semantics, type safety, and the deterministic destruction of objects are some of the features offered by C++ that makes it easier to write robust code. That is, the ability to write functions, classes, and libraries that are easy to use and hard to misuse.

C++ of today

To sum it up, the C++ of today provides programmers with the ability to write an expressive and robust code base while still having the option to target almost any hardware platform or real-time requirements. Among the most commonly used languages today, C++ alone possesses all of these properties.

I've now provided a brief rundown as to why C++ remains a relevant and widely used programming language today. In the next section, we'll look at how C++ compares to other modern programming languages.

C++ compared with other languages

A multitude of application types, platforms, and programming languages have emerged since C++ was first released. Still, C++ remains a widely used language, and its compilers are available for most platforms. The major exception, as of today, is the web platform, where JavaScript and its related technologies are the foundation. However, the web platform is evolving into being able to execute what was previously only possible in desktop applications, and in that context, C++ has found its way into web applications using technologies such as Emscripten, asm.js, and WebAssembly.

In this section, we'll begin by looking at competing languages in the context of performance. Following this, we'll look at how C++ handles object ownership and garbage collection in comparison to other languages, and how we can avoid null objects in C++. Finally, we'll cover some drawbacks of C++ that users should keep in mind when considering whether the language is appropriate for their requirements.

Competing languages and performance

In order to understand how C++ achieves its performance compared to other programming languages, let's discuss some fundamental differences between C++ and most other modern programming languages.

For simplicity, this section will focus on comparing C++ to Java, although the comparisons for most parts also apply to other programming language based upon a garbage collector, such as C# and JavaScript.

Firstly, Java compiles to bytecode, which is then compiled to machine code while the application is executing, whereas the majority of C++ implementations directly compiles the source code to machine code. Although bytecode and just-in-time compilers may theoretically be able to achieve the same (or, theoretically, even better) performance than precompiled machine code, as of today, they usually do not. To be fair, though, they perform well enough for most cases.

Secondly, Java handles dynamic memory in a completely different manner from C++. In Java, memory is automatically deallocated by a garbage collector, whereas a C++ program handles memory deallocations manually or by a reference counting mechanism. The garbage collector does prevent memory leaks, but at the cost of performance and predictability.

Thirdly, Java places all its objects in separate heap allocations, whereas C++ allows the programmer to place objects both on the stack and on the heap. In C++, it's also possible to create multiple objects in one single heap allocation. This can be a huge performance gain for two reasons: objects can be created without always allocating dynamic memory, and multiple related objects can be placed adjacent to one another in memory.

Take a look at how memory is allocated in the following example. The C++ function uses the stack for both objects and integers; Java places the objects on the heap:

C++	Java
| ```cpp
class Car {
public:
  Car(int doors)
      : doors_(doors) {}
private:
  int doors_{};
};

auto some_func() {
  auto num_doors = 2;
  auto car1 = Car{num_doors};
  auto car2 = Car{num_doors};
  // ...
}
``` | ```java
class Car {
  public Car(int doors) {
    doors_ = doors;
  }
  private int doors_;

  static void some_func() {
    int numDoors = 2;
    Car car1 = new Car(numDoors);
    Car car2 = new Car(numDoors);
    // ...
  }
}
``` |
| C++ places everything on the stack:

num_doors: int
car1: Car (object)
car1: Car (object) | Java places the Car objects on the heap:

Car (object)
num_doors: int
car1: reference
car2: reference
Car (object) |

Now take a look at the next example and see how an array of Car objects are placed in memory when using C++ and Java, respectively:

C++	Java

``auto n = 4;
auto cars = std::vector<Car>{};
cars.reserve(n);
for (auto i=0; i<n;++i) {
    cars.push_back(Car{2});
}```
	``int n = 4;
	ArrayList<Car> cars =
	    new ArrayList<Car>();
	for (int i=0; i<n; i++) {
	    cars.addElement(new Car(2));
	}```

The following diagram shows how the Car objects are laid out in memory in C++:	The following diagram shows how the Car objects are laid out in memory in Java:

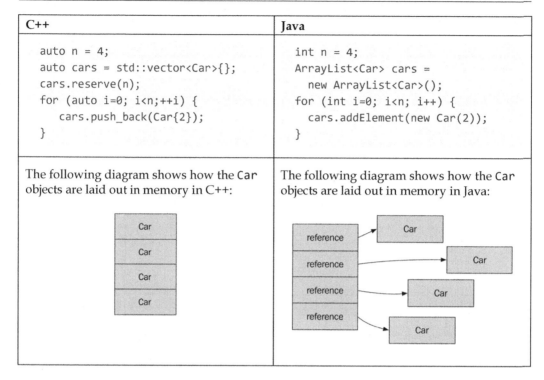

The C++ vector contains the actual Car objects placed in one contiguous memory block, whereas the equivalent in Java is a contiguous memory block of *references* to Car objects. In Java, the objects have been allocated separately, which means that they can be located anywhere on the heap.

This affects the performance, as Java, in this example, effectively has to execute five allocations in the Java heap space. It also means that whenever the application iterates the list, there is a performance win for C++, since accessing nearby memory locations is faster than accessing several random spots in memory.

Non-performance-related C++ language features

It's tempting to believe that C++ should only be used if performance is a major concern. Isn't it the case that C++ just increases the complexity of the code base due to manual memory handling, which may result in memory leaks and hard-to-track bugs?

This may have been true several C++ versions ago, but a modern C++ programmer relies on the provided containers and smart pointer types, which are part of the standard library. A substantial part of the C++ features added over the last 10 years has made the language both more powerful and simpler to use.

I would like to highlight some old but powerful features of C++ here that relate to robustness rather than performance, which are easily overlooked: value semantics, const correctness, ownership, deterministic destruction, and references.

Value semantics

C++ supports both value semantics and reference semantics. Value semantics lets us pass objects by value instead of just passing references to objects. In C++, value semantics is the default, which means that when you pass an instance of a class or struct, it behaves in the same way as passing an int, float, or any other fundamental type. To use reference semantics, we need to explicitly use references or pointers.

The C++ type system gives us the ability to explicitly state the ownership of an object. Compare the following implementations of a simple class in C++ and Java. We will start with the C++ version:

```cpp
// C++
class Bagel {
public:
  Bagel(std::set<std::string> ts) : toppings_(std::move(ts)) {}
private:
  std::set<std::string> toppings_;
};
```

The corresponding implementation in Java could look like this:

```java
// Java
class Bagel {
  public Bagel(ArrayList<String> ts) { toppings_ = ts; }
  private ArrayList<String> toppings_;
}
```

In the C++ version, the programmer states that the `toppings` are completely encapsulated by the `Bagel` class. Had the programmer intended the topping list to be shared among several bagels, it would have been declared as a pointer of some kind: `std::shared_ptr` if the ownership is shared among several bagels, or `std::weak_ptr` if someone else owns the topping list and is supposed to modify it as the program executes.

In Java, objects reference each other with shared ownership. Therefore, it's not possible to distinguish whether the topping list is intended to be shared among several bagels or not, or whether it is handled somewhere else or, if it is, as in most cases, completely owned by the `Bagel` class.

Compare the following functions; as every object is shared by default in Java (and most other languages), programmers have to take precautions for subtle bugs such as this:

C++	Java
| ```cpp
// Note how the bagels do
// not share toppings:

auto t = std::set<std::string>{};

t.insert("salt");
auto a = Bagel{t};

// 'a' is not affected
// when adding pepper
t.insert("pepper");

// 'a' will have salt
// 'b' will have salt & pepper
auto b = Bagel{t};

// No bagel is affected
t.insert("oregano");
``` | ```java
// Note how both the bagels
// share toppings:

TreeSet<String> t =
    new TreeSet<String>();
t.add("salt");
Bagel a = new Bagel(t);

// Now 'a' will subtly
// also have pepper
t.add("pepper");

// 'a' and 'b' share the
// toppings in 't'
Bagel b = new Bagel(t);

// Both bagels are affected
toppings.add("oregano");
``` |

Const correctness

Another powerful feature of C++, which Java and many other languages lack, is the ability to write fully const correct code. Const correctness means that each member function signature of a class explicitly tells the caller whether the object will be modified or not; and it will not compile if the caller tries to modify an object declared const. In Java, it is possible to declare constants using the final keyword, but this lacks the ability to declare member functions as const.

Here is an example of how we can use const member functions to prevent unintentional modifications of objects. In the following Person class, the member function age() is declared const and is therefore not allowed to mutate the Person object, whereas set_age() mutates the object and *cannot* be declared const:

```
class Person {
public:
  auto age() const { return age_; }
  auto set_age(int age) { age_ = age; }
private:
  int age_{};
};
```

It's also possible to distinguish between returning mutable and immutable references to members. In the following Team class, the member function leader() const returns an immutable Person, whereas leader() returns a Person object that may be mutated:

```
class Team {
public:
  auto& leader() const { return leader_; }
  auto& leader() { return leader_; }
private:
  Person leader_{};
};
```

Now let's see how the compiler can help us find errors when we try to mutate immutable objects. In the following example, the function argument teams is declared const, explicitly showing that this function is not allowed to modify them:

```
void nonmutating_func(const std::vector<Team>& teams) {
  auto tot_age = 0;

  // Compiles, both leader() and age() are declared const
  for (const auto& team : teams)
    tot_age += team.leader().age();
```

```
  // Will not compile, set_age() requires a mutable object
  for (auto& team : teams)
    team.leader().set_age(20);
}
```

If we want to write a function that *can* mutate the `teams` object, we simply remove const. This signals to the caller that this function may mutate the `teams`:

```
void mutating_func(std::vector<Team>& teams) {
  auto tot_age = 0;

  // Compiles, const functions can be called on mutable objects
  for (const auto& team : teams)
    tot_age += team.leader().age();

  // Compiles, teams is a mutable variable
  for (auto& team : teams)
    team.leader().set_age(20);
}
```

Object ownership

Except in very rare situations, a C++ programmer should leave the memory handling to containers and smart pointers, and never have to rely on manual memory handling.

To put it clearly, the garbage collection model in Java could almost be emulated in C++ by using `std::shared_ptr` for every object. Note that garbage-collecting languages don't use the same algorithm for allocation tracking as `std::shared_ptr`. The `std::shared_ptr` is a smart pointer based on a reference-counting algorithm that will leak memory if objects have cyclic dependencies. Garbage-collecting languages have more sophisticated methods that can handle and free cyclic dependent objects.

However, rather than relying on a garbage collector, forcing a strict ownership delicately avoids subtle bugs that may result from sharing objects by default, as in the case of Java.

If a programmer minimizes shared ownership in C++, the resulting code is easier to use and harder to abuse, as it can force the user of the class to use it as it is intended.

Deterministic destruction in C++

The destruction of objects is deterministic in C++. That means that we (can) know exactly when an object is being destroyed. This is not the case for garbage-collected languages like Java where the garbage collector decides when an unreferenced object is being finalized.

In C++, we can reliably reverse what has been done during the lifetime of an object. At first, this might seem like a small thing. But it turns out to have a great impact on how we can provide exception safety guarantees and handle resources (such as memory, file handles, mutex locks, and more) in C++.

Deterministic destruction is also one of the features that makes C++ predictable. Something that is highly valued among programmers and a requirement for performance-critical applications.

We will spend more time talking about object ownership, lifetimes, and resource management later on in the book. So don't be too worried if this doesn't make much sense at the moment.

Avoiding null objects using C++ references

In addition to strict ownership, C++ also has the concept of references, which is different from references in Java. Internally, a reference is a pointer that is not allowed to be null or repointed; therefore, no copying is involved when passing it to a function.

As a result, a function signature in C++ can explicitly restrict the programmer from passing a null object as a parameter. In Java, the programmer must use documentation or annotations to indicate non-null parameters.

Take a look at these two Java functions for computing the volume of a sphere. The first one throws a runtime exception if a null object is passed to it, whereas the second one silently ignores null objects.

This first implementation in Java throws a runtime exception if passed a null object:

```
// Java
float getVolume1(Sphere s) {
  float cube = Math.pow(s.radius(), 3);
  return (Math.PI * 4 / 3) * cube;
}
```

This second implementation in Java silently handles null objects:

```java
// Java
float getVolume2(Sphere s) {
    float rad = s == null ? 0.0f : s.radius();
    float cube = Math.pow(rad, 3);
    return (Math.PI * 4 / 3) * cube;
}
```

In both functions implemented in Java, the caller of the function has to inspect the implementation of the function in order to determine whether null objects are allowed or not.

In C++, the first function signature explicitly accepts only initialized objects by using a reference that cannot be null. The second version using a pointer as an argument explicitly shows that null objects are handled.

C++ arguments passed as references indicates that null values are not allowed:

```cpp
auto get_volume1(const Sphere& s) {
    auto cube = std::pow(s.radius(), 3.f);
    auto pi = 3.14f;
    return (pi * 4.f / 3.f) * cube;
}
```

C++ arguments passed as pointers indicates that null values are being handled:

```cpp
auto get_volume2(const Sphere* s) {
    auto rad = s ? s->radius() : 0.f;
    auto cube = std::pow(rad, 3);
    auto pi = 3.14f;
    return (pi * 4.f / 3.f) * cube;
}
```

Being able to use references or values as arguments in C++ instantly informs the C++ programmer how the function is intended to be used. Conversely, in Java, the user must inspect the implementation of the function, as objects are always passed as pointers, and there's a possibility that they could be null.

Drawbacks of C++

Comparing C++ with other programming languages wouldn't be fair without mentioning some of its drawbacks. As mentioned earlier, C++ has more concepts to learn, and is therefore harder to use correctly and to its full potential. However, if a programmer can master C++, the higher complexity turns into an advantage and the code base becomes more robust and performs better.

There are, nonetheless, some shortcomings of C++, which are simply just shortcomings. The most severe of those shortcomings are long compilation times and the complexity of importing libraries. Up until C++20, C++ has relied on an outdated import system where imported headers are simply pasted into whatever includes them. C++ modules, which are being introduced in C++20, will solve some of the problems of the system, which is based on including header files, and will also have a positive impact on compilation times for large projects.

Another apparent drawback of C++ is the lack of provided libraries. While other languages usually come with all the libraries needed for most applications, such as graphics, user interfaces, networking, threading, resource handling, and so on, C++ provides, more or less, nothing more than the bare minimum of algorithms, threads, and, as of C++17, file system handling. For everything else, programmers have to rely on external libraries.

To summarize, although C++ has a steeper learning curve than most other languages, if used correctly, the robustness of C++ is an advantage compared to many other languages. So, despite the compilation times and lack of provided libraries, I believe that C++ is a well-suited language for large-scale projects, even for projects where performance is not the highest priority.

Libraries and compilers used in this book

As mentioned earlier, C++ does not provide more than the bare necessities in terms of libraries. In this book, we will, therefore, have to rely on external libraries where necessary. The most commonly used library in the world of C++ is probably the Boost library (`http://www.boost.org`).

Some parts of this book use the Boost library where the standard C++ library is not enough. We will only use the header-only parts of the Boost library, which means that using them yourself does not require any specific build setup; rather, you just have to include the specified header file.

In addition, we will use Google Benchmark, a microbenchmark support library, to evaluate the performance of small code snippets. Google Benchmark will be introduced in *Chapter 3, Analyzing and Measuring Performance.*

The repository available at `https://github.com/PacktPublishing/Cpp-High-Performance-Second-Edition` with the accompanying source code of the book uses the Google Test framework to make it easier for you to build, run, and test the code.

It should also be mentioned that this book uses a lot of new features from C++20. At the time of writing, some of these features are not fully implemented by the compilers we use (Clang, GCC, and Microsoft Visual C++). Some of the features presented are completely missing or are only supported experimentally. An excellent up-to-date summary of the current status of the major C++ compilers can be found at `https://en.cppreference.com/w/cpp/compiler_support`.

Summary

In this chapter, I have highlighted some features and drawbacks of C++ and how it has evolved to the state it is in today. Further, we discussed the advantages and disadvantages of C++ compared with other languages, both from the perspective of performance and robustness.

In the next chapter, we will explore some modern and essential C++ features that have had a major impact on how the language has developed.

2

Essential C++ Techniques

In this chapter, we will take an in-depth look at some fundamental C++ techniques, such as move semantics, error handling, and lambda expressions, that will be used throughout this book. Some of these concepts still confuse even experienced C++ programmers and therefore we will look into both their use cases and how they work under the hood.

This chapter will cover the following topics:

- Automatic type deduction and how to use the auto keyword when declaring functions and variables.
- Move semantics and the *rule of five* and *rule of zero*.
- Error handling and contracts. Although these topics don't present anything that can be considered modern C++, both exceptions and contracts are highly debated areas within C++ today.
- Creating function objects using lambda expressions, one of the most important features from C++11.

Let's begin by taking a look at automatic type deduction.

Automatic type deduction with the auto keyword

Since the introduction of the auto keyword in C++11, there has been a lot of confusion in the C++ community about how to use the different flavors of auto, such as const auto&, auto&, auto&&, and decltype(auto).

Using auto in function signatures

Although discouraged by some C++ programmers, in my experience the use of auto in function signatures can increase readability when browsing and viewing header files.

Here is how the auto syntax looks compared to the traditional syntax with explicit types:

Traditional syntax with explicit type:	New syntax with auto:

<pre>struct Foo {
  int val() const {
    return m_;
  }
  const int& cref() const {
    return m_;
  }
  int& mref() {
    return m_;
  }
  int m_{};
};</pre>
	<pre>struct Foo {
	  auto val() const {
	    return m_;
	  }
	  auto& cref() const {
	    return m_;
	  }
	  auto& mref() {
	    return m_;
	  }
	  int m_{};
	};</pre>

The auto syntax can be used both with and without a trailing return type. The trailing return is necessary in some contexts. For example, if we are writing a virtual function, or the function declaration is put in a header file and the function definition is in a .cpp file.

Note that the auto syntax can also be used with free functions:

Return type	Syntactic variants (a, b, and c correspond to the same result):	

Value	<pre>auto val() const
	auto val() const -> int
	int val() const</pre>
		<pre>// a) auto, deduced type
		// b) auto, trailing type
		// c) explicit type</pre>

Const reference	<pre>auto& cref() const
	auto cref() const -> const int&
	const int& cref() const</pre>
		<pre>// a) auto, deduced type
		// b) auto, trailing type
		// c) explicit type</pre>

Mutable reference	<pre>auto& mref()
	auto mref() -> int&
	int& mref()</pre>
		<pre>// a) auto, deduced type
		// b) auto, trailing type
		// c) explicit type</pre>

Forwarding the return type using decltype(auto)

There is a somewhat rare version of automatic type deduction called `decltype(auto)`. Its most common use is for forwarding the exact type from a function. Imagine that we are writing wrapper functions for `val()` and `mref()` declared in the previous table, like this:

```
int val_wrapper() { return val(); }    // Returns int
int& mref_wrapper() { return mref(); } // Returns int&
```

Now, if we wanted to use return type deduction for the wrapper functions, the `auto` keyword would deduce the return type to an `int` in both cases:

```
auto val_wrapper() { return val(); }    // Returns int
auto mref_wrapper() { return mref(); } // Also returns int
```

If we wanted our `mref_wrapper()` to return an `int&`, we would need to write `auto&`. In this example, this would be fine, since we know the return type of `mref()`. However, that's not always the case. So if we want the compiler to instead choose the exact same type without explicitly saying `int&` or `auto&` for `mref_wrapper()`, we can use `decltype(auto)`:

```
decltype(auto) val_wrapper() { return val(); }    // Returns int
decltype(auto) mref_wrapper() { return mref(); } // Returns int&
```

In this way, we can avoid explicitly choosing between writing `auto` or `auto&` when we don't know what the function `val()` or `mref()` return. This is a scenario that usually happens in generic code where the type of the function that is being wrapped is a template parameter.

Using auto for variables

The introduction of the `auto` keyword in C++11 has initiated quite a debate among C++ programmers. Many people think it reduces readability, or even that it makes C++ similar to a dynamically typed language. I tend to not participate in those debates, but my personal opinion is that you should (almost) always use `auto` as, in my experience, it makes the code safer and less littered with clutter.

Overusing `auto` can make the code harder to understand. When reading code, we usually want to know which operations are supported by some object. A good IDE can provide us with this information, but it's not explicitly there in the source code. C++20 concepts address this issue by focusing on the behavior of an object. See *Chapter 8, Compile-Time Programming*, for more information about C++ concepts.

I prefer to use `auto` for local variables using the left-to-right initialization style. This means keeping the variable on the left, followed by an equals sign, and then the type on the right side, like this:

```
auto i = 0;
auto x = Foo{};
auto y = create_object();
auto z = std::mutex{};     // OK since C++17
```

With *guaranteed copy elision* introduced in C++17, the statement `auto x = Foo{}` is identical to `Foo x{};` that is, the language guarantees that there is no temporary object that needs to be moved or copied in this case. This means that we can now use the left-to-right initialization style without worrying about performance and we can also use it for non-movable/non-copyable types, such as `std::atomic` or `std::mutex`.

One big advantage of using `auto` for variables is that you will never leave a variable uninitialized since `auto x;` doesn't compile. Uninitialized variables are a particularly common source of undefined behavior that you can completely eliminate by following the style suggested here.

Using `auto` will help you with using the correct type for your variables. What you still need to do, though, is to express how you intend to use a variable by specifying whether you need a reference or a copy, and whether you want to modify the variable or just read from it.

A const reference

A `const` reference, denoted by `const auto&`, has the ability to bind to anything. The original object can never be mutated through such a reference. I believe that the `const` reference should be the default choice for objects that are potentially expensive to copy.

If the `const` reference is bound to a temporary object, the lifetime of the temporary will be extended to the lifetime of the reference. This is demonstrated in the following example:

```
void some_func(const std::string& a, const std::string& b) {
  const auto& str = a + b;  // a + b returns a temporary
  // ...
} // str goes out of scope, temporary will be destroyed
```

It's also possible to end up with a const reference by using auto&. This can be seen in the following example:

```
auto foo = Foo{};
auto& cref = foo.cref(); // cref is a const reference
auto& mref = foo.mref(); // mref is a mutable reference
```

Even though this is perfectly valid, it is preferable to always explicitly express that we are dealing with const references by using const auto&, and, more importantly, we should use auto& to *only* denote mutable references.

A mutable reference

In contrast to a const reference, a mutable reference cannot bind to a temporary. As mentioned, we use auto& to denote mutable references. Use a mutable reference only when you intend to change the object it references.

A forwarding reference

auto&& is called a forwarding reference (also referred to as a *universal reference*). It can bind to anything, which makes it useful for certain cases. Forwarding references will, just like const references, extend the lifetime of a temporary. But in contrast to the const reference, auto&& allows us to mutate objects it references, temporaries included.

Use auto&& for variables that you only forward to some other code. In those forwarding cases, you rarely care about whether the variable is a const or a mutable; you just want to pass it to some code that is actually going to use the variable.

 It's important to note that auto&& and T&& are only forwarding references if used in a function template where T is a template parameter of that function template. Using the && syntax with an explicit type, for example std::string&&, denotes an **rvalue** reference and does not have the properties of a forwarding reference (rvalues and move semantics will be discussed later in this chapter).

Practices for ease of use

Although this is my personal opinion, I recommend using const auto for fundamental types (int, float, and so on) and small non-fundamental types like std::pair and std::complex. For bigger types that are potentially expensive to copy, use const auto&. This should cover the majority of the variable declarations in a C++ code base.

auto& and auto should only be used when you require the behavior of a mutable reference or an explicit copy; this communicates to the reader of the code that those variables are important as they either copy an object or mutate a referenced object. Finally, use auto&& for forwarding code only.

Following these rules makes your code base easier to read, debug, and reason about.

 It might seem odd that while I recommend using const auto and const auto& for most variable declarations, I tend to use a simple auto in some places in this book. The reason for using plain auto is the limited space that the format of a book provides.

Before moving on, we will spend a little time talking about const and how to propagate const when using pointers.

Const propagation for pointers

By using the keyword const, we can inform the compiler about which objects are immutable. The compiler can then check that we don't try to mutate objects that aren't intended to be changed. In other words, the compiler checks our code for const-correctness. A common mistake when writing const-correct code in C++ is that a const-initialized object can still manipulate the values that member pointers point at. The following example illustrates the problem:

```cpp
class Foo {
public:
  Foo(int* ptr) : ptr_{ptr} {}
  auto set_ptr_val(int v) const {
    *ptr_ = v; // Compiles despite function being declared const!
  }
private:
  int* ptr_{};
};
```

```
int main() {
  auto i = 0;
  const auto foo = Foo{&i};
  foo.set_ptr_val(42);
}
```

Although the function `set_ptr_val()` is mutating the `int` value, it's valid to declare it `const` since the pointer `ptr_` itself is not mutated, only the `int` object that the pointer is pointing at.

In order to prevent this in a readable way, a wrapper called `std::experimental::propagate_const` has been added to the standard library extensions (included in, at the time of writing, the latest versions of Clang and GCC). Using `propagate_const`, the function `set_ptr_val()` will not compile. Note that `propagate_const` only applies to pointers, and pointer-like classes such as `std::shared_ptr` and `std::unique_ptr`, but not `std::function`.

The following example demonstrates how `propagate_const` can be used to generate compilation errors when trying to mutate an object inside a const function:

```
#include <experimental/propagate_const>
class Foo {
public:
  Foo(int* ptr) : ptr_{ptr} {}
  auto set_ptr(int* p) const {
    ptr_ = p;  // Will not compile, as expected
  }
  auto set_val(int v) const {
    val_ = v;  // Will not compile, as expected
  }
  auto set_ptr_val(int v) const {
    *ptr_ = v; // Will not compile, const is propagated
  }
private:
  std::experimental::propagate_const<int*> ptr_ = nullptr;
  int val_{};
};
```

The importance of proper use of `const` in large code bases cannot be overstated, and the introduction of `propagate_const` makes const-correctness even more effective.

Next, we will have a look at move semantics and some important rules for handling resources inside a class.

Move semantics explained

Move semantics is a concept introduced in C++11 that, in my experience, is quite hard to grasp, even by experienced programmers. Therefore, I will try to give you an in-depth explanation of how it works, when the compiler utilizes it, and, most importantly, why it is needed.

Essentially, the reason C++ even has the concept of move semantics, whereas most other languages don't, is a result of it being a value-based language, as discussed in *Chapter 1, A Brief Introduction to C++*. If C++ did not have move semantics built in, the advantages of value-based semantics would get lost in many cases and programmers would have to perform one of the following trade-offs:

- Performing redundant deep-cloning operations with high performance costs
- Using pointers for objects like Java does, losing the robustness of value semantics
- Performing error-prone swapping operations at the cost of readability

We do not want any of these, so let's have a look at how move semantics help us.

Copy-construction, swap, and move

Before we go into the details of move, I will first explain and illustrate the differences between copy-constructing an object, swapping two objects, and move-constructing an object.

Copy-constructing an object

When copying an object handling a resource, a new resource needs to be allocated, and the resource from the source object needs to be copied so that the two objects are completely separated. Imagine that we have a class, Widget, that references some sort of resource that needs to be allocated on construction. The following code default-constructs a Widget object and then copy-constructs a new instance:

```
auto a = Widget{};
auto b = a;        // Copy-construction
```

The resource allocations that are carried out are illustrated in the following figure:

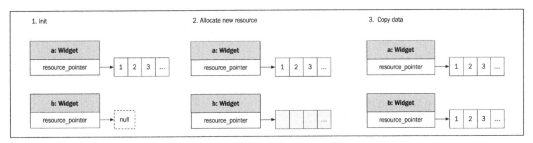

Figure 2.1: Copying an object with resources

The allocation and copying are slow processes, and, in many cases, the source object isn't needed anymore. With move semantics, the compiler detects cases like these where the old object is not tied to a variable, and instead performs a move operation.

Swapping two objects

Before move semantics were added in C++11, swapping the content of two objects was a common way to transfer data without allocating and copying. As shown next, objects simply swap their content with each other:

```
auto a = Widget{};
auto b = Widget{};
std::swap(a, b);
```

The following figure illustrates the process:

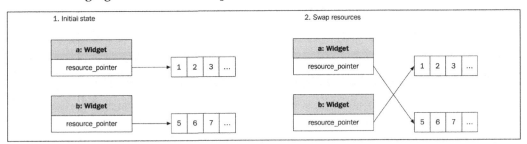

Figure 2.2: Swapping resources between two objects

The std::swap() function is a simple but useful utility used in the copy-and-swap idiom covered later in this chapter.

Move-constructing an object

When moving an object, the destination object steals the resource straight from the source object, and the source object is reset.

As you can see, it is very similar to swapping, except that the *moved-from* object does not have to receive the resources from the *moved-to* object:

```
auto a = Widget{};
auto b = std::move(a); // Tell the compiler to move the resource into b
```

The following figure illustrates the process:

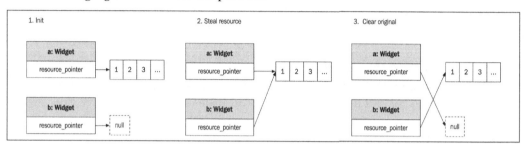

Figure 2.3: Moving resources from one object to another

Although the source object is reset, it's still in a valid state. This resetting of the source object is not something that the compiler does automatically for us. Instead, we need to implement the resetting in the move constructor to ensure that the object is in a valid state that can be destroyed or assigned to. We will talk more about valid states later on in this chapter.

Moving objects only makes sense if the object type owns a resource of some sort (the most common case being heap-allocated memory). If all data is contained within the object, the most efficient way to move an object is to just copy it.

Now that you have a basic grasp of move semantics, let's go into the details.

Resource acquisition and the rule of five

To fully understand move semantics, we need to go back to the basics of classes and resource acquisition in C++. One of the basic concepts in C++ is that a class should completely handle its resources. This means that when a class is copied, moved, copy-assigned, move-assigned, or destructed, the class should make sure its resources are handled accordingly. The necessity of implementing these five functions is commonly referred to as **the rule of five**.

Let's have a look at how the rule of five can be implemented in a class handling an allocated resource. In the `Buffer` class defined in the following code snippet, the allocated resource is an array of `floats` pointed at by the raw pointer `ptr_`:

```
class Buffer {
public:
  // Constructor
```

```
  Buffer(const std::initializer_list<float>& values)
      : size_{values.size()} {
    ptr_ = new float[values.size()];
    std::copy(values.begin(), values.end(), ptr_);
  }
  auto begin() const { return ptr_; }
  auto end() const { return ptr_ + size_; }
  /* The 5 special functions are defined below */
private:
  size_t size_{0};
  float* ptr_{nullptr};
};
```

In this case, the handled resource is a block of memory allocated in the constructor of the Buffer class. Memory is probably the most common resource for classes to handle, but a resource can be so much more: a mutex, a handle for a texture on the graphics card, a thread handle, and so on.

The five functions that are referred to in the rule of five have been left out and will follow next. We will begin with the copy-constructor, copy-assignment, and destructor, which all need to be involved in the resource handling:

```
// 1. Copy constructor
Buffer::Buffer(const Buffer& other) : size_{other.size_} {
  ptr_ = new float[size_];
  std::copy(other.ptr_, other.ptr_ + size_, ptr_);
}
// 2. Copy assignment
auto& Buffer::operator=(const Buffer& other) {
  delete [] ptr_;
  ptr_ = new float[other.size_];
  size_ = other.size_;
  std::copy(other.ptr_, other.ptr_ + size_, ptr_);
  return *this;
}
// 3. Destructor
Buffer::~Buffer() {
  delete [] ptr_; // OK, it is valid to delete a nullptr
  ptr_ = nullptr;
}
```

Before the introduction of move semantics in C++11, these three functions were usually referred to as the **rule of three**. The copy-constructor, copy-assignment, and destructor are invoked in the following cases:

```
auto func() {
  // Construct
  auto b0 = Buffer({0.0f, 0.5f, 1.0f, 1.5f});
  // 1. Copy-construct
  auto b1 = b0;
  // 2. Copy-assignment as b0 is already initialized
  b0 = b1;
} // 3. End of scope, the destructors are automatically invoked
```

Although a correct implementation of these three functions is all that is required for a class to handle its internal resources, two problems arise:

- **Resources that cannot be copied**: In the Buffer class example, our resource can be copied, but there are other types of resources where a copy wouldn't make sense. For example, the resource contained in a class might be a std::thread, a network connection, or something else that it's not possible to copy. In these cases, we cannot pass around the object.

- **Unnecessary copies**: If we return our Buffer class from a function, the entire array needs to be copied. (The compiler optimizes away the copy in some cases, though, but let's ignore that for now.)

The solution to these problems is move semantics. In addition to the copy-constructor and copy-assignment, we can add a move-constructor and a move-assignment operator to our class. Instead of taking a const reference (const Buffer&) as a parameter, the move versions accept a Buffer&& object.

The && modifier indicates that the parameter is an object that we intend to move from instead of copying it. Speaking in C++ terms, this is called an rvalue, and we will talk a little bit more about those later.

Whereas the copy() functions copy an object, the move equivalents are intended to move resources from one object to another, freeing the moved-from object from the resource.

This is how we would extend our Buffer class with the move-constructor and move-assignment. As you can see, these functions will not throw any exceptions and can therefore be marked as noexcept. This is because, as opposed to the copy-constructor/copy-assignment, they do not allocate memory or do something that might throw exceptions:

```
// 4. Move constructor
Buffer::Buffer(Buffer&& other) noexcept
    : size_{other.size_}, ptr_{other.ptr_} {
  other.ptr_ = nullptr;
  other.size_ = 0;
}
// 5. Move assignment
auto& Buffer::operator=(Buffer&& other) noexcept {
  ptr_ = other.ptr_;
  size_ = other.size_;
  other.ptr_ = nullptr;
  other.size_ = 0;
  return *this;
}
```

Now, when the compiler detects that we perform what seems to be a copy, such as returning a Buffer from a function, but the copied-from value isn't used anymore, it will utilize the no-throw move-constructor/move-assignment instead of copying.

This is pretty sweet; the interface remains as clear as when copying but, under the hood, the compiler has performed a simple move. Thus, the programmer does not need to use any esoteric pointers or out-parameters in order to avoid a copy; as the class has move semantics implemented, the compiler handles this automatically.

> Do not forget to mark your move-constructors and move-assignment operators as noexcept (unless they might throw an exception, of course). Not marking them noexcept prevents standard library containers and algorithms from utilizing them, instead resorting to using a regular copy/assignment under certain conditions.

To be able to know when the compiler is allowed to move an object instead of copying, an understanding of rvalues is necessary.

Named variables and rvalues

So, when is the compiler allowed to move objects instead of copying? As a short answer, the compiler moves an object when the object can be categorized as an rvalue. The term **rvalue** might sound complicated, but in essence it is just an object that is not tied to a named variable, for either of the following reasons:

- It's coming straight out of a function
- We make a variable an rvalue by using std::move()

The following example demonstrates both of these scenarios:

```
// The object returned by make_buffer is not tied to a variable
x = make_buffer();   // move-assigned

// The variable "x" is passed into std::move()
y = std::move(x);    // move-assigned
```

I will also use the terms **lvalue** and **named variable** interchangeably in this book. An lvalue corresponds to objects that we can refer to by name in our code.

Now we will make this a little more advanced by using a member variable of type std::string in a class. The following Button class will serve as an example:

```
class Button {
public:
  Button() {}
  auto set_title(const std::string& s) {
    title_ = s;
  }
  auto set_title(std::string&& s) {
    title_ = std::move(s);
  }
  std::string title_;
};
```

We also need a free function returning a title and a Button variable:

```
auto get_ok() {
  return std::string("OK");
}
auto button = Button{};
```

Given these prerequisites, let's look at a few cases of copying and moving in detail:

- **Case 1**: Button::title_ is copy-assigned because the string object is tied to the variable str:

  ```
  auto str = std::string{"OK"};
  button.set_title(str);                   // copy-assigned
  ```

- **Case 2**: Button::title_ is move-assigned because str is passed through std::move():

  ```
  auto str = std::string{"OK"};
  button.set_title(std::move(str));   // move-assigned
  ```

- **Case 3**: `Button::title_` is move-assigned because the new `std::string` object is coming straight out of a function:

  ```
  button.set_title(get_ok());          // move-assigned
  ```

- **Case 4**: `Button::title_` is copy-assigned because the `string` object is tied to s (this is the same as *Case 1*):

  ```
  auto str = get_ok();
  button.set_title(str);               // copy-assigned
  ```

- **Case 5**: `Button::title_` is copy-assigned because `str` is declared `const` and therefore is not allowed to mutate:

  ```
  const auto str = get_ok();
  button.set_title(std::move(str));   // copy-assigned
  ```

As you can see, determining whether an object is moved or copied is quite simple. If it has a variable name, it is copied; otherwise, it is moved. If you are using `std::move()` to move a named object, the object cannot be declared `const`.

Default move semantics and the rule of zero

 This section discusses automatically generated copy-assignment operators. It's important to know that the generated function does not have strong exception guarantees. Therefore, if an exception is thrown during the copy-assignment, the object might end up in a state where it is only partially copied.

As with the copy-constructor and copy-assignment, the move-constructor and move-assignment can be generated by the compiler. Although some compilers allow themselves to automatically generate these functions under certain conditions (more about this later), we can simply force the compiler to generate them by using the `default` keyword.

In the case of the `Button` class, which doesn't manually handle any resources, we can simply extend it like this:

```
class Button {
public:
  Button() {} // Same as before

  // Copy-constructor/copy-assignment
  Button(const Button&) = default;
  auto operator=(const Button&) -> Button& = default;
```

```
  // Move-constructor/move-assignment
  Button(Button&&) noexcept = default;
  auto operator=(Button&&) noexcept -> Button& = default;

  // Destructor
  ~Button() = default;
  // ...
};
```

To make it even simpler, if we do not declare *any* custom copy-constructor/copy-assignment or destructor, the move-constructors/move-assignments are implicitly declared, meaning that the first Button class actually handles everything:

```
class Button {
public:
  Button() {} // Same as before

  // Nothing here, the compiler generates everything automatically!
  // ...
};
```

It's easy to forget that adding just one of the five functions prevents the compiler from generating the other ones. The following version of the Button class has a custom destructor. As a result, the move operators are not generated, and the class will always be copied:

```
class Button {
public:
  Button() {}
  ~Button()
    std::cout << "destructed\n"
  }
  // ...
};
```

Let's see how we can use this insight into generated functions when implementing application classes.

Rule of zero in a real code base

In practice, the cases where you have to write your own copy/move-constructors, copy/move-assignments, and constructors should be very few. Writing your classes so that they don't require any of these special member functions to be explicitly written (or default - declared) is often referred to as **the rule of zero**. This means that if a class in the application code base is required to have any of these functions written explicitly, that piece of code would probably be better off in the library part of your code base.

Later on in this book, we will discuss std::optional, which is a handy utility class for dealing with optional members when applying the rule of zero.

A note on empty destructors

Writing an empty destructor can prevent the compiler from implementing certain optimizations. As you can see in the following snippets, copying an array of a trivial class with an empty destructor yields the same (non-optimized) assembler code as copying with a handcrafted for-loop. The first version uses an empty destructor with std::copy():

```
struct Point {
  int x_, y_;
  ~Point() {}     // Empty destructor, don't use!
};
auto copy(Point* src, Point* dst) {
  std::copy(src, src+64, dst);
}
```

The second version uses a Point class with no destructor but with a handcrafted for-loop:

```
struct Point {
  int x_, y_;
};
auto copy(Point* src, Point* dst) {
  const auto end = src + 64;
  for (; src != end; ++src, ++dst) {
    *dst = *src;
  }
}
```

Both versions generate the following x86 assembler, which corresponds to a simple loop:

```
 xor eax, eax
.L2:
 mov rdx, QWORD PTR [rdi+rax]
 mov QWORD PTR [rsi+rax], rdx
 add rax, 8
 cmp rax, 512
 jne .L2
 rep ret
```

However, if we remove the destructor or declare the destructor `default`, the compiler optimizes `std::copy()` to utilize `memmove()` instead of a loop:

```
struct Point {
  int x_, y_;
  ~Point() = default; // OK: Use default or no constructor at all
};
auto copy(Point* src, Point* dst) {
  std::copy(src, src+64, dst);
}
```

The preceding code generates the following x86 assembler, with the `memmove()` optimization:

```
 mov rax, rdi
 mov edx, 512
 mov rdi, rsi
 mov rsi, rax
 jmp memmove
```

The assembler was generated using GCC 7.1 in *Compiler Explorer*, which is available at https://godbolt.org/.

To summarize, use `default` destructors or no destructors at all in favor of empty destructors to squeeze a little bit more performance out of your application.

A common pitfall – moving non-resources

There is one common pitfall when using default-created move-assignments: classes that mix fundamental types with more advanced compound types. As opposed to compound types, fundamental types (such as `int`, `float`, and `bool`) are simply copied when moved, as they don't handle any resources.

When a simple type is mixed with a resource-owning type, the move-assignment becomes a mixture of move and copy.

Here is an example of a class that will fail:

```cpp
class Menu {
public:
  Menu(const std::initializer_list<std::string>& items)
      : items_{items} {}
  auto select(int i) {
    index_ = i;
  }
  auto selected_item() const {
      return index_ != -1 ? items_[index_] : "";
  }
  // ...
private:
  int index_{-1}; // Currently selected item
  std::vector<std::string> items_;
};
```

The Menu class will have undefined behavior if it's used like this:

```cpp
auto a = Menu{"New", "Open", "Close", "Save"};
a.select(2);
auto b = std::move(a);
auto selected = a.selected_item(); // crash
```

The undefined behavior happens as the items_ vector is moved and is therefore empty. The index_, on the other hand, is copied, and therefore still has the value 2 in the moved-from object a. When selected_item() is called, the function will try to access items_ at index 2 and the program will crash.

In these cases, the move-constructor/assignment is better implemented by simply swapping the members, like this:

```cpp
Menu(Menu&& other) noexcept {
  std::swap(items_, other.items_);
  std::swap(index_, other.index_);
}

auto& operator=(Menu&& other) noexcept {
  std::swap(items_, other.items_);
  std::swap(index_, other.index_);
```

```
    return *this;
}
```

This way, the Menu class can be safely moved while still preserving the no-throw guarantee. In *Chapter 8, Compile-Time Programming,* you will learn how to take advantage of reflection techniques in C++ in order to automate the process of creating move-constructor/assignment functions that swap the elements.

Applying the && modifier to class member functions

In addition to being applied to objects, you can also add the && modifier to a member function of a class, just as you can apply a const modifier to a member function. As with the const modifier, a member function that has the && modifier will only be considered by overload resolution if the object is an rvalue:

```
struct Foo {
  auto func() && {}
};
auto a = Foo{};
a.func();           // Doesn't compile, 'a' is not an rvalue
std::move(a).func(); // Compiles
Foo{}.func();       // Compiles
```

It might seem odd that anyone would ever want this behavior, but there are use cases. We will investigate one of them in *Chapter 10, Proxy Objects and Lazy Evaluation.*

Don't move when copies are elided anyway

It might be tempting to use std::move() when returning a value from a function, like this:

```
auto func() {
  auto x = X{};
  // ...
  return std::move(x);  // Don't, RVO is prevented
}
```

However, unless x is a move-only type, you shouldn't be doing this. This usage of std::move() prevents the compiler from using **return value optimization** (**RVO**) and thereby completely elides the copying of x, which is more efficient than moving it. So, when returning a newly created object by value, don't use std::move(); instead, just return the object:

```
auto func() {
  auto x = X{};
  // ...
  return x;  // OK
}
```

This particular example where a *named* object is elided is usually called **NRVO**, or **Named-RVO**. RVO and NRVO are implemented by all major C++ compilers today. If you want to read more about RVO and copy elision, you can find a detailed summary at https://en.cppreference.com/w/cpp/language/copy_elision.

Pass by value when applicable

Consider a function that converts a std::string to lowercase. In order to use the move-constructor where applicable, and the copy-constructor otherwise, it may seem like two functions are required:

```
// Argument s is a const reference
auto str_to_lower(const std::string& s) -> std::string {
  auto clone = s;
  for (auto& c: clone) c = std::tolower(c);
  return clone;
}
// Argument s is an rvalue reference
auto str_to_lower(std::string&& s) -> std::string {
  for (auto& c: s) c = std::tolower(c);
  return s;
}
```

However, by taking the std::string by value instead, we can write one function that covers both cases:

```
auto str_to_lower(std::string s) -> std::string {
  for (auto& c: s) c = std::tolower(c);
  return s;
}
```

Let's see why this implementation of str_to_lower() avoids unnecessary copying where possible. When passed a regular variable, shown as follows, the content of str is copy-constructed into s prior to the function call, and then move-assigned back to str when the functions returns:

```
auto str = std::string{"ABC"};
str = str_to_lower(str);
```

When passed an rvalue, as shown below, the content of str is move-constructed into s prior to the function call, and then move-assigned back to str when the function returns. Therefore, no copy is made through the function call:

```
auto str = std::string{"ABC"};
str = str_to_lower(std::move(str));
```

At first sight, it seems like this technique could be applicable to all parameters. However, this pattern is not always optimal, as you will see next.

Cases where pass-by-value is not applicable

Sometimes this pattern of accept-by-value-then-move is actually a pessimization. For example, consider the following class where the function set_data() will keep a copy of the argument passed to it:

```
class Widget {
  std::vector<int> data_{};
  // ...

public:
  void set_data(std::vector<int> x) {
    data_ = std::move(x);
  }
};
```

Assume we call set_data() and pass it an lvalue, like this:

```
auto v = std::vector<int>{1, 2, 3, 4};
widget.set_data(v);                      // Pass an lvalue
```

Since we are passing a named object, v, the code will copy-construct a new std::vector object, x, and then move-assign that object into the data_ member. Unless we pass an empty vector object to set_data(), the std::vector copy-constructor will perform a heap allocation for its internal buffer.

Now compare this with the following version of set_data() optimized for lvalues:

```
void set_data(const std::vector<int>& x) {
    data_ = x;  // Reuse internal buffer in data_ if possible
}
```

Here, there will only be a heap allocation inside the assignment operator if the capacity of the current vector, data_, is smaller than the size of the source object, x. In other words, the internal pre-allocated buffer of data_ can be reused in the assignment operator in many cases and save us from an extra heap allocation.

If we find it necessary to optimize set_data() for lvalues and rvalues, it's better, in this case, to provide two overloads:

```
void set_data(const std::vector<int>& x) {
  data_ = x;
}
void set_data(std::vector<int>&& x) noexcept {
  data_ = std::move(x);
}
```

The first version is optimal for lvalues and the second version for rvalues.

Finally, we will now look at a scenario where we can safely pass by value without worrying about the pessimization just demonstrated.

Moving constructor parameters

When initializing class members in a constructor, we can safely use the pass-by-value-then-move pattern. During the construction of a new object, there is no chance that there are pre-allocated buffers that could have been utilized to avoid heap allocations. What follows is an example of a class with one std::vector member and a constructor to demonstrate this pattern:

```
class Widget {
  std::vector<int> data_;
public:
  Widget(std::vector<int> x)        // By value
      : data_{std::move(x)} {}      // Move-construct
  // ...
};
```

We will now shift our focus to a topic that cannot be considered *modern* C++ but is frequently discussed even today.

Designing interfaces with error handling

Error handling is an important and often overlooked part of the interface of functions and classes. Error handling is a heavily debated topic in C++, but often the discussions tend to focus on exceptions versus some other error mechanism. Although this is an interesting area, there are other aspects of error handling that are even more important to understand before focusing on the actual implementation of error handling. Obviously, both exceptions and error codes have been used in numerous successful software projects, and it is not uncommon to stumble upon projects that combine the two.

A fundamental aspect of error handling, regardless of programming language, is to distinguish between **programming errors** (also known as bugs) and **runtime errors**. Runtime errors can be further divided into **recoverable runtime errors** and **unrecoverable runtime errors**. An example of an unrecoverable runtime error is *stack overflow* (see *Chapter 7, Memory Management*). When an unrecoverable error occurs, the program typically terminates immediately, so there is no point in signaling these types of errors. However, some errors might be considered recoverable in one type of application but unrecoverable in others.

An edge case that often comes up when discussing recoverable and unrecoverable errors is the somewhat unfortunate behavior of the C++ standard library when running out of memory. When your program runs out of memory, this is typically unrecoverable, yet the standard library (tries) to throw a std::bad_alloc exception when this happens. We will not spend time on unrecoverable errors here, but the talk *De-fragmenting C++: Making Exceptions and RTTI More Affordable and Usable* by Herb Sutter (https://sched.co/SiVW) is highly recommended if you want to dig deeper into this topic.

When designing and implementing an API, you should always reflect on what type of error you are dealing with, because errors from different categories should be handled in completely different ways. Deciding whether errors are programming errors or runtime errors can be done by using a methodology called **Design by Contract**; this is a topic that deserves a book on its own. However, I will here introduce the fundamentals, which are enough for our purposes.

 There are proposals for adding language support for contracts in C++, but currently contracts haven't made it to the standard yet. However, many C++ APIs and guidelines assume that you know the basics about contracts because the terminology contracts use makes it easier to discuss and document interfaces of classes and functions.

Contracts

A **contract** is a set of rules between the caller of some function and the function itself (the callee). C++ allows us to explicitly specify some rules using the C++ type system. For example, consider the following function signature:

```
int func(float x, float y)
```

It specifies that func() is returning an integer (unless it throws an exception), and that the caller has to pass two floating-point values. However, it doesn't say anything about what floating-point values that are allowed. For instance, can we pass the value 0.0 or a negative value? In addition, there might be some required relationship between x and y that cannot easily be expressed using the C++ type system. When we talk about contracts in C++, we usually refer to the rules that exist between a caller and a callee that cannot easily be expressed using the type system.

Without being too formal, a few concepts related to Design by Contract will be introduced here in order to give you some terms that you can use to reason about interfaces and error handling:

- **A precondition** specifies the *responsibilities of the caller* of a function. There may be constraints on the parameters passed to the function. Or, if it's a member function, the object might have to be in a specific state before calling the function. For example, the precondition when calling pop_back() on a std::vector is that the vector is not empty. It's the responsibility of the *caller* of pop_back() to ensure that the vector is not empty.

- **A postcondition** specifies the *responsibilities of the function* upon returning. If it's a member function, in what state does the function leave the object? For example, the postcondition of std::list::sort() is that the elements in the list are sorted in ascending order.

- **An invariant** is a condition that should always hold true. Invariants can be used in many contexts. A *loop invariant* is a condition that must be true at the beginning of every loop iteration. Further, a *class invariant* defines the valid states of an object. For example, an invariant of std::vector is that size() <= capacity(). Explicitly stating the invariants around some code gives us a better understanding of the code. Invariants are also a tool that can be used when proving that some algorithm does what it's supposed to do.

Class invariants are very important; we will therefore spend some more time discussing what they are and how they affect the design of classes.

Class invariants

As mentioned, a **class invariant** defines the valid states of an object. It specifies the relationship between the data members inside a class. An object can temporarily be in an invalid state during the time a member function is being executed. The important thing is that the invariant is upheld whenever the function passes the control to some other code that can observe the state of the object. This can happen when the function:

- Returns

- Throws an exception

- Invokes a callback function

- Calls some other function that might observe the state of the currently calling object; a common scenario is when passing a reference to this to some other function

It's important to realize that the class invariant is an implicit part of the precondition and postcondition for every member function of a class. If a member function leaves an object in an invalid state, the postcondition has not been fulfilled. Similarly, a member function can always assume that the object is in a valid state when the function is called. The exception to this rule is the constructors and the destructor of a class. If we wanted to insert code to check that the class invariant holds true, we could do that at the following points:

```cpp
struct Widget {
  Widget() {
    // Initialize object...
    // Check class invariant
  }
  ~Widget() {
    // Check class invariant
    // Destroy object...
  }
  auto some_func() {
    // Check precondition (including class invariant)
    // Do the actual work...
    // Check postcondition (including class invariant)
  }
};
```

The copy/move constructors and copy/move assignment operators were left out here, but they follow the same pattern as the constructor and some_func(), respectively.

When an object has been moved from, the object might be in some empty or reset state. This is also a valid state of the object and is therefore part of the class invariant. However, usually there are only a few member functions that can be called when the object is in this state. For example, you cannot call push_back(), empty(), or size() on a std::vector that has been moved from, but you can call clear(), which will put the vector in a state where it is ready to be used again.

You should be aware, though, that this extra reset state makes the class invariant weaker and less useful. To avoid this state completely, you should implement your classes in such a way so that moved-from objects are reset to the state the object would have after default construction. My recommendation is to always do this, except in the very rare cases where resetting the moved-from state to the default state carries an unacceptable performance penalty. In that way, you can reason much better about moved-from states, and the class is safer to use because calling member functions on that object is fine.

If you can ensure that an object is always in a valid state (the class invariant holds true), you are likely to have a class that is hard to misuse, and if you have bugs in the implementation, they will usually be easy to spot. The last thing you want is to find a class in your code base and wonder whether some behavior of that class is a bug or a feature. Violation of a contract is always a serious bug.

In order to be able to write meaningful class invariants, we are required to write classes with high cohesion and with few possible states. If you have ever written a unit test for a class that you have authored yourself, you have probably noticed that while writing the unit test, it became clear that the API could be improved from the initial version. A unit test forces you to use and reflect on the interface of the class rather than the implementation details. In the same way, a class invariant makes you think about all the valid states an object could be in. If you find it hard to define a class invariant, it's usually because your class has too many responsibilities and handles too many states. Therefore, defining class invariants usually means that you end up with well-designed classes.

Maintaining contracts

Contracts are parts of the API that you design and implement. But how do you maintain and communicate a contract to the clients using your API? C++ has no built-in support for contracts yet, but there is ongoing work to add it to future versions of C++. There are some options, though:

- Use a library such as Boost.Contract.

- Document the contracts. This has the disadvantage that the contracts are not checked when running the program. Also, documentation tends to be outdated when the code changes.

- Use static_assert() and the assert() macro defined in <cassert>. Asserts are portable, standard C++.

- Build a custom library with custom macros similar to asserts but with better control of the behavior of failed contracts.

In this book, we will use asserts, one of the most primitive ways of checking for contract violations. Still, asserts can be very effective and have an enormous impact on code quality.

Enabling and disabling asserts

Technically, we have two standard ways to assert things in C++: using static_assert() or the assert() macro from the <cassert> header. static_assert() is validated during the compilation of the code, and therefore requires an expression that can be checked during compile time rather than runtime. A failed static_assert() results in a compilation error.

For asserts that can only be evaluated during runtime, you need to use the assert() macro instead. The assert() macro is a runtime check that is typically active during debugging and testing, and completely disabled when the program is built in release mode. The assert() macro is typically defined something like this:

```
#ifdef NDEBUG
#define assert(condition) ((void)0)
#else
#define assert(condition) /* implementation defined */
#endif
```

This means that you can completely remove all the asserts and the code for checking the conditions by defining NDEBUG.

Now, with some terminology from Design by Contract under your belt, let's focus on contract violations (errors) and how to handle them in your code.

Error handling

The first thing to do when designing APIs with proper error handling is to distinguish between programming errors and runtime errors. So, before we dive into error handling strategies, we will use Design by Contract to define what type of error we are dealing with.

Programming error or runtime error?

If we find a violation of a contract, we have also found an error in our program. For example, if we can detect that someone is calling pop_back() on an empty vector, we know that there is at least one bug in our source code that needs to be fixed. Whenever a precondition is not met, we know we are dealing with a *programming error*.

On the other hand, if we have a function that loads some record from disk and cannot return the record because of a read error on the disk, then we have detected a *runtime error*:

```
auto load_record(std::uint32_t id) {
  assert(id != 0);            // Precondition
  auto record = read(id);     // Read from disk, may throw
  assert(record.is_valid()); // Postcondition
  return record;
}
```

The precondition is fulfilled, but the postcondition cannot be met because of something outside of our program. There is no bug in the source code, but the function cannot return the record found on disk because of some disk-related error. Since the postcondition cannot be fulfilled, a runtime error has to be reported back to the caller, unless the caller can recover from it itself by retrying and so on.

Programming errors (bugs)

In general, there is no point in writing code that signals and handles bugs in your code. Instead, use asserts (or some of the other alternatives mentioned previously) to make the developer aware of issues in the code. You should only use exceptions or error codes for recoverable runtime errors.

Narrowing the problem space by assumptions

An assert specifies what assumptions you, as the author of some code, have made. You can only guarantee that the code works as intended if all the asserts in your code hold true. This makes coding much easier because you can effectively limit the amount of cases that you need to handle. Asserts are also a tremendous help for your team when using, reading, and modifying code written by you. All the assumptions are clearly documented in the form of assert statements.

Finding bugs with asserts

A failed assert is always a serious bug. There are basically three options when you find an assert that fails during testing:

- The assert is correct, but the code is wrong (either because of a bug in the implementation of the function, or a bug on the call-site). In my experience, this is the most common case. Getting the asserts correct is usually easier than getting the code around them correct. Fix the code and test again.

- The code is correct, but the assert is wrong. Sometimes this happens and it is usually pretty uncomfortable if you are looking at old code. Changing or removing an assert that fails can be time consuming because you need to be 100% sure that the code actually works and understand why an old assert has suddenly started to fail. Usually, this is because of a new use case that the original authors did not think about.

- Both the assert and the code are wrong. This usually requires a redesign of the class or function. Maybe the requirements have changed, and the assumptions made by the programmer are no longer true. But don't despair; instead, you should be glad that those assumptions were explicitly written using asserts; now you know why the code is not working anymore.

Runtime asserts require testing, otherwise the asserts will not be exercised. Newly written code with many asserts usually breaks when testing. This doesn't mean that you are a bad programmer; it means that you have added meaningful asserts that catch some of the errors that otherwise could have made it to production. Also, bugs that make a test version of your program terminate are also likely to be fixed.

Performance impact

Having many runtime asserts in your code will most likely degrade the performance of your test builds. However, asserts are never meant to be used in the final version of your optimized program. If your asserts make your test build too slow to be usable, finding the set of asserts that slows down your code is usually easy to track in a profiler (see *Chapter 3, Analyzing and Measuring Performance*, for more info about profiling).

By having the release build of your program completely ignore all sorts of programming errors, your program will not spend time checking error states caused by bugs. Instead, your code will run faster and only spend time solving the actual problem it was meant to solve. It will only check for runtime errors that need to be recovered.

To summarize, programming errors should be detected when testing the program. There is no need to use exceptions or some other error handling mechanism for dealing with programming errors. Instead, a programming error should preferably log something meaningful and terminate the program to inform the programmer that the bug needs to be fixed. Following this guideline dramatically reduces the number of places we need to handle exceptions in our code. We will have better performance in our optimized build and hopefully fewer bugs since they have been detected by failed asserts. However, there are situations where errors can occur at runtime, and those errors need to be handled and recovered by the code we implement.

Recoverable runtime errors

If a function cannot uphold its part of the contract (the postcondition, that is), a runtime error has occurred and needs to be signaled to some place in the code that can handle it and recover the valid state. The purpose of handling recoverable errors is to pass an error from the place where the error occurred to the place where the valid state can be recovered. There are many ways to achieve this. There are two sides of this coin:

- For the signaling part we can choose between C++ exceptions, error codes, returning a `std::optional` or `std::pair`, or using `boost::outcome` or `std::experimental::expected`.

- Preserving the valid state of the program without leaking any resources. Deterministic destructors and automatic storage duration are the tools that make this possible in C++.

The utility classes `std::optional` and `std::pair` will be covered in *Chapter 9, Essential Utilities*. We will now focus on C++ exceptions and how to avoid leaking resources when recovering from an error.

Exceptions

Exceptions are the standard error handling mechanism provided by C++. The language was designed to be used with exceptions. One example of this is constructors that fail; the only way to signal errors from constructors is by using exceptions.

In my experience, exceptions are used in many different ways. One reason for this is that distinct applications can have vastly different requirements when dealing with runtime errors. With some applications, such as a pacemaker or a power plant control system, which may have a severe impact if they crash, we may have to deal with every possible exceptional circumstance, such as running out of memory, and keep the application in a running state. Some applications even completely stay away from using the heap memory, either because the platform doesn't have any heap available at all, or because the heap introduces an uncontrollable level of uncertainty as the mechanics of allocating new memory are out of the application's control.

I assume that you already know the syntax of throwing and catching exceptions and will not cover it here. A function that is guaranteed to not throw an exception can be marked as noexcept. It's important to understand that the compiler does *not* verify this; instead, it is up to the author of the code to figure out whether their function could throw an exception.

A function marked with noexcept makes it possible for the compiler to generate faster code in some cases. If an exception would be thrown from a function marked with noexcept, the program will call std::terminate() instead of unwinding the stack. The following code demonstrates how to mark a function as not throwing:

```
auto add(int a, int b) noexcept {
  return a + b;
}
```

You may notice that many code examples in this book don't use noexcept (or const) even if it would have been appropriate in production code. This is only because of the format of a book; it would make the code hard to read to add noexcept and const at all the places that I normally would.

Preserving the valid state

Exception handling requires us programmers to think about exception safety guarantees; that is, what is the program state before and after an exception has occurred? Strong exception safety can be seen as a transaction. A function either commits all state changes, or performs a complete rollback in the case of an exception.

To make this a bit more concrete, let's take a look at the following simple function:

```
void func(std::string& str) {
  str += f1();  // Could throw
  str += f2();  // Could throw
}
```

The function appends the result of f1() and f2() to the string, str. Now consider what would happen if an exception was thrown when calling the function f2(); only the result from f1() would be appended to str. What we want instead is to have str untouched if an exception occurs. This can be fixed by using an idiom called **copy-and-swap**. It means that we perform the operations that might throw exceptions on temporary copies before we let the application's state be modified by non-throwing swap() functions:

```cpp
void func(std::string& str) {
  auto tmp = std::string{str};   // Copy
  tmp += f1();                   // Mutate copy, may throw
  tmp += f2();                   // Mutate copy, may throw
  std::swap(tmp, str);           // Swap, never throws
}
```

The same pattern can be used in member functions to preserve the valid state of an object. Let's say we have a class with two data members and a class invariant that says that the data members cannot compare equal, as follows:

```cpp
class Number { /* ... */ };

class Widget {
public:
  Widget(const Number& x, const Number& y) : x_{x}, y_{y} {
    assert(is_valid());          // Check class invariant
  }
private:
  Number x_{};
  Number y_{};
  bool is_valid() const {        // Class invariant
   return x_ != y_;              // x_ and y_ must not be equal
  }
};
```

Next, assume we are adding a member function that updates both data members, like this:

```cpp
void Widget::update(const Number& x, const Number& y) {
  assert(x != y && is_valid());  // Precondition
  x_ = x;
  y_ = y;
  assert(is_valid());            // Postcondition
}
```

The precondition states that x and y must not compare equal. If the assignment of x_ and y_ can throw, x_ might be updated but not y_. This may result in a broken class invariant; that is, an object in an invalid state. We want the function to preserve the valid state of the object it had before the assignment operations if an error occurs. Again, one possible solution is to use the copy-and-swap idiom:

```
void Widget::update(const Number& x, const Number& y) {
    assert(x != y && is_valid());      // Precondition
    auto x_tmp = x;
    auto y_tmp = y;
    std::swap(x_tmp, x_);
    std::swap(y_tmp, y_);
    assert(is_valid());                // Postcondition
}
```

First, local copies are created without modifying the state of the object. Then, if no exception has been thrown, the state of the object can be changed using a non-throwing swap(). The copy-and-swap idiom can also be used when implementing assignment operators to achieve strong exception safety guarantees.

Another important aspect of error handling is to avoid leaking resources when an error occurs.

Resource acquisition

The destruction of C++ objects is predictable, meaning that we have full control over when, and in what order, resources that we have acquired are released. This is further illustrated in the following example, where the mutex variable m is always unlocked when exiting the function, as the scoped lock releases it when we exit the scope, regardless of how and where we exit:

```
auto func(std::mutex& m, bool x, bool y) {
  auto guard = std::scoped_lock{m}; // Lock mutex
  if (x) {
    // The guard automatically releases the mutex at early exit
    return;
  }
  if (y) {
    // The guard automatically releases if an exception is thrown
    throw std::exception{};
  }
  // The guard automatically releases the mutex at function exit
}
```

Ownership, lifetime of objects, and resource acquisition are fundamental concepts in C++, and we will cover them in *Chapter 7, Memory Management*.

Performance

Unfortunately, exceptions have a bad reputation when it comes to performance. Some concerns are legitimate, whereas some are based on historical observations when exceptions were not implemented efficiently by the compilers. However, today there are two main reasons why people abandon exceptions:

- The size of the binary program is increased even if exceptions are not being thrown. Even though this is usually not an issue, it doesn't follow the zero-overhead principle since we are paying for something that we don't use.

- Throwing and catching exceptions is relatively expensive. The runtime cost of throwing and catching exceptions is not deterministic. This makes exceptions unsuitable in contexts with hard real-time requirements. In this case, other alternatives such as returning a `std::pair` with a return value and an error code might better.

On the other hand, exceptions perform outstandingly when no exceptions are being thrown; that is, when the program follows the success path. Other error reporting mechanisms such as error codes require checking return codes in `if-else` statements even when the program runs without any errors.

Exceptions should happen rarely, and typically when an exception occurs, the extra performance penalty that exception handling adds is usually not an issue in those situations. It's usually possible to perform computations that could potentially throw before or after some performance-critical code runs. In that way, we can avoid having exceptions thrown and caught at the places in our program where we cannot afford to have exceptions.

To make a fair comparison between exceptions and some other error reporting mechanism, it's important to specify what to compare. Sometimes exceptions are compared with no error handling at all, which is unfair; exceptions need to be compared with a mechanism that offers the same functionality, of course. Don't abandon exceptions for performance reasons before you have measured the impact they might have. You can read more about analyzing and measuring performance in the next chapter.

Now we will move away from error handling and explore how we can use lambda expressions to create function objects.

Function objects and lambda expressions

Lambda expressions, introduced in C++11, and further enhanced with every C++ version since, are one of the most useful features in modern C++. Their versatility comes not only from easily passing functions to algorithms, but also their use in a lot of circumstances where you need to pass the code around, especially as you can store a lambda in a `std::function`.

Although lambdas made these programming techniques vastly simpler to work with, everything mentioned in this section is possible to perform without them. A lambda—or, more formally, a lambda expression—is a convenient way of constructing a function object. But instead of using lambda expressions, we could instead implement classes with `operator()` overloaded, and then instantiate these to create function objects.

We will explore the lambda's similarities to these kinds of classes later, but first I will introduce lambda expressions in a simple use case.

The basic syntax of a C++ lambda

In a nutshell, lambdas enable programmers to pass functions to other functions, just as easily as a variable is passed.

Let's compare passing a lambda to an algorithm with passing a variable:

```
// Prerequisite
auto v = std::vector{1, 3, 2, 5, 4};

// Look for number three
auto three = 3;
auto num_threes = std::count(v.begin(), v.end(), three);
// num_threes is 1

// Look for numbers which is larger than three
auto is_above_3 = [](int v) { return v > 3; };
auto num_above_3 = std::count_if(v.begin(), v.end(), is_above_3);
// num_above_3 is 2
```

In the first case, we pass a variable to `std::count()`, and in the latter case we pass a function object to `std::count_if()`. This is a typical use case for lambdas; we pass a function to be evaluated many times by another function (in this case, `std::count_if()`).

Also, the lambda does not need to be tied to a variable; just as we can put a variable right into an expression, we can do the same with a lambda:

```
auto num_3 = std::count(v.begin(), v.end(), 3);
auto num_above_3 = std::count_if(v.begin(), v.end(), [](int i) {
  return i > 3;
});
```

The lambdas you have seen so far are called **stateless lambdas**; they don't copy or reference any variables from outside the lambda and therefore don't need any internal state. Let's make this a little more advanced by introducing **stateful lambdas** by using capture blocks.

The capture clause

In the previous example, we hard-coded the value 3 inside the lambda so that we always counted the numbers greater than three. What if we want to use external variables inside the lambda? What we do is capture the external variables by putting them in the **capture clause**; that is, the [ ] part of the lambda:

```
auto count_value_above(const std::vector<int>& v, int x) {
  auto is_above = [x](int i) { return i > x; };
  return std::count_if(v.begin(), v.end(), is_above);
}
```

In this example, we captured the variable x by copying it into the lambda. If we want to declare x as a reference, we put an & at the beginning, like this:

```
auto is_above = [&x](int i) { return i > x; };
```

The variable is now merely a reference to the outer x variable, just like a regular reference variable in C++. Of course, we need to be very cautious about the lifetime of objects we pass by reference into a lambda since the lambda might execute in a context where the referenced objects have ceased to exist. It's therefore safer to capture by value.

Capture by reference versus capture by value

Using the capture clause for referencing and copying variables works just like regular variables. Take a look at these two examples and see if you can spot the difference:

Capture by value	Capture by reference
```auto func() { auto vals = {1,2,3,4,5,6}; auto x = 3; auto is_above = [x](int v) { return v > x; }; x = 4; auto count_b = std::count_if(vals.begin(), vals.end(), is_above); // count_b equals 3 } ```	```auto func() { auto vals = {1,2,3,4,5,6}; auto x = 3; auto is_above = [&x](int v) { return v > x; }; x = 4; auto count_b = std::count_if(vals.begin(), vals.end(), is_above); // count_b equals 2 } ```

In the first example, x was *copied* into the lambda and was therefore not affected when x was mutated; consequently `std::count_if()` counts the number of values above 3.

In the second example, x was *captured by reference,* and therefore `std::count_if()` instead counts the number of values above 4.

Similarities between a lambda and a class

I mentioned earlier that lambda expressions generate function objects. A function object is an instance of a class that has the call operator, `operator()()`, defined.

To understand what a lambda expression consists of, you can view it as a regular class with restrictions:

- The class only consists of one member function
- The capture clause is a combination of the class' member variables and its constructor

The following table shows lambda expressions and the corresponding classes. The left column uses *capture by value* and the right column *capture by reference*:

A lambda with capture by value...	A lambda with capture by reference...
``auto x = 3;
auto is_above = [x](int y) {
return y > x;
};
auto test = is_above(5);```	```auto x = 3;
auto is_above = [&x](int y) {
return y > x;
};
auto test = is_above(5);```
...corresponds to this class:	**...corresponds to this class:**
``auto x = 3;
class IsAbove {
public:
IsAbove(int x) : x{x} {}
auto operator()(int y) const {
return y > x;
}
private:
int x{}; // Value
};
auto is_above = IsAbove{x};
auto test = is_above(5);```	```auto x = 3;
class IsAbove {
public:
IsAbove(int& x) : x{x} {}
auto operator()(int y) const {
return y > x;
}
private:
int& x; // Reference
};
auto is_above = IsAbove{x};
auto test = is_above(5);```

Thanks to lambda expressions, we don't have to manually implement these function object types as classes.

Initializing variables in capture

As seen in the previous example, the capture clause initializes member variables in the corresponding class. This means that we can also initialize member variables inside a lambda. These variables will only be visible from inside the lambda. Here is an example of a lambda that initializes a capture variable called numbers:

```
auto some_func = [numbers = std::list<int>{4,2}]() {
  for (auto i : numbers)
    std::cout << i;
};
some_func();  // Output: 42
```

The corresponding class would look something like this:

```cpp
class SomeFunc {

public:
  SomeFunc() : numbers{4, 2} {}
  void operator()() const {
   for (auto i : numbers)
     std::cout << i;
  }

private:
  std::list<int> numbers;
};
auto some_func = SomeFunc{};
some_func(); // Output: 42
```

When initializing a variable inside a capture, you can imagine that there is a hidden auto keyword in front of the variable name. In this case, you can think about numbers as being defined like auto numbers = std::list<int>{4, 2}. If you want to initialize a reference, you can use an ampersand in front of the name, which would correspond to auto&. Here is an example:

```cpp
auto x = 1;
auto some_func = [&y = x]() {
  // y is a reference to x
};
```

Again, you have to be very cautious about lifetimes when referencing (and not copying) objects outside the lambda.

It's also possible to move an object inside a lambda, which is necessary when using move-only types such as std::unique_ptr. Here is how it can be done:

```cpp
auto x = std::make_unique<int>();
auto some_func = [x = std::move(x)]() {
  // Use x here..
};
```

This also demonstrates that it is possible to use the same name (x) for the variable. This is not necessary. Instead, we could have used some other name inside the lambda, for example [y = std::move(x)].

Mutating lambda member variables

As the lambda works just like a class with member variables, it can also mutate them. However, the function call operator of a lambda is const by default, so we explicitly need to specify that the lambda can mutate its members by using the mutable keyword. In the following example, the lambda mutates the counter variable every time it's invoked:

```cpp
auto counter_func = [counter = 1]() mutable {
  std::cout << counter++;
};


counter_func(); // Output: 1
counter_func(); // Output: 2
counter_func(); // Output: 3
```

If a lambda only captures variables by reference, we do not have to add the mutable modifier to the declaration, as the lambda itself doesn't mutate. The difference between mutable and non-mutable lambdas is demonstrated in the following code snippets:

Capture by value	Capture by reference
```cpp\nauto some_func() {\n auto v = 7;\n auto lambda = [v]() mutable {\n std::cout << v << " ";\n ++v;\n };\n assert(v == 7);\n lambda();\n lambda();\n assert(v == 7);\n std::cout << v;\n}\n```	```cpp\nauto some_func() {\n auto v = 7;\n auto lambda = [&v]() {\n std::cout << v << " ";\n ++v;\n };\n assert(v == 7);\n lambda();\n lambda();\n assert(v == 9);\n std::cout << v;\n}\n```
Output: 7 8 7	Output: 7 8 9

In the example to the right where v is captured by reference, the lambda will mutate the variable v, which is owned by the scope of some_func(). The mutating lambda in the left column will only mutate a copy of v, owned by the lambda itself. This is the reason why we will end up with different outputs in the two versions.

Mutating member variables from the compiler's perspective

To understand what's going on in the preceding example, take a look at how the compiler sees the previous lambda objects:

Capture by value	Capture by reference
| ```cpp
class Lambda {
public:
  Lambda(int m) : v{m} {}
  auto operator()() {
    std::cout<< v << " ";
    ++v;
  }
private:
  int v{};
};
``` | ```cpp
class Lambda {
public:
  Lambda(int& m) : v{m} {}
  auto operator()() const {
    std::cout<< v << " ";
    ++v;
  }
private:
  int& v;
};
``` |

As you can see, the first case corresponds to a class with a regular member, whereas the capture by reference case simply corresponds to a class where the member variable is a reference.

 You might have noticed that we add the modifier `const` on the `operator()` member function of the capture by reference class, and we also do not specify `mutable` on the corresponding lambda. The reason this class is still considered `const` is that we do not mutate anything inside the actual class/lambda; the actual mutation applies to the referenced value, and therefore the function is still considered `const`.

Capture all

In addition to capturing variables one by one, all variables in the scope can be captured by simply writing [=] or [&].

Using [=] means that every variable will be captured by value, whereas [&] captures all variables by reference.

If we use lambdas inside a member function, it is also possible to capture the entire object by reference using [this] or by copy by writing [*this]:

```cpp
class Foo {
public:
 auto member_function() {
   auto a = 0;
```

```
    auto b = 1.0f;
    // Capture all variables by copy
    auto lambda_0 = [=]() { std::cout << a << b; };
    // Capture all variables by reference
    auto lambda_1 = [&]() { std::cout << a << b; };
    // Capture object by reference
    auto lambda_2 = [this]() { std::cout << m_; };
    // Capture object by copy
    auto lambda_3 = [*this]() { std::cout << m_; };
  }
private:
  int m_{};
};
```

Note that using [=] does not mean that all variables in the scope are copied into the lambda; only the variables actually used inside the lambda are copied.

When capturing all variables by value, you can specify variables to be captured by reference (and vice versa). The following table shows the result of different combinations in the capture block:

Capture block	Resulting capture types
`int a, b, c;` `auto func = [=] { /*...*/ };`	Capture a, b, c by value.
`int a, b, c;` `auto func = [&] { /*...*/ };`	Capture a, b, c by reference.
`int a, b, c;` `auto func = [=, &c] { /*...*/ };`	Capture a, b by value. Capture c by reference.
`int a, b, c;` `auto func = [&, c] { /*...*/ };`	Capture a, b by reference. Capture c by value.

Although it is convenient to capture all variables with [&] or [=], I recommend capturing variables one by one, as it improves the readability of the code by clarifying exactly which variables are used inside the lambda scope.

Assigning C function pointers to lambdas

Lambdas without captures can be implicitly converted to function pointers. Let's say you are using a C library, or an older C++ library, that uses a callback function as a parameter, like this:

```
extern void download_webpage(const char* url,
                             void (*callback)(int, const char*));
```

The callback is called with a return code and some downloaded content. It is possible to pass a lambda as a parameter when calling `download_webpage()`. Since the callback is a regular function pointer, the lambda must not have any captures and you have to use a plus (+) in front of the lambda:

```
auto lambda = +[](int result, const char* str) {
  // Process result and str
};
download_webpage("http://www.packt.com", lambda);
```

This way, the lambda is converted into a regular function pointer. Note that the lambda cannot have any captures at all in order to use this functionality.

Lambda types

Since C++20, lambdas without captures are default-constructible and assignable. By using `decltype`, it's now easy to construct different lambda objects that have the same type:

```
auto x = [] {};    // A lambda without captures
auto y = x;        // Assignable
decltype(y) z;     // Default-constructible
static_assert(std::is_same_v<decltype(x), decltype(y)>); // passes
static_assert(std::is_same_v<decltype(x), decltype(z)>); // passes
```

However, this only applies to lambdas without captures. Lambdas *with* captures have their own unique type. Even if two lambda functions with captures are plain clones of each other, they still have their own unique type. Therefore, it's not possible to assign one lambda with captures to another lambda.

Lambdas and std::function

As mentioned in the previous section, lambdas with captures (stateful lambdas) cannot be assigned to each other since they have unique types, even if they look exactly the same. To be able to store and pass around lambdas with captures, we can use `std::function` to hold a function object constructed by a lambda expression.

The signature of a `std::function` is defined as follows:

```
std::function< return_type ( parameter0, parameter1...) >
```

So, a `std::function` returning nothing and having no parameters is defined like this:

```
auto func = std::function<void(void)>{};
```

A `std::function` returning a `bool` with an `int` and a `std::string` as parameters is defined like this:

```
auto func = std::function<bool(int, std::string)>{};
```

Lambda functions sharing the same signature (same parameters and same return type) can be held by the same type of `std::function` objects. A `std::function` can also be reassigned at runtime.

What is important here is that what is captured by the lambda does not affect its signature, and therefore both lambdas with and without captures can be assigned to the same `std::function` variable. The following code shows how different lambdas are assigned to the same `std::function` object called `func`:

```
// Create an unassigned std::function object
auto func = std::function<void(int)>{};

// Assign a lambda without capture to the std::function object
func = [](int v) { std::cout << v; };
func(12); // Prints 12

// Assign a lambda with capture to the same std::function object
auto forty_two = 42;
func = [forty_two](int v) { std::cout << (v + forty_two); };
func(12); // Prints 54
```

Let's put the `std::function` to use in something that resembles a real-world example next.

Implementing a simple Button class with std::function

Assume that we set out to implement a Button class. We can then use the std::function to store the action corresponding to clicking the button, so that when we call the on_click() member function, the corresponding code is executed.

We can declare the Button class like this:

```
class Button {
public:
  Button(std::function<void(void)> click) : handler_{click} {}
  auto on_click() const { handler_(); }
private:
  std::function<void(void)> handler_{};
};
```

We can then use it to create a multitude of buttons with different actions. The buttons can conveniently be stored in a container because they all have the same type:

```
auto create_buttons () {
  auto beep = Button([counter = 0]() mutable {
    std::cout << "Beep:" << counter << "! ";
    ++counter;
  });
  auto bop = Button([] { std::cout << "Bop. "; });
  auto silent = Button([] {});

  return std::vector<Button>{beep, bop, silent};
}
```

Iterating the list and calling on_click() on each button will execute the corresponding function:

```
const auto& buttons = create_buttons();
for (const auto& b: buttons) {
  b.on_click();
}
buttons.front().on_click(); // counter has been incremented

// Output: "Beep:0! Bop. Beep:1!"
```

The preceding example with buttons and click handlers demonstrates some of the benefits of using `std::function` in combination with lambdas; even though each stateful lambda will have its own unique type, a single `std::function` type can wrap lambdas that share the same signature (return type and arguments).

As a side note, you might have noticed that the `on_click()` member function is declared `const`. However, it's mutating the member variable `handler_` by increasing the `counter` variable in one of the click handlers. This might seem like it breaks const-correctness rules, as a const member function of `Button` is allowed to call a mutating function on one of its class members. The reason it is allowed is the same reason that member pointers are allowed to mutate their pointed-to value in a const context. Earlier in this chapter, we discussed how to propagate constness for pointer data members.

Performance consideration of std::function

A `std::function` has a few performance losses compared to a function object constructed by a lambda expression directly. This section will discuss some of the things related to performance to consider when using `std::function`.

Prevented inline optimizations

When it comes to lambdas, the compiler has the ability to inline the function call; that is, the overhead of the function call is eliminated. The flexible design of `std::function` make it nearly impossible for the compiler to inline a function wrapped in a `std::function`. The prevention of inline optimizations can have a negative impact on the performance if small functions wrapped in `std::function` are called very frequently.

Dynamically allocated memory for captured variables

If a `std::function` is assigned to a lambda with captured variables/references, the `std::function` will, in most cases, use heap-allocated memory to store the captured variables. Some implementations of `std::function` do not allocate additional memory if the size of the captured variable is below some threshold.

This means that not only is there a performance penalty due to the extra dynamic memory allocation, but also that it is slower, as heap-allocated memory can increase the number of cache misses (read more about cache misses in *Chapter 4, Data Structures*).

Additional run-time computation

Calling a std::function is generally a bit slower than executing a lambda, as a little more code is involved. For small and frequently called std::functions, this overhead may become significant. Imagine that we have a really small lambda defined like this:

```
auto lambda = [](int v) { return v * 3; };
```

The benchmark that follows demonstrates the difference between executing 10 million function calls for a std::vector of the explicit lambda type versus a std::vector of a corresponding std::function. We will begin with the version using the explicit lambda:

```
auto use_lambda() {
  using T = decltype(lambda);
  auto fs = std::vector<T>(10'000'000, lambda);
  auto res = 1;
  // Start clock
  for (const auto& f: fs)
    res = f(res);
  // Stop clock here
  return res;
}
```

We only measure the time it takes to execute the loop inside the function. The next version wraps our lambda in a std::function, and looks like this:

```
auto use_std_function() {
  using T = std::function<int(int)>;
  auto fs = std::vector<T>(10'000'000, T{lambda});
  auto res = 1;
  // Start clock
  for (const auto& f: fs)
    res = f(res);
  // Stop clock here
  return res;
}
```

I'm compiling this code on my MacBook Pro from 2018 using Clang with optimizations turned on (-O3). The first version, use_lambda(), executes the loop at roughly 2 ms, whereas the second version, use_std_function(), takes almost 36 ms to execute the loop.

Generic lambdas

A generic lambda is a lambda accepting auto parameters, making it possible to invoke it with any type. It works just like a regular lambda, but the operator() has been defined as a member function template.

Only the parameters are template variables, not the captured values. In other words, the captured value, v, in the following example will be of type int regardless of the types of v0 and v1:

```
auto v = 3; // int
auto lambda = [v](auto v0, auto v1) {
  return v + v0*v1;
};
```

If we translate the above lambda to a class, it would correspond to something like this:

```
class Lambda {
public:
  Lambda(int v) : v_{v} {}
  template <typename T0, typename T1>
  auto operator()(T0 v0, T1 v1) const {
    return v_ + v0*v1;
  }
private:
  int v_{};
};
auto v = 3;
auto lambda = Lambda{v};
```

Just like the templated version, the compiler won't generate the actual function until the lambda is invoked. So, if we invoke the previous lambda like this:

```
auto res_int = lambda(1, 2);
auto res_float = lambda(1.0f, 2.0f);
```

the compiler will generate something similar to the following lambdas:

```
auto lambda_int = [v](int v0, const int v1) { return v + v0*v1; };
auto lambda_float = [v](float v0, float v1) { return v + v0*v1; };
auto res_int = lambda_int(1, 2);
auto res_float = lambda_float(1.0f, 2.0f);
```

As you might have figured out, these versions are further handled just like regular lambdas.

A new feature of C++20 is that we can use `typename` instead of just auto for the parameter types of a generic lambda. The following generic lambdas are identical:

```
// Using auto
auto x = [](auto v) { return v + 1; };

// Using typename
auto y = []<typename Val>(Val v) { return v + 1; };
```

This makes it possible to name the type or refer to the type inside the body of the lambda.

Summary

In this chapter, you have learned how to use modern C++ features that will be used throughout this book. Automatic type deduction, move semantics, and lambda expressions are fundamental techniques that every C++ programmer needs to feel comfortable with today.

We also spent some time looking at error handling and how to think about bugs, along with valid states and how to recover from runtime errors. Error handling is an extremely important part of programming that is easily overlooked. Thinking about contracts between callers and callees is a way to make your code correct and avoid unnecessary defensive checks in the released version of your program.

In the next chapter, we will look into strategies for analyzing and measuring performance in C++.

3

Analyzing and Measuring Performance

Since this is a book about writing C++ code that runs efficiently, we need to cover some basics regarding how to measure software performance and estimate algorithmic efficiency. Most of the topics in this chapter are not specific to C++ and can be used whenever you are facing a problem where performance is an issue.

You will learn how to estimate algorithmic efficiency using big O notation. This is essential knowledge when choosing algorithms and data structures from the C++ standard library. If you are new to big O notation, this part might take some time to digest. But don't give up! This is a very important topic to grasp in order to understand the rest of the book, and, more importantly, to become a performance-aware programmer. If you want a more formal or more practical introduction to these concepts, there are plenty of books and online resources dedicated to this topic. On the other hand, if you have already mastered big O notation and know what amortized time complexity is, you can skim the next section and go to the later parts of this chapter.

This chapter includes sections on:

- Estimating algorithmic efficiency using big O notation
- A suggested workflow when optimizing code so that you don't spend time fine-tuning code without good reason
- CPU profilers—what they are and why you should use them
- Microbenchmarking

Let's begin by taking a look at how to estimate algorithmic efficiency using big O notation.

Asymptotic complexity and big O notation

There is usually more than one way to solve a problem, and if efficiency is a concern, you should first focus on high-level optimizations by choosing the right algorithms and data structures. A useful way of evaluating and comparing algorithms is by analyzing their asymptotic computational complexity — that is, analyzing how the running time or memory consumption grows when the size of the input increases. In addition, the C++ standard library specifies the asymptotic complexity for all containers and algorithms, which means that a basic understanding of this topic is a must if you are using this library. If you already have a good understanding of algorithm complexity and the big O notation, you can safely skip this section.

Let's start off with an example. Suppose we want to write an algorithm that returns true if it finds a specific key in an array, or false otherwise. In order to find out how our algorithm behaves when passed different sizes of the array, we would like to analyze the running time of this algorithm as a function of its input size:

```cpp
bool linear_search(const std::vector<int>& vals, int key) noexcept {
  for (const auto& v : vals) {
    if (v == key) {
      return true;
    }
  }
  return false;
}
```

The algorithm is straightforward. It iterates over the elements in the array and compares each element with the key. If we are lucky, we find the key at the beginning of the array and it returns immediately, but we might loop through the entire array without finding the key at all. This would be the worst case for the algorithm, and in general, that is the case we want to analyze.

But what happens with the running time when we increase the input size? Say we double the size of the array. Well, in the worst case, we need to compare all elements in the array that would double the running time. There seems to be a linear relationship between the input size and the running time. We call this a linear growth rate:

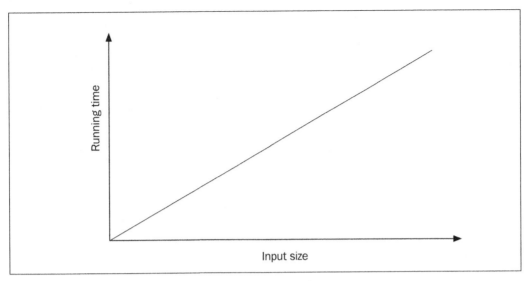

Figure 3.1: Linear growth rate

Now consider the following algorithm:

```cpp
struct Point {
  int x_{};
  int y_{};
};

bool linear_search(const std::vector<Point>& a, const Point& key) {
  for (size_t i = 0; i < a.size(); ++i) {
    if (a[i].x_ == key.x_ && a[i].y_ == key.y_) {
      return true;
    }
  }
  return false;
}
```

We are comparing points instead of integers and we are using an index with the subscript operator to access each element. How is the running time affected by these changes? The absolute running time is probably higher compared to the first algorithm since we are doing more work—for example, the comparison of points involves two integers instead of just one for each element in the array. However, at this stage, we are interested in the growth rate the algorithm exhibits, and if we plot the running time against the input size, we will still end up with a straight line, as shown in the preceding figure.

As the last example of searching for integers, let's see whether we can find a better algorithm if we assume that the elements in the array are sorted. Our first algorithm would work regardless of the order of the elements, but if we know that they are sorted, we can use a binary search. It works by looking at the element in the middle to determine whether it should continue searching in the first or second half of the array. For simplicity, the indexes high, low, and mid are of type int and requires a static_cast. A better option would be to use iterators that will be covered in succeeding chapters. Here follows the algorithm:

```cpp
bool binary_search(const std::vector<int>& a, int key) {
  auto low = 0;
  auto high = static_cast<int>(a.size()) - 1;
  while (low <= high) {
    const auto mid = std::midpoint(low, high); // C++20
    if (a[mid] < key) {
      low = mid + 1;
    } else if (a[mid] > key) {
      high = mid - 1;
    } else {
      return true;
    }
  }
  return false;
}
```

As you can see, this algorithm is harder to get correct than a simple linear scan. It looks for the specified key by *guessing* that it's in the middle of the array. If it's not, it compares the key with the element in the middle to decide which half of the array it should keep looking for the key in. So, in each iteration, it cuts the array in half.

Assume we called binary_search() with an array containing 64 elements. In the first iteration we reject 32 elements, in the next iteration we reject 16 elements, in the next iteration we reject 8 elements, and so on, until there are no more elements to compare or until we find the key. For an input size of 64, there will be, at most, 7 loop iterations. What if we *double the input size* to 128? Since we halve the size in each iteration, it means that we only need *one more loop iteration*. Clearly, the growth rate is no longer linear—it's actually logarithmic. If we measure the running time of binary_search(), we will see that the growth rate looks similar to the following:

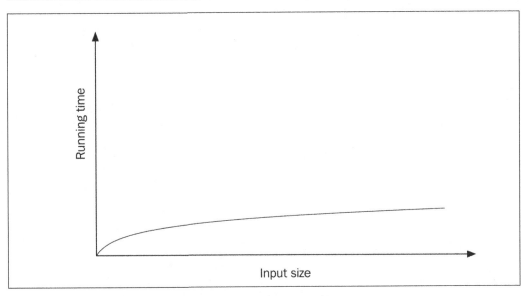

Figure 3.2: Logarithmic growth rate

On my machine, a quick timing of the three algorithms repeatedly called 10,000 times with various input sizes (n) produced the results shown in the following table:

Algorithm	n = 10	n = 1,000	n = 100,000
Linear search with `int`	0.04 ms	4.7 ms	458 ms
Linear search with `Point`	0.07 ms	6.7 ms	725 ms
Binary search with `int`	0.03 ms	0.08 ms	0.16 ms

Table 3.1: Comparison of different versions of search algorithms

Comparing algorithms 1 and 2, we can see that comparing points instead of integers takes more time, but they are still in the same order of magnitude even when the input size increases. However, if we compare all three algorithms when the input size increases, what really matters is the growth rate the algorithm exhibits. By exploiting the fact that the array was sorted, we could implement the search function with very few loop iterations. For large arrays, a binary search is practically free compared to linearly scanning the array.

 It's usually not a good idea to spend time tuning your code before you are certain that you have chosen the correct algorithms and data structures for your problem.

Wouldn't it be nice if we could express the growth rate of algorithms in a way that would help us decide which algorithm to use? Here is where the big O notation comes in handy.

Here follows an informal definition:

If *f(n)* is a function that specifies the running time of an algorithm with input size *n*, we say that *f(n)* is $O(g(n))$ if there is a constant *k* such that $f(n) \leq k * g(n)$.

This means that we could say that the time complexity of `linear_search()` is $O(n)$, for both versions (the one that operates with integers and the one that operates with points), whereas the time complexity of `binary_search()` is $O(log\ n)$ or big O of *log n*.

In practice, when we want to find the big O of a function, we can do that by eliminating all terms except the one with the largest growth rate and then remove any constant factors. For example, if we have an algorithm with a time complexity described by *f(n) = 4n² + 30n + 100*, we pick out the term with the highest growth rate, *4n²*. Next, we remove the constant factor of 4 and end up with *n²*, which means that we can say that our algorithm runs in $O(n^2)$. Finding the time complexity of an algorithm can be hard, but the more you start thinking of it while writing code, the easier it will get. For the most part, it's enough to keep track of loops and recursive functions.

Let's try to find the time complexity of the following sorting algorithm:

```cpp
void insertion_sort(std::vector<int>& a) {
  for (size_t i = 1; i < a.size(); ++i) {
    auto j = i;
    while (j > 0 && a[j-1] > a[j]) {
      std::swap(a[j], a[j-1]);
      --j;
    }
  }
}
```

The input size is the size of the array. The running time could be estimated approximately by looking at the loops that iterate over all elements. First, there is an outer loop iterating over *n - 1* elements. The inner loop is different: the first time we reach the `while`-loop, `j` is 1 and the loop only runs one iteration. On the next iteration, `j` starts at 2 and decreases to 0. For each iteration in the outer `for`-loop, the inner loop needs to do more and more work. Finally, `j` starts at *n - 1*, which means that we have, in the worst case, executed `swap()` *1 + 2 + 3 + ... + (n - 1)* times. We can express this in terms of *n* by noting that this is an arithmetic series. The sum of the series is:

$$1 + 2 + \cdots + k = \frac{k(k+1)}{2}$$

So, if we set $k = (n - 1)$, the time complexity of the sorting algorithm is:

$$\frac{(n-1)(n-1+1)}{2} = \frac{n(n-1)}{2} = \frac{n^2 - n}{2} = (1/2)\,n^2 - (1/2)\,n$$

We can now find the big O of this function by first eliminating all terms except the one with the largest growth rate, which leaves us with $(1/2)n^2$. After that, we remove the constant $1/2$ and conclude that the running time of the sorting algorithm is $O(n^2)$.

Growth rates

As stated previously, the first step in finding the big O of a complexity function is to remove all terms except the one with the highest growth rate. To be able to do that, we must know the growth rate of some common functions. In the following figure, I have plotted some of the most common functions:

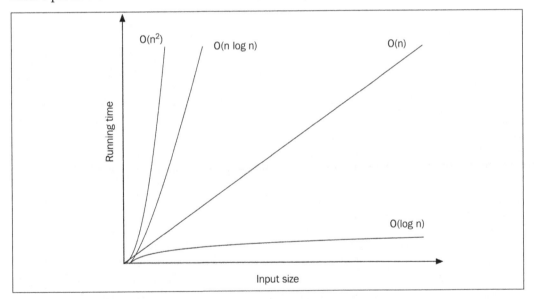

Figure 3.3: Comparison of growth rate functions

The growth rates are independent of machine or coding style and so on. When the growth rates differ between two algorithms, the one with the slowest growth rate will always win when the input size gets sufficiently large. Let's see what happens with the running time for different growth rates if we assume that it takes 1 ms to perform 1 unit of work. The following table lists the growth function, its common name, and different input sizes, n:

Big O	Name	n = 10	n = 50	n = 1000
O(1)	Constant	0.001 sec	0.001 sec	0.001 sec
O(log n)	Logarithmic	0.003 sec	0.006 sec	0.01 sec
O(n)	Linear	0.01 sec	0.05 sec	1 sec
O(n log n)	Linearithmic or *n log n*	0.03 sec	0.3 sec	10 sec
O(n²)	Quadratic	0.1 sec	2.5 sec	16.7 minutes
O(2ⁿ)	Exponential	1 sec	35,700 years	$3.4 * 10^{290}$ years

Table 3.2: Absolute running times for different growth rates and various values of input size

Note that the number in the bottom-right cell is a 291-digit number! Compare this with the age of the universe, $13.7 * 10^9$ years, which is only an 11-digit number.

Next, I will introduce amortized time complexity, which is frequently used in the C++ standard library.

Amortized time complexity

Usually, an algorithm behaves differently with different inputs. Going back to our algorithm that linearly searched for an element in an array, we were analyzing a case where the key was not in the array at all. For that algorithm, that was the worst case — that is, it used the *most* resources the algorithm will need. The best case refers to the *least* amount of resources the algorithm will need, whereas the average case specifies the amount of resources the algorithm will use on average with different inputs.

The standard library usually refers to the *amortized running time* of functions that operate on containers. If an algorithm runs in constant amortized time, it means that it will run in *O(1)* in almost all cases, except very few where it will perform worse. At first sight, amortized running time can be confused with average time, but as you will see, they are not the same.

To understand amortized time complexity, we will spend some time thinking about std::vector::push_back(). Let's assume that the vector internally has a fixed-size array to store all its elements. If there is room for more elements in the fixed-size array when calling push_back(), the operation will run in constant time, *O(1)* — that is, it's not dependent on how many elements are already in the vector as long as the internal array has room for one more:

```
if (internal_array.size() > size) {
  internal_array[size] = new_element;
  ++size;
}
```

But what happens when the internal array is full? One way to handle the growing vector is to create a new empty internal array with a bigger size and then move all the elements from the old array to the new one. This is obviously not constant time anymore since we need one move per element in the array – that is, $O(n)$. If we considered this the worst case, it would mean that push_back() is $O(n)$. However, if we call push_back() many times, we know that the expensive push_back() can't happen very often, and so it would be pessimistic, and not very useful, to say that push_back() is $O(n)$ if we know that push_back() is called many times in a row.

Amortized running time is used for analyzing a *sequence* of operations rather than a single one. We are still analyzing the worst case, but for a sequence of operations. The amortized running time can be computed by first analyzing the running time of the entire sequence and then dividing that by the length of the sequence. Suppose we are performing a sequence of m operations with the total running time $T(m)$:

$$T(m) = t_0 + t_1 + t_2 \dots + t_{m-1}$$

where $t_0 = 1, t_1 = n, t_2 = 1, t_3 = n$, and so on. In other words, half of the operations run in constant time and the other half run in linear time. The total time T for all m operations can be expressed as follows:

$$T(m) = n \cdot \frac{m}{2} + 1 \cdot \frac{m}{2} = \frac{(n+1)m}{2}$$

The amortized complexity for each operation is the total time divided by the number of operations, which turns out to be $O(n)$:

$$T(m)/m = \frac{(n+1)m}{2m} = \frac{n+1}{2} = O(n)$$

However, if we can guarantee that the number of expensive operations differs by orders of magnitude compared to the number of constant time operations, we will achieve lower amortized running costs. For example, if we can guarantee that an expensive operation only occurs once in a sequence $T(n) + T(1) + T(1) + \dots$, then the amortized running time is $O(1)$. So, depending on the frequency of the expensive operations, the amortized running time changes.

Now, back to std::vector. The C++ standard states that push_back() needs to run in amortized constant time, $O(1)$. How do the library vendors achieve this? If the capacity is increased by a fixed number of elements each time the vector becomes full, we will have a case similar to the preceding one where we had a running time of $O(n)$. Even if we use a large constant, the capacity changes would still occur at fixed intervals. The key insight is that the vector needs to grow exponentially in order to get the expensive operations to occur rarely enough. Internally, the vector uses a growth factor such that the capacity of the new array is the current size times the growth factor.

A big growth factor would potentially waste more memory but would make the expensive operation occur less frequently. To simplify the math, let's use a common strategy, namely by doubling the capacity each time the vector needs to grow. We can now estimate how often the expensive calls occur. For a vector of size n, we would need to grow the internal array $log_2(n)$ times since we are doubling the size all the time. Each time we grow the array, we need to move all the elements that are currently in the array. The ith time we grow the array there will be 2^i elements to move. So if we perform m number of push_back() operations, the total running time of the grow operations will be:

$$T(m) = \sum_{i=1}^{log_2(m)} 2^i$$

This is a geometric series and can also be expressed as:

$$\frac{2 - 2^{log_2(m)+1}}{1 - 2} = 2m - 2 = O(m)$$

Dividing this by the length of the sequence, m, we end up with the amortized running time $O(1)$.

As I have already said, amortized time complexity is used a lot in the standard library, so it's good to understand the analysis. Thinking about how push_back() could be implemented in amortized constant time has helped me remember the simplified version of amortized constant time: It will run in $O(1)$ in almost all cases, except very few where it will perform worse.

That is all we are going to cover regarding asymptotic complexity. Now we will move on to how you can tackle a performance problem and work effectively by optimizing your code.

What to measure and how?

Optimizations almost always add complexity to your code. High-level optimizations, such as choosing algorithms and data structures, can make the intention of the code clearer, but for the most part, optimizations will make the code harder to read and maintain. We therefore want to be absolutely sure that the optimizations we add have an actual impact on what we are trying to achieve in terms of performance. Do we really need to make the code faster? In what way? Does the code really use too much memory? To understand what optimizations are possible, we need to have a good understanding of the requirements, such as latency, throughput, and memory usage.

Optimizing code is fun, but it's also very easy to get lost without any measurable gains. We will start this section with a suggested workflow to follow when tuning your code:

1. **Define a goal**: It's easier to know how to optimize and when to stop optimizing if you have a well-defined, quantitative goal. For some applications, it's clear from the start what the requirements are, but in many cases it tends to be fuzzier. Even though it might be obvious that the code is running too slow, it's important to know what would be good enough. Each domain has its own limits, so make sure you understand the ones that are relevant to your application. Here are some examples to make it more concrete:

   - A response time for user-interactive applications of 100 ms; refer to https://www.nngroup.com/articles/response-times-3-important-limits.
   - Graphics with 60 Frames Per Second (FPS) give you 16 ms per frame.
   - Real-time audio with a 128 sample buffer at a 44.1 kHz sample rate means slightly less than 3 ms.

2. **Measure**: Once we know what to measure and what the limits are, we proceed by measuring how the application is performing right now. From *step 1*, it should be obvious if we are interested in average times, peaks, load, and so on. In this step, we are only concerned with measuring the goal we have set up. Depending on the application, measuring can be anything from using a stopwatch to using highly sophisticated performance analysis tools.

3. **Find the bottlenecks**: Next, we need to find the application's bottlenecks — the parts that are too slow and make the application useless. Don't trust your gut feeling at this point! Maybe you gained some insights by measuring the code at various points in *step 2* — that's fine, but you usually need to profile your code further in order to find the hot spots that matter most.

4. **Make an educated guess**: Come up with a hypothesis for how to improve the performance. Can a lookup table be used? Can we cache data to gain the overall throughput? Can we change the code so that the compiler can vectorize it? Can we decrease the number of allocations in the critical sections by reusing memory? Coming up with ideas is usually not that hard if you know that they are just educated guesses. It's okay to be wrong — you will find out later whether they had an impact or not.

5. **Optimize**: Let's implement the hypothesis we sketched in *step 4*. Don't spend too much time on this step making it perfect before you know that it actually has an effect. Be prepared to reject this optimization. It might not have the desired effect.

6. **Evaluate**: Measure again. Do the exact same test as in *step 2* and compare the results. What did we gain? If we didn't gain anything, reject the code and go back to *step 4*. If the optimization actually had a positive effect, you need to ask yourself whether it's good enough to spend more time on. How complicated is the optimization? Is it worth the effort? Is this a general performance gain or is it highly specific to a certain case/platform? Is it maintainable? Can we encapsulate it, or does it spread out all over the code base? If you can't motivate the optimization, go back to *step 4*, otherwise continue to the final step.

7. **Refactor**: If you followed the instructions in *step 5* and didn't spend too much time writing perfect code in the first place, it's time to refactor the optimization to make it cleaner. Optimizations almost always need some comments to explain why we are doing things in an unusual way.

Following this process will ensure that you stay on the right track and don't end up with complicated optimizations that aren't motivated. The importance of spending time on defining concrete goals and measuring cannot be overestimated. In order to be successful in this area, you need to understand what performance properties are relevant for your application.

Performance properties

Before you start measuring, you must know which performance properties are important for the application you are writing. In this section, I will explain some frequently used terms when measuring performance. Depending on the application you are writing, some properties are more relevant than others. For example, throughput might be a more important property than latency if you are writing an online image converter service, whereas latency is key when writing interactive applications with real-time requirements. Below are some valuable terms and concepts that are worth becoming familiar with during performance measurement:

- **Latency/response time**: Depending on the domain, latency and response time might have very precise and different meanings. However, in this book, I mean the time between the request and the response of an operation—for example, the time it takes for an image conversion service to process one image.

- **Throughput**: This refers to the number of transactions (operations, requests, and so on) processed per time unit—for example, the number of images that an image conversion service can process per second.

- **I/O bound or CPU bound**: A task usually spends the majority of its time computing things on the CPU or waiting for I/O (hard drives, networks, and so on). A task is said to be CPU bound if it would run faster if the CPU were faster. It's said to be I/O bound if it would run faster by making the I/O faster. Sometimes you hear about memory-bound tasks too, which means that the amount or speed of the main memory is the current bottleneck.

- **Power consumption**: This is a very important consideration for code that executes on mobile devices with batteries. In order to decrease the power usage, the application needs to use the hardware more efficiently, just as if we are optimizing for CPU usage, network efficiency, and so on. Other than that, high-frequency polling should be avoided since it prevents the CPU from going to sleep.

- **Data aggregation**: It's usually necessary to aggregate the data when collecting a lot of samples during performance measurement. Sometimes *mean values* are a good enough indicator of how the program performs, but more often the *median* tells you more about the actual performance since it's more robust against outliers. If you are interested in outliers, you can always measure *min* and *max* values (or the 10th percentile, for example).

This list is by no means exhaustive, but it's a good start. The important thing to remember here is that there are established terms and concepts that we can use when measuring performance. Spending some time on defining what we really mean by optimizing code helps us reach our goals faster.

Speedup of execution time

When we compare the relative performance between two versions of a program or function, it's customary to talk about **speedup**. Here I will give you a definition of speedup when comparing execution time (or latency). Assume we have measured the execution times of two versions of some code: an old slower version, and a new faster version. The speedup of execution time can then be computed accordingly:

$$Speedup\ of\ execution\ time = \frac{T_{old}}{T_{new}}$$

Where T_{old} is the execution time of the initial version of the code, and T_{new} is the execution time of the optimized version. This definition of speedup implies that a speedup of 1 means no speedup at all.

Let's make sure that you know how to measure the relative execution time with an example. Assume that we have a function that executes in 10 ms (T_{old} = 10 ms) and we manage to make it run in 4 ms after some optimization (T_{new} = 4 ms). We can then compute the speedup as follows:

$$Speedup = \frac{T_{old}}{T_{new}} = \frac{10\ ms}{4\ ms} = 2.5$$

In other words, our new optimized version provided a 2.5x speedup. If we want to express this improvement as a percentage, we can use the following formula to convert speedup to percentage improvement:

$$\%\ Improvement = 100\left(1 - \frac{1}{Speedup}\right) = 100\left(1 - \frac{1}{2.5}\right) = 60\%$$

We can then say that the new version of the code runs 60% faster than the old one and that this corresponds to a speedup of 2.5x. In this book, I will consistently use speedup, and not percentage improvement, when comparing execution time.

In the end, we are usually interested in execution time, but time is not always the best thing to measure. By inspecting other values on the hardware, the hardware might give us some other useful guidance toward optimizing our code.

Performance counters

Apart from the obvious properties, such as execution time and memory usage, it can sometimes be beneficial to measure other things. Either because they are more reliable or because they can give us better insights into what is causing our code to run slow.

Many CPUs are equipped with hardware performance counters that can provide us with metrics such as the number of instructions, CPU cycles, branch mispredictions, and cache misses. I haven't introduced these hardware aspects yet in this book, and we will not explore performance counters in depth. However, it's good to know that they exist and that there are ready-made tools and libraries (accessible through APIs) for all the major operating systems to collect **Performance Monitoring Counters (PMC)** while running a program.

The support for performance counters varies depending on the CPU and operating system. Intel provides a powerful tool called VTune, which can be used for monitoring performance counters. FreeBSD offers `pmcstat`. macOS comes with DTrace and Xcode Instruments. Microsoft Visual Studio provides support for collecting CPU counters on Windows.

Another popular tool is `perf`, which is available on GNU/Linux systems. Running the command:

```
perf stat ./your-program
```

will reveal a lot of interesting events, such as the number of context switches, page faults, mispredicted branches, and so on. Here is an example of what it output when running a small program:

```
Performance counter stats for './my-prog':

      1 129,86 msec task-clock                #  1,000 CPUs utilized
              8      context-switches          #  0,007 K/sec
              0      cpu-migrations            #  0,000 K/sec
         97 810      page-faults               #  0,087 M/sec
  3 968 043 041      cycles                    #  3,512 GHz
  1 250 538 491      stalled-cycles-frontend   #  31,52% frontend cycles idle
    497 225 466      stalled-cycles-backend    #  12,53% backend cycles idle
  6 237 037 204      instructions              #  1,57  insn per cycle
                                               #  0,20  stalled cycles per insn
  1 853 556 742      branches                  #  1640,516 M/sec
      3 486 026      branch-misses             #  0,19% of all branches


   1,130355771 sec  time elapsed

   1,026068000 sec  user
   0,104210000 sec  sys
```

We will now move on to highlight some best practices when testing and evaluating performance.

Performance testing — best practices

For some reason, it's more common to see regression tests covering functional requirements than performance requirements or other non-functional requirements covered in tests. Performance testing is usually carried out more sporadically and, more often than not, way too late in the development process. My recommendation is to measure early and detect regression as soon as possible by adding performance tests to your nightly builds.

Choose algorithms and data structures wisely if they are to handle large inputs, but don't fine-tune code without good reason. It's also important to test your application with realistic test data early on. Ask questions about data sizes early in the project. How many table rows is the application supposed to handle and still be able to scroll smoothly? Don't just try it with 100 elements and hope that your code will scale—test it!

Plotting your data is a very effective way of understanding the data you have collected. There are so many good and easy-to-use plotting tools available today, so there is really no excuse for not plotting. Both RStudio and Octave provide powerful plotting capabilities. Other examples include gnuplot and Matplotlib (Python), which can be used on various platforms and require a minimal amount of scripting to produce useful plots after collecting your data. A plot does not have to look pretty in order to be useful. Once you plot your data, you are going to see the outliers and patterns that are usually hard to find in a table full of numbers.

This concludes our *What to measure and how?* section. Next, we'll now move on to exploring ways to find the critical parts of your code that waste too many resources.

Knowing your code and hot spots

The Pareto principle, or the 80/20 rule, has been applied in various fields since it was first observed by the Italian economist Vilfredo Pareto more than 100 years ago. He was able to show that 20% of the Italian population owned 80% of the land. In computer science, it has been widely used, perhaps even overused. In software optimization, it suggests that 20% of the code is responsible for 80% of the resources that a program uses.

This is, of course, only a rule of thumb and shouldn't be taken too literally. Nevertheless, for code that has not been optimized, it's common to find some relatively small hot spots that spend the vast majority of the total resources. As a programmer, this is actually good news, because it means that we can write most of our code without tweaking it for performance reasons and instead focus on keeping the code clean. It also means that when doing optimizations, we need to know *where* to do them; otherwise, there is a good chance we will optimize code that will not have an impact on the overall performance. In this section, we will look at methods and tools for finding the 20% of your code that might be worth optimizing.

Using a profiler is usually the most efficient way of identifying hot spots in a program. Profilers analyze the execution of a program and output a statistical summary, a profile, of how often the functions or instructions in the program are being called.

In addition, profilers usually also output a call graph that shows the relationship between function calls, that is, the callers and callees for each function that was called during the profiling. In the following figure, you can see that the sort() function was called from main() (the caller) and that sort() called the function swap() (the callee):

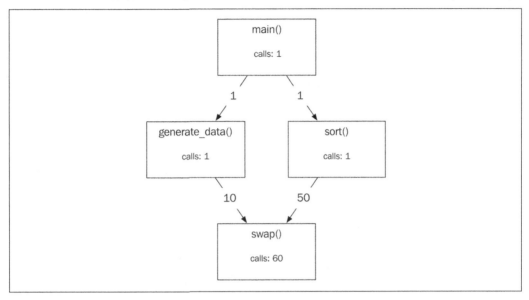

Figure 3.4: Example of a call graph. The function sort() is called once and calls swap() 50 times.

There are two main categories of profilers: sampling profilers and instrumentation profilers. The approaches can also be mixed to create a hybrid of sampling and instrumentation. gprof, the Unix performance analysis tool, is an example of this. The sections that follow focus on instrumentation profilers and sampling profilers.

Instrumentation profilers

By instrumentation, I mean inserting code into a program to be analyzed in order to gather information about how frequently each function is being executed. Typically, the inserted instrumentation code records each entry and exit point. You can write your own primitive instrumentation profiler by inserting the code manually yourself, or you can use a tool that automatically inserts the necessary code as a step in the build process.

A simple implementation might be good enough for your purposes, but be aware of the impact that the added code can have on performance, which can make the profile misleading. Another problem with a naive implementation like this is that it might prevent compiler optimizations or run the risk of being optimized away.

Just to give you an example of an instrumentation profiler, here is a simplified version of a timer class I have used in previous projects:

```cpp
class ScopedTimer {
public:
  using ClockType = std::chrono::steady_clock;

  ScopedTimer(const char* func)
      : function_name_{func}, start_{ClockType::now()} {}

  ScopedTimer(const ScopedTimer&) = delete;
  ScopedTimer(ScopedTimer&&) = delete;
  auto operator=(const ScopedTimer&) -> ScopedTimer& = delete;
  auto operator=(ScopedTimer&&) -> ScopedTimer& = delete;

  ~ScopedTimer() {
    using namespace std::chrono;
    auto stop = ClockType::now();
    auto duration = (stop - start_);
    auto ms = duration_cast<milliseconds>(duration).count();
    std::cout << ms << " ms " << function_name_ << '\n';
  }

private:
  const char* function_name_{};
  const ClockType::time_point start_{};
};
```

The `ScopedTimer` class will measure the time from when it was created to the time it went out of scope, that is, destructed. We are using the class `std::chrono::steady_clock`, available since C++11, which was designed for measuring time intervals. `steady_clock` is monotonic, which means that it will never decrease between two consecutive calls to `clock_type::now()`. This is not the case for the system clock, for example, which can be adjusted at any time.

We can now use our timer class by measuring each function in a program by creating a `ScopedTimer` instance at the beginning of each function:

```cpp
auto some_function() {
  ScopedTimer timer{"some_function"};
  // ...
}
```

Even though we don't recommend the use of preprocessor macros in general, this might be a case for using one:

```
#if USE_TIMER
#define MEASURE_FUNCTION() ScopedTimer timer{__func__}
#else
#define MEASURE_FUNCTION()
#endif
```

We are using the only predefined function-local __func__ variable available since C++11 to get the name of the function. C++20 also introduced the handy std::source_location class, which provides us with the functions function_name(), file_name(), line(), and column(). If std::source_location is not supported by your compiler yet, there are other nonstandard predefined macros that are widely supported and can be really useful for debugging purposes, for example, __FUNCTION__, __FILE__, and __LINE__.

Now, our ScopedTimer class can be used like this:

```
auto some_function() {
  MEASURE_FUNCTION();
  // ...
}
```

Assuming that we have defined USE_TIMER when compiling our timer, it will produce the following output each time some_function() returns:

```
2.3 ms some_function
```

I have demonstrated how we can manually instrument our code by inserting code that prints the elapsed time between two points in the code. Although this is a handy tool for some scenarios, please be aware of the misleading results a simple tool like this can produce. In the next section, I will introduce a profiling method that doesn't require any modifications of the executing code.

Sampling profilers

Sampling profilers create a profile by looking at the running program's state at even intervals—typically, every 10 ms. Sampling profilers usually have a minimum impact on the program's actual performance, and it's also possible to build the program in release mode with all optimizations turned on. A drawback of sampling profilers is their inaccuracy and statistical approach, which is usually not a problem as long as you are aware of it.

The following figure shows a sampling session of a running program with five functions: main(), f1(), f2(), f3(), and f4(). The t_1 - t_{10} labels indicate when each sample was taken. The boxes indicate the entry and exit point of each executing function:

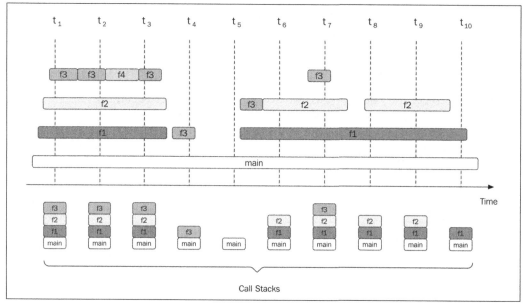

Figure 3.5: Example of a sampling profiler session

The profile is summarized in the following table:

Function	Total	Self
main()	100%	10%
f1()	80%	10%
f2()	70%	30%
f3()	50%	50%

Table 3.3: For each function, the profile shows the total percentage of call stacks that it appeared in (Total) and the percentage of call stacks where it occurred on top of the stack (Self).

The **Total** column in the preceding table shows the percentage of call stacks that contained a certain function. In our example, the main function was present in all 10 out of 10 call stacks (100%), whereas the f2() function was only detected in 7 call stacks, which corresponds to 70% of all call stacks.

The **Self** column shows, for each function, how many times it occurred on top of the call stack. The main() function was detected once on top of the call stack at the fifth sample, t_5, whereas the f2() function was on top of the call stack at samples t_6, t_8, and t_9, which corresponds to $3/10 = 30\%$.

The f3() function had the highest **Self** value (5/10) and was on top of the call stack whenever it was detected.

Conceptually, a sampling profiler stores samples of call stacks at even time intervals. It detects what is currently running on the CPU. Pure sampling profilers usually only detect functions that are currently being executed in a thread that is in a running state, since sleeping threads do not get scheduled on the CPU. This means that if a function is waiting for a lock that causes the thread to sleep, that time will not show up in the time profile. This is important because your bottlenecks might be caused by thread synchronization, which might be invisible to the sampling profiler.

What happened to the f4() function? According to the graph, it was called by the f2() function between samples two and three, but it never showed up in our statistical profile since it was never registered in any of the call stacks. This is an important property of sampling profilers. If the time between each sample is too long or the total sampling session is too short, then short and infrequently called functions will not show up in the profile. This is usually not a problem since these functions are rarely the functions you need to tune. You may note that the f3() function was also missed between t_5 and t_6, but since f3() was called very frequently, it had a big impact on the profile, anyway.

 Make sure you understand what your time profiler actually registers. Be aware of its limitations and strengths in order to use it as effectively as possible.

Microbenchmarking

Profiling can help us find the bottlenecks in our code. If these bottlenecks are caused by inefficient data structures (see *Chapter 4, Data Structures*), the wrong choice of algorithm (see *Chapter 5, Algorithms*), or unnecessary contention (see *Chapter 11, Concurrency*), these bigger issues should be addressed first. But sometimes we find a small function or a small block of code that we need to optimize, and in those cases, we can use a method called **microbenchmarking**. With this process we create a microbenchmark—a program that runs a small piece of code in isolation from the rest of the program. The process of microbenchmarking consists of the following steps:

1. Find a hot spot that needs tuning, preferably using a profiler.
2. Separate it from the rest of the code and create an isolated microbenchmark.

3. Optimize the microbenchmark. Use a benchmarking framework to test and evaluate the code during optimization.

4. Integrate the newly optimized code into the program and *measure again* to see if the optimizations are relevant when the code runs in a bigger context with more relevant input.

The four steps of the process are illustrated in the following figure:

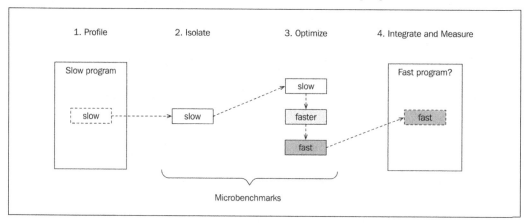

Figure 3.6: The microbenchmarking process

Microbenchmarking is fun. However, before diving into the process of trying to make a particular function faster, we should first make sure that:

- The time spent inside the function when running the program significantly affects the overall performance of the program we want to speed up. Profiling and Amdahl's law will help us understand this. Amdahl's law will be explained below.

- We cannot easily decrease the number of times the function is being called. Eliminating calls to expensive functions is usually the most effective way of optimizing the overall performance of the program.

Optimizing code using microbenchmarking should usually be seen as the last resort. The expected overall performance gains are usually small. However, sometimes we cannot avoid the fact that we need to make a relatively small piece of code run faster by tuning its implementation, and in those cases microbenchmarks can be very effective.

Next, you will learn how the speedup of a microbenchmark can affect the overall speedup of a program.

Amdahl's law

When working with microbenchmarks, it's essential to keep in mind how big (or small) an impact the optimization of the isolated code will have on the complete program. It's our experience that it is easy to get a little too excited sometimes when improving a microbenchmark, just to realize that the overall effect was nearly negligible. This risk of going nowhere is partly addressed by using a sound profiling technique, but also by keeping the overall impact of an optimization in mind.

Say that we are optimizing an isolated part of a program in a microbenchmark. The upper limit of the overall speedup of the entire program can then be computed using Amdahl's law. We need to know two values in order to compute the overall speedup:

- First, we need to know how much execution time the isolated part accounts for in proportion to the overall execution time. We denote this value of *proportional execution* time with the letter *p*.

- Secondly, we need to know the speedup of the part we are optimizing—the microbenchmark that is. We denote this value of *local speedup* with the letter *s*.

Using *p* and *s*, we can now use Amdahl's law to compute the overall speedup:

$$Overall\ speedup = \frac{1}{(1-p) + \frac{p}{s}}$$

Hopefully this doesn't look too complicated, because it's very intuitive when put in to use. To get an intuition for Amdahl's law, you can see what the overall speedup becomes when using various extreme values of *p* and *s*:

- Setting *p = 0* and *s = 5x* means that the part we optimize has no impact on the overall execution time. Therefore, the overall speedup will always be 1x regardless of the value of *s*.

- Setting *p = 1*, *s = 5x* means that we optimize a part that accounts for the entire execution time of a program, and in that case, the overall speedup will always be equal to the speedup we achieve in the part we optimize—5x in this case.

- Setting *p = 0.5* and *s = ∞* means that we completely remove the part of the program that accounted for half of the execution time. The overall speedup will then be 2x.

The results are summarized in the following table:

p	s	Overall speedup
0	5x	1x
1	5x	5x
0.5	∞	2x

Table 3.4: Extreme values of p and s and the achieved overall speedup

A complete example will demonstrate how we can use Amdahl's law in practice. Say that you are optimizing a function so that the optimized version is 2 times faster than the original version, that is, a speedup of *2x (s = 2)*. Further, let's assume that this function is only responsible for 1% of the overall execution time of a program (*p = 0.01*), then the overall speedup of the entire program can be computed as follows:

$$Overall\ speedup = \frac{1}{(1-p) + \frac{p}{s}} = \frac{1}{(1-0.01) + \frac{0.01}{2}} = 1.005$$

So, even if we managed to make our isolated code 2 times faster, the overall speedup is only a factor of 1.005 — not saying that this speedup is necessarily negligible, but we constantly need to go back and look at our gains in proportion to the bigger picture.

Pitfalls of microbenchmarking

There are plenty of hidden difficulties when measuring software performance in general and microbenchmarks in particular. Here, I will present a list of things to be aware of when working with microbenchmarks:

- Results are sometimes overgeneralized and are treated as universal truths.
- The compiler might optimize isolated code differently compared to how it is optimized in the full program. For example, a function might be inlined in the microbenchmark but not when compiled in the full program. Or, the compiler might be able to precompute parts of the microbenchmark.
- Unused returned values in a benchmark might make the compiler remove the function we are trying to measure.
- Static test data provided in the microbenchmark might give the compiler an unrealistic advantage when optimizing the code. For example, if we hardcode how many times a loop will be executed, and the compiler knows that this hardcoded value happens to be a multiple of 8, it can vectorize the loop differently, skipping the prologue and epilogue of parts that might not be aligned with the SIMD register size. And then in the real code, where this hardcoded compile-time constant is replaced with a runtime value, that optimization doesn't happen.

- Unrealistic test data can have an impact on branch prediction when running the benchmark.

- Results between multiple measurements might vary because of factors such as frequency scaling, cache pollution, and the scheduling of other processes.

- The limiting factor of a code's performance could be due to cache misses, not the time it actually takes to execute instructions. Therefore, in many scenarios, an important rule of microbenchmarking is that you have to thrash the cache before you measure, otherwise you're not really measuring anything.

I wish I had a simple formula for avoiding all the pitfalls listed above, but unfortunately, I don't. However, in the next section, we will have a look at a concrete example to see how some of those pitfalls can be addressed by using a microbenchmarking support library.

A microbenchmark example

We will wrap this chapter up by going back to our initial examples with linear search and binary search from this chapter and demonstrate how they can be benchmarked using a benchmarking framework.

We began this chapter by comparing two ways of searching for an integer in a `std::vector`. If we knew that the vector was already sorted, we could use a binary search, which outperformed the simple linear search algorithm. I will not repeat the definition of the functions here, but the declaration looked like this:

```
bool linear_search(const std::vector<int>& v, int key);
bool binary_search(const std::vector<int>& v, int key);
```

The difference in the execution time of these functions is very obvious once the input is sufficiently large, but it will serve as a good enough example for our purpose. We will begin by only measuring `linear_search()`. Then, when we have a working benchmark in place, we will add `binary_search()` and compare the two versions.

In order to make a testing program, we first need a way to generate a sorted vector of integers. A simple implementation, as follows, will be sufficient for our needs:

```
auto gen_vec(int n) {
  std::vector<int> v;
  for (int i = 0; i < n; ++i) {
    v.push_back(i);
  }
```

```
    return v;
  }
```

The vector that is returned will contain all integers between 0 and *n - 1*. Once we have that in place, we can create a naive test program like this:

```
int main() { // Don't do performance tests like this!
  ScopedTimer timer("linear_search");
  int n = 1024;
  auto v = gen_vec(n);
  linear_search(v, n);
}
```

We are searching for the value n, which we know isn't in the vector, so the algorithm will exhibit its worst-case performance using this test data. That's the good part of this test. Other than that, it is afflicted with many flaws that will make this benchmark useless:

- Compiling this code using optimizations will most likely completely remove the code because the compiler can see that the results from the functions are not being used.

- We don't want to measure the time it takes to create and fill the std::vector.

- By only running the linear_search() function once, we will not achieve a statistically stable result.

- It's cumbersome to test for different input sizes.

Let's see how these problems can be addressed by using a microbenchmarking support library. There are various tools/libraries for benchmarking, but we will use **Google Benchmark**, https://github.com/google/benchmark, because of its widespread use, and as a bonus, it can also be easily tested online on the page http://quick-bench.com without the need for any installation.

Here is how a simple microbenchmark of linear_search() might look when using Google Benchmark:

```
#include <benchmark/benchmark.h> // Non-standard header
#include <vector>

bool linear_search(const std::vector<int>& v, int key) { /* ... */ }
auto gen_vec(int n) { /* ... */ }

static void bm_linear_search(benchmark::State& state) {
  auto n = 1024;
```

```
  auto v = gen_vec(n);
  for (auto _ : state) {
    benchmark::DoNotOptimize(linear_search(v, n));
  }
}

BENCHMARK(bm_linear_search); // Register benchmarking function
BENCHMARK_MAIN();
```

That's it! The only thing we haven't addressed yet is the fact that the input size is hardcoded to 1024. We will fix that in a while. Compiling and running this program will generate something like this:

```
-------------------------------------------------------------
Benchmark              Time    CPU         Iterations
-------------------------------------------------------------
bm_linear_search     361 ns  361 ns         1945664
```

The number of iterations reported in the rightmost column reports the number of times the loop needed to execute before a statistically stable result was achieved. The state object passed to our benchmarking function determines when to stop. The average time per iteration is reported in two columns: **Time** is the wall-clock time and **CPU** is the time spent on the CPU by the main thread. In this case they were the same, but if linear_search() had been blocked waiting for I/O (for example), the CPU time would have been lower than the wall-clock time.

Another important thing to note is that the code that generates the vector is not included in the reported time. The only code that is being measured is the code inside this loop:

```
for (auto _ : state) {   // Only this loop is measured
  benchmark::DoNotOptimize(binary_search(v, n));
}
```

The boolean value returned from our search functions is wrapped inside benchmark::DoNotOptimize(). This is the mechanism used to ensure that the returned value is not optimized away, which could make the entire call to linear_search() disappear.

Now let's make this benchmark a little more interesting by varying the input size. We can do that by passing arguments to our benchmarking function using the state object. Here is how to do it:

```
static void bm_linear_search(benchmark::State& state) {
  auto n = state.range(0);
  auto v = gen_vec(n);
  for (auto _ : state) {
    benchmark::DoNotOptimize(linear_search(v, n));
  }
}
BENCHMARK(bm_linear_search)->RangeMultiplier(2)->Range(64, 256);
```

This will start with an input size of 64 and double the size until it reaches 256. On my machine, the test generated the following output:

```
----------------------------------------------------------------
Benchmark                   Time     CPU        Iterations
----------------------------------------------------------------
bm_linear_search/64      17.9 ns  17.9 ns       38143169
bm_linear_search/128     44.3 ns  44.2 ns       15521161
bm_linear_search/256     74.8 ns  74.7 ns        8836955
```

As a final example, we will benchmark both the linear_search() and the binary_search() functions using a variable input size and also try to let the framework estimate the time complexity of our functions. This can be done by providing the input size to the state object using the SetComplexityN() function. The complete microbenchmark example looks like this:

```
#include <benchmark/benchmark.h>
#include <vector>

bool linear_search(const std::vector<int>& v, int key) { /* ... */ }
bool binary_search(const std::vector<int>& v, int key) { /* ... */ }
auto gen_vec(int n) { /* ... */ }

static void bm_linear_search(benchmark::State& state) {
  auto n = state.range(0);
  auto v = gen_vec(n);
  for (auto _ : state) {
    benchmark::DoNotOptimize(linear_search(v, n));
  }
  state.SetComplexityN(n);
}
```

```
static void bm_binary_search(benchmark::State& state) {
  auto n = state.range(0);
  auto v = gen_vec(n);
  for (auto _ : state) {
    benchmark::DoNotOptimize(binary_search(v, n));
  }
  state.SetComplexityN(n);
}

BENCHMARK(bm_linear_search)->RangeMultiplier(2)->
  Range(64, 4096)->Complexity();
BENCHMARK(bm_binary_search)->RangeMultiplier(2)->
  Range(64, 4096)->Complexity();
BENCHMARK_MAIN();
```

When running the benchmark, we will get the following results printed to the console:

Benchmark	Time	CPU	Iterations
bm_linear_search/64	18.0 ns	18.0 ns	38984922
bm_linear_search/128	45.8 ns	45.8 ns	15383123
...			
bm_linear_search/8192	1988 ns	1982 ns	331870
bm_linear_search_BigO	0.24 N	0.24 N	
bm_linear_search_RMS	4 %	4 %	
bm_binary_search/64	4.16 ns	4.15 ns	169294398
bm_binary_search/128	4.52 ns	4.52 ns	152284319
...			
bm_binary_search/4096	8.27 ns	8.26 ns	80634189
bm_binary_search/8192	8.90 ns	8.90 ns	77544824
bm_binary_search_BigO	0.67 lgN	0.67 lgN	
bm_binary_search_RMS	3 %	3 %	

The output is aligned with our initial results in this chapter, where we concluded that the algorithms exhibit linear runtime and logarithmic runtime, respectively. If we plot the values in a table, we can clearly see the linear and logarithmic growth rates of the functions.

The following figure was generated using Python with Matplotlib:

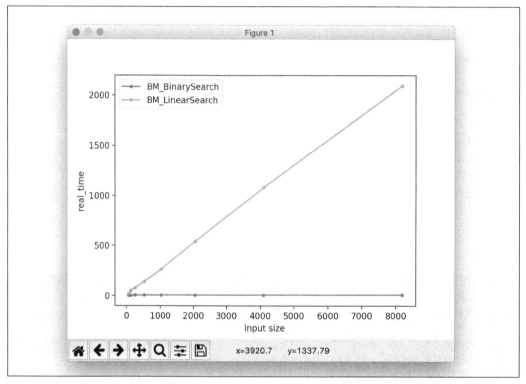

Figure 3.7: Plotting the execution time for various input sizes reveals the growth rates of the search functions

You now have a lot of tools and insights for finding and improving the performance of your code. I cannot stress enough the importance of measuring and setting goals when working with performance. A quote from Andrei Alexandrescu will conclude this section:

"Measuring gives you a leg up on experts who don't need to measure."

- Andrei Alexandrescu, 2015, Writing Fast Code I, code::dive conference 2015, https://codedive.pl/2015/writing-fast-code-part-1.

Summary

In this chapter, you learned how to compare the efficiency of algorithms by using big O notation. You now know that the C++ standard library provides complexity guarantees for algorithms and data structures. All standard library algorithms specify their worst-case or average-case performance guarantees, whereas containers and iterators specify amortized or exact complexity.

You also discovered how to quantify software performance by measuring latency and throughput.

Lastly, you learned how to detect hot spots in your code by using CPU profilers and how to perform microbenchmarkings to improve isolated parts of your program.

In the next chapter, you will find out how to use data structures provided by the C++ standard library efficiently.

4

Data Structures

In the last chapter, we discussed how to analyze time and memory complexity and how to measure performance. In this chapter, we are going to talk about how to choose and use data structures from the standard library. To understand why certain data structures work very well on the computers of today, we first need to cover some basics about computer memory. In this chapter, you will learn about:

- The properties of computer memory
- The standard library containers: sequence containers and associative containers
- The standard library container adaptors
- Parallel arrays

Before we start walking through the containers offered by the standard library and some other useful data structures, we will briefly discuss some properties of computer memory.

The properties of computer memory

C++ treats memory as a sequence of cells. The size of each cell is 1 byte, and each cell has an address. Accessing a byte in memory by its address is a constant-time operation, $O(1)$, in other words, it's independent of the total number of memory cells. On a 32-bit machine, you can theoretically address 2^{32} bytes, that is, around 4 GB, which restricts the amount of memory a process is allowed to use at once. On a 64-bit machine, you can theoretically address 2^{64} bytes, which is so big that there is hardly any risk of running out of addresses.

The following figure shows a sequence of memory cells laid out in memory. Each cell contains 8 bits. The hexadecimal numbers are the addresses of the memory cells:

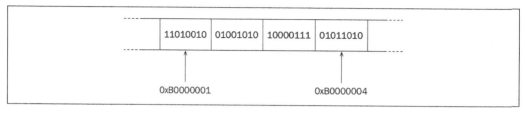

Figure 4.1: A sequence of memory cells

Since accessing a byte by its address is an $O(1)$ operation, from a programmer's perspective, it's tempting to believe that each memory cell is equally quick to access. This approach to memory is simple and useful in many cases, but when choosing data structures for efficient use, you need to take into account the memory hierarchy that exists in modern computers. The importance of the memory hierarchy has increased, since the time it takes to read and write from the main memory has become more expensive when compared to the speed of today's processors. The following figure shows the architecture of a machine with one CPU and four cores:

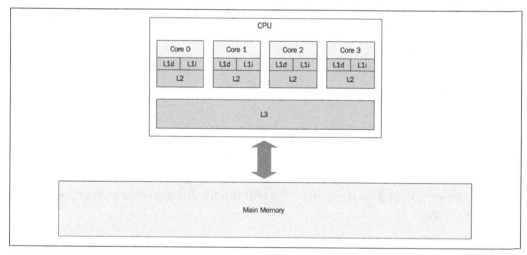

Figure 4.2: An example of a processor with four cores; the boxes labeled L1i, L1d, L2, and L3 are memory caches

I'm currently writing this chapter on a MacBook Pro from 2018, which is equipped with an Intel Quad-Core i7 CPU. On this processor, each core has its own L1 and L2 caches, whereas the L3 cache is shared among all four cores. Running the following command from a terminal:

```
sysctl -a hw
```

gives me, among other things, the following information:

```
hw.memsize: 17179869184
hw.cachelinesize: 64
hw.l1icachesize: 32768
hw.l1dcachesize: 32768
hw.l2cachesize: 262144
hw.l3cachesize: 8388608
```

The reported `hw.memsize` is the total amount of main memory, which is 16 GB in this case.

The `hw.cachelinesize`, which is reported to be 64 bytes, is the size of the cache lines, also known as blocks. When accessing a byte in memory, the machine is not only fetching the byte that is asked for; instead, the machine always fetches a cache line, which, in this case, is 64 bytes. The various caches between the CPU and main memory keep track of 64-byte blocks, instead of individual bytes.

The `hw.l1icachesize` is the size of the L1 instruction cache. This is a 32 KB cache dedicated to storing instructions that have been recently used by the CPU. The `hw.l1dcachesize` is also 32 KB and is dedicated to data, as opposed to instructions.

Lastly, we can read the size of the L2 cache and the L3 cache, which is 256 KB and 8 MB, respectively. An important observation is that the caches are tiny compared to the amount of main memory available.

Without presenting any detailed facts about the actual number of cycles required to access data from each layer in the cache hierarchy, a very rough guideline is that there are orders of magnitude differences of latency between two adjacent layers (for example, L1 and L2). The following table shows an extract from the latency numbers presented in an article by Peter Norvig called *Teach yourself programming in ten years, 2001* (`http://norvig.com/21-days.html`). The full table is usually referred to as *Latency numbers every programmer should know* and is credited to Jeff Dean:

L1 cache reference	0.5 ns
L2 cache reference	7 ns
Main memory reference	100 ns

Structuring the data in such a way that the caches can be fully utilized can have a dramatic effect on performance. Accessing data that has recently been used and, therefore, potentially already resides in the cache will make your program faster. This is known as **temporal locality**.

Also, accessing data located near some other data you are using will increase the likelihood that the data you need is already in a cache line that was fetched from the main memory earlier. This is known as **spatial locality**.

Constantly wiping out the cache lines in inner loops might result in very bad performance. This is sometimes called **cache thrashing**. Let's look at an example:

```cpp
constexpr auto kL1CacheCapacity = 32768; // The L1 Data cache size
constexpr auto kSize = kL1CacheCapacity / sizeof(int);
using MatrixType = std::array<std::array<int, kSize>, kSize>;

auto cache_thrashing(MatrixType& matrix) {
  auto counter = 0;
  for (auto i = 0; i < kSize; ++i) {
    for (auto j = 0; j < kSize; ++j) {
      matrix[i][j] = counter++;
    }
  }
}
```

This version takes about 40 ms to run on my computer. However, by only changing the line in the inner loop to the following, the time it takes to complete the function increases from 40 ms to over 800 ms:

```cpp
matrix[j][i] = counter++;
```

In the first example, when using `matrix[i][j]`, most of the time we will access memory that is already in the L1 cache, whereas, in the modified version using `matrix[j][i]`, every access will generate an L1 cache miss. A few images might help you to understand what's going on. Instead of drawing the full 32768 x 32768 matrix, a tiny 3 x 3 matrix, as shown here, will serve as an example:

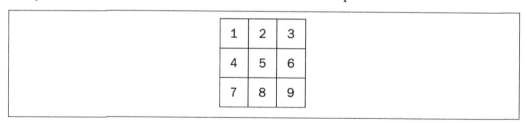

Figure 4.3: A 3x3 matrix

Even if this might be our mental image of how a matrix resides in memory, there is no such thing as 2-dimensional memory. Instead, when this matrix is laid out in a 1-dimensional memory space, it looks like this:

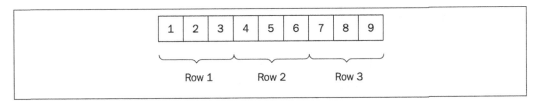

Figure 4.4: A 2-dimensional matrix in a 1-dimensional memory space

That is, it's a contiguous array of elements laid out row by row. In the fast version of our algorithm, the numbers are accessed sequentially in the same order in which they are contiguously laid out in memory, like this:

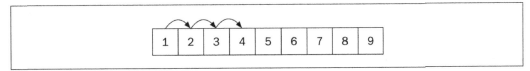

Figure 4.5: Fast sequential stride-1 accesses

Whereas in the slow version of the algorithm, the elements are accessed in a completely different pattern. Accessing the first four elements using the slow version would now look like this instead:

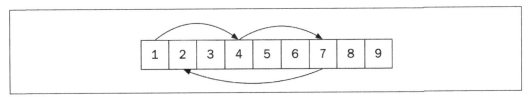

Figure 4.6: Slow access using a larger stride

Accessing data in this way is substantially slower due to poor spatial locality. Modern processors are usually also equipped with a **prefetcher**, which can automatically recognize memory access patterns and try to prefetch data from memory into the caches that are likely to be accessed in the near future. Prefetchers tend to perform best for smaller strides. You can read a lot more about this in the excellent book, *Computer Systems, A Programmer's Perspective*, by Randal E. Bryant and David R. O'Hallaron.

To summarize this section, even if memory accesses are constant-time operations, caching can have dramatic effects on the actual time it takes to access the memory. This is something to always bear in mind when using or implementing new data structures.

Next, I will introduce a set of data structures from the C++ standard library, called containers.

The standard library containers

The C++ standard library offers a set of very useful container types. A container is a data structure that contains a collection of elements. The container manages the memory of the elements it holds. This means that we don't have to explicitly create and delete the objects that we put in a container. We can pass objects created on the stack to a container and the container will copy and store them on the free store.

Iterators are used to access elements in containers, and are, therefore, a fundamental concept for understanding algorithms and data structures from the standard library. The iterator concept is covered in *Chapter 5, Algorithms*. For this chapter, it's enough to know that an iterator can be thought of as a pointer to an element and that iterators have different operators defined depending on the container they belong to. For example, array-like data structures provide random access iterators to their elements. These iterators support arithmetic expressions using + and -, whereas an iterator to a linked list, for example, only supports ++ and -- operators.

The containers are divided into three categories: sequence containers, associative containers, and container adaptors. This section will contain a brief introduction to the containers in each of the three categories and also address the most important things to consider when performance is an issue.

Sequence containers

Sequence containers keep the elements in the order we specify when adding the elements to the container. The sequence containers from the standard library are std::array, std::vector, std::deque, std::list, and std::forward_list. I will also address std::basic_string in this section, although it's not formally a generic sequence container because it only handles elements of character types.

We should know the answers to the following questions before choosing a sequence container:

1. What is the number of elements (order of magnitude)?
2. What are the usage patterns? How often are you going to add data? Read/ traverse data? Delete data? Rearrange data?
3. Where in the sequence are you going to add data most often? At the end, at the beginning, or in the middle of the sequence?
4. Do you need to sort the elements? Or do you even care about the order?

Depending on the answers to these questions, we can determine which sequence containers are more or less suitable for our needs. But, to do that, we need a basic understanding of the interfaces and performance characteristics of each type of sequence container.

The sections that follow will briefly present the different sequence containers, starting with one of the most widely used containers overall.

Vectors and arrays

`std::vector` is probably the most commonly used container type, and for good reason. A vector is an array that grows dynamically when needed. The elements added to a vector are guaranteed to be laid out contiguously in memory, which means that you can access any element in the array by its index in constant time. It also means that it provides excellent performance when traversing the elements in the order they are laid out, thanks to the spatial locality mentioned earlier.

A vector has a **size** and a **capacity**. The size is the number of elements that are currently held in the container, and the capacity is the number of elements that the vector can hold until it needs to allocate more space:

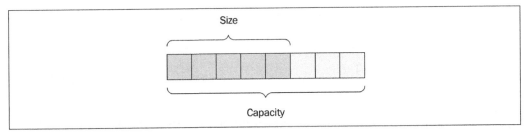

Figure 4.7: Size and capacity of a std::vector

Adding elements to the end of a vector using the `push_back()` function is fast, as long as the size is less than the capacity. When adding an element and there is no room for more, the vector will allocate a new internal buffer and then move all of the elements to the new space. The capacity will grow in such a way that resizing the buffer rarely happens, thus making `push_back()` an amortized constant-time operation, as we discussed in *Chapter 3, Analyzing and Measuring Performance*.

A vector template instance of type `std::vector<Person>` will store `Person` objects by value. When the vector needs to rearrange the `Person` objects (for example, as a result of an insert), the values will be copy constructed or moved. Objects will be moved if they have a `nothrow` move constructor. Otherwise, the objects will be copy constructed in order to guarantee strong exception safety:

```
Person(Person&& other) {          // Will be copied
    // ...
}
Person(Person&& other) noexcept { // Will be moved
    // ...
}
```

Internally, std::vector uses std::move_if_noexcept in order to determine whether the object should be copied or moved. The <type_traits> header can help you to verify at compile time that your classes are guaranteed to not throw an exception when moved:

```
static_assert(std::is_nothrow_move_constructible<Person>::value);
```

If you are adding newly created objects to the vector, you can take advantage of the emplace_back() function, which will create the object in place for you, instead of creating an object and then copying/moving it to the vector using the push_back() function:

```
persons.emplace_back("John", 65);
```

The capacity of the vector can change in the following ways:

- By adding an element to the vector when the capacity == size
- By calling reserve()
- By calling shrink_to_fit()

Other than that, the vector will not change the capacity, and hence will not allocate or deallocate dynamic memory. For example, the member function clear() empties a vector, but it does not change its capacity. These memory guarantees make the vector usable even in real-time contexts.

Since C++20, there are also two free functions that erase elements from a std::vector. Prior to C++20, we had to use the *erase-remove idiom*, which we will discuss in *Chapter 5, Algorithms*. However, now the recommended way to erase elements from a std::vector is by using std::erase() and std::erase_if(). Here is a short example of how to use these functions:

```
auto v = std::vector{-1, 5, 2, -3, 4, -5, 5};
std::erase(v, 5);                               // v: [-1,2,-3,4,-5]
std::erase_if(v, [](auto x) { return x < 0; }); // v: [2, 4]
```

As an alternative to the dynamically sized vector, the standard library also provides a fixed size version named `std::array` that manages its elements by using the stack as opposed to the free store. The size of the array is a template argument specified at compile time, which means that the size and type elements become a part of the concrete type:

```
auto a = std::array<int, 16>{};
auto b = std::array<int, 1024>{};
```

In this example, a and b are not the same type, which means that you have to specify the size when using the type as a function parameter:

```
auto f(const std::array<int, 1024>& input) {
  // ...
}

f(a);  // Does not compile, f requires an int array of size 1024
```

This might seem a bit tedious at first, but this is, in fact, the big advantage over the built-in array type (the C arrays), which loses the size information when passed to a function, since it automatically converts a pointer into the first element of the array:

```
// input looks like an array, but is in fact a pointer
auto f(const int input[]) {
  // ...
}

int a[16];
int b[1024];
f(a); // Compiles, but unsafe
```

An array losing its size information is usually referred to as **array decay**. You will see later on in this chapter how array decay can be avoided by using `std::span` when passing contiguous data to functions.

Deque

Sometimes, you'll find yourself in a situation where you need to frequently add elements to both the beginning and end of a sequence. If you are using a `std::vector` and need to speed up the inserts at the front, you can instead use `std::deque`, which is short for **double-ended queue**. `std::deque` is usually implemented as a collection of fixed-size arrays, which makes it possible to access elements by their index in constant time. However, as you can see in the following figure, all of the elements are not stored contiguously in memory, which is the case with `std::vector` and `std::array`.

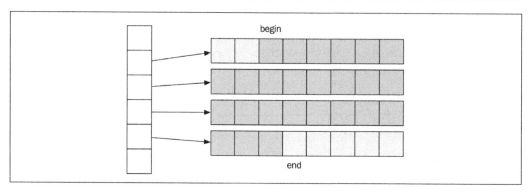

Figure 4.8: A possible layout of std::deque

List and forward_list

The std::list is a **doubly linked list,** meaning that each element has one link to the next element and one link to its previous element. This makes it possible to iterate over the list both backward and forward. There is also a **singly linked list** named std::forward_list. The reason you wouldn't always choose the doubly linked list over std::forward_list is because of the excessive memory that is occupied by the back pointers in the doubly linked list. So, if you don't need to traverse the list backward, use std::forward_list. Another interesting feature of the forward list is that it's optimized for very short lists. When the list is empty, it only occupies one word, which makes it a viable data structure for sparse data.

Note that even if the elements are ordered in a sequence, they are *not* laid out contiguously in memory like the vector and array are, which means that iterating a linked list will most likely generate a lot more cache misses compared to the vector.

To recap, the std::list is a doubly linked list with pointers to the next and previous elements:

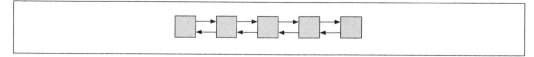

Figure 4.9: std::list is a doubly linked list

The std::forward_list is a singly linked list with pointers to the next element:

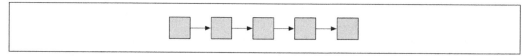

Figure 4.10: std::forward_list is a singly linked list

The `std::forward_list` is more memory efficient since it only has one pointer to the next element.

Lists are also the only containers that support **splicing**, which is a way to transfer elements between lists without copying or moving the elements. This means, for example, that it is possible to concatenate two lists into one in constant time, *O(1)*. Other containers require at least linear time for such operations.

The basic_string

The last template class that we will cover in this section is the `std::basic_string`. The `std::string` is a typedef for `std::basic_string<char>`. Historically, `std::basic_string` was not guaranteed to be laid out contiguously in memory. This changed with C++17, which makes it possible to pass the string to APIs that require an array of characters. For example, the following code reads an entire file into a string:

```
auto in = std::ifstream{"file.txt", std::ios::binary | std::ios::ate};
if (in.is_open()) {
  auto size = in.tellg();
  auto content = std::string(size, '\0');
  in.seekg(0);
  in.read(&content[0], size);
  // "content" now contains the entire file
}
```

By opening the file using `std::ios::ate`, the position indicator is set to the end of the stream so that we can use `tellg()` to retrieve the size of the file. After that, we set the input position to the beginning of the stream and start reading.

Most implementations of `std::basic_string` utilize something called **small object optimization**, which means that they do not allocate any dynamic memory if the size of the string is small. We will discuss small object optimization later in the book. For now, let's move on to discuss associative containers.

Associative containers

The associative containers place their elements based on the element itself. For example, it's not possible to add an element at the back or front in an associative container as we do with `std::vector::push_back()` or `std::list::push_front()`. Instead, the elements are added in a way that makes it possible to find the element without the need to scan the entire container. Therefore, the associative containers have some requirements for the objects we want to store in a container. We will look at these requirements later.

There are two main categories of associative containers:

- **Ordered associative containers**: These containers are based on trees; the containers use a tree for storing their elements. They require that the elements are ordered by the less than operator (<). The functions for adding, deleting, and finding elements are all *O(log n)* in the tree-based containers. The containers are named std::set, std::map, std::multiset, and std::multimap.

- **Unordered associative containers**: These containers are based on hash tables; the containers use a hash table for storing their elements. They require that the elements are compared with the equality operator (==) and that there is a way to compute a hash value based on an element. More on that later. The functions for adding, deleting, and finding elements are all *O(1)* in the hash table-based containers. The containers are named std::unordered_set, std::unordered_map, std::unordered_multiset, and std::unordered_multimap.

Since C++20, all associative containers are equipped with a function named contains(), which should be used when you want to know whether a container contains some specific elements. In earlier versions of C++, it was necessary to use count() or find() to find out whether a container contained an element.

Always use the specialized functions, such as contains() and empty(), instead of using count() > 0 or size() == 0. The specialized functions are guaranteed to be the most efficient ones.

Ordered sets and maps

The ordered associative containers guarantee that insert, delete, and search can be done in logarithmic time, *O(log n)*. How that is achieved is up to the implementation of the standard library. However, the implementations we know about do use some kind of self-balancing binary search tree. The fact that the tree stays approximately balanced is necessary for controlling the height of the tree, and, hence, also the worst-case running time when accessing elements. There is no need for the tree to pre-allocate memory, so, typically, a tree will allocate memory on the free store each time an element is inserted and also free up memory whenever elements are erased. Take a look at the following diagram, which shows that the height of a balanced tree is *O(log n)*:

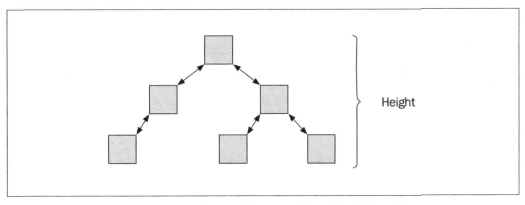

Figure 4.11: The height of the tree is O(log n) if it's balanced

Unordered sets and maps

The unordered versions of sets and maps offer a hash-based alternative to the tree-based versions. This data structure is, in general, referred to as hash tables. In theory, hash tables offer amortized constant-time insert, add, and delete operations, which can be compared to the tree-based versions that operate in $O(log\ n)$. However, in practice, the difference might not be so obvious, especially if you are not storing a very large number of elements in your container.

Let's see how a hash table can offer $O(1)$ operations. A hash table keeps its elements in some sort of array of buckets. When adding an element to the hash table, an integer is computed for the element using a hash function. The integer is usually called the **hash** of the element. The hash value is then limited to the size of the array (by using the modulo operation, for example) so that the new limited value can be used as an index in the array. Once the index is computed, the hash table can store the element in the array at that index. The lookup of an element works in a similar manner by first computing a hash value for the element we are looking for and then accessing the array.

Apart from computing the hash value, this technique seems straightforward. This is just half of the story, though. What if two different elements generate the same index, either because they produced the same hash value, or because two different hash values are being limited to the same index? When two non-equal elements end up at the same index, we call that a **hash collision**. This is not just an edge case: this will happen a lot, even if we are using a good hash function, and especially if the array is small when compared to the number of elements we are adding. There are various ways of dealing with hash collisions. Here, we will focus on the one that is being used in the standard library, which is called **separate chaining**.

Separate chaining solves the problem of two unequal elements ending up at the same index. Instead of just storing the elements directly in the array, the array is a sequence of **buckets**. Each bucket can contain multiple elements, that is, all of the elements that are hashed to the same index. So, each bucket is also some sort of container. The exact data structure used for the buckets is not defined, and it can vary for different implementations. However, we can think of it as a linked list and assume that finding an element in a specific bucket is slow, since it needs to scan the elements in the buckets linearly.

The following figure shows a hash table with eight buckets. The elements have landed in three separate buckets. The bucket with index **2** contains four elements, the bucket with index **4** contains two elements, and the bucket with index **5** contains only one element. The other buckets are empty:

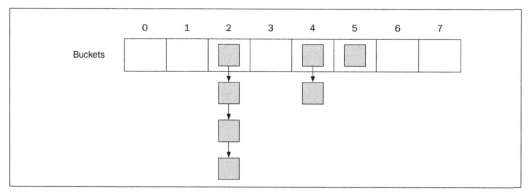

Figure 4.12: Each bucket contains 0 or more elements

Hash and equals

The hash value, which can be computed in constant time with respect to the size of the container, determines which bucket an element will be placed in. Since it's possible that more than one object will generate the same hash value, and therefore end up in the same bucket, each key also needs to provide an equals function, which is used to compare the key we are looking for with all of the keys in the bucket.

If two keys are equal, they are required to generate the same hash value. However, it's perfectly legal for two objects to return the same hash value while not being equal to each other.

A good hash function is quick to compute and will also distribute the keys evenly among the buckets in order to minimize the number of elements in each bucket.

The following is an example of a *very bad*, but valid, hash function:

```
auto my_hash = [](const Person& person) {
  return 47; // Bad, don't do this!
};
```

It is valid because it will return the same hash value for two objects that are equal. The hash function is also very quick. However, since all elements will produce the same hash value, all keys will end up in the same bucket, which means finding an element will be *O(n)* instead of *O(1)*, which we are aiming for.

A good hash function, on the other hand, ensures that the elements are distributed evenly among the buckets to minimize hash collisions. The C++ standard actually has a note about this, which states that it should be very rare for a hash function to produce the same hash value for two different objects. Fortunately, the standard library already provides us with good hash functions for basic types. In many cases, we can reuse these functions when writing our own hash functions for user-defined types.

Suppose we want to use a Person class as a key in an unorordered_set. The Person class has two data members: age, which is an int, and name, which is a std::string. We start by writing the equal predicate:

```
auto person_eq = [](const Person& lhs, const Person& rhs) {
  return lhs.name() == rhs.name() && lhs.age() == rhs.age();
};
```

For two Person objects to be equal, they need to have the same name and the same age. We can now define the hash predicate by combining the hash values of all of the data members that are included in the equals predicate. Unfortunately, there is no function in the C++ standard yet to combine hash values, but there is a good one available in Boost, which we will use here:

```
#include <boost/functional/hash.hpp>
auto person_hash = [](const Person& person) {
  auto seed = size_t{0};
  boost::hash_combine(seed, person.name());
  boost::hash_combine(seed, person.age());
  return seed;
};
```

 If, for some reason, you cannot use Boost, boost::hash_combine() is really just a one-liner that can be copied from the documentation found at https://www.boost.org/doc/libs/1_55_0/doc/html/hash/reference.html#boost.hash_combine.

With the equality and hash functions defined, we can finally create our `unordered_set`:

```
using Set = std::unordered_set<Person, decltype(person_hash),
                               decltype(person_eq)>;
auto persons = Set{100, person_hash, person_eq};
```

A good rule of thumb is to always use all of the data members that are being used in the equal function when producing the hash value. That way, we adhere to the contract between equals and hash, and, at the same time, this enables us to provide an effective hash value. For example, it would be correct but inefficient to only use the name when computing the hash value, since that would mean that all `Person` objects with the same name would end up in the same bucket. Even worse, though, would be to include data members in the hash function that are not being used in the equals function. This would most likely result in a disaster where you cannot find objects in your `unordered_set` that, in fact, compare equally.

Hash policy

Apart from creating hash values that distribute the keys evenly among the buckets, we can reduce the number of collisions by having many buckets. The average number of elements per bucket is called the **load factor**. In the preceding example, we created an `unordered_set` with 100 buckets. If we add 50 `Person` objects to the set, `load_factor()` would return 0.5. The `max_load_factor` is an upper limit of the load factor, and when that value is reached, the set will need to increase the number of buckets, and, as a consequence, also rehash all the elements that are currently in the set. It's also possible to trigger a rehash manually with the `rehash()` and `reserve()` member functions.

Let's move on to look at the third category: container adaptors.

Container adaptors

There are three container adaptors in the standard library: `std::stack`, `std::queue`, and `std::priority_queue`. Container adaptors are quite different from sequence containers and associative containers because they represent **abstract data types** that can be implemented by the underlying sequence container. For example, the stack, which is a **last in, first out (LIFO)** data structure supporting push and pop on the top of the stack, can be implemented by using a `vector`, `list`, deque, or any other custom sequence container that supports `back()`, `push_back()`, and `pop_back()`. The same goes for queue, which is a **first in, first out (FIFO)** data structure, and `priortiy_queue`.

In this section, we will focus on `std::priority_queue`, which is a pretty useful data structure that is easy to forget.

Priority queues

A **priority queue** offers a constant-time lookup of the element with the highest priority. The priority is defined using the less than operator of the elements. Insert and delete both run in logarithmic time. A priority queue is a partially ordered data structure, and it might not be obvious when to use one instead of a completely sorted data structure, for example, a tree or a sorted vector. However, in some cases, a priority queue can offer you the functionality you need, and for a lower cost than a completely sorted container.

The standard library already provides a partial sort algorithm, so we don't need to write our own. But let's look at how we can implement a partial sort algorithm using a priority queue. Suppose that we are writing a program for searching documents given a query. The matching documents (search hits) should be ordered by rank, and we are only interested in finding the first 10 search hits with the highest rank.

A document is represented by the following class:

```
class Document {
public:
  Document(std::string title) : title_{std::move(title)} {}
private:
  std::string title_;
  // ...
};
```

When searching, an algorithm selects the documents that match the query and computes a rank of the search hits. Each matching document is represented by a Hit:

```
struct Hit {
  float rank_{};
  std::shared_ptr<Document> document_;
};
```

Finally, we need to sort the hits and return the top *m* documents. What are the options for sorting the hits? If the hits are contained in a container that provides random access iterators, we could use std::sort() and only return the *m* first elements. Or, if the total number of hits is much larger than the *m* documents we are to return, we could use std::partial_sort(), which would be more efficient than std::sort().

But what if we don't have random access iterators? Maybe the matching algorithm only provides forward iterators to the hits. In that case, we could use a priority queue and still come up with an efficient solution. Our sort interface would look like this:

```
template<typename It>
auto sort_hits(It begin, It end, size_t m) -> std::vector<Hit> {
```

We could call this function with any iterator that has the increment operator defined. Next, we create a std::priority_queue backed by a std::vector, using a custom compare function for keeping the *lowest* ranking hits at the top of the queue:

```
auto cmp = [](const Hit& a, const Hit& b) {
  return a.rank_ > b.rank_; // Note, we are using greater than
};
auto queue = std::priority_queue<Hit, std::vector<Hit>,
                                 decltype(cmp)>{cmp};
```

We will only insert, at most, *m* elements in the priority queue. The priority queue will contain the highest-ranking hits seen so far. Among the elements that are currently in the priority queue, the hit with the lowest rank will be the topmost element:

```
for (auto it = begin; it != end; ++it) {
  if (queue.size() < m) {
    queue.push(*it);
  }
  else if (it->rank_ > queue.top().rank_) {
    queue.pop();
    queue.push(*it);
  }
}
```

Now, we have collected the highest-ranking hits in the priority queue, so the only thing left to do is to put them in a vector in reverse order and return the *m*-sorted hits:

```
auto result = std::vector<Hit>{};
while (!queue.empty()) {
  result.push_back(queue.top());
  queue.pop();
```

```
  }
  std::reverse(result.begin(), result.end());
  return result;
} // end of sort_hits()
```

What is the complexity of this algorithm? If we denote the number of hits with *n* and the number of returned hits with *m*, we can see that the memory consumption is *O(m)*, whereas the time complexity is *O(n * log m)*, since we are iterating over *n* elements. Additionally, in each iteration, we might have to do a push and/or pop, which both run in *O(log m)* time.

We will now leave the standard library containers and focus on a couple of new useful class templates that are closely related to standard containers.

Using views

In this section, we will discuss some relatively new class templates in the C++ standard library: `std::string_view` from C++17 and `std::span`, which was introduced in C++20.

These class templates are not containers but lightweight views (or slices) of a sequence of contiguous elements. Views are small objects that are meant to be copied by value. They don't allocate memory, nor do they provide any guarantees regarding the lifetime of the memory they point to. In other words, they are non-owning reference types, which differ significantly from the containers described previously in this chapter. At the same time, they are closely related to `std::string`, `std::array`, and `std::vector`, which we will look at soon. I will start by describing `std::string_view`.

Avoiding copies with string_view

A `std::string_view` contains a pointer to the beginning of an immutable string buffer and a size. Since a string is a contiguous sequence of characters, the pointer and the size fully define a valid substring range. Typically, a `std::string_view` points to some memory that is owned by a `std::string`. But it could also point to a string literal with static storage duration or something like a memory-mapped file. The following diagram shows a `std::string_view` pointing at memory owned by a `std::string`:

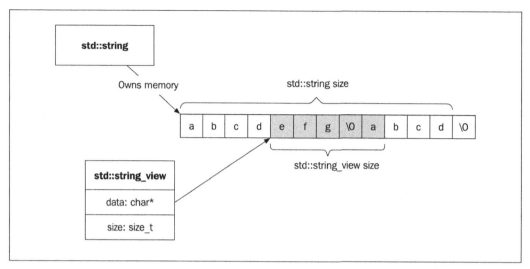

Figure 4.13: A std::string_view object pointing at memory owned by an instance of std::string

The character sequence defined by a `std::string_view` is not required to be terminated by a null character, but it is perfectly valid to have a sequence of characters that contains null characters. The `std::string`, on the other hand, needs to be able to return a null-terminated string from `c_str()`, which means that it always stores an extra null character at the end of the sequence.

The fact that `string_view` does not need a null terminator means that it can handle substrings much more efficiently than a C-style string or a `std::string` because it does not have to create new strings just to add the null terminator. The complexity of `substr()` using a `std::string_view` is constant, which should be compared to the `substr()` version of `std::string`, which runs in linear time.

There is also a performance win when passing strings to functions. Consider the following code:

```
auto some_func(const std::string& s) {
  // process s ...
}
some_func("A string literal"); // Creates a std::string
```

When passing a string literal to `some_func()`, the compiler needs to construct a new `std::string` object to match the type of the argument. However, if we let `some_func()` accept a `std::string_view`, there is no longer any need to construct a `std::string`:

```
auto some_func(std::string_view s) { // Pass by value
  // process s ...
```

```
}
some_func("A string literal");
```

A `std::string_view` instance can be constructed efficiently both from a `std::string` and a string literal and is, therefore, a well-suited type for function parameters.

Eliminating array decay with std::span

When discussing `std::vector` and `std::array` earlier in this chapter, I mentioned that array decay (losing the size information of an array) happens with built-in arrays when they are passed to a function:

```
// buffer looks like an array, but is in fact a pointer
auto f1(float buffer[]) {
  const auto n = std::size(buffer);   // Does not compile!
  for (auto i = 0u; i < n; ++i) {     // Size is lost!
    // ...
  }
}
```

We could get around this problem by adding a size parameter:

```
auto f2(float buffer[], size_t n) {
  for (auto i = 0u; i < n; ++i) {
    // ...
  }
}
```

Although this technically works, passing the correct data to this function is both error-prone and tedious, and if f2() passes the buffer to other functions, it needs to remember to pass the correctly sized variable n. This is what the call site of f2() might look like:

```
float a[256];
f2(a, 256);
f2(a, sizeof(a)/sizeof(a[0])); // A common tedious pattern
f2(a, std::size(a));
```

Array decay is the source of many bound-related bugs, and in situations where built-in arrays are used (for one reason or another), `std::span` offers a safer way to pass arrays to functions. Since the span holds both the pointer to the memory and the size together in one object, we can use it as the single type when passing sequences of elements to functions:

```
auto f3(std::span<float> buffer) {  // Pass by value
  for (auto&& b : buffer) {          // Range-based for-loop
    // ...
  }
}
float a[256];
f3(a);           // OK! Array is passed as a span with size
auto v = std::vector{1.f, 2.f, 3.f, 4.f};
f3(v);           // OK!
```

A span is also more convenient to use over a built-in array since it acts more like a regular container with support for iterators.

There are many similarities between std::string_view and std::span when it comes to the data members (pointer and size) and the member functions. But there are also some notable differences: the memory pointed to by std::span is mutable, whereas the std::string_view always points to constant memory. std::string_view also contains string-specific functions such as hash() and substr(), which are naturally not part of std::span. Lastly, there is no compare() function in std::span, so it's not possible to directly use the comparison operators on std::span objects.

It's now time to highlight a few general points related to performance when using data structures from the standard library.

Some performance considerations

We have now covered the three major container categories: sequence containers, associative containers, and container adaptors. This section will provide you with some general performance advice to consider when working with containers.

Balancing between complexity guarantees and overhead

Knowing the time and memory complexity of data structures is important when choosing between containers. But it's equally important to remember that each container is afflicted with an overhead cost, which has a bigger impact on the performance for smaller datasets. The complexity guarantees only become interesting for sufficiently large datasets. It's up to you, though, to decide what sufficiently large means in your use cases. Here, again, you need to measure your program while executing it to gain insights.

In addition, the fact that computers are equipped with memory caches makes the use of data structures that are friendly to the cache more likely to perform better. This usually speaks in favor of the std::vector, which has a low memory overhead and stores its elements contiguously in memory, making access and traversal faster.

The following diagram shows the actual running time of two algorithms. One runs in linear time, *O(n)*, and the other runs in logarithmic time, *O(log n)*, but with a larger overhead. The logarithmic algorithm is slower than the linear time algorithm when the input size is below the marked threshold:

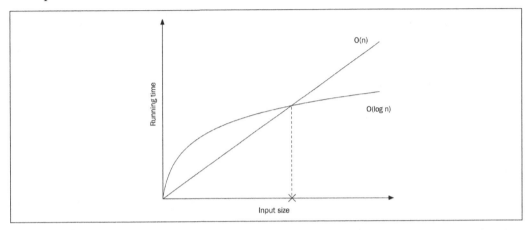

Figure 4.14: For small sizes of n, the linear algorithm, O(n), is faster than the algorithm running in O(log n)

Our next point to keep in mind is more concrete and highlights the importance of using the most suitable API functions.

Knowing and using the appropriate API functions

In C++, there is usually more than one way to do something. The language and the library continue to evolve, but very few features are being deprecated. When new functions are added to the standard library, we should learn when to use them and reflect on what patterns we might have used to compensate for a previously missing function.

Here, we will focus on two small, but important, functions that can be found in the standard library: contains() and empty(). Use contains() when checking whether an element exists in an associated container. Use empty() if you want to know whether a container has any elements or is empty. Apart from expressing the intent more clearly, it also has performance benefits. Checking the size of a linked list is an *O(n)* operation, whereas calling empty() on a list runs in constant time, *O(1)*.

Before C++20 and the introduction of the contains() function, we had to take a detour every time we wanted to check for the existence of some value in an associative container. You have most likely stumbled upon code that uses various ways to look for the existence of an element. Suppose we have a bag-of-words implemented using a std::multiset:

```
auto bag = std::multiset<std::string>{}; // Our bag-of-words
// Fill bag with words ...
```

If we want to know whether some specific word is in our bag-of-words, there are numerous ways to go forward. One alternative would be to use count(), like this:

```
auto word = std::string{"bayes"}; // Our word we want to find

if (bag.count(word) > 0) {
  // ...
}
```

It seems reasonable, but it may have a slight overhead since it counts *all* elements that match our word. Another alternative is to use find(), but it has the same overhead since it returns all the matching words, not just the first occurrence:

```
if (bag.find(word) != bag.end()) {
  // ...
}
```

Before C++20, the recommended way was to use lower_bound(), since it only returns the first matching element, like this:

```
if (bag.lower_bound(word) != bag.end()) {
  // ...
}
```

Now, with C++20 and the introduction of contains(), we can express our intent more clearly and also be sure that the library will provide us with the most efficient implementation when we only want to check for existence of an element:

```
if (bag.contains(word)) { // Efficient and with clear intent
  // ...
}
```

The general rule is that if there is a specific member function or a free function designed for a specific container, then use it if it matches your needs. It will be efficient, and it will express the intent more clearly. Don't use detours like the ones shown earlier just because you haven't learned the full API or because you have old habits of doing things in a certain way.

It should also be said that the zero-overhead principle applies particularly well to functions like these, so don't spend time trying to outsmart the library implementors by handcrafting your own functions.

We will now go ahead and look at a lengthier example of how we can reorder data in different ways to optimize runtime performance for a specific use case.

Parallel arrays

We will finish this chapter by talking about iterating over elements and exploring ways to improve performance when iterating over array-like data structures. I have already mentioned two important factors for performance when accessing data: spatial locality and temporal locality. When iterating over elements stored contiguously in memory, we will increase the probability that the data we need is already cached if we manage to keep our objects small, thanks to spatial locality. Obviously, this will have a great impact on performance.

Recall the cache-thrashing example, shown at the beginning of this chapter, where we iterated over a matrix. It demonstrated that we sometimes need to think about the way we access data, even if we have a fairly compact representation of the data.

Next, we will compare how long it takes to iterate over objects of different sizes. We will start by defining two structs, SmallObject and BigObject:

```
struct SmallObject {
  std::array<char, 4> data_{};
  int score_{std::rand()};
};

struct BigObject {
  std::array<char, 256> data_{};
  int score_{std::rand()};
};
```

SmallObject and BigObject are identical, except for the size of the initial data array. Both structs contain an int named score_, which we initialize to a random value just for testing purposes. We can let the compiler tell us the size of the objects by using the sizeof operator:

```
std::cout << sizeof(SmallObject); // Possible output is 8
std::cout << sizeof(BigObject);   // Possible output is 260
```

We need plenty of objects in order to evaluate the performance. Create one million objects of each kind:

```
auto small_objects = std::vector<SmallObject>(1'000'000);
auto big_objects = std::vector<BigObject>(1'000'000);
```

Now for the iteration. Let's say that we want to sum the scores of all the objects. Our preference would be to use `std::accumulate()`, which we will cover later in the book, but, for now, a simple `for`-loop will do. We write this function as a template so that we don't have to manually write one version for each type of object. The function iterates over the objects and sums all the scores:

```
template <class T>
auto sum_scores(const std::vector<T>& objects) {
  ScopedTimer t{"sum_scores"};     // See chapter 3

  auto sum = 0;
  for (const auto& obj : objects) {
    sum += obj.score_;
  }
  return sum;
}
```

Now, we are ready to see how long it takes to sum the scores in the small objects compared to the big objects:

```
auto sum = 0;
sum += sum_scores(small_objects);
sum += sum_scores(big_objects);
```

To achieve reliable results, we need to repeat the test a couple of times. On my computer, it takes about 1 ms to compute the sum of the small objects and 10 ms to compute the sum of the big objects. This example is similar to the cache thrashing example at the beginning of the chapter, and one reason for the big difference is, again, because of the way the computer uses the cache hierarchy to fetch data from the main memory.

How can we utilize the fact that it's faster to iterate over collections of smaller objects than bigger objects when working with more realistic scenarios than the preceding example?

Obviously, we can do our best to keep the size of our classes small, but it's often easier said than done. Also, if we are working with an old code base that has been growing for some time, the chances are high that we will stumble across some really large classes with too many data members and too many responsibilities.

We will now look at a class that represents a user in an online game system and see how we can split it into smaller parts. The class has the following data members:

```
struct User {
    std::string name_;
    std::string username_;
    std::string password_;
    std::string security_question_;
    std::string security_answer_;
    short level_{};
    bool is_playing_{};
};
```

A user has a name that is frequently used and some information for authentication that are rarely used. The class also keeps track of which level the player is currently playing at. Finally, the User struct also knows whether the user is currently playing by storing the is_playing_ boolean.

The sizeof operator reports that the User class is 128 bytes when compiling for a 64-bit architecture. An approximate layout of the data members can be seen in the following figure:

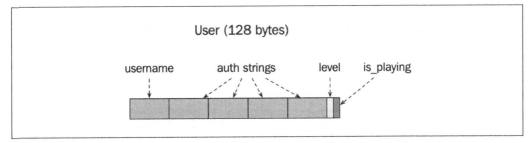

Figure 4.15: Memory layout of the User class

All users are kept in a std::vector, and there are two global functions that are called very often and need to run quickly: num_users_at_level() and num_playing_users(). Both functions iterate over all users, and therefore we need to make iterations over the user vector quick.

The first function returns the number of users who have reached a certain level:

```
auto num_users_at_level(const std::vector<User>& users, short level) {
  ScopedTimer t{"num_users_at_level (using 128 bytes User)"};

  auto num_users = 0;
  for (const auto& user : users)
    if (user.level_ == level)
      ++num_users;

  return num_users;
}
```

The second function computes how many users are currently playing:

```
auto num_playing_users(const std::vector<User>& users) {
  ScopedTimer t{"num_playing_users (using 128 bytes User)"};

  return std::count_if(users.begin(), users.end(),
    [](const auto& user) {
      return user.is_playing_;
    });
}
```

Here, we use the algorithm `std::count_if()` instead of a handwritten loop, as we did in `num_users_at_level()`. `std::count_if()` will call the predicate we provide for each user in the user vector and return the number of times the predicate returns true. This is basically what we are doing in the first function as well, so we could also have used `std::count_if()` in the first case. Both functions run in linear time.

Calling the two functions with a vector of one million users results in the following output:

```
11 ms num_users_at_level (using 128 bytes User)
10 ms num_playing_users (using 128 bytes User)
```

We hypothesize that by making the `User` class smaller, it would be faster to iterate over the vector. As mentioned, the password and security data fields are rarely used and could be grouped in a separate struct. That would give us the following classes:

```
struct AuthInfo {
  std::string username_;
  std::string password_;
  std::string security_question_;
  std::string security_answer_;
};

struct User {
  std::string name_;
  std::unique_ptr<AuthInfo> auth_info_;
  short level_{};
  bool is_playing_{};
};
```

This change decreases the size of the User class from 128 bytes to 40 bytes. Instead of storing four strings in the User class, we use a pointer to refer to the new AuthInfo object. The following figure shows you how we have split up the User class into two smaller classes:

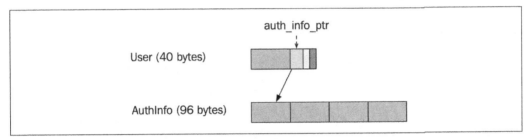

Figure 4.16: Memory layout when authentication information is kept in a separate class

This change makes sense from a design perspective too. Keeping the authentication data in a separate class increases the cohesion of the User class. The User class contains a pointer to the authentication information. The total amount of memory that the user data occupies has not decreased, of course, but the important thing right now is to shrink the User class in order to speed up the functions that iterate over all users.

From an optimization point of view, we have to measure this again to verify that our hypothesis regarding smaller data is valid. It turns out that both functions run more than twice as fast with the smaller User class. The output when running the modified version is:

```
4 ms num_users_at_level with User
3 ms num_playing_users with User
```

Next, we are going to try a more aggressive way of shrinking the amount of data we need to iterate through by using **parallel arrays**. First, a warning: this is an optimization that, in many cases, has too many drawbacks to be a viable alternative. Don't take this as a general technique and apply it without thinking twice. We will come back to the pros and cons of parallel arrays after looking at a few examples.

By using parallel arrays, we simply split the large structures into smaller types, similar to what we did with the authentication information for our User class. But instead of using pointers to relate objects, we store the smaller structures in separate arrays of equal size. The smaller objects in the different arrays that share the same index form the complete original object.

An example will clarify this technique. The User class we have worked with consists of 40 bytes. It now only contains a username string, a pointer to the authentication information, an integer for the current level, and the is_playing_ boolean. By making the user objects smaller, we saw that the performance improved when iterating over the objects. The memory layout of an array of user objects would look something like the one shown in the following figure. We will ignore memory alignment and padding for now, but will get back to these topics in *Chapter 7, Memory Management*:

Figure 4.17: User objects stored contiguously in a vector

Instead of having one vector with user objects, we can store all the short levels and is_playing_ flags in separate vectors. The current level for the user at index 0 in the user array is also stored at index 0 in the level array. In that way, we can avoid having pointers to the levels, and instead just use the index for connecting the data fields. We could do the same thing with the boolean is_playing_ field and end up with three parallel arrays instead of just one. The memory layout of the three vectors would look something like this:

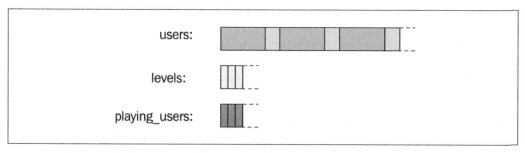

Figure 4.18: Memory layout when using three parallel arrays

We are using three parallel arrays to make iterations over one particular field quickly. The num_users_at_level() function can now compute the number of users at a specific level by only using the level array. The implementation is now simply a wrapper around std::count():

```
auto num_users_at_level(const std::vector<int>& users, short level) {
  ScopedTimer t{"num_users_at_level using int vector"};
  return std::count(users.begin(), users.end(), level);
}
```

Likewise, the num_playing_users() function only needs to iterate over the vector of booleans to determine the number of playing users. Again, we use std::count():

```
auto num_playing_users(const std::vector<bool>& users) {
  ScopedTimer t{"num_playing_users using vector<bool>"};
  return std::count(users.begin(), users.end(), true);
}
```

With parallel arrays, we don't have to use the user array at all. The amount of memory occupied by the extracted arrays is substantially smaller than the user array, so let's check whether we have improved on performance when running the functions on one million users again:

```
auto users = std::vector<User>(1'000'000);
auto levels = std::vector<short>(1'000'000);
auto playing_users = std::vector<bool>(1'000'000);

// Initialize data
// ...

auto num_at_level_5 = num_users_at_level(levels, 5);
auto num_playing = num_playing_users(playing_users);
```

Counting the number of users at a certain level only takes about 0.7 ms when using the array of integers. To recap, the initial version using the User class with a size of 128 bytes took around 11 ms. The smaller User class executed in 4 ms, and now, by only using the levels array, we are down to 0.7 ms. This is quite a dramatic change.

For the second function, `num_playing_users()`, the change is even bigger — it only takes around 0.03 ms to count how many users are currently playing. The reason why it can be so fast is thanks to a data structure called **bit arrays**. It turns out that `std::vector<bool>` is not at all a standard vector of C++ `bool` objects. Instead, internally, it's a bit array. Operations such as `count()` and `find()` can be optimized very efficiently in a bit array since it can process 64 bits at a time (on a 64-bit machine), or possibly even more by using SIMD registers. The future of `std::vector<bool>` is unclear, and it might be deprecated soon in favor of the fixed-size `std::bitset` and a new dynamically sized bitset. There is already a version in Boost named `boost::dynamic_bitset`.

This is all fantastic, but I warned you about some drawbacks. First of all, extracting the fields from the classes where they actually belong will have a big impact on the structure of the code. In some cases, it makes perfect sense to split large classes into smaller parts, but in other cases, it totally breaks encapsulation and exposes data that could have been hidden behind interfaces with higher abstraction.

It's also cumbersome to ensure that the arrays are in sync, such that we always need to ensure that fields that comprise one object are stored at the same index in all arrays. Implicit relationships like this can be hard to maintain and are error-prone.

The last drawback is actually related to performance. In the preceding example, you saw that for algorithms that iterate over one field at a time, there was a big performance gain. However, if we have an algorithm that would need to access multiple fields that have been extracted into different arrays, it would be substantially slower than iterating over one array with bigger objects.

So, as is always the case when working with performance, there is nothing that comes without a cost, and the cost for exposing data and splitting one simple array into multiple arrays may or may not be too high. It all depends on the scenario you are facing and what performance gain you encounter after measuring. Don't consider parallel arrays before you actually face a real performance issue. Always opt for sound design principles first, and favor explicit ways of expressing relationships between objects rather than implicit ones.

Summary

In this chapter, the container types from the standard library were introduced. You learned that the way we structure data has a big impact on how efficiently we can perform certain operations on a collection of objects. The asymptotic complexity specifications of the standard library containers are key factors to consider when choosing among the different data structures.

In addition, you learned how the cache hierarchy in modern processors impacts the way we need to organize data for efficient access to memory. The importance of utilizing the cache levels efficiently cannot be stressed enough. This is one of the reasons why containers that keep their elements contiguously in memory have become the most used, such as `std::vector` and `std::string`.

In the next chapter, we will look at how we can use iterators and algorithms to operate on containers efficiently.

5
Algorithms

The use of containers from the standard library is widely employed among C++ programmers. It's rare to find C++ code bases without references to std::vector or std::string, for example. However, in my experience, standard library algorithms are much less frequently used, even though they offer the same kind of benefits as containers:

- They can be used as building blocks when solving complex problems
- They are well documented (including references, books, and videos)
- Many C++ programmers are already familiar with them
- Their space and runtime costs are known (complexity guarantees)
- Their implementations are well crafted and efficient

If this wasn't enough, C++ features such as lambdas, execution policies, concepts, and ranges have all made the standard algorithms more powerful and, at the same time, friendlier to use.

In this chapter, we will take a look at how we can write efficient algorithms in C++ using the **Algorithm library**. You will learn the benefits of using the standard library algorithms as building blocks in your application, both performance-wise and readability-wise.

In this chapter, you will learn about:

- The algorithms in the C++ standard library
- Iterators and ranges – the glue between the containers and the algorithms
- How to implement a generic algorithm that can operate on standard containers

- Best practices when using C++ standard algorithms

Let's begin by taking a look at the standard library algorithms and how they came to be what they are today.

Introducing the standard library algorithms

Integrating the standard library algorithms into your C++ vocabulary is important. In this introduction, I will present a set of common problems that can be solved effectively by using the standard library algorithms.

C++20 comes with a dramatic change to the Algorithm library by the introduction of the **Ranges library** and the language feature of C++ *concepts*. So, before we start, we need a brief background of the history of the C++ standard library.

Evolution of the standard library algorithms

You have probably heard about STL algorithms or STL containers. And hopefully, you have heard about the new **Ranges library** introduced with C++20. There have been a lot of additions to the standard library in C++20. And before going further, I need to clear up some terminology. We'll start with the STL.

The **STL**, or the **Standard Template Library**, was initially the name of a library added to the C++ standard library in the 1990s. It contained algorithms, containers, iterators, and function objects. The name has been sticky, and we have become accustomed to hearing and talking about the STL algorithms and containers. The C++ standard does not mention the STL however; instead, it talks about the *standard library* and their individual components such as the **Iterator library** and the **Algorithm library**. I will try to avoid using the name STL in this book and instead talk about the standard library or individual libraries when needed.

Now on to the Ranges library and what I will call the **constrained algorithms**. The Ranges library is a library added to the standard library in C++20 that introduced a completely new header called <ranges>, which we will talk more about in the next chapter. But the addition of the Ranges library also had a big impact on the <algorithm> header by introducing overloaded versions of all previously existing algorithms. I will refer to these algorithms as the *constrained algorithms* because they are constrained using C++ concepts. So, the <algorithm> header now includes the old iterator-based algorithms and the new algorithms constrained with C++ concepts that can operate on ranges. This means that the algorithms we will discuss in this chapter come in two flavors, as demonstrated in the following example:

```
#include <algorithm>
#include <vector>

auto values = std::vector{9, 2, 5, 3, 4};

// Sort using the std algorithms
std::sort(values.begin(), values.end());

// Sort using the constrained algorithms under std::ranges
std::ranges::sort(values);
std::ranges::sort(values.begin(), values.end());
```

Note that both versions of sort() live in the <algorithm> header but they are distinguished by different namespaces and signatures. This chapter will use both flavors, but in general, I recommend using the new constrained algorithms whenever possible. The benefits will hopefully become apparent after reading this chapter.

Now you are ready to start learning about how you can use ready-made algorithms to solve common problems.

Solving everyday problems

I will list here some common scenarios and useful algorithms just to give you a taste of the algorithms that are available in the standard library. The are many algorithms in the library, and I will only present a few in this section. For a quick but complete overview of the standard library algorithms, I recommend the talk from *CppCon 2018, 105 STL Algorithms in Less Than an Hour*, by Jonathan Boccara, available at https://sched.co/FnJh.

Iterating over a sequence

It's useful to have a short helper function that can print the elements of a sequence. The following generic function works with any container that holds elements that can be printed to an output stream using operator<<():

```
void print(auto&& r) {
  std::ranges::for_each(r, [](auto&& i) { std::cout << i << ' '; });
}
```

The print() function is using for_each(), which is an algorithm imported from the <algorithm> header. for_each() calls the function that we provide once for each element in the range. The return value of the function we provide is ignored and has no effect on the sequence we pass to for_each(). We can use for_each() for side effects such as printing to stdout (which we do in this example).

A similar, very general algorithm is transform(). It also calls a function for each element in a sequence, but instead of ignoring the return value, it stores the return value of the function in an output sequence, like this:

```
auto in = std::vector{1, 2, 3, 4};
auto out = std::vector<int>(in.size());
auto lambda = [](auto&& i) { return i * i; };

std::ranges::transform(in, out.begin(), lambda);

print(out);
// Prints: "1 4 9 16"
```

This code snippet also demonstrates how we can use our print() function defined earlier. The transform() algorithm will call our lambda once for each element in the input range. To specify where the output will be stored, we provide transform() with an output iterator, out.begin(). We will talk a lot more about iterators later on in this chapter.

With our print() function in place and a demonstration of some of the most general algorithms, we will move on to look at some algorithms for generating elements.

Generating elements

Sometimes we need to assign a sequence of elements with some initial values or reset an entire sequence. The following example fills a vector with the value -1:

```
auto v = std::vector<int>(4);
std::ranges::fill(v, -1);
print(v);
// Prints "-1 -1 -1 -1 "
```

The next algorithm, generate(), calls a function for each element and stores the return value at the current element:

```
auto v = std::vector<int>(4);
std::ranges::generate(v, std::rand);
print(v);
// Possible output: "1804289383 846930886 1681692777 1714636915 "
```

In the preceding example, the `std::rand()` function is called once for each element.

The last generating algorithm I will mention is `std::iota()` from the `<numeric>` header. It generates values in increasing order. The start value must be specified as a second argument. Here is a short example that generates values between 0 and 5:

```
auto v = std::vector<int>(6);
std::iota(v.begin(), v.end(), 0);
print(v); // Prints: "0 1 2 3 4 5 "
```

This sequence is already sorted, but it more commonly happens that you have an unordered collection of elements that needs sorting, which we will look at next.

Sorting elements

Sorting elements is a very common operation. There are sorting-algorithm alternatives that are good to know about, but in this introduction, I will only show the most conventional version, simply named `sort()`:

```
auto v = std::vector{4, 3, 2, 3, 6};
std::ranges::sort(v);
print(v);      // Prints: "2 3 3 4 6 "
```

As mentioned, this is not the only way to sort, and sometimes we can use a partial sorting algorithm to gain performance. We will talk more abort sorting later in this chapter.

Finding elements

Another very common task is to find out whether a specific value is in a collection or not. Maybe we want to know how many instances of some specific value there are in a collection. These algorithms that search for values can be implemented more efficiently if we know that the collection is already sorted. You saw this in *Chapter 3, Analyzing and Measuring Performance*, where we compared linear search with binary search.

Here we begin with the `find()` algorithm, which doesn't require a sorted collection:

```
auto col = std::list{2, 4, 3, 2, 3, 1};
auto it = std::ranges::find(col, 2);
if (it != col.end()) {
  std::cout << *it << '\n';
}
```

If the element we are looking for could not be found, `find()` returns the `end()` iterator of the collection. In the worst case, `find()` needs to inspect all elements in the sequence, therefore it runs in $O(n)$ time.

Finding using binary search

If we know that the collection is already sorted, we can use one of the binary search algorithms: `binary_search()`, `equal_range()`, `upper_bound()`, or `lower_bound()`. If we are using these functions with containers that provide random access to their elements, they are all guaranteed to run in $O(log\ n)$ time. You will gain a better understanding of how algorithms can provide complexity guarantees, even though they are operating on different containers, when we talk about iterators and ranges later in this chapter (there's a section coming up named, funnily enough, *Iterators and Ranges*).

In the following examples, we will use a sorted `std::vector` with the following elements:

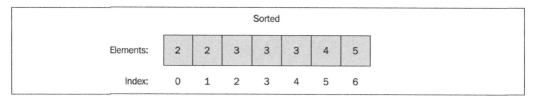

Figure 5.1: An sorted std::vector with seven elements

The `binary_search()` function returns `true` or `false` depending on whether the value we searched for could be found:

```
auto v = std::vector{2, 2, 3, 3, 3, 4, 5};    // Sorted!
bool found = std::ranges::binary_search(v, 3);
std::cout << std::boolalpha << found << '\n'; //   Output: true
```

Before calling `binary_search()`, you should be absolutely sure that the collection is sorted. We can easily assert this in our code with the use of `is_sorted()` as follows:

```
assert(std::ranges::is_sorted(v));
```

This check will run in $O(n)$, but will only be called when asserts are activated and hence will not affect the performance of your final program.

The sorted collection we are working with contains multiple 3s. What if we want to know the position of the first 3 or last 3 in the collection? In that case, we can use `lower_bound()` for finding the first 3, or `upper_bound()` for finding the element past the last 3:

```
auto v = std::vector{2, 2, 3, 3, 3, 4, 5};
auto it = std::ranges::lower_bound(v, 3);
if (it != v.end()) {
  auto index = std::distance(v.begin(), it);
  std::cout << index << '\n'; // Output: 2
}
```

This code will output 2 since that is the index of the first 3. To get the index of an element from an iterator, we use std::distance() from the <iterator> header.

In the same manner, we can use upper_bound() to get an iterator to the element *past* the last 3:

```
const auto v = std::vector{2, 2, 3, 3, 3, 4, 5};
auto it = std::ranges::upper_bound(v, 3);
if (it != v.end()) {
  auto index = std::distance(v.begin(), it);
  std::cout << index << '\n'; // Output: 5
}
```

If you want both the upper bound and lower bound, you can instead use equal_range(), which returns the subrange of the collection containing the 3s:

```
const auto v = std::vector{2, 2, 3, 3, 3, 4, 5};
auto subrange = std::ranges::equal_range(v, 3);
if (subrange.begin() != subrange.end()) {
  auto pos1 = std::distance(v.begin(), subrange.begin());
  auto pos2 = std::distance(v.begin(), subrange.end());
  std::cout << pos1 << " " << pos2 << '\n';
} // Output: "2 5"
```

Now let's explore some other useful algorithms for inspecting a collection.

Testing for certain conditions

There are three very handy algorithms called all_of(), any_of(), and none_of(). They all take a range, a unary predicate (a function that takes one argument and returns true or false), and an optional projection function.

Let's say we have a list of numbers and a small lambda that determines whether a number is negative or not:

```
const auto v = std::vector{3, 2, 2, 1, 0, 2, 1};
const auto is_negative = [](int i) { return i < 0; };
```

We can check if none of the numbers are negative by using `none_of()`:

```
if (std::ranges::none_of(v, is_negative)) {
  std::cout << "Contains only natural numbers\n";
}
```

Further, we can ask if all elements in the list are negative by using `all_of()`:

```
if (std::ranges::all_of(v, is_negative)) {
  std::cout << "Contains only negative numbers\n";
}
```

Lastly, we can see whether the list contains at least one negative number using `any_of()`:

```
if (std::ranges::any_of(v, is_negative)) {
  std::cout << "Contains at least one negative number\n";
}
```

It's easy to forget about these small, handy building blocks that reside in the standard library. But once you get into the habit of using them, you will never look back and start writing these by hand again.

Counting elements

The most obvious way to count the number of elements that equals some value is to call `count()`:

```
const auto numbers = std::list{3, 3, 2, 1, 3, 1, 3};
int n = std::ranges::count(numbers, 3);
std::cout << n;                    // Prints: 4
```

The `count()` algorithm runs in linear time. However, if we know that the sequence is sorted and we are using a vector or some other random-access data structure, we could instead use `equal_range()`, which will run in $O(log\ n)$ time. The following is an example:

```
const auto v = std::vector{0, 2, 2, 3, 3, 4, 5};
assert(std::ranges::is_sorted(v)); // O(n), but not called in release
auto r = std::ranges::equal_range(v, 3);
int n = std::ranges::size(r);
std::cout << n;                    // Prints: 2
```

The `equal_range()` function finds the subrange that contains all elements with the value we want to count. Once the subrange is found, we can retrieve the length of the subrange using `size()` from the `<ranges>` header.

Minimum, maximum, and clamping

I want to mention a set of small but extremely useful algorithms that are essential knowledge for a seasoned C++ programmer. The functions `std::min()`, `std::max()`, and `std::clamp()` are sometimes forgotten and instead we too often find ourselves writing code like this:

```
const auto y_max = 100;
auto y = some_func();
if (y > y_max) {
  y = y_max;
}
```

The code ensures that the value of y is within a certain limit. This code works, but we can avoid the mutable variable and the `if` statement by using `std::min()` as follows:

```
const auto y = std::min(some_func(), y_max);
```

Both the mutable variable and the `if` statement that clutter our code have been eliminated by instead using `std::min()`. We can use `std::max()` for similar scenarios. If we want to limit a value to within both a minimum and a maximum value, we might do it like this:

```
const auto y = std::max(std::min(some_func(), y_max), y_min);
```

But, since C++17, we now have `std::clamp()` that does this for us in one function. So instead, we could just use `clamp()` as follows:

```
const auto y = std::clamp(some_func(), y_min, y_max);
```

Sometimes we need to find the extreme values in an unsorted collection of elements. For this purpose, we can use `minmax()`, which (unsurprisingly) returns the minimum and maximum values of a sequence. Combined with structured binding, we can print the extreme values as follows:

```
const auto v = std::vector{4, 2, 1, 7, 3, 1, 5};
const auto [min, max] = std::ranges::minmax(v);
std::cout << min << " " << max;      // Prints: "1 7"
```

We can also find the position of the minimum or maximum element by using `min_element()` or `max_element()`. Instead of returning the value, it returns an iterator pointing at the element we are looking for. In the following example, we are finding the minimum element:

```
const auto v = std::vector{4, 2, 7, 1, 1, 3};
const auto it = std::ranges::min_element(v);
std::cout << std::distance(v.begin(), it); // Output: 3
```

This snippet of code prints 3, which is the index of the first minimum value that was found.

This was a brief introduction to some of the most common algorithms from the standard library. The runtime cost of algorithms is specified in the C++ standard and all library implementations need to adhere to these, even though the exact implementation can vary between different platforms. To understand how the complexity guarantees can be withheld for generic algorithms working with many different types of containers, we need to take a closer look at iterators and ranges.

Iterators and ranges

As seen in the previous examples, the standard library algorithms operate on iterators and ranges rather than container types. This section will focus on iterators and the new concept of ranges introduced in C++20. Using containers and algorithms correctly becomes easy once you have grasped iterators and ranges.

Introducing iterators

Iterators form the basis of the standard library algorithms and ranges. Iterators are the glue between data structures and algorithms. As you have already seen, C++ containers store their elements in very different ways. Iterators provide a generic way to navigate through the elements in a sequence. By having algorithms operate on iterators rather than container types, the algorithms become more generic and flexible since they do not depend on the type of container and the way the containers arrange their elements in memory.

At its core, an iterator is an object that represents a position in a sequence. It has two main responsibilities:

- Navigating in the sequence
- Reading and writing the value at its current position

The iterator abstraction is not at all a C++ exclusive concept, rather it exists in most programming languages. What differentiates the C++ implementation of the iterator concept from other programming languages is that C++ mimics the syntax of raw memory pointers.

Basically, an iterator could be considered an object with the same properties as a raw pointer; it can be stepped to the next element and dereferenced (if pointing to a valid address). The algorithms only use a few of the operations that a pointer allows, although the iterator may internally be a heavy object traversing a tree-like `std::map`.

Most of the algorithms found directly under the `std` namespace operate only on iterators, not containers (that is, `std::vector`, `std::map`, and so on). Many algorithms return iterators rather than values.

To be able to navigate in a sequence without going out of bounds, we need a generic way to tell when the iterator has reached the end of a sequence. That is what we have sentinel values for.

Sentinel values and past-the-end iterators

A **sentinel value** (or simply a sentinel) is a special value that indicates the end of a sequence. Sentinel values make it possible to iterate a sequence of values without knowing the size of the sequence in advance. An example usage of sentinel values are C-style strings that are null-terminated (in this case, the sentinel is the `'\0'` character). Instead of keeping track of the length of null-terminated strings, the pointer to the beginning of the string and the sentinel at the end is enough to define a sequence of characters.

The constrained algorithms use an iterator to define the first element in a sequence and a sentinel to indicate the end of the sequence. The only requirement of the sentinel is that it can be compared against the iterator, which in practice means that `operator==()` and `operator!=()` should be defined to accept combinations of a sentinel and an iterator:

```
bool operator=!(sentinel s, iterator i) {
  // ...
}
```

Now that you know what a sentinel is, how would we create a sentinel to indicate the end of a sequence? The trick here is to use something called a **past-the-end iterator** as a sentinel. It is simply an iterator that points to an element *after* (or past) the last element in the sequence we define. Take a look at the following code snippet and diagram:

```
auto vec = std::vector {
  'a','b','c','d'
};

auto first = vec.begin();
auto last = vec.end();
```

As seen in the preceding diagram, the `last` iterator now points to an imagined element after `'d'`. This makes it possible to iterate over all the elements in the sequence by using a loop:

```
for (; first != last; ++first) {
  char value = *first; // Dereference iterator
  // ...
```

We can use the past-the-end sentinel to compare it against our iterator, `it`, but we cannot dereference the sentinel since it doesn't point to an element of the range. This concept of past-the-end iterators has a long history and even works for built-in C arrays:

```
char arr[] = {'a', 'b', 'c', 'd'};
char* end = arr + sizeof(arr);
for (char* it = arr; it != end; ++it) { // Stop at end
    std::cout << *it << ' ';
}
// Output: a b c d
```

Again, note that end actually points out of bounds, so we are not allowed to dereference it, but we are allowed to read the pointer value and compare it with our it variable.

Ranges

A range is a replacement for the iterator-sentinel pairs that we have used when referring to a sequence of elements. The `<range>` header contains multiple concepts that define requirements for different kinds of ranges, for example, `input_range`, `random_access_range`, and so forth. These are all refinements of the most basic concept called `range`, which is defined like this:

```
template<class T>
concept range = requires(T& t) {
  ranges::begin(t);
  ranges::end(t);
};
```

This means that any type that exposes `begin()` and `end()` functions is considered a range (given that these functions return iterators).

For C++ standard containers, the `begin()` and `end()` functions will return iterators of the same type, whereas for C++20 ranges, this is not true in general. A range with identical iterator and sentinel types fulfills the concept of `std::ranges::common_range`. The new C++20 views (covered in the next chapter) return iterator-sentinel pairs that can be of different types. However, they can be transformed to a view that has the same type for the iterator and sentinel using `std::views::common`.

The constrained algorithms found in the `std::ranges` namespace can operate on ranges instead of iterator pairs. And since all standard containers (`vector`, `map`, `list`, and so on) fulfill the range concept, we can pass ranges directly to the constrained algorithms as follows:

```
auto vec = std::vector{1, 1, 0, 1, 1, 0, 0, 1};
std::cout << std::ranges::count(vec, 0); // Prints 3
```

Ranges are an abstraction of something iterable (something that can be looped over), and to some extent, they hide the immediate use of C++ iterators. However, iterators are still a major part of the C++ standard library and are also used extensively in the Ranges library.

The next thing you need to understand is the different kinds of iterators that exist.

Iterator categories

Now that you have a better understanding of how a range is defined and how we can know when we have reached the end of a sequence, it's time to look more closely at the operations that iterators can support in order to navigate, read, and write values.

Iterator navigation in a sequence can be done with the following operations:

- Step forward: `std::next(it)` or `++it`
- Step backward: `std::prev(it)` or `--it`
- Jump to an arbitrary position: `std::advance(it, n)` or `it += n`

Reading and writing a value at the position that the iterator represents is done by *dereferencing* the iterator. Here is how it looks:

- Read: `auto value = *it`
- Write: `*it = value`

These are the most common operations for iterators that are exposed by containers. But in addition, iterators might operate on data sources where a write or read implies a step forward. Examples of such data sources could be user input, a network connection, or a file. These data sources require the following operations:

- Read only *and* step forward: `auto value = *it; ++it;`
- Write only *and* step forward: `*it = value; ++it;`

These operations are only possible to express with two succeeding expressions. The post-condition of the first expression is that the second expression must be valid. This also means that we can only read or write a value to a position once. If we want to read or write a new value, we must first advance the iterator to the next position.

Not all iterators support all of the operations in the preceding list. For example, some iterators can only *read* values and *step forward*, whereas others can both *read*, *write*, and *jump* to arbitrary positions.

Now if we think about a few basic algorithms, it becomes obvious that the requirements on the iterators vary between different algorithms:

- If an algorithm counts the number of occurrences of a value, it requires the *read* and *step forward* operations
- If an algorithm fills a container with a value, it requires the *write* and *step forward* operations
- A binary search algorithm on a sorted collection requires the *read* and *jump* operations

Some algorithms can be implemented more efficiently depending on what operations the iterators support. Just like containers, all algorithms in the standard library have complexity guarantees (using big O notation). For an algorithm to fulfill a certain complexity guarantee, it puts *requirements* on the iterators it operates on. These requirements are categorized into six basic iterator categories that relate to each other as shown in the following diagram:

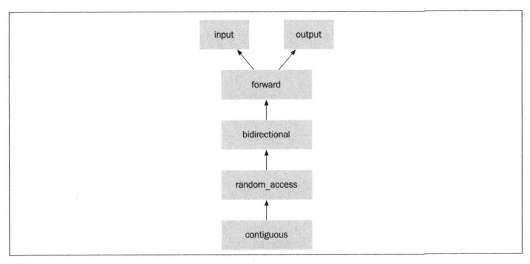

Figure 5.2: The six iterator categories and their relation to each other

The arrows indicate that an iterator category also has all the capabilities of the category it points at. For example, if an algorithm requires a forward iterator, we can just as well pass it a bidirectional iterator, since a bidirectional iterator has all the capabilities of a forward iterator.

The six requirements are formally specified by the following concepts:

- `std::input_iterator`: Supports *read only and step forward* (once). One-pass algorithms such as `std::count()` can use input iterators. `std::istream_iterator` is an example of an input iterator.

- `std::output_iterator`: Supports *write only and step forward* (once). Note that an output iterator can only write, not read. `std::ostream_iterator` is an example of an output iterator.

- `std::forward_iterator`: Supports *read* and *write* and *step forward*. The value at the current position can be read or written multiple times. Singly linked lists such as `std::forward_list` expose forward iterators.

- `std::bidirectional_iterator`: Supports *read, write, step forward*, and *step backward*. The doubly linked `std::list` exposes bidirectional iterators.

- `std::random_access_iterator`: Supports *read, write, step forward, step backward*, and *jump* to an arbitrary position in constant time. The elements inside `std::deque` can be accessed with random access iterators.

- `std::contiguous_iterator`: The same as random access iterators, but also guarantees that the underlying data is a contiguous block of memory, such as `std::string`, `std::vector`, `std::array`, `std::span`, and the (rarely used) `std::valarray`.

The iterator categories are very important for understanding the time-complexity requirements of the algorithms. Having a good understanding of the underlying data structures makes it fairly easy to know what iterators typically belong to which containers.

We are now ready to dig a little deeper into the common patterns used by most of the standard library algorithms.

Features of the standard algorithms

To get a better understanding of the standard algorithms, it's good to know a bit about the features and common patterns used by all algorithms in the `<algorithm>` header. As already stated, the algorithms under the `std` and `std::ranges` namespaces have a lot in common. We will start here with the general principles that are true for both the `std` algorithms and the constrained algorithms under `std::range`. Then, in the next section, we will move on to discuss the features that are specific to the constrained algorithms found under `std::ranges`.

Algorithms do not change the size of the container

Functions from `<algorithm>` can only modify the elements in a specified range; elements are never added or deleted from the underlying container. Therefore, these functions never alter the size of the container that they operate on.

For example, `std::remove()` or `std::unique()` do not actually remove elements from a container (despite their names). Rather, it moves the elements that should be kept to the front of the container and then returns a sentinel that defines the new end of the valid range of elements:

Code example	Resulting vector
``// Example with std::remove()
auto v = std::vector{1,1,2,2,3,3};
auto new_end = std::remove(
v.begin(), v.end(), 2);
v.erase(new_end, v.end());```	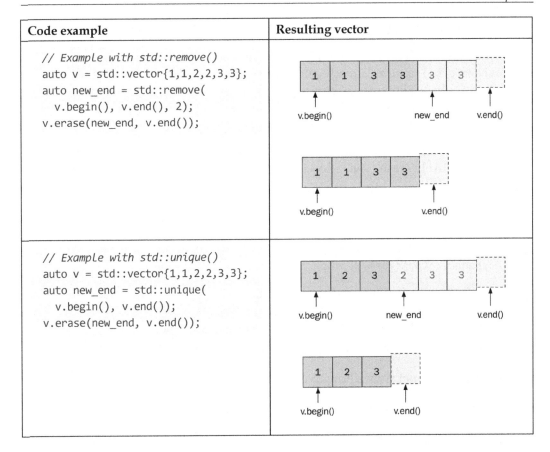
``// Example with std::unique()
auto v = std::vector{1,1,2,2,3,3};
auto new_end = std::unique(
v.begin(), v.end());
v.erase(new_end, v.end());```	

 C++20 added new versions of the std::erase() and std::erase_if() functions to the <vector> header, which erases values immediately from the vector without the need to first call remove() followed by erase().

The fact that standard library algorithms never change the size of a container means that we need to allocate data ourselves when calling algorithms that produce output.

Algorithms with output require allocated data

Algorithms that write data to an output iterator, such as `std::copy()` or `std::transform()`, require already allocated data reserved for the output. As the algorithms only use iterators as arguments, they cannot allocate data by themselves. To enlarge the container the algorithms operate on, they rely on the iterator being capable of enlarging the container it iterates.

If an iterator to an empty container is passed to the algorithms for output, the program will likely crash. The following example, where squared is empty, illustrates the problem:

```
const auto square_func = [](int x) { return x * x; };
const auto v = std::vector{1, 2, 3, 4};
auto squared = std::vector<int>{};
std::ranges::transform(v, squared.begin(), square_func);
```

Instead, you have to do either of the following:

- Preallocate the required size for the resulting container, or
- Use an insert iterator, which inserts elements into a container while iterating

The following snippet shows how to use preallocated space:

```
const auto square_func = [](int x) { return x * x; };
const auto v = std::vector{1, 2, 3, 4};
auto squared = std::vector<int>{};
squared.resize(v.size());
std::ranges::transform(v, squared.begin(), square_func);
```

The following snippet shows how to use `std::back_inserter()` and `std::inserter()` to insert values into a container that is not preallocated:

```
const auto square_func = [](int x) { return x * x; };
const auto v = std::vector{1, 2, 3, 4};

// Insert into back of vector using std::back_inserter
auto squared_vec = std::vector<int>{};
auto dst_vec = std::back_inserter(squared_vec);
std::ranges::transform(v, dst_vec, square_func);
```

```
// Insert into a std::set using std::inserter
auto squared_set = std::set<int>{};
auto dst_set = std::inserter(squared_set, squared_set.end());
std::ranges::transform(v, dst_set, square_func);
```

 If you are operating on `std::vector` and know the expected size of the resulting container, you can use the `reserve()` member function before executing the algorithm in order to avoid unnecessary allocations. Otherwise, the vector may reallocate new chunks of memory several times during the algorithm.

Algorithms use operator==() and operator<() by default

For comparison, an algorithm relies on the fundamental == and < operators, as in the case of an integer. To be able to use your own classes with algorithms, operator==() and operator<() must either be provided by the class or as an argument to the algorithm.

By using the three-way comparison operator, operator<=>(), we can have the necessary operators generated by the compiler. The following example shows a simple Flower class, where operator==() is utilized by std::find(), and operator<() is utilized by std::max_element():

```
struct Flower {
    auto operator<=>(const Flower& f) const = default;
    bool operator==(const Flower&) const = default;
    int height_{};
};
auto garden = std::vector<Flower>{{67}, {28}, {14}};
// std::max_element() uses operator<()
auto tallest = std::max_element(garden.begin(), garden.end());
// std::find() uses operator==()
auto perfect = *std::find(garden.begin(), garden.end(), Flower{28});
```

Apart from using the default comparison functions for the current type, it's also possible to use a custom comparator function, which we will explore next.

Custom comparator functions

Sometimes we need to compare objects without using the default comparison operators, for example, when sorting or finding a string by length. In those cases, a custom function can be provided as an additional argument. While the original algorithm uses a value (for example, `std::find()`), the version with a specific operator has the same name with _if attached at the end (`std::find_if()`, `std::count_if()`, and so on):

```
auto names = std::vector<std::string> {
  "Ralph", "Lisa", "Homer", "Maggie", "Apu", "Bart"
};
std::sort(names.begin(), names.end(),
        [](const std::string& a,const std::string& b) {
            return a.size() < b.size(); });
// names is now "Apu", "Lisa", "Bart", "Ralph", "Homer", "Maggie"

// Find names with Length 3
auto x = std::find_if(names.begin(), names.end(),
  [](const auto& v) { return v.size() == 3; });
// x points to "Apu"
```

Constrained algorithms use projections

The constrained algorithms under `std::ranges` provide us with a handy feature called **projections**, which decreases the need for writing custom comparison functions. The preceding example in the previous section could be rewritten using the standard predicate `std::less` combined with a custom projection:

```
auto names = std::vector<std::string>{
  "Ralph", "Lisa", "Homer", "Maggie", "Apu", "Bart"
};
std::ranges::sort(names, std::less<>{}, &std::string::size);
// names is now "Apu", "Lisa", "Bart", "Ralph", "Homer", "Maggie"

// Find names with Length 3
auto x = std::ranges::find(names, 3, &std::string::size);
// x points to "Apu"
```

It's also possible to pass a lambda as a projection parameter, which can be handy when you want to combine multiple properties in a projection:

```cpp
struct Player {
  std::string name_{};
  int level_{};
  float health_{};
  // ...
};
auto players = std::vector<Player>{
  {"Aki", 1, 9.f},
  {"Nao", 2, 7.f},
  {"Rei", 2, 3.f}};
auto level_and_health = [](const Player& p) {
  return std::tie(p.level_, p.health_);
};
// Order players by level, then health
std::ranges::sort(players, std::greater<>{}, level_and_health);
```

The possibility to pass a projection object to the standard algorithms is a very welcome feature and really simplifies the use of custom comparisons.

Algorithms require move operators not to throw

All algorithms use `std::swap()` and `std::move()` when moving elements around, but only if the move constructor and move assignment are marked `noexcept`. Therefore, it is important to have these implemented for heavy objects when using algorithms. If they are not available and exception free, the elements will be copied instead.

 Note that if you implement a move constructor and a move assignment operator in your class, `std::swap()` will utilize them and, therefore, a specified `std::swap()` overload is not needed.

Algorithms have complexity guarantees

The complexity of each algorithm in the standard library is specified using big O notation. Algorithms are created with performance in mind. Therefore, they do not allocate memory nor do they have a time complexity higher than $O(n \log n)$. Algorithms that do not fit these criteria are not included even if they are fairly common operations.

 Note the exceptions of `stable_sort()`, `inplace_merge()`, and `stable_partition()`. Many implementations tend to temporarily allocate memory during these operations.

For example, let's consider an algorithm that tests whether a non-sorted range contains duplicates. One option is to implement it by iterating through the range and search the rest of the range for a duplicate. This will result in an algorithm with $O(n^2)$ complexity:

```
template <typename Iterator>
auto contains_duplicates(Iterator first, Iterator last) {
  for (auto it = first; it != last; ++it)
    if (std::find(std::next(it), last, *it) != last)
      return true;
  return false;
}
```

Another option is to make a copy of the full range, sort it, and look for adjacent equal elements. This will result in a time complexity of $O(n \log n)$, the complexity of `std::sort()`. However, since it needs to make a copy of the full range, it still doesn't qualify as a building block algorithm. Allocating means that we cannot trust it not to throw:

```
template <typename Iterator>
auto contains_duplicates(Iterator first, Iterator last) {
  // As (*first) returns a reference, we have to get
  // the base type using std::decay_t
  using ValueType = std::decay_t<decltype(*first)>;
  auto c = std::vector<ValueType>(first, last);
```

```
    std::sort(c.begin(), c.end());
    return std::adjacent_find(c.begin(),c.end()) != c.end();
}
```

The complexity guarantees have been a part of the C++ standard library from the very beginning and are one of the major reasons behind its great success. Algorithms in the C++ standard library are designed and implemented with performance in mind.

Algorithms perform just as well as C library function equivalents

The standard C library comes with a number of low-level algorithms, including `memcpy()`, `memmove()`, `memcmp()`, and `memset()`. In my experience, sometimes people use these functions instead of their equivalents in the standard Algorithm library. The reason is that people tend to believe that the C library functions are faster and, therefore, accept the trade-off in type safety.

This is not true for modern standard library implementation; the equivalent algorithms, `std::copy()`, `std::equal()`, and `std::fill()`, resort to these low-level C functions where plausible; hence, they provide both performance and type safety.

Sure, there might be exceptions where the C++ compiler is not able to detect that it is safe to resort to the low-level C-functions. For example, if a type is not trivially copyable, `std::copy()` cannot use `memcpy()`. But that's for good reason; hopefully, the author of a class that is not trivially copyable had good reasons for designing the class in such a way, and we (or the compiler) should not ignore that by not calling the appropriate constructors.

Sometimes, functions from the C++ Algorithm library even outperform their C library equivalents. The most prominent example is `std::sort()` versus `qsort()` from the C library. A big difference between `std::sort()` and `qsort()` is that `qsort()` is a *function* and `std::sort()` is a *function template*. When `qsort()` calls the comparison function, which is provided as a function pointer, it is generally a lot slower than calling an ordinary comparison function that may be inlined by the compiler when using `std::sort()`.

We will spend the remainder of this chapter going through some best practices when using the standard algorithms and implementing custom algorithms.

Writing and using generic algorithms

The Algorithm library contains generic algorithms. To keep things as concrete as possible here, I will show an example of how a generic algorithm can be implemented. This will provide you with some insights into how to use the standard algorithms and at the same time demonstrate that implementing a generic algorithm is not that hard. I will intentionally avoid explaining all the details about the example code here, because we will spend a lot of time on generic programming later on in this book.

In the examples that follow, we will transform a simple non-generic algorithm into a full-fledged generic algorithm.

Non-generic algorithms

A generic algorithm is an algorithm that can be used with various ranges of elements, not only one specific type, such as `std::vector`. The following algorithm is an example of a non-generic algorithm that only works with `std::vector<int>`:

```
auto contains(const std::vector<int>& arr, int v) {
  for (int i = 0; i < arr.size(); ++i) {
    if (arr[i] == v) { return true; }
  }
  return false;
}
```

To find the element we are looking for, we rely on the interface of `std::vector` that provides us with the `size()` function and the subscript operator (`operator[]()`). However, not all containers provide us with these functions, and I don't recommend you write raw loops like this anyway. Instead, we need to create a function template that operates on iterators.

Generic algorithms

By replacing the `std::vector` with two iterators, and the `int` with a template parameter, we can transform our algorithm to a generic version. The following version of `contains()` can be used with any container:

```
template <typename Iterator, typename T>
auto contains(Iterator begin, Iterator end, const T& v) {
  for (auto it = begin; it != end; ++it) {
    if (*it == v) { return true; }
  }
```

```
    return false;
  }
```

To use it with, for example, std::vector, you would have to pass the begin() and end() iterators:

```
  auto v = std::vector{3, 4, 2, 4};
  if (contains(v.begin(), v.end(), 3)) {
  // Found the value...
  }
```

We could improve this algorithm by offering a version that accepts a range instead of two separate iterator parameters:

```
  auto contains(const auto& r, const auto& x) {
    auto it = std::begin(r);
    auto sentinel = std::end(r);
    return contains(it, sentinel, x);
  }
```

This algorithm does not force the client to provide the begin() and end() iterators because we have moved that inside the function. We are using the **abbreviated function template** syntax from C++20 to avoid spelling out explicitly that this is a function template. As a last step, we could add constraints to our parameter types:

```
  auto contains(const std::ranges::range auto& r, const auto& x) {
    auto it = std::begin(r);
    auto sentinel = std::end(r);
    return contains(it, sentinel, x);
  }
```

As you can see, there is really not that much code needed to create a robust generic algorithm. The only requirement on the data structure we pass to the algorithm is that it can expose begin() and end() iterators. You will learn more about constraints and concepts in *Chapter 8, Compile-Time Programming*.

Data structures that can be used by generic algorithms

This leads us to the insight that new custom data structures we create can be used by the standard generic algorithms as long as they expose the begin() and end() iterators or a range. As a simple example, we could implement a two-dimensional Grid structure where rows are exposed as a pair of iterators, like this:

```
struct Grid {
  Grid(std::size_t w, std::size_t h) : w_{w}, h_{h} {
    data_.resize(w * h);
  }
  auto get_row(std::size_t y); // Returns iterators or a range

  std::vector<int> data_{};
  std::size_t w_{};
  std::size_t h_{};
};
```

The following diagram illustrates the layout of the Grid structure with the iterator pairs:

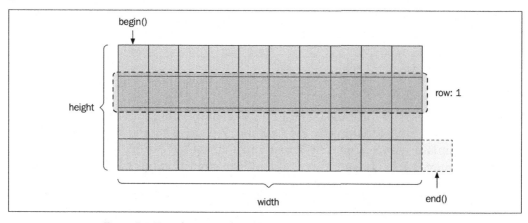

Figure 5.3: Two-dimensional grid built upon a one-dimensional vector

A possible implementation of get_row() would return a std::pair holding iterators that represent the beginning and the end of the row:

```
auto Grid::get_row(std::size_t y) {
  auto left = data_.begin() + w_ * y;
  auto right = left + w_;
  return std::make_pair(left, right);
}
```

The iterator pair representing a row can then be utilized by standard library algorithms. In the following example, we are using std::generate() and std::count():

```
auto grid = Grid{10, 10};
auto y = 3;
```

```
auto row = grid.get_row(y);
std::generate(row.first, row.second, std::rand);
auto num_fives = std::count(row.first, row.second, 5);
```

While this works, it is a bit clumsy to work with std::pair, and it also requires the client to know how to handle the iterator pair. There is nothing that explicitly says that the first and second members actually denote a half-open range. Wouldn't it be nice if it could expose a strongly typed range instead? Fortunately, the Ranges library that we will explore in the next chapter provides us with a view type called std::ranges::subrange. Now, the get_row() function could be implemented like this:

```
auto Grid::get_row(std::size_t y) {
  auto first = data_.begin() + w_ * y;
  auto sentinel = first + w_;
  return std::ranges::subrange{first, sentinel};
}
```

We could be even lazier and use the handy view that is tailor-made for this scenario, called std::views::counted()

```
auto Grid::get_row(std::size_t y) {
  auto first = data_.begin() + w_ * y;
  return std::views::counted(first, w_);
}
```

A row returned from the Grid class could now be used with any of the constrained algorithms that accept ranges instead of iterator pairs:

```
auto row = grid.get_row(y);
std::ranges::generate(row, std::rand);
auto num_fives = std::ranges::count(row, 5);
```

That completes our example of writing and using a generic algorithm that supports both iterator pairs and a range. Hopefully, this has given you some insights about how to write data structures and algorithms in a generic way to avoid the combinatorial explosion that would occur if we had to write specialized algorithms for all types of data structures.

Best practices

Let's consider practices that will help you out when working with the algorithms we've been discussing. I will start by highlighting the importance of actually exploiting the standard algorithms.

Using the constrained algorithms

The constrained algorithms under std::ranges introduced with C++20 offer some benefits over the iterator-based algorithms under std. The constrained algorithms do the following:

- Support projections, which simplifies custom comparisons of elements.

- Support ranges instead of iterator pairs. There is no need to pass begin() and end() iterators as separate arguments.

- Are easy to use correctly and provide descriptive error messages during compilation as a result of being constrained by C++ concepts.

It's my recommendation to start using the constrained algorithms over the iterator-based algorithms.

 You may have noticed that this book uses iterator-based algorithms in a lot of places. The reason for this is that not all standard library implementations support the constrained algorithms at the time of writing this book.

Sorting only for the data you need to retrieve

The Algorithm library contains three basic sorting algorithms: sort(), partial_sort(), and nth_element(). In addition, it also contains a few variants of those, including stable_sort(), but we will focus on these three as, in my experience, it is easy to forget that, in many cases, a complete sort can be avoided by using nth_element() or partial_sort() instead.

While sort() sorts the entire range, partial_sort() and nth_element() could be thought of as algorithms for inspecting parts of that sorted range. In many cases, you are only interested in a certain part of the sorted range, for example:

- If you want to calculate the median of a range, you require the value in the middle of the sorted range.

- If you want to create a body scanner that can be used by the mean 80% by height of a population, you require two values in the sorted range: the value located 10% from the tallest person, and the value located 10% from the shortest person.

The following diagram illustrates how `std::nth_element` and `std::partial_sort` process a range, compared to a fully sorted range:

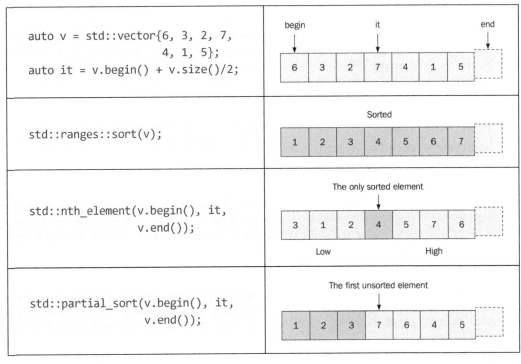

Figure 5.1: Sorted and non-sorted elements of a range using different algorithms

The following table shows their algorithmic complexity; note that *m* denotes the subrange which is being fully sorted:

Algorithm	Complexity
`std::sort()`	$O(n \log n)$
`std::partial_sort()`	$O(n \log m)$
`std::nth_element()`	$O(n)$

Table 5.2: Algorithmic complexity

Use cases

Now that you have insights into std:nth_element() and std::partial_sort(), let's see how we can combine them to inspect parts of a range as if the entire range were sorted:

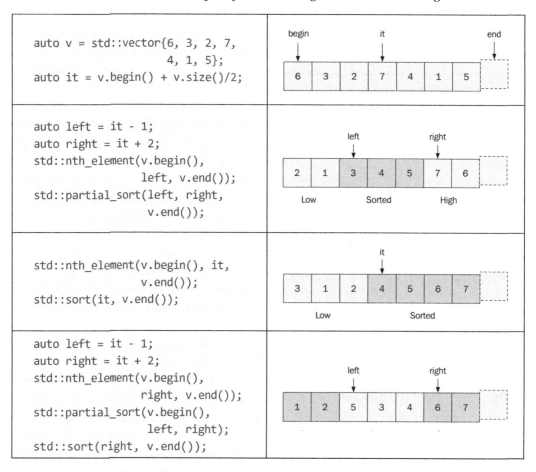

Figure 5.3: Combining algorithms and corresponding partially ordered results

As you can see, by using combinations of std::sort(), std::nth_element(), and std::partial_sort(), there are many ways to avoid sorting the entire range when not absolutely needed. This is an effective way to gain performance.

Performance evaluation

Let's see how std::nth_element() and std::partial_sort() measure up against std::sort(). We've measured this with a std::vector with 10,000,000 random int elements:

Operation	Code, where r is the range operated on	Time (Speedup)
Sort	`std::sort(r.begin(), r.end());`	760 ms (1.0x)
Find median	`auto it = r.begin() + r.size() / 2;` `std::nth_element(r.begin(), it, r.end());`	83 ms (9.2x)
Sort first tenth of range	`auto it = r.begin() + r.size() / 10;` `std::partial_sort(r.begin(), it, r.end());`	378 ms (2.0x)

Table 5.3: Benchmark results for partial sort algorithms

Use standard algorithms over raw for-loops

It's easy to forget that complex algorithms can be implemented by combining algorithms from the standard library. Maybe because of an old habit of trying to solve problems by hand and immediately starting to handcraft for-loops and working through the problem using an imperative approach. If this sounds familiar to you, my recommendation is to get to know the standard algorithms well enough so that you start considering them as the first choice.

I promote the use of standard library algorithms over raw for-loops, for a number of reasons:

- Standard algorithms deliver performance. Even though some of the algorithms in the standard library may seem trivial, they are often optimally designed in ways that are not obvious at first glance.

- Standard algorithms provide safety. Even simpler algorithms may have corner cases, which are easy to overlook.

- Standard algorithms are future-proof; a given algorithm can be replaced by a more suitable algorithm if you want to take advantage of SIMD extensions, parallelism, or even the GPU at a later stage (see *Chapter 14, Parallel Algorithms*).

- Standard algorithms are thoroughly documented.

In addition, by using algorithms instead of for-loops, the intention of each operation is clearly indicated by the name of the algorithm. The readers of your code do not need to inspect details inside raw for-loop to determine what your code does if you use standard algorithms as building blocks.

Once you get into the habit of thinking in terms of algorithms, you'll realize that many for-loops are most often a variation of a few simple algorithms such as `std::transform()`, `std::any_of()`, `std::copy_if()`, and `std::find()`.

Using algorithms will also make the code cleaner. You can often implement functions without nested code blocks and at the same time avoid mutable variables. This will be demonstrated in the following example.

Example 1: Readability issues and mutable variables

Our first example is from a real-world code base, although variable names have been disguised. As it is only a cut-out, you don't have to understand the logic of the code. The example here is just to show you how the complexity is lowered when using algorithms compared with nested for-loops.

The original version looked like this:

```
// Original version using a for-loop
auto conflicting = false;
for (const auto& info : infos) {
  if (info.params() == output.params()) {
    if (varies(info.flags())) {
      conflicting = true;
      break;
    }
  }
  else {
    conflicting = true;
    break;
  }
}
```

In the for-loop version, it's hard to grasp when or why `conflicting` is set to `true`, whereas in the following versions of the algorithm, you can instinctively see that it happens if `info` fulfills a predicate. Further, the standard algorithm version uses no mutable variables and can be written using a combination of a short lambda and `any_of()`. Here is how it looks:

```
// Version using standard algorithms
const auto in_conflict = [&](const auto& info) {
  return info.params() != output.params() || varies(info.flags());
};
const auto conflicting = std::ranges::any_of(infos, in_conflict);
```

Although it may overstate the point, imagine if we were to track a bug or parallelize it, the standard algorithm version using a lambda and `any_of()` would be far easier to understand and reason about.

Example 2: Unfortunate exceptions and performance problems

To further state the importance of using algorithms rather than for-loops, I'd like to show a few not-so-obvious problems that you may bump into when using handcrafted for-loops rather than standard algorithms.

Let's say we need a function that moves the first *n* elements from the front of a container to the back, like this:

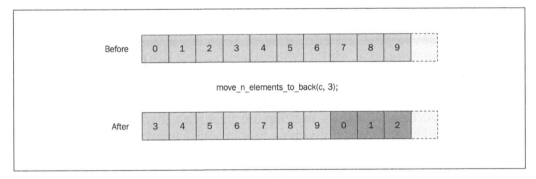

Figure 5.4: Moving the first three elements to the back of a range

Approach 1: Use a traditional for-loop

A naive approach would be to copy the first n elements to the back while iterating over them and then erasing the first n elements:

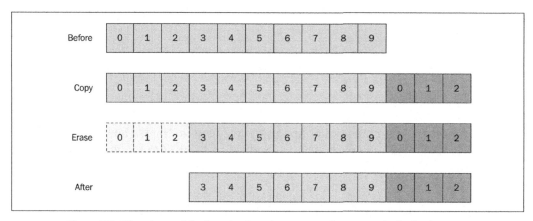

Figure 5.5: Allocating and deallocating in order to move elements to the back of a range

Here's the corresponding implementation:

```cpp
template <typename Container>
auto move_n_elements_to_back(Container& c, std::size_t n) {
  // Copy the first n elements to the end of the container
  for (auto it = c.begin(); it != std::next(c.begin(), n); ++it) {
    c.emplace_back(std::move(*it));
  }
  // Erase the copied elements from front of container
  c.erase(c.begin(), std::next(c.begin(), n));
}
```

At first glance, it might look plausible, but inspecting it reveals a severe problem — if the container reallocates during the iteration due to emplace_back(), the iterator it will no longer be valid. As the algorithm tries to access an invalid iterator, the algorithm will go into undefined behavior and, in the best case, crash.

Approach 2: Safe for-loop (safe at the expense of performance)

As undefined behaviors are an obvious problem, we'll have to rewrite the algorithm. We are still using a handcrafted for-loop, but we'll utilize the index instead of the iterator:

```
template <typename Container>
auto move_n_elements_to_back(Container& c, std::size_t n) {
  for (size_t i = 0; i < n; ++i) {
    auto value = *std::next(c.begin(), i);
    c.emplace_back(std::move(value));
  }
  c.erase(c.begin(), std::next(c.begin(), n));
}
```

The solution works; it doesn't crash anymore. But now, it has a subtle performance problem. The algorithm is significantly slower on std::list than on std::vector. The reason is that std::next(it, n) used with std::list::iterator is *O(n)*, and *O(1)* on a std::vector::iterator. As std::next(it, n) is invoked in every step of the for-loop, this algorithm will have a time complexity of $O(n^2)$ on containers such as std::list. Apart from this performance limitation, the preceding code also has the following limitations:

- It doesn't work with containers of a static size, such as std::array, due to emplace_back()
- It might throw an exception, since emplace_back() may allocate memory and fail (this is probably rare though)

Approach 3: Find and use a suitable standard library algorithm

When we have reached this stage, we should browse through the standard library and see whether it contains a suitable algorithm to be used as a building block. Conveniently, the <algorithm> header provides an algorithm called std::rotate(), which does exactly what we are looking for while avoiding all the disadvantages mentioned before. Here is our final version using the std::rotate() algorithm:

```
template <typename Container>
auto move_n_elements_to_back(Container& c, std::size_t n) {
  auto new_begin = std::next(c.begin(), n);
  std::rotate(c.begin(), new_begin, c.end());
}
```

Let's have a look at the advantages of using std::rotate():

- The algorithm does not throw exceptions, as it does not allocate memory (the contained object might throw exceptions though)
- It works with containers whose size cannot be changed, such as std::array

- Performance is $O(n)$ regardless of the container it operates on
- The implementation may very well be optimized with specific hardware in mind

Maybe you find this comparison between for-loops and standard algorithms unfair because there are other solutions to this problem that are both elegant and efficient. Still, in the real world, it's not uncommon to see implementations like the ones you just saw, when there are algorithms in the standard library just waiting to solve your problems.

Example 3: Exploiting the standard library optimizations

This last example highlights the fact that even algorithms that may seem very simple might contain optimizations you wouldn't consider. Let's have a look at std::find(), for example. At a glance, it seems that the obvious implementation couldn't be optimized further. Here is a possible implementation of the std::find() algorithm:

```
template <typename It, typename Value>
auto find_slow(It first, It last, const Value& value) {
  for (auto it = first; it != last; ++it)
    if (*it == value)
      return it;
  return last;
}
```

However, looking through the GNU libstdc++ implementation, when being used with random_access_iterator (in other words, std::vector, std::string, std::deque, and std::array), the libc++ implementers have unrolled the main loop into chunks of four loops at a time, resulting in the comparison (it != last) being executed one-fourth as many times.

Here is the optimized version of std::find() taken from the libstdc++ library:

```
template <typename It, typename Value>
auto find_fast(It first, It last, const Value& value) {
  // Main loop unrolled into chunks of four
  auto num_trips = (last - first) / 4;
  for (auto trip_count = num_trips; trip_count > 0; --trip_count) {
    if (*first == value) {return first;} ++first;
    if (*first == value) {return first;} ++first;
    if (*first == value) {return first;} ++first;
    if (*first == value) {return first;} ++first;
```

```
    }
    // Handle the remaining elements
    switch (last - first) {
      case 3: if (*first == value) {return first;} ++first;
      case 2: if (*first == value) {return first;} ++first;
      case 1: if (*first == value) {return first;} ++first;
      case 0:
      default: return last;
    }
  }
```

Note that it is actually std::find_if(), not std::find(), that utilizes this loop-unrolling optimization. But std::find() is implemented using std::find_if().

In addition to std::find(), a multitude of algorithms in libstdc++ are implemented using std::find_if(), for example, any_of(), all_of(), none_of(), find_if_not(), search(), is_partitioned(), remove_if(), and is_permutation(), which means that all of these are slightly faster than a handcrafted for-loop.

And by slightly, I really mean slightly; the speedup is roughly 1.07x, as shown in the following table:

Find an integer in a std::vector of 10,000,000 elements		
Algorithm	Time	Speedup
find_slow()	3.06 ms	1.00x
find_fast()	3.26 ms	1.07x

Table 5.5: find_fast() uses optimizations found in libstdc++. The benchmark shows that find_fast() is slightly faster than find_slow().

However, even though the benefit is almost negligible, using standard algorithms, you get it for free.

"Compare with zero" optimization

In addition to the loop unrolling, a very subtle optimization is that trip_count is iterated backward in order to compare with zero instead of a value. On some CPUs, comparing with zero is slightly faster than any other value, as it uses another assembly instruction (on the x86 platform, it uses test instead of cmp).

The following table shows the difference in assembly output using gcc 9.2:

Action	C++	Assembler x86
Compare with zero	```auto cmp_zero(size_t val) { return val > 0; }```	**test** edi, edi setne al ret
Compare with the other value	```auto cmp_val(size_t val) { return val > 42; }```	**cmp** edi, 42 setba al ret

Table 5.6: The difference in assembly output

Even though this kind of optimization is encouraged in the standard library implementation, do not rearrange your handmade loops in order to benefit from this optimization unless it's a (very) hot spot. Doing so will heavily reduce the readability of your code; let the algorithms handle these kinds of optimizations instead.

This was the end of my recommendations about using algorithms rather than for-loops. If you are not already using the standard algorithms, I hope that I have given you some arguments to convince you to give it a try. Now we will move on to my very last suggestion on using algorithms effectively.

Avoiding container copies

We will finish this chapter by highlighting a common problem when trying to combine multiple algorithms from the Algorithm library: it's hard to avoid unnecessary copies of the underlying containers.

An example will clarify what I mean here. Let's say we have some sort of Student class to represent a student in a particular year and with a particular exam score, like this:

```
struct Student {
  int year_{};
  int score_{};
  std::string name_{};
  // ...
};
```

If we want to find the student in the second year with the highest score in a big collection of students, we would probably use max_element() on score_, but as we only want to take the students from the second year into account, it gets tricky. Essentially, we want to compose a new algorithm out of a combination of copy_if() and max_element(), but composing algorithms is not possible with the Algorithm library. Instead, we would have to make a copy of all the students in the second year to a new container and then iterate the new container to find the maximum score:

```cpp
auto get_max_score(const std::vector<Student>& students, int year) {
  auto by_year = [=](const auto& s) { return s.year_ == year; };
  // The student list needs to be copied in
  // order to filter on the year
  auto v = std::vector<Student>{};
  std::ranges::copy_if(students, std::back_inserter(v), by_year);
  auto it = std::ranges::max_element(v, std::less{}, &Student::score_);
  return it != v.end() ? it->score_ : 0;
}
```

This is one of the places where it is tempting to start writing a custom algorithm from scratch without taking advantage of the standard algorithms. But as you will see in the next chapter, there is no need to abandon the standard library for tasks like this. The ability to compose algorithms is one of the key motivations for using the Ranges library, which we will cover next.

Summary

In this chapter, you learned how to use the basic concepts in the Algorithm library, the advantages of using them as building blocks instead of handwritten for-loops, and why using the standard Algorithm library is beneficial for optimizing your code at a later stage. We also discussed the guarantees and trade-offs of the standard algorithms, meaning that you can, from now on, use them with confidence.

By using the advantages of the algorithms instead of manual for-loops, your code base is well prepared for the parallelization techniques that will be discussed in the coming chapters of this book. One key feature that the standard algorithms are missing is the possibility to compose algorithms, something that was highlighted when we tried to avoid unnecessary container copies. In the next chapter, you will learn how to use views from the C++ Ranges library to overcome this limitation of standard algorithms.

6

Ranges and Views

This chapter will pick up right where we left off in the previous chapter about algorithms and their limitations. Views from the Ranges library are a powerful complement to the Algorithm library, which allows us to compose multiple transformations into a lazy evaluated view over a sequence of elements. After reading this chapter, you will understand what range views are and how to use them in combination with containers, iterators, and algorithms from the standard library.

Specifically, we'll cover the following major topics:

- The composability of algorithms
- Range adaptors
- Materializing views into containers
- Generating, transforming, and sampling elements in a range

Before we get into the Ranges library itself, let's discuss why it's been added to C++20, and why we'd want to use it.

The motivation for the Ranges library

With the introduction of the Ranges library to C++20 came some major improvements to how we benefit from the standard library when implementing algorithms. The following list shows the new features:

- Concepts that define requirements on iterators and ranges can now be better checked by the compiler and provide more help during development

- New overloads of all functions in the <algorithm> header are constrained with the concepts just mentioned and accept ranges as arguments rather than iterator pairs

- Constrained iterators in the iterator header

- Range views, which make it possible to compose algorithms

This chapter will focus on the last item: the concept of views, which allow us to compose algorithms to avoid the unnecessary copying of data to owning containers. To fully understand the importance of this, let's begin by demonstrating the lack of composability within the algorithm library.

Limitations of the Algorithm library

standard library algorithms are lacking in one fundamental aspect: composability. Let's examine what is meant by that by looking at the last example from *Chapter 5, Algorithms*, where we discussed this briefly. If you remember, we had a class to represent a Student in a particular year and with a particular exam score:

```cpp
struct Student {
  int year_{};
  int score_{};
  std::string name_{};
  // ...
};
```

If we wanted to find the highest score from a big collection of students in their second year, we would probably use max_element() on score_, but as we only want to take the students in a specific year into account, it gets tricky. By using the new algorithms that accept both ranges and projections (refer to *Chapter 5, Algorithms*), we might end up with something like this:

```cpp
auto get_max_score(const std::vector<Student>& students, int year) {
  auto by_year = [=](const auto& s) { return s.year_ == year; };
  // The student list needs to be copied in
  // order to filter on the year
  auto v = std::vector<Student>{};
  std::ranges::copy_if(students, std::back_inserter(v), by_year);
  auto it = std::ranges::max_element(v, std::less{}, &Student::score_);
  return it != v.end() ? it->score_ : 0;
}
```

Here is an example of how it can be used:

```
auto students = std::vector<Student>{
  {3, 120, "Niki"},
  {2, 140, "Karo"},
  {3, 190, "Sirius"},
  {2, 110, "Rani"},
  // ...
};
auto score = get_max_score(students, 2);
std::cout << score << '\n';
// Prints 140
```

This implementation of get_max_score() is easy to understand, but it creates unnecessary copies of Student objects when using copy_if() and std::back_inserter().

You may now be thinking that get_max_score() could be written as a simple for-loop, which relieves us of extra allocation(s) due to copy_if():

```
auto get_max_score(const std::vector<Student>& students, int year) {
  auto max_score = 0;
  for (const auto& student : students) {
    if (student.year_ == year) {
      max_score = std::max(max_score, student.score_);
    }
  }
  return max_score;
}
```

Although this is easily achievable in this small example, we would like to be able to implement this algorithm by composing small algorithmic building blocks, rather than implementing it from scratch using a single for-loop.

What we would like is a syntax that is as readable as using algorithms, but with the ability to avoid constructing new containers for every step in the algorithm. This is where the views from the Ranges library come into play. Although the Ranges library contains a lot more than views, the major difference from the Algorithm library is the ability to compose what is essentially a different kind of iterator into a lazy evaluated range.

This is what the previous example would look if it was written using views from the Ranges library:

```
auto max_value(auto&& range) {
  const auto it = std::ranges::max_element(range);
  return it != range.end() ? *it : 0;
}

auto get_max_score(const std::vector<Student>& students, int year) {
  const auto by_year = [=](auto&& s) { return s.year_ == year; };
  return max_value(students
    | std::views::filter(by_year)
    | std::views::transform(&Student::score_));
}
```

Now we are back to using algorithms and can, therefore, avoid mutable variables, for-loops, and if-statements. The extra vector that held students in a specific year in our initial example has now been eliminated. Instead, we have composed a range view, which represents all of the students filtered by the by_year predicate, and then transformed to only expose the score. The view is then passed to a small utility function max_value(), which uses the max_element() algorithm to compare the scores of the selected students in order to find the maximum value.

This way of composing algorithms by chaining them together and, at the same time, avoiding unnecessary copying is what motivates us to start using views from the Ranges library.

Understanding views from the Ranges library

Views in the Ranges library are lazy evaluated iterations over a range. Technically, they are only iterators with built-in logic, but syntactically, they provide a very pleasant syntax for many common operations.

The following is an example of how to use a view to square each number in a vector (via iteration):

```
auto numbers = std::vector{1, 2, 3, 4};
auto square = [](auto v) {  return v * v; };
```

```
auto squared_view = std::views::transform(numbers, square);
for (auto s : squared_view) {  // The square Lambda is invoked here
  std::cout << s << " ";
}
// Output: 1 4 9 16
```

The variable squared_view is not a copy of the numbers vector with the values squared; it is a proxy object for numbers with one slight difference — every time you access an element, the std::transform() function is invoked. This is why we say that a view is lazy evaluated.

From the outside, you can still iterate over squared_view in the same way as any regular container and, therefore, you can perform regular algorithms such as find() or count(), but, internally, you haven't created another container.

If you want to store the range, the view can be materialized to a container using std::ranges::copy(). (This will be demonstrated later on in this chapter.) Once the view has been copied back to a container, there is no longer any dependency between the original and the transformed container.

With ranges, it is also possible to create a filtered view where only a part of the range is visible. In this case, only the elements that satisfy the condition are visible when iterating the view:

```
auto v = std::vector{4, 5, 6, 7, 6, 5, 4};
auto odd_view =
  std::views::filter(v, [](auto i){ return (i % 2) == 1; });
for (auto odd_number : odd_view) {
  std::cout << odd_number << " ";
}
// Output: 5 7 5
```

Another example of the versatility of the Ranges library is the possibility it offers to create a view that can iterate over several containers as if they were a single list:

```
auto list_of_lists = std::vector<std::vector<int>> {
  {1, 2},
  {3, 4, 5},
  {5},
  {4, 3, 2, 1}
};
```

```
auto flattened_view = std::views::join(list_of_lists);
for (auto v : flattened_view)
  std::cout << v << " ";
// Output: 1 2 3 4 5 5 4 3 2 1

auto max_value = *std::ranges::max_element(flattened_view);
// max_value is 5
```

Now that we have looked briefly at some examples using views, let's examine the requirements and properties that are common for all views

Views are composable

The full power of views comes from the ability to combine them. As they don't copy the actual data, you can express multiple operations on a dataset while, internally, only iterating over it once. To understand how views are composed, let's look at our initial example, but without using the pipe operator for composing the views; instead, let's construct the actual view classes directly. Here is how this looks:

```
auto get_max_score(const std::vector<Student>& s, int year) {
  auto by_year = [=](const auto& s) { return s.year_ == year; };

  auto v1 = std::ranges::ref_view{s}; // Wrap container in a view
  auto v2 = std::ranges::filter_view{v1, by_year};
  auto v3 = std::ranges::transform_view{v2, &Student::score_};

  auto it = std::ranges::max_element(v3);
  return it != v3.end() ? *it : 0;
}
```

We begin by creating a `std::ranges::ref_view`, which is a thin wrapper around a container. In our case, it turns the vector s into a view that is cheap to copy. We need this because our next view, `std::ranges::filter_view`, requires a view as its first parameter. As you can see, we compose our next view by referring to the previous view in the chain.

This chain of composable views can, of course, be made arbitrarily long. The algorithm `max_element()` doesn't need to know anything about the complete chain; it only needs to iterate the range v3, as it was an ordinary container.

The following diagram is a simplified view of the relationships between the `max_element()` algorithm, the views, and the input container:

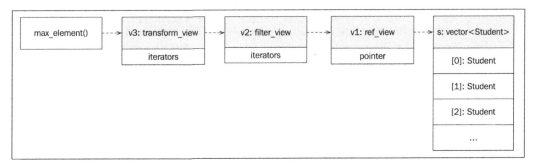

Figure 6.1: The top level algorithm, std::ranges::max_element(), pulls values from the views which lazyily process elements from the underlying container (std::vector)

Now, this style of composing views is a bit verbose, and if we were to try to remove the intermediate variables v1 and v2, we would end up with something like this:

```
using namespace std::ranges; // _view classes live in std::ranges
auto scores =
  transform_view{filter_view{ref_view{s}, by_year},
    &Student::score_};
```

Now, this might not look syntactically elegant. By getting rid of the intermediate variables, we have something that is hard to read even to a trained eye. We are also forced to read the code from the inside out to understand the dependencies. Fortunately, the Ranges library provides us with range adaptors, which is the preferred way of composing views.

Range views come with range adaptors

As you have seen earlier, the Ranges library also allows us to compose views using range adaptors and pipe operators for a much more elegant syntax (you will learn more about using the pipe operator in your own code in *Chapter 10, Proxy Objects and Lazy Evaluation*). The previous code example could be rewritten by using range adaptor objects, and we would have something like this:

```
using namespace std::views; // range adaptors live in std::views
auto scores = s | filter(by_year) | transform(&Student::score_);
```

The ability to read a statement from left to right, rather than inside out, makes the code much easier to read. If you have used a Unix shell, you are probably familiar with this notation for chaining commands.

Each view in the Ranges library has a corresponding range adaptor object that can be used together with the pipe operator. When using the range adaptors, we can also skip the extra `std::ranges::ref_view` since the range adaptors work directly with `viewable_ranges`, namely, a range that can be safely converted into a `view`.

You can think of a range adaptor as a global stateless object that has two functions implemented: `operator()()` and `operator|()`. Both functions construct and return view objects. The pipe operator is what is being used in the preceding example. But it is also possible to use the call operator to form a view using a nested syntax with parentheses, like this:

```
using namespace std::views;
auto scores = transform(filter(s, by_year), &Student::score_);
```

Again, when using range adaptors, there is no need to wrap the input container in a `ref_view`.

To summarize, each view in the Ranges library consists of:

- A class template (the actual view type) that operates on view objects, for example, `std::ranges::transform_view`. These view types can be found under the namespace `std::ranges`.

- A range adaptor object that creates instances of the view class from ranges, for example, `std::views::transform`. All range adaptors implement `operator()()` and `operator|()`, which makes it possible to compose transformations using the pipe operator or by nesting. The range adaptor objects live under the namespace `std::views`.

Views are non-owning ranges with complexity guarantees

In the previous chapter, the concept of a range was introduced. Any type that provides the functions `begin()` and `end()`, where `begin()` returns an iterator and `end()` returns a sentinel, qualifies as a range. We concluded that all standard containers are ranges. Containers own their elements, so we can, therefore, call them owning ranges.

A view is also a range, that is, it provides `begin()` and `end()` functions. However, unlike containers, a view does not own the elements in the range that the view spans over.

The construction of a view is required to be a constant-time operation, *O(1)*. It cannot perform any work that depends on the size of the underlying container. The same goes for assigning, copying, moving, and destructing a view. This makes it easy to reason about performance when using views to combine multiple algorithms. It also makes it impossible for views to own elements, since that would require linear time complexity upon construction and destruction.

Views don't mutate the underlying container

At first glance, a view might look like a mutated version of the input container. However, the container is not mutated at all: all the processing is performed in the iterators. A view is simply a proxy object that, when iterated, *looks* like a mutated container.

This also makes it possible for a view to expose elements of types that are different from the types of the input elements. The following snippet demonstrates how a view transforms the element type from int to std::string:

```
auto ints = std::list{2, 3, 4, 2, 1};
auto strings = ints
  | std::views::transform([](auto i) { return std::to_string(i); });
```

Perhaps we have a function that operates on a container that we want to transform using range algorithms, and then we want to return and store it back in a container. For example, in the example above, we might want to actually store the strings in a separate container. You will learn how to do that in the next section.

Views can be materialized into containers

Sometimes, we want to store the view in a container, that is, **materialize** the view. All views can be materialized into containers, but it is not as easy as you would have hoped. A function template called std::ranges::to<T>(), which could turn a view into an arbitrary container type T, was proposed for C++20 but didn't quite make it. Hopefully we will get something similar in a future version of C++. Until then, we need to do a little more work ourselves in order to materialize views.

In the previous example, we converted ints into std::strings, as follows:

```
auto ints = std::list{2, 3, 4, 2, 1};
auto r = ints
  | std::views::transform([](auto i) { return std::to_string(i); });
```

Now, if we want to materialize the range r to a vector, we could use
`std::ranges::copy()` like this:

```
auto vec = std::vector<std::string>{};
std::ranges::copy(r, std::back_inserter(vec));
```

Materializing views is a common operation, so it would be handy if we had a
generic utility for this case. Say that we want to materialize some arbitrary view
into a `std::vector`; we could use some generic programming to come up with the
following convenient utility function:

```
auto to_vector(auto&& r) {
  std::vector<std::ranges::range_value_t<decltype(r)>> v;

  if constexpr(std::ranges::sized_range<decltype(r)>) {
    v.reserve(std::ranges::size(r));
  }

  std::ranges::copy(r, std::back_inserter(v));
  return v;
}
```

This snippet is taken from Timur Doumler's blog post, `https://timur.audio/how-to-`
`make-a-container-from-a-c20-range`, which is well worth a read.

We haven't talked much about generic programming yet in this book, but the next
few chapters will explain the use of `auto` argument types and `if constexpr`.

We are using `reserve()` to optimize the performance of this function. It will preallocate
enough room for all of the elements in the range to avoid further allocations. However,
we can only call `reserve()` if we know the size of the range, and therefore we have to
use the `if constexpr` statement to check whether the range is a `size_range` at compile
time.

With this utility in place, we can transform a container of some type into a vector
holding elements of another arbitrary type. Let's see how to convert a list of integers
to a vector of `std::strings` using `to_vector()`. Here is an example:

```
auto ints = std::list{2, 3, 4, 2, 1};
auto r = ints
  | std::views::transform([](auto i) { return std::to_string(i); });
auto strings = to_vector(r);
// strings is now a std::vector<std::string>
```

Remember that once the view has been copied back to a container, there is no longer any dependency between the original and the transformed container. This also means that the materialization is an eager operation, whereas all view operations are lazy.

Views are lazy evaluated

All of the work that is performed by a view happens lazily. This is the opposite of the functions found in the <algorithm> header, which perform their work immediately on all elements when they are called.

You have seen that the std::views::filter view can replace the algorithm std::copy_if(), and that the std::views::transform view can replace the std::transform() algorithm. When we use the views as building blocks and chain them together, we benefit from lazy evaluation by avoiding unnecessary copies of the container elements required by the eager algorithms.

But what about std::sort()? Is there a corresponding sorting view? The answer is no because it would require the view to first collect all the elements eagerly in order to find the first element to return. Instead, we have to do that ourselves by explicitly calling sort on our view. In most cases, we also need to materialize the view before sorting. We can clarify this with an example. Assume that we have a vector of numbers that we have filtered by some predicate, like this:

```
auto vec = std::vector{4, 2, 7, 1, 2, 6, 1, 5};
auto is_odd = [](auto i) { return i % 2 == 1; };
auto odd_numbers = vec | std::views::filter(is_odd);
```

If we try to sort our view odd_numbers using std::ranges::sort() or std::sort(), we will get a compilation error:

```
std::ranges::sort(odd_numbers); // Doesn't compile
```

The compiler complains about the types of iterators provided by the odd_numbers range. The sorting algorithm requires random access iterators, but that's not the type of iterators that our view provides, even though the underlying input container is a std::vector. What we need to do is to materialize the view before sorting:

```
auto v = to_vector(odd_numbers);
std::ranges::sort(v);
// v is now 1, 1, 5, 7
```

But why is this necessary? The answer is that this is a consequence of lazy evaluation. The filter view (and many other views) cannot preserve the iterator types of the underlying range (in this case, the `std::vector`) when evaluation needs to be lazy by reading one element at a time.

So, are there any views that can be sorted? Yes, an example would be `std::views::take`, which returns the first *n* elements in a range. The following example compiles and runs fine without the need for materializing the view before sorting:

```
auto vec = std::vector{4, 2, 7, 1, 2, 6, 1, 5};
auto first_half = vec | std::views::take(vec.size() / 2);
std::ranges::sort(first_half);
// vec is now 1, 2, 4, 7, 2, 6, 1, 5
```

The quality of the iterators has been preserved and it's therefore possible to sort the `first_half` view. The end result is that the first half of the elements in the underlying vector vec have been sorted.

You now have a good understanding of what views from the Ranges library are and how they work. In the next section, we will explore how to use the views that are included in the standard library.

Views in the standard library

So far in this chapter, we have been talking about views from the Ranges library. As was described earlier, these view types need to be constructed in constant time and also have constant-time copy, move, and assignment operators. However, in C++, we have talked about view classes before the Ranges library was added to C++20. These view classes are non-owning types, just like `std::ranges::view`, but without the complexity guarantees.

In this section, we will begin by exploring the views from the Ranges library that are associated with the `std::ranges::view` concept, and then move on to `std::string_view` and `std::span`, which are not associated with `std::ranges::view`.

Range views

There are already many views in the Ranges library, and I think we will see even more of them in future versions of C++. This section will provide a quick overview of some of the available views and also put them in different categories based on what they do.

Generating views

Generating views produce values. They can generate a finite or infinite range of values. The most obvious example in this category is std::views::iota, which produces values within a half-open range. The following snippet prints the values -2, -1, 0, and 1:

```
for (auto i : std::views::iota(-2, 2)) {
  std::cout << i << ' ';
}
// Prints -2 -1 0 1
```

By omitting the second argument, std::views::iota will produce an infinite number of values on request.

Transforming views

Transforming views are views that transform the elements of a range or the structure of the range itself. Some examples include:

- std::views::transform: Transforms the value and/or the type of each element
- std::views::reverse: Returns a reversed version of the input range
- std::views::split: Takes an element apart and splits each element into a subrange. The resulting range is a range of ranges
- std::views::join: The opposite of split; flattens out all subranges

The following example uses split and join to extract all digits from a string of comma-separated values:

```
auto csv = std::string{"10,11,12"};
auto digits = csv
  | std::views::split(',')      // [ [1, 0], [1, 1], [1, 2] ]
  | std::views::join;           // [ 1, 0, 1, 1, 1, 2 ]

for (auto i : digits) {
  std::cout << i;
}
// Prints 101112
```

Sampling views

Sampling views are views that select a subset of elements in a range, for example:

- `std::views::filter`: Returns only the elements that fulfill a provided predicate
- `std::views::take`: Returns the *n* first elements of a range
- `std::views::drop`: Returns all the remaining elements in a range after dropping the first *n* elements

You have seen plenty of examples using `std::views::filter` in this chapter; it's an extremely useful view. Both `std::views::take` and `std::views::drop` have a `_while` version, which accepts a predicate instead of a number. Here is an example using take and drop_while:

```
auto vec = std::vector{1, 2, 3, 4, 5, 4, 3, 2, 1};
auto v = vec
  | std::views::drop_while([](auto i) { return i < 5; })
  | std::views::take(3);

for (auto i : v) { std::cout << i << " "; }
// Prints 5 4 3
```

This example uses `drop_while` to discard values from the front that are less than 5. The remaining elements are passed to `take`, which returns the first three elements. Now to our last category of range views.

Utility views

You have already seen some of the utility views in action in this chapter. They come in handy when you have something that you want to convert or treat as a view. Some examples in this category of views are `ref_view`, `all_view`, `subrange`, `counted`, and `istream_view`.

The following example shows you how to read a text file with floating-point numbers and then print them.

Assume that we have a text file called `numbers.txt` full of important floating-point numbers, like this:

```
1.4142 1.618 2.71828 3.14159 6.283 ...
```

We could then create a view of floats by using std::ranges::istream_view:

```
auto ifs = std::ifstream("numbers.txt");
for (auto f : std::ranges::istream_view<float>(ifs)) {
  std::cout << f << '\n';
}
ifs.close();
```

By creating a std::ranges::istream_view and passing it an istream object, we have a succinct way of processing data from files or any other input stream.

The views in the Ranges library have been carefully chosen and designed. There will most likely be more of them in upcoming versions of the standard. Being aware of the different categories of views helps us to keep them apart and make them easy to find when we need them.

Revisiting std::string_view and std::span

It's worth noting that the standard library provides us with other views outside of the Ranges library. Both std::string_view and std::span introduced in *Chapter 4, Data Structures* are non-owning ranges that are perfect to use in combination with the Ranges view.

There is no guarantee that these views can be constructed in constant time, as is the case with the views from the Ranges library. For example, constructing a std::string_view from a null-terminated C-style string could invoke a call to strlen(), which is an $O(n)$ operation.

Suppose, for some reason, we have a function that resets the first n values in a range:

```
auto reset(std::span<int> values, int n) {
  for (auto& i : std::ranges::take_view{values, n}) {
    i = int{};
  }
}
```

There is no need to use a range adaptor with values in this case because values is already a view. By using std::span, we can pass both built-in arrays or a container such as std::vector:

```
int a[]{33, 44, 55, 66, 77};
reset(a, 3);
// a is now [0, 0, 0, 66, 77]
```

```
auto v = std::vector{33, 44, 55, 66, 77};
reset(v, 2);
// v is now [0, 0, 55, 66, 77]
```

In a similar way, we can use `std::string_view` together with the Ranges library. The following function splits the content of a `std::string_view` into a `std::vector` of `std::string` elements:

```
auto split(std::string_view s, char delim) {
  const auto to_string = [](auto&& r) -> std::string {
    const auto cv = std::ranges::common_view{r};
    return {cv.begin(), cv.end()};
  };
  return to_vector(std::ranges::split_view{s, delim}
    | std::views::transform(to_string));
}
```

The lambda `to_string` transforms a range of `chars` into a `std::string`. The `std::string` constructor requires identical iterator and sentinel types, therefore, the range is wrapped in a `std::ranges::common_view`. The utility `to_vector()` materializes the view and returns a `std::vector<std::string>`. `to_vector()` was defined earlier in this chapter.

Our `split()` function can now be used with both `const char*` strings and `std::string` objects, like this:

```
const char* c_str = "ABC,DEF,GHI";  // C style string
const auto v1 = split(c_str, ',');  // std::vector<std::string>

const auto s = std::string{"ABC,DEF,GHI"};
const auto v2 = split(s, ',');       // std::vector<std::string>

assert(v1 == v2);                    // true
```

We will now wrap this chapter up by talking a little bit about what we expect to see in the Ranges library in future versions of C++.

The future of the Ranges library

The Ranges library that got accepted in C++20 was based on a library authored by Eric Niebler, and is available at `https://github.com/ericniebler/range-v3`. Only a small subset of the components of this library have made their way into the standard at present, but more things are likely to be added soon.

In addition to many useful views that haven't been accepted yet, such as `group_by`, `zip`, `slice`, and `unique`, there is the concept of **actions** that can be piped in the same way that views can. However, instead of being lazy evaluated like views, actions perform eager mutations of ranges. Sorting is an example of a typical action.

If you cannot wait for these features to be added to the standard library, I recommend that you take a look at the range-v3 library.

Summary

This chapter presented a number of motivations behind using Range views to construct algorithms. By using views, we can compose algorithms efficiently, and with a succinct syntax, using the pipe operator. You also learned what it means for a class to be a view and how to use range adaptors that turn ranges into views.

A view does not own its elements. Constructing a range view is required to be a constant time operation and all views are evaluated lazily. You have seen examples of how we can convert a container into a view, and how to materialize a view back into an owning container.

Finally, we covered a brief overview of the views that come with the standard library, and the likely future of ranges in C++.

This chapter is the last in the series about containers, iterators, algorithms, and ranges. We will now move on to memory management in C++.

7
Memory Management

After reading the previous chapters, it should no longer come as a surprise that the way we handle memory can have a huge impact on performance. The CPU spends a lot of time shuffling data between the CPU registers and the main memory (loading and storing data to and from the main memory). As shown in *Chapter 4, Data Structures*, the CPU uses memory caches to speed up access to memory, and programs need to be cache-friendly in order to run quickly.

This chapter will reveal more aspects of how computers work with memory so that you know which things must be considered when tuning memory usage. In addition, this chapter covers:

- Automatic memory allocation and dynamic memory management.

- The life cycle of a C++ object and how to manage object ownership.

- Efficient memory management. Sometimes, there are hard memory limits that force us to keep our data representation compact, and sometimes, we have plenty of memory available but need the program to go faster by making memory management more efficient.

- How to minimize dynamic memory allocations. Allocating and deallocating dynamic memory is relatively expensive and, at times, we need to avoid unnecessary allocations to make the program run faster.

We will start this chapter by explaining some concepts that you need to understand before we dig deeper into C++ memory management. This introduction will explain virtual memory and virtual address spaces, stack memory versus heap memory, paging, and swap space.

Computer memory

The physical memory of a computer is shared among all the processes running on a system. If one process uses a lot of memory, the other processes will most likely be affected. But from a programmer's perspective, we usually don't have to bother about the memory that is being used by other processes. This isolation of memory is due to the fact that most operating systems today are **virtual memory** operating systems, which provide the illusion that a process has all the memory for itself. Each process has its own **virtual address space**.

The virtual address space

Addresses in the virtual address space that programmers see are mapped to physical addresses by the operating system and the **memory management unit (MMU)**, which is a part of the processor. This mapping or translation happens each time we access a memory address.

This extra layer of indirection makes it possible for the operating system to use physical memory for the parts of a process that are currently being used, and back up the rest of the virtual memory on disk. In this sense, we can look at the physical main memory as a cache for the virtual memory space, which resides on secondary storage. The areas of the secondary storage that are used for backing up memory pages are usually called **swap space**, **swap file**, or simply **pagefile**, depending on the operating system.

Virtual memory makes it possible for processes to have a virtual address space bigger than the physical address space, since virtual memory that is not in use does not have to occupy physical memory.

Memory pages

The most common way to implement virtual memory today is to divide the address space into fixed-size blocks called **memory pages**. When a process accesses memory at a virtual address, the operating system checks whether the memory page is backed by physical memory (a page frame). If the memory page is not mapped in the main memory, a hardware exception occurs, and the page is loaded from disk into memory. This type of hardware exception is called a **page fault**. This is not an error but a necessary interrupt in order to load data from disk to memory. As you may have guessed, though, this is very slow compared to reading data that is already resident in memory.

When there are no more available page frames in the main memory, a page frame has to be evicted. If the page to be evicted is dirty, that is, it has been modified since it was last loaded from disk, it needs to be written to disk before it can be replaced. This mechanism is called **paging**. If the memory page has not been modified, the memory page is simply evicted.

Not all operating systems that support virtual memory support paging. iOS, for example, does have virtual memory but dirty pages are never stored on disk; only clean pages can be evicted from memory. If the main memory is full, iOS will start terminating processes until there is enough free memory again. Android uses a similar strategy. One reason for not writing memory pages back to the flash storage of the mobile devices is that it drains the battery, and it also shortens the lifespan of the flash storage itself.

The following diagram shows two running processes. They both have their own virtual memory space. Some of the pages are mapped to the physical memory, while some are not. If process 1 needs to use memory in the memory page that starts at address 0x1000, a page fault will occur. The memory page will then be mapped to a vacant memory frame. Also, note that the virtual memory addresses are not the same as the physical addresses. The first memory page of process 1, which starts at the virtual address 0x0000, is mapped to a memory frame that starts at the physical address 0x4000:

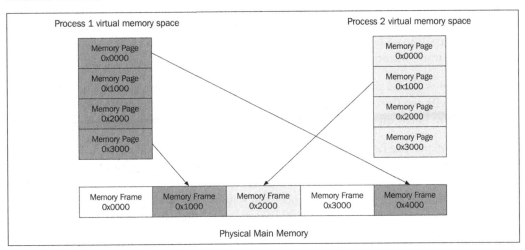

Figure 7.1: Virtual memory pages, mapped to memory frames in physical memory.
Virtual memory pages that are not in use do not have to occupy physical memory.

Thrashing

Thrashing can happen when a system runs low on physical memory and is, therefore, constantly paging. Whenever a process gets time scheduled on the CPU, it tries to access memory that has been paged out. Loading new memory pages means that the other pages first have to be stored on disk. Moving data back and forth between disk and memory is usually very slow; in some cases, this more or less stalls the computer since the system spends all its time paging. Looking at the system's page fault frequency is a good way to determine whether the program has started thrashing.

Knowing the basics of how memory is being handled by the hardware and the OS is important when optimizing performance. Next, we will see how memory is handled during the execution of a C++ program.

Process memory

The stack and the heap are the two most important memory segments in a C++ program. There is also static storage and thread local storage, but we will talk more about that later. Actually, to be formally correct, C++ doesn't talk about stack and heap; instead, it talks about the free store, storage classes, and the storage duration of objects. However, since the concepts of stack and heap are widely used in the C++ community, and all the implementations of C++ that we are aware of use a stack to implement function calls and manage the automatic storage of local variables, it is important to understand what stack and heap are.

In this book, I will also use the terms *stack* and *heap* rather than the storage duration of objects. I will use the terms *heap* and *free store* interchangeably and will not make any distinction between them.

Both the stack and the heap reside in the process' virtual memory space. The stack is a place where all the local variables reside; this also includes arguments to functions. The stack grows each time a function is called and contracts when a function returns. Each thread has its own stack and, hence, stack memory can be considered thread-safe. The heap, on the other hand, is a global memory area that is shared among all the threads in a running process. The heap grows when we allocate memory with new (or the C library functions malloc() and calloc()) and contracts when we free the memory with delete (or free()). Usually, the heap starts at a low address and grows in an upward direction, whereas the stack starts at a high address and grows in a downward direction. *Figure 7.2* shows how the stack and heap grow in opposite directions in a virtual address space:

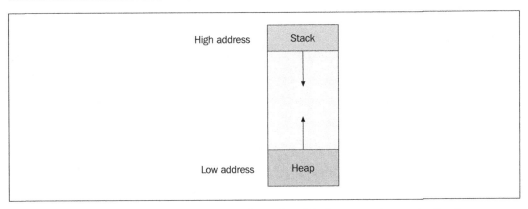

Figure 7.2: An address space of a process. The stack and the heap grow in opposite directions.

The next sections will provide more details about the stack and the heap, and also explain when we are using each of these memory areas in the C++ programs we write.

Stack memory

The stack differs in many ways compared to the heap. Here are some of the unique properties of the stack:

- The stack is a contiguous memory block.
- It has a fixed maximum size. If a program exceeds the maximum stack size, the program will crash. This condition is called stack overflow.
- The stack memory never becomes fragmented.
- Allocating memory from the stack is (almost) always fast. Page faults are possible but rare.
- Each thread in a program has its own stack.

The code examples that follow in this section will examine some of these properties. Let's start with allocations and deallocations to get a feel for how the stack is used in a program.

We can easily find out in which direction the stack grows by inspecting the address of the stack-allocated data. The following example code demonstrates how the stack grows and contracts when entering and leaving functions:

```
void func1() {
  auto i = 0;
  std::cout << "func1(): " << std::addressof(i) << '\n';
}
```

```
void func2() {
  auto i = 0;
  std::cout << "func2(): " << std::addressof(i) << '\n';
  func1();
}

int main() {
  auto i = 0;
  std::cout << "main():  " << std::addressof(i) << '\n';
  func2();
  func1();
}
```

A possible output when running the program could look like this:

```
main():  0x7ea075ac
func2(): 0x7ea07594
func1(): 0x7ea0757c
func1(): 0x7ea07594
```

By printing the address of the stack allocated integer, we can determine how much and in which direction the stack grows on my platform. The stack grows by 24 bytes each time we enter either func1() or func2(). The integer i, which will be allocated on the stack, is 4 bytes long. The remaining 20 bytes contain data needed when the function ends, such as the return address, and perhaps some padding for alignment.

The following diagram illustrates how the stack grows and contracts during the execution of the program. The first box illustrates how the memory looks when the program has just entered the main() function. The second box shows how the stack has increased when we execute func1(), and so on:

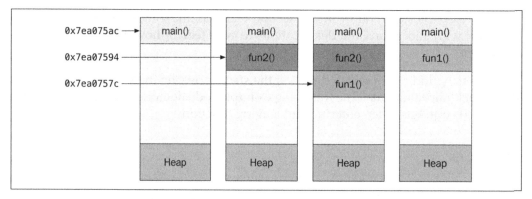

Figure 7.3: The stack grows and contracts when functions are entered

The total memory allocated for the stack is a fixed-size contiguous memory block created at thread startup. So, how big is the stack and what happens when we reach the limit of the stack?

As mentioned earlier, the stack grows each time the program enters a function and contracts when the function returns. The stack also grows whenever we create a new stack variable within the same function and contracts when such a variable goes out of scope. The most common reason for the stack to overflow is by deep recursive calls and/or by using large, automatic variables on the stack. The maximum size of the stack differs among platforms and can also be configured for individual processes and threads.

Let's see if we can write a program to see how big the stack is by default on my system. We will begin by writing a function, func(), which will recurse infinitely. At the beginning of each function, we'll allocate a 1-kilobyte variable, which will be placed onto the stack every time we enter func(). Every time func() is executed, we print the current size of the stack:

```cpp
void func(std::byte* stack_bottom_addr) {
  std::byte data[1024];
  std::cout << stack_bottom_addr - data << '\n';
  func(stack_bottom_addr);
}

int main() {
  std::byte b;
  func(&b);
}
```

The size of the stack is only an estimate. We compute it by subtracting the address of the first local variable in main() from the first local variable defined in func().

When I compiled the code with Clang, I got a warning that func() will never return. Normally, this is a warning that we should not ignore, but this time, this is exactly the result we want, so we ignore the warning and run the program anyway. The program crashes after a short while when the stack has reached its limit. Before the program crashes, it manages to print out thousands of lines with the current size of the stack. The last lines of the output look like this:

```
...
8378667
8379755
8380843
```

Since we are subtracting `std::byte` pointers, the size is in bytes, so it looks like the maximum size of the stack is around 8 MB on my system. On Unix-like systems, it is possible to set and get the stack size for processes by using the `ulimit` command with the option `-s`:

```
$ ulimit -s
$ 8192
```

`ulimit` (short for user limit) returns the current setting for the maximum stack size in kilobytes. The output of `ulimit` confirms the results from our experiment: the stack is about 8 MB on my Mac if I don't configure it explicitly.

On Windows, the default stack size is usually set to 1 MB. A program running fine on macOS might crash due to a stack overflow on Windows if the stack size is not correctly configured.

With this example, we can also conclude that we don't want to run out of stack memory since the program will crash when that happens. Later in this chapter, we will see how to implement a rudimentary memory allocator to handle fixed-size allocations. We will then understand that the stack is just another type of memory allocator that can be implemented very efficiently because the usage pattern is always sequential. We always request and release memory at the top of the stack (the end of the contiguous memory). This ensures that the stack memory will never become fragmented and that we can allocate and deallocate memory by only moving a stack pointer.

Heap memory

The heap (or the free store, which is a more correct term in C++) is where data with dynamic storage lives. As mentioned earlier, the heap is shared among multiple threads, which means that memory management for the heap needs to take concurrency into account. This makes memory allocations in the heap more complicated than stack allocations, which are local per thread.

The allocation and deallocation pattern for stack memory is sequential, in the sense that memory is always deallocated in the reverse order to that in which it was allocated. On the other hand, for dynamic memory, the allocations and deallocations can happen arbitrarily. The dynamic lifetime of objects and the variable sizes of memory allocations increase the risk of **fragmented memory**.

An easy way to understand the issue with memory fragmentation is to go through an example of how fragmented memory can occur. Suppose that we have a small contiguous memory block of 16 KB that we are allocating memory from. We are allocating objects of two types: type **A**, which is 1 KB, and type **B**, which is 2 KB. We first allocate an object of type **A**, followed by an object of type **B**. This repeats until the memory looks like the following image:

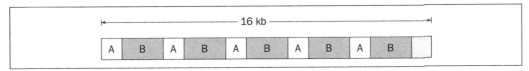

Figure 7.4: The memory after allocating objects of type A and B

Next, all objects of type **A** are no longer needed, so they can be deallocated. The memory now looks like this:

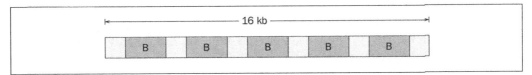

Figure 7.5: The memory after objects of type A are deallocated

There is now 10 KB of memory in use and 6 KB is available. Now, suppose we want to allocate a new object of type **B**, which is 2 KB. Although there is 6 KB of free memory, there is nowhere we can find a 2 KB memory block because the memory has become fragmented.

Now that you have a good understanding of how computer memory is structured and used in a running process, it's time to explore how C++ objects live in memory.

Objects in memory

All the objects we use in a C++ program reside in memory. Here, we will explore how objects are created and deleted from memory, and also describe how objects are laid out in memory.

Creating and deleting objects

In this section, we will dig into the details of using new and delete. Consider the following way of using new to create an object on the free store and then deleting it using delete:

```
auto* user = new User{"John"}; // allocate and construct
```

```
user->print_name();            // use object
delete user;                   // destruct and deallocate
```

I don't recommend that you call new and delete explicitly in this manner, but let's ignore that for now. Let's get to the point; as the comments suggest, new actually does two things, namely:

- Allocates memory to hold a new object of the User type
- Constructs a new User object in the allocated memory space by calling the constructor of the User class

The same thing goes with delete, it:

- Destructs the User object by calling its destructor
- Deallocates/frees the memory that the User object was placed in

It is actually possible to separate these two actions (memory allocation and object construction) in C++. This is rarely used but has some important and legitimate use cases when writing library components.

Placement new

C++ allows us to separate memory allocation from object construction. We could, for example, allocate a byte array with malloc() and construct a new User object in that region of memory. Have a look at the following code snippet:

```
auto* memory = std::malloc(sizeof(User));
auto* user = ::new (memory) User("john");
```

The perhaps unfamiliar syntax that's using ::new (memory) is called **placement new**. It is a non-allocating form of new, which only constructs an object. The double colon (::) in front of new ensures that the resolution occurs from the global namespace to avoid picking up an overloaded version of operator new.

In the preceding example, placement new constructs the User object and places it at the specified memory location. Since we are allocating the memory with std::malloc() for a single object, it is guaranteed to be correctly aligned (unless the class User has been declared to be overaligned). Later on, we will explore cases where we have to take alignment into account when using placement new.

There is no placement delete, so in order to destruct the object and free the memory, we need to call the destructor explicitly and then free the memory:

```
user->~User();
std::free(memory);
```

This is the only time you should call a destructor explicitly. Never call a destructor like this unless you have created an object with placement new.

C++17 introduces a set of utility functions in <memory> for constructing and destroying objects without allocating or deallocating memory. So, instead of calling placement new, it is now possible to use some of the functions from <memory> whose names begin with std::uninitialized_ for constructing, copying, and moving objects to an uninitialized memory area. And instead of calling the destructor explicitly, we can now use std::destroy_at() to destruct an object at a specific memory address without deallocating the memory.

The previous example could be rewritten using these new functions. Here is how it would look:

```
auto* memory = std::malloc(sizeof(User));
auto* user_ptr = reinterpret_cast<User*>(memory);
std::uninitialized_fill_n(user_ptr, 1, User{"john"});
std::destroy_at(user_ptr);
std::free(memory);
```

C++20 also introduces std::construct_at(), which makes it possible to replace the std::uninitialized_fill_n() call with:

```
std::construct_at(user_ptr, User{"john"});        // C++20
```

Please keep in mind that we are showing these naked low-level memory facilities to get a better understanding of memory management in C++. Using reinterpret_cast and the memory utilities demonstrated here should be kept to an absolute minimum in a C++ code base.

Next, you will see what operators are called when we use the new and delete expressions.

The new and delete operators

The function operator new is responsible for allocating memory when a new expression is invoked. The new operator can be either a globally defined function or a static member function of a class. It is possible to overload the global operators new and delete. Later in this chapter, we will see that this can be useful when analyzing memory usage.

Here is how to do it:

```
auto operator new(size_t size) -> void* {
  void* p = std::malloc(size);
  std::cout << "allocated " << size << " byte(s)\n";
  return p;
}

auto operator delete(void* p) noexcept -> void {
  std::cout << "deleted memory\n";
  return std::free(p);
}
```

We can verify that our overloaded operators are actually being used when creating and deleting a char object:

```
auto* p = new char{'a'}; // Outputs "allocated 1 byte(s)"
delete p;                // Outputs "deleted memory"
```

When creating and deleting an array of objects using the new[] and delete[] expressions, there is another pair of operators that are being used, namely operator new[] and operator delete[]. We can overload these operators in the same way:

```
auto operator new[](size_t size) -> void* {
  void* p = std::malloc(size);
  std::cout << "allocated " << size << " byte(s) with new[]\n";
  return p;
}

auto operator delete[](void* p) noexcept -> void {
  std::cout << "deleted memory with delete[]\n";
  return std::free(p);
}
```

Keep in mind that if you overload operator new, you should also overload operator delete. Functions for allocating and deallocating memory come in pairs. Memory should be deallocated by the allocator that the memory was allocated by. For example, memory allocated with std::malloc() should always be freed using std::free(), while memory allocated with operator new[] should be deallocated using operator delete[].

It is also possible to override a class-specific operator new or operator delete. This is probably more useful than overloading the global operators, since it is more likely that we need a custom dynamic memory allocator for a specific class.

Here, we are overloading `operator new` and `operator delete` for the `Document` class:

```
class Document {
// ...
public:
  auto operator new(size_t size) -> void* {
    return ::operator new(size);
  }
  auto operator delete(void* p) -> void {
    ::operator delete(p);
  }
};
```

The class-specific version of `new` will be used when we create new dynamically allocated `Document` objects:

```
auto* p = new Document{}; // Uses class-specific operator new
delete p;
```

If we instead want to use global `new` and `delete`, it is still possible by using the global scope (`::`):

```
auto* p = ::new Document{}; // Uses global operator new
::delete p;
```

We will discuss memory allocators later in this chapter and we will then see the overloaded `new` and `delete` operators in use.

To summarize what we have seen so far, a `new` expression involves two things: allocation and construction. `operator new` allocates memory and you can overload it globally or per class to customize dynamic memory management. Placement new can be used to construct an object in an already allocated memory area.

Another important, but rather low-level, topic that we need to understand in order to use memory efficiently is the **alignment** of memory.

Memory alignment

The CPU reads memory into its registers one word at a time. The word size is 64 bits on a 64-bit architecture, 32 bits on a 32-bit architecture, and so forth. For the CPU to work efficiently when working with different data types, it has restrictions on the addresses where objects of different types are located. Every type in C++ has an alignment requirement that defines the addresses at which an object of a certain type should be located in memory.

If the alignment of a type is 1, it means that the objects of that type can be located at any byte address. If the alignment of a type is 2, it means that the number of bytes between successive allowed addresses is 2. Or to quote the C++ standard:

> *"An alignment is an implementation-defined integer value representing the number of bytes between successive addresses at which a given object can be allocated."*

We can use `alignof` to find out the alignment of a type:

```
// Possible output is 4
std::cout << alignof(int) << '\n';
```

When I run this code, it outputs 4, which means that the alignment requirement of the type `int` is 4 bytes on my platform.

The following figure shows two examples of memory from a system with 64-bit words. The upper row contains three 4-byte integers, which are located on addresses that are 4 bytes aligned. The CPU can load these integers into registers in an efficient way and never need to read multiple words when accessing one of the `int` members. Compare this with the second row, which contains two `int` members, which are located at unaligned addresses. The second `int` even spans over two-word boundaries. In the best case, this is just inefficient, but on some platforms, the program will crash:

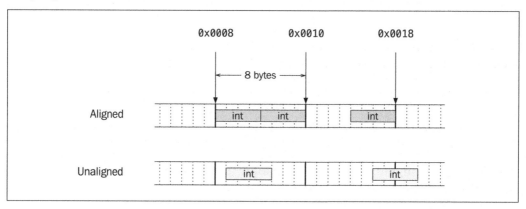

Figure 7.6: Two examples of memory that contain ints at aligned and unaligned memory addresses

Let's say that we have a type with an alignment requirement of 2. The C++ standard doesn't say whether the valid addresses are 1, 3, 5, 7... or 0, 2, 4, 6.... All platforms that we are aware of start counting addresses at 0, so, in practice we could check if an object is correctly aligned by checking if its address is a multiple of the alignment using the modulo operator (%).

However, if we want to write fully portable C++ code, we need to use `std::align()` and not modulo to check the alignment of an object. `std::align()` is a function from `<memory>` that will adjust a pointer according to an alignment that we pass as an argument. If the memory address we pass to it is already aligned, the pointer will not be adjusted. Therefore, we can use `std::align()` to implement a small utility function called `is_aligned()`, as follows:

```cpp
bool is_aligned(void* ptr, std::size_t alignment) {
  assert(ptr != nullptr);
  assert(std::has_single_bit(alignment)); // Power of 2

  auto s = std::numeric_limits<std::size_t>::max();
  auto aligned_ptr = ptr;
  std::align(alignment, 1, aligned_ptr, s);
  return ptr == aligned_ptr;
}
```

At first, we make sure that the `ptr` argument isn't null and that `alignment` is a power of 2, which is stated as a requirement in the C++ standard. We are using C++20 `std::has_single_bit()` from the `<bit>` header to check this. Next, we are calling `std::align()`. The typical use case for `std::align()` is when we have a memory buffer of some size in which we want to store an object with some alignment requirement. In this case, we don't have a buffer, and we don't care about the size of the objects, so we say that the object is of size 1 and the buffer is the maximum value of a `std::size_t`. Then, we can compare the original `ptr` and the adjusted `aligned_ptr` to see if the original pointer was already aligned. We will have use for this utility in the examples to come.

When allocating memory with `new` or `std::malloc()`, the memory we get back should be correctly aligned for the type we specify. The following code shows that the memory allocated for `int` is at least 4 bytes aligned on my platform:

```cpp
auto* p = new int{};
assert(is_aligned(p, 4ul)); // True
```

In fact, `new` and `malloc()` are guaranteed to always return memory suitably aligned for any scalar type (if it manages to return memory at all). The `<cstddef>` header provides us with a type called `std::max_align_t`, whose alignment requirement is at least as strict as all the scalar types. Later on, we will see that this type is useful when writing custom memory allocators. So, even if we only request memory for `char` on the free store, it will be aligned suitably for `std::max_align_t`.

The following code shows that the memory returned from new is correctly aligned for std::max_align_t and also for any scalar type:

```
auto* p = new char{};
auto max_alignment = alignof(std::max_align_t);
assert(is_aligned(p, max_alignment)); // True
```

Let's allocate char two times in a row with new:

```
auto* p1 = new char{'a'};
auto* p2 = new char{'b'};
```

Then, the memory may look something like this:

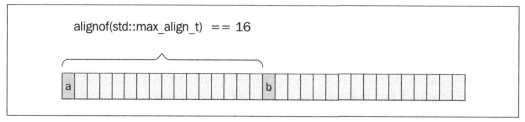

Figure 7.7: Memory layout after two separate allocations of one char each

The space between p1 and p2 depends on the alignment requirements of std::max_align_t. On my system, it was 16 bytes and, therefore, there are 15 bytes between each char instance, even though the alignment of a char is only 1.

It is possible to specify custom alignment requirements that are stricter than the default alignment when declaring a variable using the alignas specifier. Let's say we have a cache line size of 64 bytes and that we, for some reason, want to ensure that two variables are placed on separate cache lines. We could do the following:

```
alignas(64) int x{};
alignas(64) int y{};
// x and y will be placed on different cache lines
```

It's also possible to specify a custom alignment when defining a type. The following is a struct that will occupy exactly one cache line when being used:

```
struct alignas(64) CacheLine {
    std::byte data[64];
};
```

Now, if we were to create a stack variable of the type CacheLine, it would be aligned according to the custom alignment of 64 bytes:

```
int main() {
  auto x = CacheLine{};
  auto y = CacheLine{};
  assert(is_aligned(&x, 64));
  assert(is_aligned(&y, 64));
  // ...
}
```

The stricter alignment requirements are also satisfied when allocating objects on the heap. In order to support dynamic allocation of types with non-default alignment requirements, C++17 introduced new overloads of operator new() and operator delete() which accept an alignment argument of type std::align_val_t. There is also an aligned_alloc() function defined in <cstdlib> which can be used to manually allocate aligned heap memory.

As follows is an example in which we allocate a block of heap memory that should occupy exactly one memory page. In this case, the alignment-aware versions of operator new() and operator delete() will be invoked when using new and delete:

```
constexpr auto ps = std::size_t{4096};        // Page size

struct alignas(ps) Page {
    std::byte data_[ps];
};

auto* page = new Page{};                       // Memory page
assert(is_aligned(page, ps));                  // True
// Use page ...
delete page;
```

Memory pages are not part of the C++ abstract machine, so there is no portable way to programmatically get hold of the page size of the currently running system. However, you could use boost::mapped_region::get_page_size() or a platform-specific system call, such as getpagesize(), on Unix systems.

A final caveat to be aware of is that the supported set of alignments are defined by the implementation of the standard library you are using, and not the C++ standard.

Padding

The compiler sometimes needs to add extra bytes, **padding**, to our user-defined types. When we define data members in a class or struct, the compiler is forced to place the members in the same order as we define them.

However, the compiler also has to ensure that the data members inside the class have the correct alignment; hence, it needs to add padding between data members if necessary. For example, let's assume we have a class defined as follows:

```cpp
class Document {
  bool is_cached_{};
  double rank_{};
  int id_{};
};
std::cout << sizeof(Document) << '\n'; // Possible output is 24
```

The reason for the possible output being 24 is that the compiler inserts padding after `bool` and `int`, to fulfill the alignment requirements of the individual data members and the entire class. The compiler converts the `Document` class into something like this:

```cpp
class Document {
  bool is_cached_{};
  std::byte padding1[7]; // Invisible padding inserted by compiler
  double rank_{};
  int id_{};
  std::byte padding2[4]; // Invisible padding inserted by compiler
};
```

The first padding between `bool` and `double` is 7 bytes, since the `rank_` data member of the `double` type has an alignment of 8 bytes. The second padding that is added after `int` is 4 bytes. This is needed in order to fulfill the alignment requirements of the `Document` class itself. The member with the largest alignment requirement also determines the alignment requirement for the entire data structure. In our example, this means that the total size of the `Document` class must be a multiple of 8, since it contains a `double` value that is 8-byte aligned.

We now realize that we can rearrange the order of the data members in the `Document` class in a way that minimizes the padding inserted by the compiler, by starting with types with the biggest alignment requirements. Let's create a new version of the `Document` class:

```
// Version 2 of Document class
class Document {
  double rank_{}; // Rearranged data members
  int id_{};
  bool is_cached_{};
};
```

With the rearrangement of the members, the compiler now only needs to pad after the is_cached_ data member to adjust for the alignment of Document. This is how the class will look after padding:

```
// Version 2 of Document class after padding
class Document {
  double rank_{};
  int id_{};
  bool is_cached_{};
  std::byte padding[3]; // Invisible padding inserted by compiler
};
```

The size of the new Document class is now only 16 bytes, compared to the first version, which was 24 bytes. The insight here should be that the size of an object can change just by changing the order in which its members are declared. We can also verify this by using the sizeof operator again on our updated version of Document:

```
std::cout << sizeof(Document) << '\n'; // Possible output is 16
```

The following image shows the memory layout of version 1 and version 2 of the Document class:

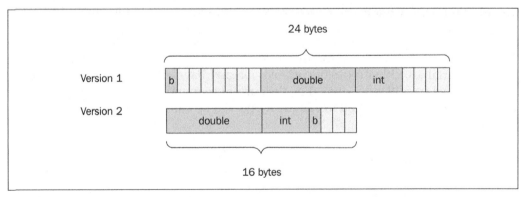

Figure 7.8: Memory layouts of the two versions of the Document class.
The size of an object can change just by changing the order in which its members are declared.

As a general rule, you can place the biggest data members at the beginning and the smallest members at the end. In this way, you can minimize the memory overhead caused by padding. Later on, we will see that we need to think about alignment when placing objects in memory regions that we have allocated, before we know the alignment of the objects that we are creating.

From a performance perspective, there can also be cases where you want to align objects to cache lines to minimize the number of cache lines an object spans over. While we are on the subject of cache friendliness, it should also be mentioned that it can be beneficial to place multiple data members that are frequently used together next to each other.

Keeping your data structures compact is important for performance. Many applications are bound by memory access time. Another important aspect of memory management is to never leak or waste memory for objects that are no longer needed. We can effectively avoid all sorts of resource leaks by being clear and explicit about the ownership of resources. This is the topic of the following section.

Memory ownership

Ownership of resources is a fundamental aspect to consider when programming. An owner of a resource is responsible for freeing the resource when it is no longer needed. A resource is typically a block of memory but could also be a database connection, a file handle, and so on. Ownership is important, regardless of which programming language you are using. However, it is more apparent in languages such as C and C++, since dynamic memory is not garbage-collected by default. Whenever we allocate dynamic memory in C++, we have to think about the ownership of that memory. Fortunately, there is now very good support in the language for expressing various types of ownership by using smart pointers, which we will cover later in this section.

The smart pointers from the standard library help us specify the ownership of dynamic variables. Other types of variables already have a defined ownership. For example, local variables are owned by the current scope. When the scope ends, the objects that have been created inside the scope will be automatically destroyed:

```
{
  auto user = User{};
} // user automatically destroys when it goes out of scope
```

Static and global variables are owned by the program and will be destroyed when the program terminates:

```
static auto user = User{};
```

Data members are owned by the instances of the class that they belong to:

```
class Game {
  User user; // A Game object owns the User object
  // ...
};
```

It is only dynamic variables that do not have a default owner, and it is up to the programmer to make sure that all the dynamically allocated variables have an owner to control the lifetime of the variables:

```
auto* user = new User{}; // Who owns user now?
```

With modern C++, we can write most of our code without explicit calls to new and delete, which is a great thing. Manually keeping track of calls to new and delete can very easily become an issue with memory leaks, double deletes, and other nasty bugs as a result. Raw pointers do not express any ownership, which makes ownership hard to track if we are only using raw pointers to refer to dynamic memory.

I recommend that you make ownership clear and explicit, but do strive to minimize manual memory management. By following a few fairly simple rules for dealing with the ownership of memory, you will increase the likelihood of getting your code clean and correct without leaking resources. The coming sections will guide you through some best practices for that purpose.

Handling resources implicitly

First, make your objects implicitly handle the allocation/deallocation of dynamic memory:

```
auto func() {
  auto v = std::vector<int>{1, 2, 3, 4, 5};
}
```

In the preceding example, we are using both stack and dynamic memory, but we don't have to explicitly call new and delete. The std::vector object we create is an automatic object that will live on the stack. Since it is owned by the scope, it will be automatically destroyed when the function returns. The std::vector object itself uses dynamic memory to store the integer elements. When v goes out of scope, its destructor can safely free the dynamic memory. This pattern of letting destructors free dynamic memory makes it fairly easy to avoid memory leaks.

While we are on the subject of freeing resources, I think it makes sense to mention RAII. **RAII** is a well-known C++ technique, short for **Resource Acquisition Is Initialization**, where the lifetime of a resource is controlled by the lifetime of an object. The pattern is simple but extremely useful for handling resources (memory included). But let's say, for a change, that the resource we need is some sort of connection for sending requests. Whenever we are done using the connection, we (the owners) must remember to close it. Here is an example of how it looks when we open and close the connection manually to send a request:

```
auto send_request(const std::string& request) {
  auto connection = open_connection("http://www.example.com/");
  send_request(connection, request);
  close(connection);
}
```

As you can see, we have to remember to close the connection after we have used it, or the connection will stay open (leak). In this example, it seems hard to forget, but once the code gets more complicated after inserting proper error handling and multiple exit paths, it will be hard to guarantee that the connection will always be closed. RAII solves this by relying on the fact that the lifetime of automatic variables is handled for us in a predictable way. What we need is an object that will have the same lifetime as the connection we get from the open_connection() call. We can create a class for this, called RAIIConnection:

```
class RAIIConnection {
public:
  explicit RAIIConnection(const std::string& url)
      : connection_{open_connection(url)} {}
  ~RAIIConnection() {
    try {
      close(connection_);
    }
    catch (const std::exception&) {
      // Handle error, but never throw from a destructor
    }
  }
  auto& get() { return connection_; }

private:
  Connection connection_;
};
```

The `Connection` object is now wrapped in a class that controls the lifetime of the connection (the resource). Instead of manually closing the connection, we can now let `RAIIConnection` handle this for us:

```
auto send_request(const std::string& request) {
  auto connection = RAIIConnection("http://www.example.com/");
  send_request(connection.get(), request);
  // No need to close the connection, it is automatically handled
  // by the RAIIConnection destructor
}
```

RAII makes our code safer. Even if `send_request()` would throw an exception here, the connection object would still be destructed and close the connection. We can use RAII for many types of resources, not just memory, file handles, and connections. Another example is `std::scoped_lock` from the C++ standard library. It tries to acquire a lock (mutex) on creation and then releases the lock on destruction. You can read more about `std::scoped_lock` in *Chapter 11, Concurrency*.

Now, we will explore more ways to make memory ownership explicit in C++.

Containers

You can use standard containers to handle a collection of objects. The container you use will own the dynamic memory it needs to store the objects you add to it. This is a very effective way of minimizing manual `new` and `delete` expressions in your code.

It's also possible to use `std::optional` to handle the lifetime of an object that might or might not exist. `std::optional` can be seen as a container with a maximum size of 1.

We won't talk more about the containers here, since they have already been covered in *Chapter 4, Data Structures*.

Smart pointers

The smart pointers from the standard library wrap a raw pointer and make the ownership of the object it points to explicit. When used correctly, there is no doubt about who is responsible for deleting a dynamic object. The three smart pointer types are: `std::unique_ptr`, `std::shared_ptr`, and `std::weak_ptr`. As their names suggest, they represent three types of ownership of an object:

- Unique ownership expresses that I, and only I, own the object. When I'm done using it, I will delete it.

- Shared ownership expresses that I own the object along with others. When no one needs the object anymore, it will be deleted.
- Weak ownership expresses that I'll use the object if it exists, but don't keep it alive just for me.

We'll deal with each of these types, respectively, in the following sections.

Unique pointer

The safest and least complicated ownership is unique ownership and should be the first thing that pops into your mind when thinking about smart pointers. Unique pointers represent unique ownership; that is, a resource is owned by exactly one entity. Unique ownership can be transferred to someone else, but it cannot be copied, since that would break its uniqueness. Here is how to use a `std::unique_ptr`:

```
auto owner = std::make_unique<User>("John");
auto new_owner = std::move(owner); // Transfer ownership
```

Unique pointers are also very efficient since they add very little performance overhead compared to ordinary raw pointers. The slight overhead is incurred by the fact that `std::unique_ptr` has a non-trivial destructor, which means that (unlike a raw pointer) it cannot be passed in a CPU register when being passed to a function. This makes them slower than raw pointers.

Shared pointer

Shared ownership means that an object can have multiple owners. When the last owner ceases to exist, the object will be deleted. This is a very useful pointer type but is also more complicated than the unique pointer.

The `std::shared_ptr` object uses reference counting to keep track of the number of owners an object has. When the counter reaches 0, the object will be deleted. The counter needs to be stored somewhere, so it does have some memory overhead compared to the unique pointer. Also, `std::shared_ptr` is internally thread-safe, so the counter needs to be updated atomically to prevent race conditions.

The recommended way of creating objects owned by shared pointers is to use `std::make_shared<T>()`. It is both safer (from an exception-safety point of view) and more efficient than creating the object manually with `new` and then passing it to a `std::shared_ptr` constructor. By overloading `operator new()` and `operator delete()` again to track allocations, we can conduct an experiment to find out why using `std::make_shared<T>()` is more efficient:

```
auto operator new(size_t size) -> void* {
  void* p = std::malloc(size);
  std::cout << "allocated " << size << " byte(s)" << '\n';
  return p;
}

auto operator delete(void* p) noexcept -> void {
  std::cout << "deleted memory\n";
  return std::free(p);
}
```

Now, let's try the recommended way first, using `std::make_shared()`:

```
int main() {
  auto i = std::make_shared<double>(42.0);
  return 0;
}
```

The output when running the program is as follows:

```
allocated 32 bytes
deleted memory
```

Now, let's allocate the `int` value explicitly by using `new` and then pass it to the `std::shared_ptr` constructor:

```
int main() {
  auto i = std::shared_ptr<double>{new double{42.0}};
  return 0;
}
```

The program will generate the following output:

```
allocated 4 bytes
allocated 32 bytes
deleted memory
deleted memory
```

We can conclude that the second version needs two allocations, one for the `double` and one for the `std::shared_ptr`, whereas the first version only needed one allocation. This also means that, by using `std::make_shared()`, our code will be more cache-friendly, thanks to spatial locality.

Weak pointer

Weak ownership doesn't keep any objects alive; it only allows us to use an object if someone else owns it. Why would you want such a fuzzy ownership as weak ownership? One common reason for using a weak pointer is to break a reference cycle. A reference cycle occurs when two or more objects refer to each other using shared pointers. Even if all external `std::shared_ptr` constructors are gone, the objects are kept alive by referring to themselves.

Why not just use a raw pointer? Isn't the weak pointer exactly what a raw pointer already is? Not at all. A weak pointer is safe to use since we cannot reference the object unless it actually exists, which is not the case with a dangling raw pointer. An example will clarify this:

```
auto i = std::make_shared<int>(10);
auto weak_i = std::weak_ptr<int>{i};

// Maybe i.reset() happens here so that the int is deleted...
if (auto shared_i = weak_i.lock()) {
  // We managed to convert our weak pointer to a shared pointer
  std::cout << *shared_i << '\n';
}
else {
  std::cout << "weak_i has expired, shared_ptr was nullptr\n";
}
```

Whenever we try to use the weak pointer, we need to convert it into a shared pointer first using the member function `lock()`. If the object hasn't expired, the shared pointer will be a valid pointer to that object; otherwise, we will get an empty `std::shared_ptr` back. This way, we can avoid dangling pointers when using `std::weak_ptr` instead of raw pointers.

This will end our section about objects in memory. C++ offers excellent support for dealing with memory, both regarding low-level concepts such as alignment and padding and high-level concepts such as object ownership.

Having a sound understanding of ownership, RAII, and reference counting are very important when working with C++. Programmers that are new to C++ and haven't been exposed to these concepts earlier might need some time to fully grasp this. At the same time, these concepts are not unique to C++. In most languages, they are more diffused, but in others, they are even more prominent (Rust is an example of the latter). So, once mastered, it will improve your programming skills in other languages as well. Thinking about object ownership will have a positive impact of the design and architecture of the programs you write.

Now, we will move on to an optimization technique that will reduce the usage of dynamic memory allocations and instead use the stack whenever possible.

Small object optimization

One of the great things about containers such as `std::vector` is that they automatically allocate dynamic memory when needed. Sometimes, though, the use of dynamic memory for container objects that only contain a few small elements can hurt performance. It would be more efficient to keep the elements in the container itself and only use stack memory, instead of allocating small regions of memory on the heap. Most modern implementations of `std::string` will take advantage of the fact that a lot of strings in a normal program are short, and that short strings are more efficient to handle without the use of heap memory.

One alternative is to keep a small separate buffer in the string class itself, which can be used when the string's content is short. This would increase the size of the string class, even when the short buffer is not used.

So, a more memory-efficient solution is to use a union, which can hold a short buffer when the string is in short mode and, otherwise, hold the data members it needs to handle a dynamically allocated buffer. The technique for optimizing a container for handling small data is usually referred to as small string optimization for strings, or small object optimization and small buffer optimization for other types. We have many names for the things we love.

A short code example will demonstrate how `std::string` from libc++ from LLVM behaves on my 64-bit system:

```
auto allocated = size_t{0};
// Overload operator new and delete to track allocations
void* operator new(size_t size) {
  void* p = std::malloc(size);
  allocated += size;
  return p;
}

void operator delete(void* p) noexcept {
  return std::free(p);
}

int main() {
  allocated = 0;
  auto s = std::string{""}; // Elaborate with different string sizes
```

```
    std::cout << "stack space = " << sizeof(s)
      << ", heap space = " << allocated
      << ", capacity = " << s.capacity() << '\n';
}
```

The code starts by overloading global operator new and operator delete for the purpose of tracking dynamic memory allocations. We can now start testing different sizes of the string s to see how std::string behaves. When building and running the preceding example in release mode on my system, it generates the following output:

```
stack space = 24, heap space = 0, capacity = 22
```

This output tells us that std::string occupies 24 bytes on the stack and that it has a capacity of 22 chars without using any heap memory. Let's verify that this is actually true by replacing the empty string with a string of 22 chars:

```
auto s = std::string{"1234567890123456789012"};
```

The program still produces the same output and verifies that no dynamic memory has been allocated. But what happens when we increase the string to hold 23 characters instead?

```
auto s = std::string{"12345678901234567890123"};
```

Running the program now produces the following output:

```
stack space = 24, heap space = 32, capacity = 31
```

The std::string class has now been forced to use the heap to store the string. It allocates 32 bytes and reports that the capacity is 31. This is because libc++ always stores a null-terminated string internally and, therefore, needs an extra byte at the end for the null character. It is still quite remarkable that the string class can be only 24 bytes and can hold strings of 22 characters in length without allocating any memory. How does it do this? As mentioned earlier, it is common to save memory by using a union with two different layouts: one for the short mode and one for the long mode. There is a lot of cleverness in the real libc++ implementation to make the maximum use of the 24 bytes that are available. The code here is simplified for the purpose of demonstrating this concept. The layout for the long mode looks like this:

```
struct Long {
  size_t capacity_{};
  size_t size_{};
  char* data_{};
};
```

Each member in the long layout is 8 bytes, so the total size is 24 bytes. The char pointer `data_` is a pointer to the dynamically allocated memory that will hold long strings. The layout of the short mode looks something like this:

```
struct Short {
  unsigned char size_{};
  char data_[23]{};
};
```

In the short mode, there is no need to use a variable for the capacity, since it is a compile-time constant. It is also possible to use a smaller type for the `size_` data member in this layout, since we know that the length of the string can only range from 0 to 22 if it is a short string.

Both layouts are combined using a union:

```
union u_ {
  Short short_layout_;
  Long long_layout_;
};
```

There is one piece missing, though: how can the string class know whether it is currently storing a short string or a long string? A flag is needed to indicate this, but where is it stored? It turns out that libc++ uses the least significant bit on the `capacity_` data member in the long mode, and the least significant bit on the `size_` data member in the short mode. For the long mode, this bit is redundant anyway since the string always allocates memory sizes that are multiples of 2. In the short mode, it is possible to use only 7 bits for storing the size so that one bit can be used for the flag. It becomes even more complicated when writing this code to handle big endian byte order, since the bit needs to be placed in memory at the same location, regardless of whether we are using the short struct or the long struct of the union. You can look up the details in the libc++ implementation at https://github.com/llvm/llvm-project/tree/master/libcxx.

Figure 7.9 summarizes our simplified (but still rather complicated) memory layout of the union used by an efficient implementation of the small string optimization:

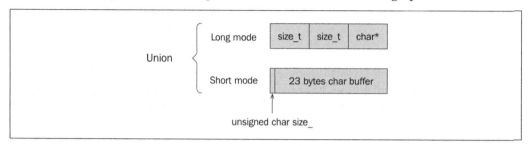

Figure 7.9: The union of the two different layouts used for handling short strings and long strings, respectively

Clever tricks like this are the reason that you should strive to use the efficient and well-tested classes provided by the standard library before you try to roll out your own. Nevertheless, knowing about these optimizations and how they work is important and useful, even if you never need to write one yourself.

Custom memory management

We have come a long way in this chapter now. We have covered the basics of virtual memory, the stack and the heap, the new and delete expressions, memory ownership, and alignment and padding. But before we close this chapter, we are going to show how to customize memory management in C++. We will see how the parts that we went through earlier in this chapter will come in handy when writing a custom memory allocator.

But first, what is a custom memory manager and why do we need one?

When using new or malloc() to allocate memory, we use the built-in memory management system in C++. Most implementations of operator new use malloc(), which is a general-purpose memory allocator. Designing and building a general-purpose memory manager is a complicated task, and there are many people who have already spent a lot of time researching this topic. Still, there are several reasons why you might want to write a custom memory manager. Here are some examples:

- **Debugging and diagnostics**: We have already done this a couple of times in this chapter by overloading operator new and operator delete, just to print out some debugging information.

- **Sandboxing**: A custom memory manager can provide a sandbox for code that isn't allowed to allocate unrestricted memory. The sandbox can also track memory allocations and release memory when the sandboxed code finishes executing.

- **Performance**: If we need dynamic memory and can't avoid allocations, we may have to write a custom memory manager that performs better for our specific needs. Later on, we will cover some of the circumstances that we could utilize to outperform `malloc()`.

With that said, many experienced C++ programmers have never faced a problem that actually required them to customize the standard memory manager that comes with the system. This is a good indication of how good the general-purpose memory managers actually are today, despite all the requirements they have to fulfill without any knowledge about our specific use cases. The more we know about the memory usage patterns in our application, the better the chances are that we can actually write something more efficient than `malloc()`. Remember the stack, for example? Allocating and deallocating memory from the stack is very fast compared to the heap, thanks to the fact that it doesn't need to handle multiple threads and that deallocations are guaranteed to always happen in reverse order.

Building a custom memory manager usually starts with analyzing the exact memory usage patterns and then implementing an arena.

Building an arena

Two frequently used terms when working with memory allocators are **arena** and **memory pool**. We will not distinguish between these terms in this book. By arena, I mean a block of contiguous memory, including a strategy for handing out parts of that memory and reclaiming it later on.

An arena could technically also be called a *memory resource* or an *allocator*, but those terms will be used to refer to abstractions from the standard library. The custom allocator we will develop later will be implemented using the arena we create here.

There are some general strategies that can be used when designing an arena that will make allocations and deallocations likely to perform better than `malloc()` and `free()`:

- **Single-threaded**: If we know that an arena will only be used from one thread, there is no need to protect data with synchronization primitives, such as locks or atomics. There is no risk that the client using the arena may be blocked by some other thread, which is important in real-time contexts.
- **Fixed-size allocations**: If the arena only hands out memory blocks of a fixed size, it is relatively easy to reclaim memory efficiently without memory fragmentation by using a free list.

- **Limited lifetime**: If you know that objects allocated from an arena only need to live during a limited and well-defined lifetime, the arena can postpone reclamation and free the memory all at once. An example could be objects created while handling a request in a server application. When the request has finished, all the memory that was handed out during the request can be reclaimed in one step. Of course, the arena needs to be big enough to handle all the allocations during the request without reclaiming memory continually; otherwise, this strategy will not work.

I will not go into further details about these strategies, but it is good to be aware of the possibilities when looking for ways to improve memory management in your program. As is often the case with optimizing software, the key is to understand the circumstances under which your program will run and to analyze the specific memory usage patterns. We do this to find ways to improve a custom memory manager compared to a general-purpose one.

Next, we will have a look at a simple arena class template, which can be used for small or few objects that need dynamic storage duration, but where the memory it needs usually is so small that it can be placed on the stack. This code is based on Howard Hinnant's `short_alloc`, published at `https://howardhinnant.github.io/stack_alloc.html`. This is a great place to start if you want to dig deeper into custom memory management. I think it is a good example for demonstration purposes because it can handle multiple sizes of objects, which require proper handling of alignment.

But again, keep in mind that this is a simplified version for demonstrating the concept rather than providing you with production-ready code:

```
template <size_t N>
class Arena {
  static constexpr size_t alignment = alignof(std::max_align_t);
public:
  Arena() noexcept : ptr_(buffer_) {}
  Arena(const Arena&) = delete;
  Arena& operator=(const Arena&) = delete;

  auto reset() noexcept { ptr_ = buffer_; }
  static constexpr auto size() noexcept { return N; }
  auto used() const noexcept {
    return static_cast<size_t>(ptr_ - buffer_);
  }
  auto allocate(size_t n) -> std::byte*;
  auto deallocate(std::byte* p, size_t n) noexcept -> void;
```

```
  private:
    static auto align_up(size_t n) noexcept -> size_t {
      return (n + (alignment-1)) & ~(alignment-1);
    }
    auto pointer_in_buffer(const std::byte* p) const noexcept -> bool {
      return std::uintptr_t(p) >= std::uintptr_t(buffer_) &&
             std::uintptr_t(p) < std::uintptr_t(buffer_) + N;
    }
    alignas(alignment) std::byte buffer_[N];
    std::byte* ptr_{};
};
```

The arena contains an `std::byte` buffer, whose size is determined at compile time. This makes it possible to create an arena object on the stack or as a variable with a static or thread local storage duration. The alignment might be allocated on the stack; hence, there is no guarantee that it will be aligned for types other than `char` unless we apply the `alignas` specifier to the array. The helper `align_up()` function may look complicated if you are not used to bitwise operations. However, it basically just rounds up to the alignment requirement that we use. The memory that this version will hand out will be the same as when using `malloc()` as it's suitable for any type. This is a bit wasteful if we use the arena for small types with smaller alignment requirements, but we'll ignore this here.

When reclaiming memory, we need to know whether the pointer we are asked to reclaim actually belongs to our arena. The `pointer_in_buffer()` function checks this by comparing a pointer address with the address range of the arena. As a side note, relationally comparing raw pointers to disjoint objects is undefined behavior; this might be used by an optimizing compiler and result in surprising effects. To avoid this, we are casting the pointers to `std::uintptr_t` before comparing the addresses. If you are curious about the details behind this, you can find a thorough explanation in the article *How to check if a pointer is in range of memory* by Raymond Chen at `https://devblogs.microsoft.com/oldnewthing/20170927-00/?p=97095`.

Next, we need the implementation of allocate and deallocate:

```
template<size_t N>
auto Arena<N>::allocate(size_t n) -> std::byte* {
  const auto aligned_n = align_up(n);
  const auto available_bytes =
    static_cast<decltype(aligned_n)>(buffer_ + N - ptr_);
  if (available_bytes >= aligned_n) {
    auto* r = ptr_;
```

```
      ptr_ += aligned_n;
      return r;
    }
    return static_cast<std::byte*>(::operator new(n));
}
```

The `allocate()` function returns a pointer to a correctly aligned memory with the specified size, n. If there is no available space in the buffer for the requested size, it will fall back to using operator new instead.

The following `deallocate()` function first checks whether the pointer to the memory to be deallocated is from the buffer, or has been allocated with operator new. If it is not from the buffer, we simply delete it with operator delete. Otherwise, we check whether the memory to be deallocated is the last memory we handed out from the buffer and, then, reclaim it by moving the current ptr_, just as a stack would do. We simply ignore other attempts to reclaim the memory:

```
template<size_t N>
auto Arena<N>::deallocate(std::byte* p, size_t n) noexcept -> void {
  if (pointer_in_buffer(p)) {
    n = align_up(n);
    if (p + n == ptr_) {
      ptr_ = p;
    }
  }
  else {
    ::operator delete(p);
  }
}
```

That's about it; our arena is now ready to be used. Let's use it when allocating User objects:

```
auto user_arena = Arena<1024>{};

class User {
public:
  auto operator new(size_t size) -> void* {
    return user_arena.allocate(size);
  }
  auto operator delete(void* p) -> void {
    user_arena.deallocate(static_cast<std::byte*>(p), sizeof(User));
  }
```

```
  auto operator new[](size_t size) -> void* {
    return user_arena.allocate(size);
  }
  auto operator delete[](void* p, size_t size) -> void {
    user_arena.deallocate(static_cast<std::byte*>(p), size);
  }
private:
  int id_{};
};

int main() {
  // No dynamic memory is allocated when we create the users
  auto user1 = new User{};
  delete user1;

  auto users = new User[10];
  delete [] users;

  auto user2 = std::make_unique<User>();
  return 0;
}
```

The `User` objects created in this example will all reside in the buffer of the `user_area` object. That is, no dynamic memory is allocated when we call `new` or `make_unique()` here. But there are other ways to create `User` objects in C++ that this example doesn't show. We will cover them in the next section.

A custom memory allocator

When trying out our custom memory manager with a specific type, it worked great! There is a problem, though. It turns out that the class-specific `operator new` is not called on all the occasions that we might have expected. Consider the following code:

```
auto user = std::make_shared<User>();
```

What happens when we want to have a `std::vector` of 10 users?

```
auto users = std::vector<User>{};
users.reserve(10);
```

In neither of the two cases is our custom memory manager being used. Why? Starting with the shared pointer, we have to go back to the example earlier where we saw that `std::make_shared()` actually allocates memory for both reference counting data and the object it should point to. There is no way that `std::make_shared()` can use an expression such as `new User()` to create the user object and the counter with only one allocation. Instead, it allocates memory and constructs the user object using placement new.

The `std::vector` object is similar. It doesn't construct 10 objects by default in an array when we call `reserve()`. This would have required a default constructor for all the classes to be used with the vector. Instead, it allocates memory that can be used for holding 10 user objects when they are being added. Again, placement new is the tool for making this possible.

Fortunately, we can provide a custom memory allocator to both `std::vector` and `std::shared_ptr` in order to have them use our custom memory manager. This is true for the rest of the containers in the standard library as well. If we don't supply a custom allocator, the containers will use the default `std::allocator<T>` class. So, what we need in order to use our arena is to write an allocator that can be used by the containers.

Custom allocators have been a hotly debated topic for a long time in the C++ community. Many custom containers have been implemented to control how memory is managed instead of using the standard containers with custom allocators, probably for good reasons.

However, the support and requirements for writing a custom allocator were improved in C++11, and are now a lot better. Here, we will only focus on allocators from C++11 and beyond.

A minimal allocator in C++11 now looks like this:

```
template<typename T>
struct Alloc {
  using value_type = T;
  Alloc();
  template<typename U> Alloc(const Alloc<U>&);
  T* allocate(size_t n);
  auto deallocate(T*, size_t) const noexcept -> void;
};
template<typename T>
auto operator==(const Alloc<T>&, const Alloc<T>&) -> bool;
template<typename T>
auto operator!=(const Alloc<T>&, const Alloc<T>&) -> bool;
```

It's really not that much code anymore, thanks to the improvements in C++11. The container that uses the allocator actually uses `std::allocator_traits`, which provides reasonable defaults if the allocator omits them. I recommend you have a look at the `std::allocator_traits` to see what traits can be configured and what the defaults are.

By using `malloc()` and `free()`, we could quite easily implement a minimal custom allocator. Here, we will show the old and famous `Mallocator`, first published in a blog post by Stephan T. Lavavej, to demonstrate how to write a minimal custom allocator using `malloc()` and `free()`. Since then, it has been updated for C++11 to make it even slimmer. Here is how it looks:

```cpp
template <class T>
struct Mallocator {

  using value_type = T;
  Mallocator() = default;

  template <class U>
  Mallocator(const Mallocator<U>&) noexcept {}

  template <class U>
  auto operator==(const Mallocator<U>&) const noexcept {
    return true;
  }

  template <class U>
  auto operator!=(const Mallocator<U>&) const noexcept {
    return false;
  }

  auto allocate(size_t n) const -> T* {
    if (n == 0) {
      return nullptr;
    }
    if (n > std::numeric_limits<size_t>::max() / sizeof(T)) {
      throw std::bad_array_new_length{};
    }
    void* const pv = malloc(n * sizeof(T));
    if (pv == nullptr) {
      throw std::bad_alloc{};
    }
    return static_cast<T*>(pv);
```

```
  }
  auto deallocate(T* p, size_t) const noexcept -> void {
    free(p);
  }
};
```

`Mallocator` is a **stateless allocator**, which means that the allocator instance itself doesn't have any mutable state; instead, it uses global functions for allocation and deallocation, namely `malloc()` and `free()`. A stateless allocator should always compare equal to the allocators of the same type. It indicates that memory allocated with `Mallocator` should also be deallocated with `Mallocator`, regardless of the `Mallocator` instance. A stateless allocator is the least complicated allocator to write, but it is also limited, since it depends on the global state.

To use our arena as a stack-allocated object, we will need a **stateful allocator** that can reference the arena instance. Here, the arena class that we implemented really starts to make sense. Say, for example, that we want to use one of the standard containers in a function to do some processing. We know that, most of the time, we are dealing with very small amounts of data that will fit on the stack. But once we use the containers from the standard library, they will allocate memory from the heap, which, in this case, will hurt our performance.

What are the alternatives to using the stack to manage data and avoid unnecessary heap allocations? One alternative is to build a custom container that uses a variation of the small object optimization we looked at for `std::string`.

It is also possible to use a container from Boost, such as `boost::container::small_vector`, which is based on LLVM's small vector. We advise you to check it out if you haven't already: `http://www.boost.org/doc/libs/1_74_0/doc/html/container/non_standard_containers.html`.

Yet another alternative, though, is to use a custom allocator, which we will explore next. Since we already have an arena template class ready, we could simply create the instance of an arena on the stack and have a custom allocator use it for the allocations. What we then need to do is implement a stateful allocator, which could hold a reference to the stack-allocated arena object.

Again, this custom allocator that we will implement is a simplified version of Howard Hinnant's `short_alloc`:

```
template <class T, size_t N>
struct ShortAlloc {

  using value_type = T;
  using arena_type = Arena<N>;
```

```
ShortAlloc(const ShortAlloc&) = default;
ShortAlloc& operator=(const ShortAlloc&) = default;

ShortAlloc(arena_type& arena) noexcept : arena_{&arena} { }

template <class U>
ShortAlloc(const ShortAlloc<U, N>& other) noexcept
    : arena_{other.arena_} {}

template <class U> struct rebind {
  using other = ShortAlloc<U, N>;
};
auto allocate(size_t n) -> T* {
  return reinterpret_cast<T*>(arena_->allocate(n*sizeof(T)));
}
auto deallocate(T* p, size_t n) noexcept -> void {
  arena_->deallocate(reinterpret_cast<std::byte*>(p), n*sizeof(T));
}
template <class U, size_t M>
auto operator==(const ShortAlloc<U, M>& other) const noexcept {
  return N == M && arena_ == other.arena_;
}
template <class U, size_t M>
auto operator!=(const ShortAlloc<U, M>& other) const noexcept {
  return !(*this == other);
}
template <class U, size_t M> friend struct ShortAlloc;

private:
  arena_type* arena_;
};
```

The allocator holds a reference to the arena. This is the only state the allocator has. The functions `allocate()` and `deallocate()` simply forward their requests to the arena. The compare operators ensure that two instances of the `ShortAlloc` type are using the same arena.

Now, the allocator and arena we implemented can be used with a standard container to avoid dynamic memory allocations. When we are using small data, we can handle all allocations using the stack instead. Let's see an example using `std::set`:

```
int main() {

  using SmallSet =
    std::set<int, std::less<int>, ShortAlloc<int, 512>>;

  auto stack_arena = SmallSet::allocator_type::arena_type{};
  auto unique_numbers = SmallSet{stack_arena};

  // Read numbers from stdin
  auto n = int{};
  while (std::cin >> n)
    unique_numbers.insert(n);

  // Print unique numbers
  for (const auto& number : unique_numbers)
    std::cout << number << '\n';
}
```

The program reads integers from standard input until the end-of-file is reached
(*Ctrl + D* on Unix-like systems and *Ctrl + Z* on Windows). It then prints the unique
numbers in ascending order. Depending on how many numbers are read from stdin,
the program will use stack memory or dynamic memory by using our ShortAlloc
allocator.

Using polymorphic memory allocators

If you have followed this chapter, you now know how to implement a custom
allocator that can be used with arbitrary containers, including those from the
standard library. Suppose we want to use our new allocator for some code we find
in our code base that is processing buffers of the type std::vector<int>, like this:

```
void process(std::vector<int>& buffer) {
  // ...
}

auto some_func() {
  auto vec = std::vector<int>(64);
  process(vec);
  // ...
}
```

We are eager to try out our new allocator, which is utilizing stack memory, and try to inject it like this:

```
using MyAlloc = ShortAlloc<int, 512>;  // Our custom allocator

auto some_func() {
  auto arena = MyAlloc::arena_type();
  auto vec = std::vector<int, MyAlloc>(64, arena);
  process(vec);
  // ...
}
```

When compiling, we come to the painful realization that `process()` is a function that expects `std::vector<int>`, and our vec variable is now of another type. GCC gives us the following error:

```
error: invalid initialization of reference of type 'const
std::vector<int>&' from expression of type 'std::vector<int,
ShortAlloc<int, 512> >
```

The reason for the type mismatch is that the custom allocator, `MyAlloc`, that we want to use is passed to `std::vector` as a template parameter and therefore becomes part of the type we instantiate. As a result, `std::vector<int>` and `std::vector<int, MyAlloc>` cannot be interchanged.

This may or may not be a problem for the use cases you are working on, and you could solve it by making the `process()` function accept a `std::span` or make it a generic function working with ranges instead of requiring a `std::vector`. Regardless, it's important to realize that the allocator actually becomes a part of the type when using allocator-aware template classes from the standard library.

What allocator is `std::vector<int>` using then? The answer is that `std::vector<int>` uses the default template argument which is `std::allocator`. So, writing `std::vector<int>` is equivalent to `std::vector<int, std::allocator<int>>`. The template class `std::allocator` is an empty class that uses global new and global delete when it fulfills allocation and deallocation requests from the container. This also means that the size of a container using an empty allocator is smaller than that of a container using our custom allocator:

```
std::cout << sizeof(std::vector<int>) << '\n';
// Possible output: 24

std::cout << sizeof(std::vector<int, MyAlloc>) << '\n';
// Possible output: 32
```

Checking the implementation of `std::vector` from libc++, we can see that it is using a nifty type called **compressed pair**, which, in turn, is based on the *empty base-class optimization* to get rid of the unnecessary storage usually occupied by a member of an empty class. We will not cover the details here, but if you are interested, you could have a look at the boost version of `compressed_pair`, which is documented at `https://www.boost.org/doc/libs/1_74_0/libs/utility/doc/html/compressed_pair.html`.

This problem of ending up with different types when using different allocators was addressed in C++17 by introducing an extra layer of indirection; all standard containers under the namespace `std::pmr` use the same allocator, namely `std::pmr::polymorphic_allocator`, which dispatches all allocation/deallocation requests to a **memory resource** class. So, instead of writing new custom memory allocators, we could use the general polymorphic memory allocator named `std::pmr::polymorphic_allocator` and instead write new custom memory resources that will be handed to the polymorphic allocator during construction. The memory resource is analogous to our `Arena` class, and the `polymorphic_allocator` is the extra layer of indirection that contains a pointer to the resource.

The following diagram shows the control flow as the vector delegates to its allocator instance and the allocator, in turn, delegates to the memory resource to which it points:

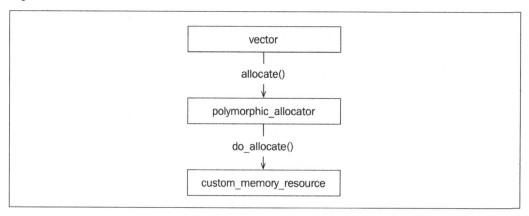

Figure 7.10: Allocating memory using a polymorphic_allocator

To start using the polymorphic allocator, we need to change the namespace from `std` to `std::pmr`:

```
auto v1 = std::vector<int>{};            // Uses std::allocator
auto v2 = std::pmr::vector<int>{/*...*/}; // Uses polymorphic_allocator
```

Writing a custom memory resource is relatively straightforward, especially with knowledge about memory allocators and arenas. But we might not even have to write a custom memory resource in order to achieve what we want. C++ already provides us with a few useful implementations that we should consider before writing our own. All memory resources derive from the base class `std::pmr::memory_resource`. The following memory resources live in the `<memory_resource>` header:

- `std::pmr::monotonic_buffer_resource`: This is quite similar to our `Arena` class. This class is preferable in scenarios when we're creating many objects with a short lifetime. Memory is freed only when the `monotonic_buffer_resource` instance is destructed, which makes allocations very fast.

- `std::pmr::unsynchronized_pool_resource`: This uses memory pools (also known as "slabs") containing fixed-size memory blocks, which avoids fragmentation within each pool. Each pool hands out memory for objects of a certain size. If you are creating many objects of a few different sizes, this class can be beneficial to use. This memory resource is not thread-safe and cannot be used from multiple threads unless you provide external synchronization.

- `std::pmr::synchronized_pool_resource`: This is a thread-safe version of `unsynchronized_pool_resource`.

Memory resources can be chained. When creating an instance of a memory resource, we can provide it with an **upstream memory resource**. This will be used if the current resource cannot handle the request (similar to what we did in `ShortAlloc` by using `malloc()` once our small buffer was full), or when the resource itself needs to allocate memory (such as when `monotonic_buffer_resource` needs to allocate its next buffer). The `<memory_resource>` header provides us with free functions that return pointers to global resource objects that are useful when specifying upstream resources:

- `std::pmr::new_delete_resource()`: Uses the global `operator new` and `operator delete`.

- `std::pmr::null_memory_resource()`: A resource that always throws `std::bad_alloc` whenever it is asked to allocate memory.

- `std::pmr::get_default_resource()`: Returns a globally default memory resource that can be set at runtime by `set_default_resource()`. The initial default resource is `new_delete_resource()`.

Let's see how we could rewrite our example from the last section, but this time using a `std::pmr::set`:

```
int main() {
    auto buffer = std::array<std::byte, 512>{};
```

```
auto resource = std::pmr::monotonic_buffer_resource{
  buffer.data(), buffer.size(), std::pmr::new_delete_resource()};

auto unique_numbers = std::pmr::set<int>{&resource};

auto n = int{};
while (std::cin >> n) {
  unique_numbers.insert(n);
}

for (const auto& number : unique_numbers) {
  std::cout << number << '\n';
}
}
```

We are passing a stack-allocated buffer to the memory resource, and then providing it with the object returned from new_delete_resource() as an upstream resource to be used if the buffer becomes full. If we would have omitted the upstream resource, it would have used the default memory resource, which, in this case, would have been the same since our code does not change the default memory resource.

Implementing a custom memory resource

Implementing a custom memory resource is fairly simple. We need to publicly inherit from std::pmr::memory_resource and then implement three pure virtual functions that will be invoked by the base class (std::pmr::memory_resource). Let's implement a simple memory resource that prints allocations and deallocations and then forwards the request to the default memory resource:

```
class PrintingResource : public std::pmr::memory_resource {
public:
  PrintingResource() : res_{std::pmr::get_default_resource()} {}

private:
  void* do_allocate(std::size_t bytes, std::size_t alignment)override {
    std::cout << "allocate: " << bytes << '\n';
    return res_->allocate(bytes, alignment);
  }
  void do_deallocate(void* p, std::size_t bytes,
                     std::size_t alignment) override {
    std::cout << "deallocate: " << bytes << '\n';
    return res_->deallocate(p, bytes, alignment);
  }
```

```
  bool do_is_equal(const std::pmr::memory_resource& other)
    const noexcept override {
    return (this == &other);
  }
  std::pmr::memory_resource* res_;   // Default resource
};
```

Note that we are saving the default resource in the constructor rather than calling get_default_resource() directly from do_allocate() and do_deallocate(). The reason for this is that someone could potentially change the default resource by calling set_default_resource() in the time between an allocation and a deallocation.

We can use a custom memory resource to track allocations made by a std::pmr container. Here is an example of using a std::pmr::vector:

```
auto res = PrintingResource{};
auto vec = std::pmr::vector<int>{&res};

vec.emplace_back(1);
vec.emplace_back(2);
```

A possible output when running the program is:

```
allocate: 4
allocate: 8
deallocate: 4
deallocate: 8
```

Something to be very careful about when using polymorphic allocators is that we are passing around raw non-owning pointers to memory resources. This is not specific to polymorphic allocators; we actually had the same problem with our Arena class and ShortAlloc as well, but this might be even easier to forget when using containers from std::pmr since these containers are using the same allocator type. Consider the following example:

```
auto create_vec() -> std::pmr::vector<int> {
  auto resource = PrintingResource{};
  auto vec = std::pmr::vector<int>{&resource}; // Raw pointer
  return vec;                                  // Ops! resource
}                                              // destroyed here

auto vec = create_vec();
vec.emplace_back(1);                           // Undefined behavior
```

Since the resource is destroyed when it goes out if scope at the end of `create_vec()`, our newly created `std::pmr::vector` is useless and will most likely crash when used.

This concludes our section on custom memory management. It is a complicated subject and if you feel tempted to use custom memory allocators to gain performance, I encourage you to carefully measure and analyze the memory access patterns in your application before you use and/or implement custom allocators. Typically, there are only a small set of classes or objects in an application that really need to be tweaked using custom allocators. At the same time, reducing the number of dynamic memory allocations in an application or grouping objects together, in certain regions of memory, can have a dramatic effect on performance.

Summary

This chapter has covered a lot of ground, starting with the basics of virtual memory and finally implementing a custom allocator that can be used by containers from the standard library. A good understanding of how your program uses memory is important. Overuse of dynamic memory can be a performance bottleneck that you might need to optimize away.

Before you start implementing your own containers or custom memory allocators, bear in mind that many people before you have probably had very similar memory issues to the ones you may face. So, there is a good chance that the right tool for you is already out there in a library. Building custom memory managers that are fast, safe, and robust is a challenge.

In the next chapter, you will learn how to benefit from the newly introduced feature of C++ concepts, and how we can use template metaprogramming to have the compiler generate code for us.

8

Compile-Time Programming

C++ has the ability to evaluate expressions at compile time, meaning that values are already calculated when the program executes. Even though metaprogramming has been possible since C++98, it was initially very complicated due to its complex template-based syntax. With the introduction of constexpr, if constexpr, and recently, C++ *concepts*, metaprogramming has become much more similar to writing regular code.

This chapter will give you a brief introduction to compile-time expression evaluations in C++ and how they can be used for optimization.

We will cover the following topics:

- Metaprogramming using C++ templates and how to write abbreviated function templates in C++20
- Inspecting and manipulating types at compile time using type traits
- Constant expressions that are evaluated by the compiler
- C++20 concepts and how to use them to add constraints to our template parameters
- Some real-world examples of metaprogramming

We will begin with an introduction to template metaprogramming.

Introduction to template metaprogramming

When writing regular C++ code, it is eventually transformed into machine code. **Metaprogramming**, on the other hand, allows us to write code that transforms itself into regular C++ code. In a more general sense, metaprogramming is a technique where we write code that transforms or generates some other code. By using metaprogramming, we can avoid duplicating code that only differs slightly based on the data types we use, or we can minimize runtime costs by precomputing values that can be known before the final program executes. There is nothing that stops us from generating C++ code by using other languages. We could, for example, do metaprogramming by using preprocessor macros extensively or writing a Python script that generates or modifies C++ files for us:

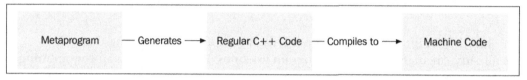

Figure 8.1: A metaprogram generates regular C++ code that will later be compiled into machine code

Even though we could use any language to produce regular code, with C++, we have the privilege of writing metaprograms within the language itself using **templates** and **constant expressions**. The C++ compiler can execute our metaprogram and generate regular C++ code that the compiler will further transform into machine code.

There are many advantages to doing metaprogramming directly within C++ using templates and constant expressions rather than using some other technique:

- We don't have to parse the C++ code (the compiler does that for us).
- There is excellent support for analyzing and manipulating C++ types when using C++ template metaprogramming.
- The code of the metaprogram and the regular non-generic code is mixed in the C++ source. Sometimes, this can make it hard to understand what parts are executed at runtime and compile time, respectively. However, in general, this is a very important aspect of making C++ metaprogramming effective to use.

In its simplest and most common form, template metaprogramming in C++ is used to generate functions, values, and classes that accept different types. A template is said to be **instantiated** when the compiler uses that template to generate a class or a function. Constant expressions are **evaluated** by the compiler to generate constant values:

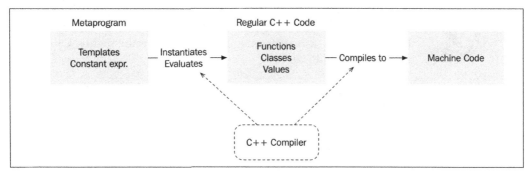

Figure 8.2: Compile-time programming in C++. The metaprogram that will generate regular C++ code is written in C++ itself.

This is a somewhat simplified view; there is nothing that says that the C++ compiler is required to perform the transformations in this way. However, it's useful to think about C++ metaprogramming being carried out in these two distinct phases:

- An initial phase, where templates and constant expressions produce regular C++ code of functions, classes, and constant values. This phase is usually called **constant evaluation**.

- A second phase, where the compiler eventually compiles the regular C++ code into machine code.

Later in this chapter, I will refer to C++ code generated from metaprogramming as *regular C++ code*.

When using metaprogramming, it is important to remember that its main use case is to make great libraries and, thereby, hide complex constructs/optimizations from the user code. Please note that however complex the interior of the code for the metaprogram may be, it's important to hide it behind a good interface so that the user codebase is easy to read and use.

Let's move on and create our first templates for generating function and classes.

Creating templates

Let's take a look at a simple pow() function and a Rectangle class. By using a **type template parameter**, the pow() function and the Rectangle class can be used with any integer or floating-point type. Without templates, we would have to create a separate function/class for every base type.

Writing metaprogramming code can be very complex; something that can make it easier is to imagine how the expected regular C++ code is intended to be.

Here is an example of a simple function template:

```
// pow_n accepts any number type
template <typename T>
auto pow_n(const T& v, int n) {
  auto product = T{1};
  for (int i = 0; i < n; ++i) {
    product *= v;
  }
  return product;
}
```

Using this function will generate a function whose return type is dependent on the template parameter type:

```
auto x = pow_n<float>(2.0f, 3); // x is a float
auto y = pow_n<int>(3, 3);      // y is an int
```

The explicit template argument types (`float` and `int` in this case) can (preferably) be omitted, and instead the compiler can figure this out on its own. This mechanism is called **template argument deduction** because the compiler *deduces* the template arguments. The following example will result in the same template instantiation as the one shown previously:

```
auto x = pow_n(2.0f, 3);  // x is a float
auto y = pow_n(3, 3);     // y is an int
```

Correspondingly, a simple class template can be defined as follows:

```
// Rectangle can be of any type
template <typename T>
class Rectangle {
public:
  Rectangle(T x, T y, T w, T h) : x_{x}, y_{y}, w_{w}, h_{h} {}
  auto area() const { return w_ * h_; }
  auto width() const { return w_; }
  auto height() const { return h_; }
private:
  T x_{}, y_{}, w_{}, h_{};
};
```

When a class template is utilized, we can explicitly specify the types that the template should generate the code for, like this:

```
auto r1 = Rectangle<float>{2.0f, 2.0f, 4.0f, 4.0f};
```

But it's also possible to benefit from **class template argument deduction (CTAD)**, and have the compiler deduce the argument type for us. The following code will instantiate a Rectangle<int>:

```
auto r2 = Rectangle{-2, -2, 4, 4};    // Rectangle<int>
```

A function template can then accept a Rectangle object where the rectangle dimensions are defined using an arbitrary type T, as follows:

```
template <typename T>
auto is_square(const Rectangle<T>& r) {
  return r.width() == r.height();
}
```

Type template parameters are the most common template parameters. Next, you will see how to use numeric parameters instead of type parameters.

Using integers as template parameters

Beyond general types, a template can also be of other types, such as integral types and floating-point types. In the following example, we will use an int in the template, which means that the compiler will generate a new function for every unique integer passed as a template argument:

```
template <int N, typename T>
auto const_pow_n(const T& v) {
  auto product = T{1};
  for (int i = 0; i < N; ++i) {
    product *= v;
  }
  return product;
}
```

The following code will oblige the compiler to instantiate two distinct functions: one squares the value and one cubes the value:

```
auto x2 = const_pow_n<2>(4.0f);   // Square
auto x3 = const_pow_n<3>(4.0f);   // Cube
```

Note the difference between the template parameter N and the function parameter v. For every value of N, the compiler generates a new function. However, v is passed as a regular parameter and, as such, does not result in a new function.

Providing specializations of a template

By default, the compiler will generate regular C++ code whenever we use a template with new parameters. But it's also possible to provide a custom implementation for certain values of the template parameters. Say, for example, that we want to provide the regular C++ code of our const_pow_n() function when it's used with integers and the value of N is 2. We could write a **template specialization** for this case, as follows:

```
template<>
auto const_pow_n<2, int>(const int& v) {
  return v * v;
}
```

For function templates, we need to fix *all* template parameters when writing a specialization. For example, it's not possible to only specify the value of N and let the type argument T be unspecified. However, for class templates, it is possible to specify only a subset of the template parameters. This is called **partial template specialization**. The compiler will choose the most specific template first.

The reason we cannot apply partial template specialization to functions is that functions can be overloaded (and classes cannot). If we were allowed to mix overloads and partial specialization, it would be very hard to comprehend.

How the compiler handles a template function

When the compiler handles a template function, it constructs a regular function with the template parameters expanded. The following code will make the compiler generate regular functions since it utilizes templates:

```
auto a = pow_n(42, 3);        // 1. Generate new function
auto b = pow_n(42.f, 2);      // 2. Generate new function
auto c = pow_n(17.f, 5);      // 3.
auto d = const_pow_n<2>(42.f); // 4. Generate new function
auto e = const_pow_n<2>(99.f); // 5.
auto f = const_pow_n<3>(42.f); // 6. Generate new function
```

Thus, when compiled, as distinguished from regular functions, the compiler will generate new functions for every unique set of *template parameters*. This means that it is the equivalent of manually creating four different functions that look something like this:

```
auto pow_n__float(float v, int n) {/*...*/}   // Used by: 1
auto pow_n__int(int v, int n) {/*...*/}       // Used by: 2 and 3
auto const_pow_n__2_float (float v) {/*...*/} // Used by: 4 and 5
auto const_pow_n__3_float(float v) {/*...*/}  // Used by: 6
```

This is important for understanding how metaprogramming works. The template code generates non-templated C++ code, which is then executed as regular code. If the generated C++ code does not compile, the error will be caught at compile time.

Abbreviated function templates

C++20 introduced a new abbreviated syntax for writing function templates by adopting the same style used by generic lambdas. By using auto for function parameter types, we are actually creating a function template rather than a regular function. Recall our initial pow_n() template, which was declared like this:

```
template <typename T>
auto pow_n(const T& v, int n) {
  // ...
```

Using the abbreviated function template syntax, we can instead declare it by using auto:

```
auto pow_n(const auto& v, int n) { // Declares a function template
  // ...
```

The difference between these two versions is that the abbreviated version doesn't have an explicit placeholder for the type of the variable v. And since we were using the placeholder T in our implementation, this code will unfortunately fail to compile:

```
auto pow_n(const auto& v, int n) {
  auto product = T{1}; // Error: What is T?
  for (int i = 0; i < n; ++i) {
    product *= v;
  }
  return product;
}
```

To fix this, we can use the decltype specifier.

Receiving the type of a variable with decltype

The `decltype` specifier is used to retrieve the type of a variable and is used when an explicit type name is not available.

Sometimes, we need an explicit placeholder for a type but none are available, only the variable name is. This happened to us in our implementation of the `pow_n()` function previously, when using the abbreviated function template syntax.

Let's look at an example of using `decltype` by fixing our implementation of `pow_n()`:

```
auto pow_n(const auto& v, int n) {
  auto product = decltype(v){1};    // Instead of T{1}
  for (int i = 0; i < n; ++i) { product *= v; }
  return product;
}
```

Although this code compiles and works, we are a bit lucky since the type of v is actually a const reference and not the type we want for the variable `product`. We can get around this by using the left-to-right declaration style. But trying to rewrite the line where the product is defined to something that would appear to be identical reveals a problem:

```
auto pow_n(const auto& v, int n) {
  decltype(v) product{1};
  for (int i = 0; i < n; ++i) { product *= v; } // Error!
  return product;
}
```

Now, we are getting a compilation error since `product` is a const reference and may not be assigned to a new value.

What we really want is to get rid of the const reference from the type of v when defining the variable `product`. We could use a handy template called `std::remove_cvref` for this purpose. Our definition of `product` would then look like this instead:

```
typename std::remove_cvref<decltype(v)>::type product{1};
```

Phew! In this particular case, it would probably have been easier to stick with our initial `template <typename T>` syntax. But now, you have learned how to use `std::remove_cvref` together with `decltype`, which is a common pattern when writing generic C++ code.

Before C++20, it was common to see `decltype` in the body of generic lambdas. However, it is now possible to avoid the rather inconvenient `decltype` by adding explicit template parameters to generic lambdas:

```
auto pow_n = []<class T>(const T& v, int n) {
  auto product = T{1};
  for (int i = 0; i < n; ++i) { product *= v; }
  return product;
};
```

In the definition of the lambda, we are writing `<class T>` in order to get an identifier for the type of the argument that can be used inside the body of the function.

It might take some time to get accustomed to using `decltype` and utilities for manipulating types. Maybe `std::remove_cvref` looks a bit mysterious at first. It's a template from the `<type_traits>` header, which we will look further into in the next section.

Type traits

When doing template metaprogramming, you may often find yourself in situations where you need information about the types you are dealing with at compile time. When writing regular (non-generic) C++ code, we work with concrete types that we have complete knowledge about, but this is not the case when writing a template; the concrete types are not determined until a template is being instantiated by the compiler. Type traits let us extract information about the types our templates are dealing with in order to generate efficient and correct C++ code.

In order to extract information about template types, the standard library provides a type traits library, which is available in the `<type_traits>` header. All type traits are evaluated at compile time.

Type trait categories

There are two categories of type traits:

- Type traits that return information about a type as a boolean or an integer value.
- Type traits that return a new type. These type traits are also called metafunctions.

The first category returns `true` or `false`, depending on the input, and ends with `_v` (short for value).

 The `_v` postfix was added in C++17. If your library implementation does not provide `_v` postfixes for type traits, then you can use the older version, `std::is_floating_point<float>::value`. In other words, remove the `_v` extension and add `::value` at the end.

Here are some examples of compile-time type checking using type traits for fundamental types:

```
auto same_type = std::is_same_v<uint8_t, unsigned char>;
auto is_float_or_double = std::is_floating_point_v<decltype(3.f)>;
```

Type traits can also be used on user-defined types:

```
class Planet {};
class Mars : public Planet {};
class Sun {};
static_assert(std::is_base_of_v<Planet, Mars>);
static_assert(!std::is_base_of_v<Planet, Sun>);
```

The second category of type traits returns a new type and ends with _t (short for type). These type trait transformations (or metafunctions) come in handy when dealing with pointers and references:

```
// Examples of type traits which transforms types
using value_type = std::remove_pointer_t<int*>;  // -> int
using ptr_type = std::add_pointer_t<float>;      // -> float*
```

The type trait std::remove_cvref that we used earlier is also part of this category. It removes the reference part (if any) and the const and volatile qualifiers from a type. std::remove_cvref was introduced in C++20. Before that, it was conventional to use std::decay for this task.

Using type traits

As already mentioned, all type traits are evaluated at compile time. For example, this function, which returns 1 if the value is greater than or equal to zero and -1 otherwise, can immediately return 1 for unsigned integers, as follows:

```
template<typename T>
auto sign_func(T v) -> int {
  if (std::is_unsigned_v<T>) {
    return 1;
  }
  return v < 0 ? -1 : 1;
}
```

Since type traits are evaluated at compile time, the compiler will generate the code shown in the following table when invoked with an unsigned and signed integer, respectively:

Used with an unsigned integer...	...generated function:
```auto unsigned_v = uint32_t{42};``` ```auto sign = sign_func(unsigned_v);```	```int sign_func(uint32_t v) {``` ``` if (true) {``` ``` return 1;``` ``` }``` ``` return v < 0 ? -1 : 1;``` ```}```
Used with a signed integer...	**...generated function:**
```auto signed_v = int32_t{-42};``` ```auto sign = sign_func(signed_v);```	```int sign_func(int32_t v) {``` ``` if (false) {``` ``` return 1;``` ``` }``` ``` return v < 0 ? -1 : 1;``` ```}```

Table 8.1: Based on the type we pass to sign_func() (in the left column), different functions is generated by the compiler (in the right column).

Next, let's talk about constant expressions.

Programming with constant expressions

An expression prefixed with the constexpr keyword tells the compiler that the expression should be evaluated at compile time:

```
constexpr auto v = 43 + 12; // Constant expression
```

The constexpr keyword can also be used with functions. In that case, it tells the compiler that a certain function is intended to be evaluated at compile time if all the conditions allowing for compile-time evaluation are fulfilled. Otherwise, it will execute at runtime, like a regular function.

A constexpr function has a few restrictions; it is not allowed to do the following:

- Handle local static variables
- Handle thread_local variables
- Call any function, which, in itself, is not a constexpr function

With the constexpr keyword, writing a compile-time evaluated function is as easy as writing a regular function since its parameters are regular parameters instead of template parameters.

Consider the following `constexpr` function:

```
constexpr auto sum(int x, int y, int z) { return x + y + z; }
```

Let's call the function like this:

```
constexpr auto value = sum(3, 4, 5);
```

Since the result of `sum()` is used in a constant expression and all its parameters can be determined at compile time, the compiler will generate the following regular C++ code:

```
const auto value = 12;
```

This is then compiled into machine code, as usual. In other words, the compiler evaluates a `constexpr` function and generates regular C++ code where the result is calculated.

If we called `sum()` instead and stored the result in a variable that is *not* marked with `constexpr`, the compiler *might* (most likely) evaluate `sum()` at compile time:

```
auto value = sum(3, 4, 5); // value is not constexpr
```

In summary, if a `constexpr` function is invoked from a constant expression and all its arguments are constant expressions, it is guaranteed to be evaluated at compile time.

Constexpr functions in a runtime context

In the previous example, the summed values (3, 4, 5) were known to the compiler at compile time, but how do `constexpr` functions handle variables whose values are not known until runtime? As mentioned in the previous section, `constexpr` is an indicator to the compiler that a function, under certain conditions, can be evaluated at compile time. If variables with values are unknown until the runtime is invoked, they will be evaluated just like regular functions.

In the following example, the values of x, y, and z are provided from the user at runtime, and therefore, it would be impossible for the compiler to calculate the sum at compile time:

```
int x, y, z;
std::cin >> x >> y >> z;       // Get user input
auto value = sum(x, y, z);
```

If we didn't intend to use `sum()` during runtime at all, we could prohibit such usage by making it an immediate function.

Declaring immediate functions using consteval

A `constexpr` function can be called at runtime or compile time. If we want to limit the uses of a function so that it's only invoked at compile time, we can do that by using the keyword `consteval` instead of `constexpr`. Let's assume that we want to prohibit all uses of `sum()` at runtime. With C++20, we can do that with the following code:

```
consteval auto sum(int x, int y, int z) { return x + y + z; }
```

A function that is declared using `consteval` is called an **immediate function** and can only produce constants. If we want to call `sum()`, we need to call it from within a constant expression, or the compilation will fail:

```
constexpr auto s = sum(1, 2, 3); // OK
auto x = 10;
auto s = sum(x, 2, 3);           // Error, expression is not const
```

The compiler will also complain if we try to use `sum()` with parameters that are not known at compile time:

```
int x, y, z;
std::cin >> x >> y >> z;
constexpr auto s = sum(x, y, z); // Error
```

Let's discuss the `if constexpr` statement next.

The if constexpr statement

The `if constexpr` statement allows template functions to evaluate different scopes in the same function at compile time (also called compile-time polymorphism). Take a look at the following example, where a function template called `speak()` tries to differentiate member functions, depending on the type:

```
struct Bear { auto roar() const { std::cout << "roar\n"; } };
struct Duck { auto quack() const { std::cout << "quack\n"; } };

template <typename Animal>
auto speak(const Animal& a) {
  if (std::is_same_v<Animal, Bear>) { a.roar(); }
  else if (std::is_same_v<Animal, Duck>) { a.quack(); }
}
```

Let's say we compile the following lines:

```
auto bear = Bear{};
speak(bear);
```

The compiler will then generate a `speak()` function, similar to this:

```
auto speak(const Bear& a) {
  if (true) { a.roar(); }
  else if (false) { a.quack(); } // This line will not compile
}
```

As you can see, the compiler will keep the call to the member function, `quack()`, which will then fail to compile since `Bear` does not contain a `quack()` member function. This happens even though the `quack()` member function will never be executed due to the `else if (false)` statement.

In order to make the `speak()` function compile, regardless of the type, we need to inform the compiler that we'd like to completely ignore the scope if the `if` statement is `false`. Conveniently, this is exactly what `if constexpr` does.

Here is how we can write the `speak()` function with the ability to handle both `Bear` and `Duck`, even though they do not share a common interface:

```
template <typename Animal>
auto speak(const Animal& a) {
  if constexpr (std::is_same_v<Animal, Bear>) { a.roar(); }
  else if constexpr (std::is_same_v<Animal, Duck>) { a.quack(); }
}
```

When `speak()` is invoked with `Animal == Bear`, as follows:

```
auto bear = Bear{};
speak(bear);
```

the compiler generates the following function:

```
auto speak(const Bear& animal) { animal.roar(); }
```

When `speak()` is invoked with `Animal == Duck`, as follows:

```
auto duck = Duck{};
speak(duck);
```

the compiler generates the following function:

```
auto speak(const Duck& animal) { animal.quack(); }
```

If speak() is invoked with any other primitive type, such as Animal == int, as follows:

```
speak(42);
```

the compiler generates an empty function:

```
auto speak(const int& animal) {}
```

Unlike a regular if statement, the compiler is now able to generate multiple different functions: one using Bear, another one using Duck, and a last one if the type is neither Bear nor Duck. If we want to make this third case a compilation error, we can do that by adding an else case with a static_assert:

```
template <typename Animal>
auto speak(const Animal& a) {
  if constexpr (std::is_same_v<Animal, Bear>) { a.roar(); }
  else if constexpr (std::is_same_v<Animal, Duck>) { a.quack(); }
  else { static_assert(false); } // Trig compilation error
}
```

We will talk more about the usefulness of static_assert later.

As mentioned earlier, the way constexpr is being used here can be referred to as compile-time polymorphism. So, how does it relate to runtime polymorphism?

Comparison with runtime polymorphism

As a side note, if we were to implement the previous example with traditional runtime polymorphism, using inheritance and virtual functions to achieve the same functionality, the implementation would look as follows:

```
struct AnimalBase {
  virtual ~AnimalBase() {}
  virtual auto speak() const -> void {}
};
struct Bear : public AnimalBase {
  auto roar() const { std::cout << "roar\n"; }
  auto speak() const -> void override { roar(); }
};
struct Duck : public AnimalBase {
  auto quack() const { std::cout << "quack\n"; }
  auto speak() const -> void override { quack(); }
};
```

```
auto speak(const AnimalBase& a) {
  a.speak();
}
```

The objects have to be accessed using pointers or references, and the type is inferred at *runtime*, which results in a performance loss compared with the compile-time version, where everything is available when the application executes. The following image shows the difference between the two types of polymorphism in C++:

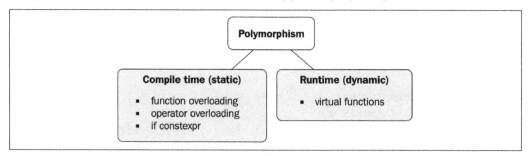

Figure 8.3: Runtime polymorphism is supported by virtual functions whereas compile time polymorphism is supported by function/operator overloading and if constexpr.

Now, we will continue to see how we can use if constexpr for something more useful.

Example of the generic modulus function using if constexpr

This example will show you how to use if constexpr to distinguish between operators and global functions. In C++, the % operator is used to get the modulus of integers, while std::fmod() is used for floating-point types. Say we'd like to generalize our codebase and create a generic modulus function called generic_mod().

If we were to implement generic_mod() with a regular if statement, as follows:

```
template <typename T>
auto generic_mod(const T& v, const T& n) -> T {
  assert(n != 0);
  if (std::is_floating_point_v<T>) { return std::fmod(v, n); }
  else { return v % n; }
}
```

it would fail if invoked with T == float as the compiler would generate the following function, which would fail to compile:

```
auto generic_mod(const float& v, const float& n) -> float {
  assert(n != 0);
  if (true) { return std::fmod(v, n); }
  else { return v % n; } // Will not compile
}
```

Even though the application cannot reach it, the compiler will generate the line `return v % n;`, which isn't compliant with `float`. The compiler doesn't care that the application cannot reach it—since it cannot generate an assembly for it, it will fail to compile.

As in the previous example, we will change the `if` statement to an `if constexpr` statement:

```
template <typename T>
auto generic_mod(const T& v, const T& n) -> T {
  assert(n != 0);
  if constexpr (std::is_floating_point_v<T>) {
    return std::fmod(v, n);
  } else {                    // If T is a floating point,
    return v % n;             // this code is eradicated
  }
}
```

Now, when the function is invoked with a floating-point type, it will generate the following function, where the `v % n` operation is eradicated:

```
auto generic_mod(const float& v, const float& n) -> float {
  assert(n != 0);
  return std::fmod(v, n);
}
```

The runtime `assert()` tells us that we cannot call this function if the second argument is 0.

Checking programming errors at compile time

Assert statements are a simple but very powerful tool for validating invariants and contracts between callers and callees in a codebase, (see *Chapter 2, Essential C++ Techniques*.) It's possible to check programming errors while executing the program using `assert()`. But we should always strive to detect errors as early as possible, and if we have a constant expression, we can catch programming errors when compiling the program using `static_assert()`.

Using assert to trigger errors at runtime

Review the templated version of pow_n(). Let's say we want to prevent it from being called with negative exponents (the n value). To prevent this in the runtime version, where n is a regular argument, we can add a runtime assertion:

```
template <typename T>
auto pow_n(const T& v, int n) {
  assert(n >= 0); // Only works for positive numbers
  auto product = T{1};
  for (int i = 0; i < n; ++i) {
    product *= v;
  }
  return product;
}
```

If the function is called with a negative value for n, the program will break and inform us where we should start looking for the bug. This is good, but it would be even better if we could track this error at compile time rather than runtime.

Using static_assert to trigger errors at compile time

If we do the same to the template version, we can utilize static_assert(). The static_assert() declaration, unlike a regular assert, will refuse to compile if the condition isn't fulfilled. So, it's better to break the build than have a program break at runtime. In the following example, if the template parameter N is a negative number, static_assert() will prevent the function from compiling:

```
template <int N, typename T>
auto const_pow_n(const T& v) {
  static_assert(N >= 0, "N must be positive");
  auto product = T{1};
  for (int i = 0; i < N; ++i) {
    product *= v;
  }
  return product;
}

auto x = const_pow_n<5>(2);  // Compiles, N is positive
auto y = const_pow_n<-1>(2); // Does not compile, N is negative
```

In other words, with regular variables, the compiler is only aware of the type and has no idea what it contains. With compile-time values, the compiler knows both the type and the value. This allows the compiler to calculate other compile-time values.

 Instead of using an int and assert that it's non-negative, we could (should) have used an unsigned int instead. We are only using a signed int in this example to demonstrate the use of assert() and static_assert().

Using compile-time asserts is one way to check constraints at compile time. It is a simple but very useful tool. The support for compile-time programming has seen some very exciting progress over the last few years in C++. Now, we will move on to one of the biggest features from C++20 that takes constraints checking to a new level.

Constraints and concepts

So far, we have covered quite a few important techniques for writing C++ metaprograms. You have seen how templates can generate concrete classes and functions for us with excellent support from the type traits library. Furthermore, you have seen how the use of constexpr, consteval, and if constexpr can help us move computations from runtime to compile time. In that way, we can detect programming errors at compile time and write programs with lower runtime costs. This is great, but there is still plenty of room for improvement when it comes to writing and consuming generic code in C++. Some of the issues that we haven't addressed yet include:

1. Interfaces are too generic. When using a template with some arbitrary type, it's hard to know what the requirements of that type are. This makes the templates hard to use if we only inspect the template interface. Instead, we have to rely on documentation or dig deep into the implementation of a template.

2. Type errors are caught late by the compiler. The compiler will eventually check the types when compiling the regular C++ code, but the error messages are usually hard to interpret. Instead, we would like type errors to be caught in the instantiation phase.

3. Unconstrained template parameters make metaprogramming hard. The code we have written so far in this chapter has used unconstrained template parameters, with the exception of a few static asserts. This is manageable for small examples, but it would be much easier to write and reason about our metaprograms if we could have access to more meaningful types, in the same way the type system helps us write correct non-generic C++ code.

4. Conditional code generation (compile-time polymorphism) can be performed using `if constexpr`, but it quickly becomes hard to read and write at a larger scale.

As you will see in this section, C++ concepts address these issues in an elegant and effective way by introducing two new keywords: `concept` and `requires`. Before exploring constraints and concepts, we will spend some time considering the shortcomings of template metaprogramming without concepts. Then, we will use constraints and concepts to strengthen our code.

An unconstrained version of a Point2D template

Suppose we are writing a program that deals with a two-dimensional coordinate system. We have a class template that represents a point with x and y coordinates, as follows:

```
template <typename T>
class Point2D {
public:
  Point2D(T x, T y) : x_{x}, y_{y} {}
  auto x() { return x_; }
  auto y() { return y_; }
  // ...
private:
  T x_{};
  T y_{};
};
```

Let's assume that we need to find the Euclidean distance between two points, **p1** and **p2**, as illustrated here:

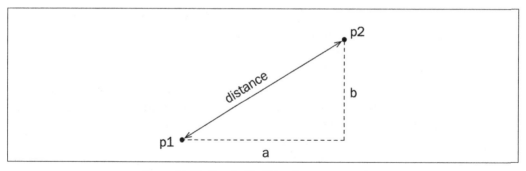

Figure 8.4: Finding the Euclidean between p1 and p2

To compute the distance, we implement a free function that takes two points and uses the Pythagorean theorem (the actual math is of less importance here):

```cpp
auto dist(auto p1, auto p2) {
  auto a = p1.x() - p2.x();
  auto b = p1.y() - p2.y();
  return std::sqrt(a*a + b*b);
}
```

A small test program verifies that we can instantiate the Point2D template with integers and compute the distance between the two points:

```cpp
int main() {
  auto p1 = Point2D{2, 2};
  auto p2 = Point2D{6, 5};
  auto d = dist(p1, p2);
  std::cout << d;
}
```

This code compiles and runs fine and outputs 5 to the console.

Generic interfaces and bad error messages

Before moving on, let's take a short detour and reflect for a while on the function template dist(). Let's imagine that we didn't have easy access to the implementation of dist() and only could read the interface:

```cpp
auto dist(auto p1, auto p2) // Interface part
```

What can we say about the return type and the types of p1 and p2? Practically nothing—because p1 and p2 are completely *unconstrained*, the interface of dist() does not reveal anything for us. This doesn't mean that we can pass anything to dist(), though, because in the end, the generated regular C++ code has to compile.

For example, if we try to instantiate our dist() template with two integers instead of Point2D objects like this:

```cpp
auto d = dist(3, 4);
```

the compiler will gladly generate a regular C++ function, similar to this:

```cpp
auto dist(int p1, int p2) {
  auto a = p1.x() - p2.x();  // Will generate an error:
  auto b = p1.y() - p2.y();  // int does not have x() and y()
```

```
    return std::sqrt(a*a + b*b);
}
```

The error will be caught later on when the regular C++ code is checked by the compiler. Clang generates the following error message when trying to instantiate dist() with two integers:

```
error: member reference base type 'int' is not a structure or union
auto a = p1.x() - p2.y();
```

This error message refers to the *implementation* of dist(), something that the caller of the function dist() shouldn't need to know about. This is a trivial example, but trying to interpret error messages caused by providing wrong types to templates from sophisticated template libraries can be a real challenge.

Even worse, if we are really unlucky, we get through the entire compilation by providing types that don't make sense at all. In this case, we are instantiating a Point2D with const char*:

```
int main() {
    auto from = Point2D{"2.0", "2.0"}; // Ouch!
    auto to = Point2D{"6.0", "5.0"};   // Point2D<const char*>
    auto d = dist(from, to);
    std::cout << d;
}
```

It compiles and runs, but the output is probably not what we would expect. We want to catch these sorts of errors earlier on in the process, something we can achieve by using constraints and concepts as shown in the image below:

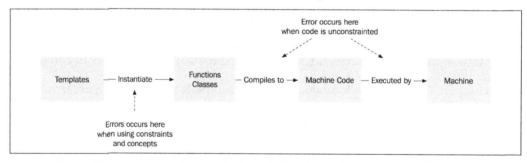

Figure 8.5: Type errors can be caught at instantiation phase using constraints and concepts

Later on, you will see how this code can be made more expressive so that it is easier to use correctly and harder to misuse. We will do this by adding concepts and constraints to our code. But first, I will provide a quick overview of how to define and use concepts.

A syntactic overview of constraints and concepts

This section is a short introduction to constraints and concepts. We will not cover them completely in this book but I will provide you with enough material to be productive.

Defining new concepts

Defining new concepts is straightforward with some help from the type traits that you are already familiar with. The following example defines the concept FloatingPoint using the keyword concept:

```
template <typename T>
concept FloatingPoint = std::is_floating_point_v<T>;
```

The right-hand side of the assignment expression is where we can specify the constraints of the type T. It's also possible to combine multiple constraints using || (logical OR) and && (logical AND). The following example uses || to combine floats and integrals into a Number concept:

```
template <typename T>
concept Number = FloatingPoint<T> || std::is_integral_v<T>;
```

You will note that, it's possible to build concepts using already defined concepts on the right-hand side as well. The standard library contains a <concepts> header, which defines many useful concepts, such as std::floating_point (which we should use rather than defining our own).

Furthermore, we can use the requires keyword to add a set of statements that should be added to our concept definition. For example, this is the definition of the concept std::range from the Ranges library:

```
template<typename T>
concept range = requires(T& t) {
  ranges::begin(t);
  ranges::end(t);
};
```

In short, this concept states that a range is something that we can pass to std::ranges::begin() and std::ranges::end().

It's possible to write more sophisticated requires clauses than this, and you will see more on that later on.

Constraining types with concepts

We can add constraints to template parameter types by using the `requires` keyword. The following template can only be instantiated with the parameters of integral types by using the concept `std::integral`:

```
template <typename T>
requires std::integral<T>
auto mod(T v, T n) {
  return v % n;
}
```

We can use the same technique when defining class templates:

```
template <typename T>
requires std::integral<T>
struct Foo {
  T value;
};
```

An alternative syntax allows us to write this in a more compact way by replacing the `typename` directly with the concept:

```
template <std::integral T>
auto mod(T v, T n) {
  return v % n;
}
```

This form can also be used with class templates:

```
template <std::integral T>
struct Foo {
  T value;
};
```

If we want to use the abbreviated function template form when defining a function template, we can add the concept in front of the `auto` keyword:

```
auto mod(std::integral auto v, std::integral auto n) {
  return v % n;
}
```

The return type can also be constrained by using concepts:

```
std::integral auto mod(std::integral auto v, std::integral auto n) {
  return v % n;
}
```

As you can see, there are many ways to specify the same thing. The abbreviated form combined with concepts has really made it easy to both read and write constrained function templates. Another powerful feature of C++ concepts is the ability to overload functions in a clear and expressive way.

Function overloading

Recall the generic_mod() function we implemented earlier using if constexpr. It looked something like this:

```
template <typename T>
auto generic_mod(T v, T n) -> T {
  if constexpr (std::is_floating_point_v<T>) {
    return std::fmod(v, n);
  } else {
    return v % n;
  }
}
```

By using concepts, we can overload a function template similar to how we would have done if we'd written a regular C++ function:

```
template <std::integral T>
auto generic_mod(T v, T n) -> T {          // Integral version
  return v % n;
}

template <std::floating_point T>
auto generic_mod(T v, T n) -> T {          // Floating point version
  return std::fmod(v, n);
}
```

With your new knowledge of constraints and concepts, it's time to go back to our example with the Point2D template and see how it can be improved.

A constrained version of the Point2D template

Now that you know how to define and use concepts, let's put them to use by writing a better version of our templates, Point2D and dist(). Remember that what we're aiming for is a more expressive interface and to have errors caused by irrelevant parameter types appear at template instantiation.

We will begin by creating a concept for arithmetic types:

```
template <typename T>
concept Arithmetic = std::is_arithmetic_v<T>;
```

Next, we will create a concept called `Point` that defines that a point should have the member functions `x()` and `y()` return the same type, and that this type should support arithmetic operations:

```
template <typename T>
concept Point = requires(T p) {
  requires std::is_same_v<decltype(p.x()), decltype(p.y())>;
  requires Arithmetic<decltype(p.x())>;
};
```

This concept can now make the interface of `dist()` much better with explicit constraints:

```
auto dist(Point auto p1, Point auto p2) {
  // Same as before ...
```

This is starting to look really promising, so let's just add a constraint to our return type as well. Although `Point2D` might be instantiated with an integral type, we know that the distance can be a floating-point number. The concept `std::floating_point` from the standard library is well suited for this. Here is the final version of `dist()`:

```
std::floating_point auto dist(Point auto p1, Point auto p2) {
  auto a = p1.x() - p2.x();
  auto b = p1.y() - p2.y();
  return std::sqrt(a*a + b*b);
}
```

Our interface is now more descriptive, and when we try to instantiate it with wrong parameter types, we will get errors during the instantiation phase rather than the final compilation phase.

We should now do the same to our `Point2D` template to avoid someone accidentally instantiating it with types that it wasn't intended to handle. For example, we would like to prevent someone from instantiating a `Point2D` class with `const char*`, like this:

```
auto p1 = Point2D{"2.0", "2.0"}; // How can we prevent this?
```

We have already created the `Arithmetic` concept, which we can use here to put constraints in the template parameter of `Point2D`. Here is how we do this:

```
template <Arithmetic T> // T is now constrained!
class Point2D {
public:
  Point2D(T x, T y) : x_{x}, y_{y} {}
  auto x() { return x_; }
  auto y() { return y_; }
  // ...
private:
  T x_{};
  T y_{};
};
```

The only thing we needed to change was to specify that the type `T` should support the operations specified by the concept `Arithmetic`. Trying to instantiate a template using `const char*` will now generate a direct error message while the compiler tries to instantiate a `Point2D<const char*>` class.

Adding constraints to your code

The usefulness of concepts reaches far beyond template metaprogramming. It's a fundamental feature of C++20 that changes how we write and reason about code using concepts other than concrete types or completely unconstrained variables declared with `auto`.

A concept is very similar to a type (such as `int`, `float`, or `Plot2D<int>`). Both types and concepts specify a set of supported operations on an object. By inspecting a type or a concept, we can determine how certain objects can be constructed, moved, compared, and accessed by member functions and so on. A big difference, though, is that a concept does not say anything about how an object is stored in memory, whereas a type provides this information in addition to its set of supported operations. For example, we can use the `sizeof` operator on a type but not on a concept.

With concepts and `auto`, we can declare variables without the need for spelling out the exact type, but still express the intent with our code very clearly. Have a look at the following code snippet:

```
const auto& v = get_by_id(42); // What can I do with v?
```

Most of the time, when we stumble upon code like this, we are interested in knowing what operations we can perform on v rather than knowing the exact type. Adding a concept in front of auto makes the difference:

```
const Person auto& v = get_by_id(42);
v.get_name();
```

It's possible to use concepts in almost all contexts where we can use the keyword auto: local variables, return values, function arguments, and so forth. Using concepts in our code makes it easier to read. At the time of writing this book (mid 2020), there is currently no additional support for concepts in the established C++ IDEs. However, it is just a matter of time before code completion, as well as other useful editor features based on concepts, will be available and make C++ coding both more fun and safer.

Concepts in the standard library

C++20 also included a new <concepts> header with predefined concepts. You have already seen some of them in action. Many concepts are based on the traits from the type traits library. However, there are a few fundamental concepts that have not been expressed with traits previously. Among the most important ones are the comparison concepts such as std::equality_comparable and std::totally_ordered, as well as the object concepts such as std::movable, std::copyable, std::regular, and std::semiregular. We will not spend any more time on the concepts from the standard library but remember to keep them in mind before starting to define your own. Defining concepts on the correct level of generality is not trivial and it's usually wise to define new concepts based on the already existing ones.

Let's end this chapter by having a look at some real-world examples of metaprogramming in C++.

Real-world examples of metaprogramming

Advanced metaprogramming can appear to be very academic, so in order to demonstrate its usefulness, let's look at some examples that not only demonstrate the syntax of metaprogramming, but how it can be used in practice.

Example 1: creating a generic safe cast function

When casting between data types in C++, there is a multitude of different ways things can go wrong:

- You might lose a value if casting to an integer type of a lower bit length.
- You might lose a value if casting a negative value to an unsigned integer.
- If casting from a pointer to any other integer than uintptr_t, the correct address might become incorrect. This is because C++ only guarantees that uintptr_t is the only integer type that can withhold an address.
- If casting from double to float, the result might be int if the double value is too large for float to withhold.
- If casting between pointers with a static_cast(), we might get undefined behavior if the types aren't sharing a common base class.

In order to make our code more robust, we can create a generic checked cast function that verifies our casts in debug mode and performs our casts as fast as possible if in release mode.

Depending on the types that are being cast, different checks are performed. If we try to cast between types that are not verified, it won't compile.

These are the cases safe_cast() is intended to handle:

- **Same type**: Obviously, if we're casting the same type, we just return the input value.
- **Pointer to pointer**: If casting between pointers, safe_cast() performs a dynamic cast in debug mode to verify it is castable.
- **Double to floating point**: safe_cast() accepts precision loss when casting from double to float with one exception – if casting from a double to a float, there is a chance the double is too large for the float to handle the result.
- **Arithmetic to arithmetic**: If casting between arithmetic types, the value is cast back to its original type to verify no precision has been lost.
- **Pointer to non-pointer**: If casting from a pointer to a non-pointer type, safe_cast() verifies that the destination type is an uintptr_t or intptr_t, the only integer types that are guaranteed to hold an address.

In any other case, the safe_cast() function fails to compile.

Let's see how we can implement this. We start by fetching information about our cast operation in constexpr booleans. The reason they are constexpr booleans and not const booleans is that we will utilize them later in if constexpr expressions, which require constexpr conditions:

```cpp
template <typename T> constexpr auto make_false() { return false; }
template <typename Dst, typename Src>
auto safe_cast(const Src& v) -> Dst{
  using namespace std;
  constexpr auto is_same_type = is_same_v<Src, Dst>;
  constexpr auto is_pointer_to_pointer =
    is_pointer_v<Src> && is_pointer_v<Dst>;
  constexpr auto is_float_to_float =
    is_floating_point_v<Src> && is_floating_point_v<Dst>;
  constexpr auto is_number_to_number =
    is_arithmetic_v<Src> && is_arithmetic_v<Dst>;
  constexpr auto is_intptr_to_ptr =
    (is_same_v<uintptr_t,Src> || is_same_v<intptr_t,Src>)
    && is_pointer_v<Dst>;
  constexpr auto is_ptr_to_intptr =
    is_pointer_v<Src> &&
    (is_same_v<uintptr_t,Dst> || is_same_v<intptr_t,Dst>);
```

So, now that we have all the necessary information about the cast as constexpr booleans, we assert at compile time that we can perform the cast. As mentioned previously, a static_assert() will fail to compile if the condition is not satisfied (unlike a regular assert, which verifies conditions at runtime).

Note the usage of static_assert() and make_false<T> at the end of the if/else chain. We cannot just type static_assert(false) as that would prevent safe_cast() from compiling at all; instead, we utilize the template function make_false<T>() to delay the generation until required.

When the actual static_cast() is performed, we cast back to the original type and verify that the result is equal to the uncasted argument using a regular runtime assert() This way, we can make sure the static_cast() has not lost any data:

```cpp
if constexpr(is_same_type) {
  return v;
}
else if constexpr(is_intptr_to_ptr || is_ptr_to_intptr){
  return reinterpret_cast<Dst>(v);
}
else if constexpr(is_pointer_to_pointer) {
```

```
    assert(dynamic_cast<Dst>(v) != nullptr);
    return static_cast<Dst>(v);
  }
  else if constexpr (is_float_to_float) {
    auto casted = static_cast<Dst>(v);
    auto casted_back = static_cast<Src>(v);
    assert(!isnan(casted_back) && !isinf(casted_back));
    return casted;
  }
  else if constexpr (is_number_to_number) {
    auto casted = static_cast<Dst>(v);
    auto casted_back = static_cast<Src>(casted);
    assert(casted == casted_back);
    return casted;
  }
  else {
    static_assert(make_false<Src>(),"CastError");
    return Dst{}; // This can never happen,
    // the static_assert should have failed
  }
}
```

Note how we use the `if constexpr` in order for the function to conditionally compile. If we use a regular `if` statement, the function will fail to compile:

```
auto x = safe_cast<int>(42.0f);
```

This is because the compiler will try to compile the following line and `dynamic_cast` only accepts pointers:

```
// type To is an integer
assert(dynamic_cast<int>(v) != nullptr); // Does not compile
```

However, thanks to the `if constexpr` and `safe_cast<int>(42.0f)` constructs, the following function compiles properly:

```
auto safe_cast(const float& v) -> int {
  constexpr auto is_same_type = false;
  constexpr auto is_pointer_to_pointer = false;
  constexpr auto is_float_to_float = false;
  constexpr auto is_number_to_number = true;
  constexpr auto is_intptr_to_ptr = false;
  constexpr auto is_ptr_to_intptr = false
  if constexpr(is_same_type) { /* Eradicated */ }
```

```
    else if constexpr(is_intptr_to_ptr||is_ptr_to_intptr){/* Eradicated */}
    else if constexpr(is_pointer_to_pointer) {/* Eradicated */}
    else if constexpr(is_float_to_float) {/* Eradicated */}
    else if constexpr(is_number_to_number) {
      auto casted = static_cast<int>(v);
      auto casted_back = static_cast<float>(casted);
      assert(casted == casted_back);
      return casted;
    }
    else { /* Eradicated */ }
  }
```

As you can see, except for the is_number_to_number clause, everything in-between the if constexpr statements has been completely eradicated, allowing the function to compile.

Example 2: hash strings at compile time

Let's say we have a resource system consisting of an unordered map of strings that identifies bitmaps. If a bitmap is already loaded, the system returns the loaded bitmap; otherwise, it loads the bitmap and returns it:

```
// External function which loads a bitmap from the filesystem
auto load_bitmap_from_filesystem(const char* path) -> Bitmap {/* ... */}

// Bitmap cache
auto get_bitmap_resource(const std::string& path) -> const Bitmap& {
  // Static storage of all loaded bitmaps
  static auto loaded = std::unordered_map<std::string, Bitmap>{};
  // If the bitmap is already in loaded_bitmaps, return it
  if (loaded.count(path) > 0) {
    return loaded.at(path);
  }
  // The bitmap isn't already loaded, load and return it
  auto bitmap = load_bitmap_from_filesystem(path.c_str());
  loaded.emplace(path, std::move(bitmap));
  return loaded.at(path);
}
```

The bitmap cache is then utilized wherever a bitmap resource is needed:

- If it's not loaded yet, the get_bitmap_resource() function will load and return it

- If it's already been loaded somewhere else, the get_bitmap_resource() will simply return the loaded function

So, independent of which of these draw functions is executed first, the second one will not have to load the bitmap from disk:

```
auto draw_something() {
  const auto& bm = get_bitmap_resource("my_bitmap.png");
  draw_bitmap(bm);
}
auto draw_something_again() {
  const auto& bm = get_bitmap_resource("my_bitmap.png");
  draw_bitmap(bm);
}
```

Since we are using an unordered map, we need to compute a hash value whenever we check for a bitmap resource. You will now see how we can optimize the runtime code by moving computations to compile time.

The advantages of the compile-time hash sum calculation

The problem that we will try to solve is that every time the line get_bitmap_resource("my_bitmap.png") is executed, the application will compute the hash sum of the string "my_bitmap.png" at runtime. What we would like to do is perform this calculation at compile time so that when the application executes, the hash sum has already been calculated. In other words, just as you have learned to use metaprogramming to generate functions and classes at compile time, we will now have it generate the hash sum at compile time.

You might have already come to the conclusion that this is a so-called *micro-optimization*: calculating the hash sum of a small string won't affect the application's performance at all as it is such a tiny operation. That is probably completely true; this is just an example of how to move a calculation from runtime to compile time, and there might be other instances where this can make a significant performance impact.

As a side note, when writing software for weak hardware, string hashing is a pure luxury, but hashing strings at compile time gives us this luxury on any platform since everything is computed at compile time.

Implementing and verifying a compile-time hash function

In order to enable the compiler to calculate the hash sum at compile time, we rewrite hash_function() so that it takes a raw null-terminated char string as a parameter of an advanced class like std::string, which cannot be evaluated at compile time. Now, we can mark hash_function() as constexpr:

```
constexpr auto hash_function(const char* str) -> size_t {
  auto sum = size_t{0};
  for (auto ptr = str; *ptr != '\0'; ++ptr)
    sum += *ptr;
  return sum;
}
```

Now, let's invoke this with a raw literal string known at compile time:

```
auto hash = hash_function("abc");
```

The compiler will generate the following piece of code, which is the sum of the ASCII values corresponding to a, b, and c (97, 98, and 99):

```
auto hash = size_t{294};
```

Just accumulating the individual values is a very bad hash function; do not do this in a real-world application. It's only here because it's easy to grasp. A better hash function would be to combine all the individual characters with boost::hash_combine(), as explained in *Chapter 4, Data Structures.*

hash_function() will only evaluate at compile time if the compiler knows the string at compile time; if not, the compiler will execute constexpr at runtime, just like any other expression.

Now that we have the hash function in place, it's time to create a string class that uses it.

Constructing a PrehashedString class

We are now ready to implement a class for pre-hashed strings that will use the hash function we created. This class consists of the following:

- A constructor that takes a raw string as a parameter and calculates the hash at construction.

- Comparison operators.

- A get_hash() member function, which returns the hash.

- An overload of std::hash(), which simply returns the hash value. This overload is used by std::unordered_map, std::unordered_set, or any other class from the standard library that uses hash values. To put it simply, this makes the container aware that a hash function exists for the PrehashedString.

Here is a basic implementation of a PrehashedString class:

```cpp
class PrehashedString {
public:
  template <size_t N>
  constexpr PrehashedString(const char(&str)[N])
      : hash_{hash_function(&str[0])},
        size_{N - 1}, // The subtraction is to avoid null at end
        strptr_{&str[0]} {}
  auto operator==(const PrehashedString& s) const {
    return
      size_ == s.size_ &&
      std::equal(c_str(), c_str() + size_, s.c_str());
  }
  auto operator!=(const PrehashedString& s) const {
    return !(*this == s); }
  constexpr auto size()const{ return size_; }
  constexpr auto get_hash()const{ return hash_; }
  constexpr auto c_str()const->const char*{ return strptr_; }
private:
  size_t hash_{};
  size_t size_{};
  const char* strptr_{nullptr};
};

namespace std {
template <>
struct hash<PrehashedString> {
  constexpr auto operator()(const PrehashedString& s) const {
    return s.get_hash();
  }
};
} // namespace std
```

Note the template trick in the constructor. This forces the `PrehashedString` to only accept compile-time string literals. The reason for this is that the `PrehashedString` class does not own the `const char*` ptr and therefore we may only use it with string literals created at compile time:

```
// This compiles
auto prehashed_string = PrehashedString{"my_string"};

// This does not compile
// The prehashed_string object would be broken if the str is modified
auto str = std::string{"my_string"};
auto prehashed_string = PrehashedString{str.c_str()};

// This does not compile.
// The prehashed_string object would be broken if the strptr is deleted
auto* strptr = new char[5];
auto prehashed_string = PrehashedString{strptr};
```

So, now that we have everything in place, let's see how the compiler handles `PrehashedString`.

Evaluating PrehashedString

Here is a simple test function that returns the hash value for the string "abc" (used for simplicity):

```
auto test_prehashed_string() {
  const auto& hash_fn = std::hash<PrehashedString>{};
  const auto& str = PrehashedString("abc");
  return hash_fn(str);
}
```

Since our hash function simply sums the values, and the letters in "abc" have ASCII values of $a = 97$, $b = 98$, and $c = 99$, the assembler (generated by Clang) should output the sum $97 + 98 + 99 = 294$ somewhere. Inspecting the assembler, we can see that the `test_prehashed_string()` function compiles to exactly one `return` statement, which returns 294:

```
mov eax, 294
ret
```

This means that the whole `test_prehashed_string()` function has been executed at compile time; when the application executes, the hash sum has already been calculated!

Evaluating get_bitmap_resource() with PrehashedString

Let's return to our original get_bitmap_resource() function, the std::string, which was originally used and exchanged for a PrehashedString:

```
// Bitmap cache
auto get_bitmap_resource(const PrehashedString& path) -> const Bitmap&
{
  // Static storage of all loaded bitmaps
  static auto loaded_bitmaps =
    std::unordered_map<PrehashedString, Bitmap>{};
  // If the bitmap is already in loaded_bitmaps, return it
  if (loaded_bitmaps.count(path) > 0) {
    return loaded_bitmaps.at(path);
  }
  // The bitmap isn't already loaded, load and return it
  auto bitmap = load_bitmap_from_filesystem(path.c_str());
  loaded_bitmaps.emplace(path, std::move(bitmap));
  return loaded_bitmaps.at(path);
}
```

We also need a function to test with:

```
auto test_get_bitmap_resource() { return get_bitmap_resource("abc"); }
```

What we would like to know is whether this function precalculated the hash sum. Since get_bitmap_resource() does quite a lot (constructing a static std::unordered_map, inspecting the map, and so on), the resulting assembly is about 500 lines. Nevertheless, if our magic hash sum is found in the assembler, this means that we have succeeded.

When inspecting the assembler generated by Clang, we will find a line that corresponds to our hash sum, 294:

```
.quad   294                     # 0x126
```

To confirm this, we will change the string from "abc" to "aaa", which should change this line in the assembler to 97 * 3 = 291, but everything else should be exactly the same.

We're doing this to make sure this wasn't just some other magic number that popped up, totally unrelated to the hash sum.

Inspecting the resulting assembler, we will find the desired result:

```
.quad    291                    # 0x123
```

Everything, except this line, is the same, so we can safely assume that the hash is calculated at compile time.

The examples we have looked at demonstrate that we can use compile-time programming for very different things. Adding safety checks that can be verified at compile time allows us to find bugs without running the program and searching for errors with coverage tests. And moving expensive runtime operations to compile time makes our final program faster.

Summary

In this chapter, you have learned how to use metaprogramming to generate functions and values at compile time instead of runtime. You also discovered how to do this in a modern C++ way by using templates, the constexpr, static_assert(), and if constexpr, type traits, and concepts. Moreover, with constant string hashing, you saw how to use compile-time evaluation in a practical context.

In the next chapter, you will learn how to further expand your C++ toolbox so that you can create libraries by constructing hidden proxy objects.

9

Essential Utilities

This chapter will introduce some essential classes from the C++ **Utility library**. Some of the metaprogramming techniques presented in the previous chapter will be used in order to work effectively with collections that contain elements of different types.

C++ containers are homogenous, meaning that they can only store elements of one single type. A `std::vector<int>` stores a collection of integers and all objects stored in a `std::list<Boat>` are of type `Boat`. But sometimes, we need to keep track of a collection of elements of different types. I will refer to these collections as **heterogenous collections**. In a heterogeneous collection, the elements may have different types. The following figure shows an example of a homogenous collection of `int`s and a heterogenous collection with elements of different types:

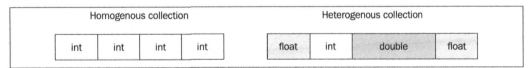

Figure 9.1: Homogenous and heterogenous collections

This chapter will cover a set of useful templates from the C++ Utility library that can be used to store multiple values of various types. The chapter is divided into four sections:

- Representing optional values with `std::optional`
- Fixed size collections using `std::pair`, `std::tuple`, and `std::tie()`
- Dynamically sized collections using the standard containers with elements of type `std::any` and `std::variant`
- Some real-world examples that demonstrate the usefulness of `std::tuple` and `std::tie()`, together with the metaprogramming concepts we covered in *Chapter 8, Compile-Time Programming*

Let's begin by exploring `std::optional` and some of its important use cases.

Representing optional values with std::optional

Although quite a minor feature from C++17, `std::optional` is a nice addition to the standard library. It simplifies a common case that couldn't be expressed in a clean and straightforward way prior to `std::optional`. In a nutshell, it is a small wrapper for any type where the wrapped type can be either initialized or uninitialized.

To put it in C++ lingo, `std::optional` is a *stack-allocated container with a max size of one*.

Optional return values

Before the introduction of `std::optional`, there was no clear way to define functions that may not return a defined value, such as the intersection point of two line segments. With the introduction of `std::optional`, such optional return values can be clearly expressed. What follows is an implementation of a function that returns an optional intersection between two lines:

```cpp
// Prerequisite
struct Point { /* ... */ };
struct Line { /* ... */ };

auto lines_are_parallel(Line a, Line b) -> bool { /* ... */ }
auto compute_intersection(Line a, Line b) -> Point { /* ... */ }

auto get_intersection(const Line& a, const Line& b)
  -> std::optional<Point>
{
  if (lines_are_parallel(a, b))
    return std::optional{compute_intersection(a, b)};
  else
    return {};
}
```

The syntax of std::optional resembles that of a pointer; the value is accessed by operator*() or operator->(). Trying to access the value of an empty optional using operator*() or operator->() is undefined behavior. It's also possible to access the value using the value() member function, which instead will throw an std::bad_optional_access exception if the optional contains no value. What follows is a simple example of a returned std::optional:

```
auto set_magic_point(Point p) { /* ... */ }
auto intersection = get_intersection(line0, line1);
if (intersection.has_value()) {
  set_magic_point(*intersection);
}
```

> The object held by a std::optional is always stack allocated, and the memory overhead for wrapping a type into a std::optional is the size of a bool (usually one byte), plus possible padding.

Optional member variables

Let's say we have a class that represents a human head. The head can have a hat of some sort, or no hat at all. By using std::optional to represent the hat member variable, the implementation is as expressive as it can be:

```
struct Hat { /* ... */ };

class Head {
public:
  Head() { assert(!hat_); }      // hat_ is empty by default
  auto set_hat(const Hat& h) {
    hat_ = h;
  }
  auto has_hat() const {
    return hat_.has_value();
  }
  auto& get_hat() const {
    assert(hat_.has_value());
    return *hat_;
```

```
  }
  auto remove_hat() {
    hat_ = {};         // Hat is cleared by assigning to {}
  }
private:
  std::optional<Hat> hat_;
};
```

Without `std::optional`, representing an optional member variable would rely on, for example, a pointer or an extra `bool` member variable. Both have disadvantages such as allocating on the heap, or accidentally accessing an optional considered empty without a warning.

Avoiding empty states in enums

A pattern that can be seen in old C++ code bases is *empty states* or *null states* in enums. Here is an example:

```
enum class Color { red, blue, none };  // Don't do this!
```

In the preceding enum, none is a so-called null state. The reason for adding the none value in the `Color` enum is to make it possible to represent an optional color, for example:

```
auto get_color() -> Color; // Returns an optional color
```

However, with this design, there is no way to represent a non-optional color, which makes it necessary for *all* code to handle the extra null state none.

A better alternative is to avoid the extra null state, and instead represent an optional color with the type `std::optional<Color>`:

```
enum class Color { red, blue };
auto get_color() -> std::optional<Color>;
```

This clearly indicates that we might not get a color back. But we also know that once we have a `Color` object, there is no way it can be null:

```
auto set_color(Color c) { /* c is a valid color, now use it ... */ }
```

When implementing `set_color()`, we know that the client has passed a valid color.

Sorting and comparing std::optional

The `std::optional` is equally comparable and sortable using the rules shown in the following table:

Two *empty* optional values are considered equal.	An empty optional is considered *less* than a non-empty.
```auto a = std::optional<int>{}; auto b = std::optional<int>{}; auto c = std::optional<int>{4}; assert(a == b); assert(b != c);```	```auto a = std::optional<int>{}; auto b = std::optional<int>{4}; auto c = std::optional<int>{5}; assert(a < b); assert(b < c);```

Therefore, if you sort a container of `std::optional<T>`, the empty optional values will end up at the beginning of the container, whereas the non-empty optionals will be sorted as usual, as follows:

```
auto c = std::vector<std::optional<int>>{{3}, {}, {1}, {}, {2}};
std::sort(c.begin(), c.end());
// c is {}, {}, {1}, {2}, {3}
```

If you are in the habit of representing optional values using pointers, designing APIs using out parameters, or adding special null states in enums, it's time to add `std::optional` to your toolbox, as it provides an efficient and safe alternative to these anti-patterns.

Let's continue by exploring collections of a fixed size that can hold elements of different types.

Fixed size heterogenous collections

The C++ Utility library includes two class templates that can be used for storing multiple values of different types: `std::pair` and `std::tuple`. They are both collections with a fixed size. Just like `std::array`, it's not possible to add more values dynamically at runtime.

The big difference between `std::pair` and `std::tuple` is that `std::pair` can only hold two values, whereas `std::tuple` can be instantiated with an arbitrary size at compile time. We will begin with a brief introduction to `std::pair` before moving on to `std::tuple`.

Using std::pair

The class template `std::pair` lives in the `<utility>` header and has been available in C++ since the introduction of the standard template library. It is used in the standard library where algorithms need to return two values, such as `std::minmax()`, which can return both the smallest and the greatest value of an initializer list:

```
std::pair<int, int> v = std::minmax({4, 3, 2, 4, 5, 1});
std::cout << v.first << " " << v.second;     // Outputs: "1 5"
```

The preceding example shows that the elements of a `std::pair` can be accessed through the members `first` and `second`.

Here, the `std::pair` holds values of the same type, so, it would have been possible to return an array here as well. But what makes `std::pair` even more interesting is that it can hold values of *different* types. This is the reason why we consider this a heterogeneous collection, despite the fact that it can only hold two values.

An example from the standard library where `std::pair` holds different values is the associative container `std::map`. The value type of `std::map` is a pair that consists of the key and the element that the key is associated with:

```
auto scores = std::map<std::string, int>{};
scores.insert(std::pair{"Neo", 12}); // Correct but ineffecient
scores.emplace("Tri", 45);           // Use emplace() instead
scores.emplace("Ari", 33);

for (auto&& it : scores) { // "it" is a std::pair
  auto key = it.first;
  auto val = it.second;
  std::cout << key << ": " << val << '\n';
}
```

The requirement to explicitly name the `std::pair` type has decreased, and in modern C++, it's common to use initializer lists and structured bindings to hide the fact that we are dealing with values of `std::pair`. The following example expresses the same thing but without mentioning the underlying `std::pair` explicitly:

```
auto scores = std::map<std::string, int> {
  {"Neo", 12},                            // Initializer Lists
  {"Tri", 45},
  {"Ari", 33}
};
```

```
for (auto&& [key, val] : scores) {        // Structured bindings
  std::cout << key << ": " << val << '\n';
}
```

We will talk more about structured binding later in this chapter.

As the name suggests, `std::pair` can only hold two values. C++11 introduced a new utility class called `std::tuple`, which is a generalization of `std::pair` that can hold an arbitrary number of elements.

The std::tuple

The `std::tuple` can be used as a fixed-size heterogeneous collection that can be declared to be of any size. In contrast to `std::vector`, for example, its size cannot change at runtime; you cannot add or remove elements.

A tuple can be constructed with its member types explicitly specified like this:

```
auto t = std::tuple<int, std::string, bool>{};
```

Or, we can initialize it using class template argument deduction, as follows:

```
auto t = std::tuple{0, std::string{}, false};
```

This will make the compiler generate a class, which can roughly be viewed like this:

```
struct Tuple {
  int data0_{};
  std::string data1_{};
  bool data2_{};
};
```

As with many other classes in the C++ standard library, `std::tuple` also has a corresponding `std::make_tuple()` function, which deduces the types automatically from the parameters:

```
auto t = std::make_tuple(42, std::string{"hi"}, true);
```

But as stated earlier, from C++17 and onward, many of these `std::make_` functions are superfluous, since C++17 classes can deduce these types from the constructor.

Accessing the members of a tuple

The individual elements of std::tuple can be accessed using the free function template std::get<Index>(). You may wonder why the members can't be accessed like a regular container with the at(size_t index) member function. The reason is that a member function such as at() is only allowed to return one type, whereas a tuple consists of different types at different indices. Instead, the function template std::get() is used with the index as a template parameter:

```
auto a = std::get<0>(t);    // int
auto b = std::get<1>(t);    // std::string
auto c = std::get<2>(t);    // bool
```

We can imagine the std::get() function being implemented something like this:

```
template <size_t Index, typename Tuple>
auto& get(const Tuple& t) {
  if constexpr(Index == 0) {
    return t.data0_;
  } else if constexpr(Index == 1) {
    return t.data1_;
  } else if constexpr(Index == 2) {
    return t.data2_;
  }
}
```

This means that when we create and access a tuple as follows:

```
auto t = std::tuple(42, true);
auto v = std::get<0>(t);
```

the compiler roughly generates the following code:

```
// The Tuple class is generated first:
class Tuple {
  int data0_{};
  bool data1_{};
public:
  Tuple(int v0, bool v1) : data0_{v0}, data1_{v1} {}
};
// get<0>(Tuple) is then generated to something like this:
auto& get(const Tuple& tpl) { return data0_; }

// The generated function is then utilized:
```

```
auto t = Tuple(42, true);
auto v = get(t);
```

Note that this example can merely be thought of as a simplistic way to imagine what the compiler generates when constructing `std::tuple`; the interior of `std::tuple` is very complex. Still, it is important to understand that a `std::tuple` class is basically a simple struct whose members can be accessed by a compile-time index.

> The `std::get()` function template can also use the typename as a parameter. It is used like this:
>
> ```
> auto number = std::get<int>(tuple);
> auto str = std::get<std::string>(tuple);
> ```
>
> This is only possible if the specified type is contained once in the tuple.

Iterating std::tuple members

From a programmer's perspective, it may seem that `std::tuple` can be iterated with a regular range-based `for`-loop, just like any other container, as follows:

```
auto t = std::tuple(1, true, std::string{"Jedi"});
for (const auto& v : t) {
  std::cout << v << " ";
}
```

The reason this is not possible is that the type of `const auto& v` is only evaluated once, and since `std::tuple` contains elements of different types, this code simply does not compile.

The same goes for regular algorithms, as iterators don't mutate the type pointed to; therefore, `std::tuple` does not provide a `begin()` or `end()` member function, nor does it provide a subscript operator, `[]`, for accessing the values. So, we need to come up with some other way to unroll the tuple.

Unrolling the tuple

As tuples cannot be iterated as usual, what we need to do is use metaprogramming to unroll the loop. From the previous example, we want the compiler to generate something like this:

```
auto t = std::tuple(1, true, std::string{"Jedi"});
std::cout << std::get<0>(t) << " ";
```

```
std::cout << std::get<1>(t) << " ";
std::cout << std::get<2>(t) << " ";
// Prints "1 true Jedi"
```

As you can see, we iterate every index of the tuple, which means we need the number of types/values contained in the tuple. Then, since the tuple contains different types, we need to write a meta-function that generates a new function for every type in the tuple.

If we start with a function that generates the call for a specific index, it will look like this:

```
template <size_t Index, typename Tuple, typename Func>
void tuple_at(const Tuple& t, Func f) {
  const auto& v = std::get<Index>(t);
  std::invoke(f, v);
}
```

We can then combine it with a generic lambda, as you learned in *Chapter 2, Essential C++ Techniques:*

```
auto t = std::tuple{1, true, std::string{"Jedi"}};
auto f = [](const auto& v) { std::cout << v << " "; };
tuple_at<0>(t, f);
tuple_at<1>(t, f);
tuple_at<2>(t, f);
// Prints "1 true Jedi"
```

With the function `tuple_at()` in place, we can then move on to the actual iteration. The first thing we need is the number of values in the tuple as a compile-time constant. Fortunately, this value can be obtained by the type trait `std::tuple_size_v<Tuple>`. Using `if constexpr`, we can then unfold the iteration by creating a similar function, which takes different actions, depending on the index:

- If the index is equal to the tuple size, it generates an empty function
- Otherwise, it executes the lambda at the passed index and generates a new function with 1 added to the index

This is how the code will look:

```
template <typename Tuple, typename Func, size_t Index = 0>
void tuple_for_each(const Tuple& t, const Func& f) {
  constexpr auto n = std::tuple_size_v<Tuple>;
```

```
    if constexpr(Index < n) {
      tuple_at<Index>(t, f);
      tuple_for_each<Tuple, Func, Index+1>(t, f);
    }
  }
}
```

As you can see, the default index is set to zero so that we don't have to specify it when iterating. This `tuple_for_each()` function can then be called like this, with the lambda directly in place:

```
auto t = std::tuple{1, true, std::string{"Jedi"}};
tuple_for_each(t, [](const auto& v) { std::cout << v << " "; });
// Prints "1 true Jedi"
```

Quite nice; syntactically, it looks pretty similar to the `std::for_each()` algorithm.

Implementing other algorithms for tuples

Expanding upon `tuple_for_each()`, different algorithms iterating a tuple can be implemented in a similar manner. Here is an example of how `std::any_of()` for tuples is implemented:

```
template <typename Tuple, typename Func, size_t Index = 0>
auto tuple_any_of(const Tuple& t, const Func& f) -> bool {
  constexpr auto n = std::tuple_size_v<Tuple>;
  if constexpr(Index < n) {
    bool success = std::invoke(f, std::get<Index>(t));
    if (success) {
      return true;
    }
    return tuple_any_of<Tuple, Func, Index+1>(t, f);
  } else {
    return false;
  }
}
```

It can be used like this:

```
auto t = std::tuple{42, 43.0f, 44.0};
auto has_44 = tuple_any_of(t, [](auto v) { return v == 44; });
```

The function template `tuple_any_of()` iterates through every type in the tuple and generates a lambda function for the element at the current index, which it then compares with 44. In this case, has_44 will evaluate to true, as the last element, a double value, is 44. If we add an element of a type that is not comparable with 44, such as `std::string`, we will get a compilation error.

Accessing tuple elements

Prior to C++17, there were two standard ways of accessing elements of a `std::tuple`:

- For accessing single elements, the function `std::get<N>(tuple)` was used.
- For accessing multiple elements, the function `std::tie()` was used.

Although they both worked, the syntax for performing such a simple task was very verbose, as shown in the following example:

```
// Prerequisite
using namespace std::string_literals;  // "..."s
auto make_saturn() { return std::tuple{"Saturn"s, 82, true}; }

int main() {
  // Using std::get<N>()
  {
    auto t = make_saturn();
    auto name = std::get<0>(t);
    auto n_moons = std::get<1>(t);
    auto rings = std::get<2>(t);
    std::cout << name << ' ' << n_moons << ' ' << rings << '\n';
    // Output: Saturn 82 true
  }
  // Using std::tie()
  {
    auto name = std::string{};
    auto n_moons = int{};
    auto rings = bool{};
    std::tie(name, n_moons, rings) = make_saturn();
    std::cout << name << ' ' << n_moons << ' ' << rings << '\n';
  }
}
```

In order to be able to perform this common task elegantly, structured bindings were introduced in C++17.

Structured bindings

Using structured bindings, multiple variables can be initialized at once using auto and a bracket declaration list. As with the auto keyword in general, you can apply control over whether the variables should be mutable references, forward references, const references, or values by using the corresponding modifier. In the following example, a structured binding of const references is being constructed:

```cpp
const auto& [name, n_moons, rings] = make_saturn();
std::cout << name << ' ' << n_moons << ' ' << rings << '\n';
```

Structured bindings can also be used to extract the individual members of a tuple in a for-loop, as follows:

```cpp
auto planets = {
  std::tuple{"Mars"s, 2, false},
  std::tuple{"Neptune"s, 14, true}
};
for (auto&& [name, n_moons, rings] : planets) {
    std::cout << name << ' ' << n_moons << ' ' << rings << '\n';
}
// Output:
// Mars 2 false
// Neptune 14 true
```

Here's a quick tip. If you want to return multiple arguments with named variables instead of tuple indices, it is possible to return a struct defined inside a function and use automatic return type deduction:

```cpp
auto make_earth() {
  struct Planet { std::string name; int n_moons; bool rings; };
  return Planet{"Earth", 1, false};
}
// ...
auto p = make_earth();
std::cout << p.name << ' ' << p.n_moons << ' ' << p.rings << '\n';
```

Structured bindings also work with structs, so, we might capture the individual data members directly as follows, even if it is a struct:

```cpp
auto [name, num_moons, has_rings] = make_earth();
```

In this case, we can choose arbitrary names for our identifiers since it's the order of the data members of `Planet` that is relevant, just like when returning a tuple.

Now, we will look at another use case for `std::tuple` and `std::tie()` when handling an arbitrary number of function arguments.

The variadic template parameter pack

The **variadic template parameter pack** enables programmers to create template functions that can accept any number of arguments.

An example of a function with a variadic number of arguments

If we were to create a function that makes a string out of any number of arguments without variadic template parameter packs, we would need to use C-style variadic arguments (just like `printf()` does) or create a separate function for every number of arguments:

```
auto make_string(const auto& v0) {
  auto ss = std::ostringstream{};
  ss << v0;
  return ss.str();
}

auto make_string(const auto& v0, const auto& v1) {
    return make_string(v0) + " " + make_string(v1);
}

auto make_string(const auto& v0, const auto& v1, const auto& v2) {
    return make_string(v0, v1) + " " + make_string(v2);
}
// ... and so on for as many parameters we might need
```

This is the intended use of our function:

```
auto str0 = make_string(42);
auto str1 = make_string(42, "hi");
auto str2 = make_string(42, "hi", true);
```

If we require a large number of arguments, this becomes tedious, but with a parameter pack, we can implement this as a function that accepts an arbitrary number of arguments.

How to construct a variadic parameter pack

The parameter pack is identified by putting three dots in front of the typename and three dots after the variadic argument expands the pack, with a comma in-between:

```
template<typename ...Ts>
auto f(Ts... values) {
  g(values...);
}
```

Here's the syntactic explanation:

- `Ts` is a list of types
- `<typename ...Ts>` indicates that the function deals with a list
- `values...` expands the pack such that a comma is added between every value

To put it into code, consider this `expand_pack()` function template:

```
template <typename ...Ts>
auto expand_pack(const Ts& ...values) {
    auto tuple = std::tie(values...);
}
```

Let's call the preceding function like this:

```
expand_pack(42, std::string{"hi"});
```

In this case, the compiler will generate a function similar to this:

```
auto expand_pack(const int& v0, const std::string& v1) {
    auto tuple = std::tie(v0, v1);
}
```

This is what the individual parameter pack parts expand to:

Expression:	Expands to:
`template <typename... Ts>`	`template <typename T0, typename T1>`
`expand_pack(const Ts& ...values)`	`expand_pack(const T0& v0, const T1& v1)`
`std::tie(values...)`	`std::tie(v0, v1)`

Table 9.1: Expanding expressions

Now, let's see how we can create a `make_string()` function with a variadic parameter pack.

Going further with the initial `make_string()` function, in order to create a string out of every parameter, we need to iterate the pack. There is no way to directly iterate a parameter pack, but a simple workaround would be to make a tuple out of it and then iterate it with the `tuple_for_each()` function template, as follows:

```cpp
template <typename ...Ts>
auto make_string(const Ts& ...values) {
  auto ss = std::ostringstream{};
  // Create a tuple of the variadic parameter pack
  auto tuple = std::tie(values...);
  // Iterate the tuple
  tuple_for_each(tuple, [&ss](const auto& v) { ss << v; });
  return ss.str();
}
// ...
auto str = make_string("C++", 20);  // OK: str is "C++"
```

The parameter pack is converted into a `std::tuple` with `std::tie()` and then iterated using `tuple_for_each()`. To recap, the reason we need to use `std::tuple` to handle the parameters are because we want to support an arbitrary number of parameters of various types. If we only had to support parameters of one specific type, we could instead have used a `std::array` with a range-based `for`-loop, like this:

```cpp
template <typename ...Ts>
auto make_string(const Ts& ...values) {
  auto ss = std::ostringstream{};
  auto a = std::array{values...};      // Only supports one type
  for (auto&& v : a) { ss << v; }
  return ss.str();
}
// ...
auto a = make_string("A", "B", "C");  // OK: Only one type
auto b = make_string(100, 200, 300);  // OK: Only one type
auto c = make_string("C++", 20);      // Error: Mixed types
```

As you have seen, `std::tuple` is a heterogenous collection with a fixed size and fixed element positions—more or less like a regular struct but without named member variables.

How can we expand upon this to create a dynamically sized collection (such as `std::vector` and `std::list`) but with the ability to store elements of mixed types? We'll look at a solution to this in the following section.

Dynamically sized heterogenous collections

We started this chapter by noting that the dynamically sized containers offered by C++ are homogenous, meaning that we can only store elements of one single type. But sometimes, we need to keep track of a collection that's dynamic in size that contains elements of different types. To be able to do that, we will use containers that contain elements of type std::any or std::variant.

The simplest solution is to use std::any as the base type. The std::any object can store any type of value in it:

```
auto container = std::vector<std::any>{42, "hi", true};
```

It has some drawbacks, though. First, every time a value in it is accessed, the type must be tested for at runtime. In other words, we completely lose the type information of the stored value at compile time. Rather, we have to rely on runtime type checks for the information. Secondly, it allocates the object on the heap rather than the stack, which can have significant performance implications.

If we want to iterate our container, we need to explicitly say this to every std::any object: *if you are an int, do this, and if you are a char pointer, do that*. This is not desirable as it requires repeated source code, and it is also less efficient than using other alternatives, which we will cover later in this chapter.

The following example compiles; the type is explicitly tested for and casted upon:

```cpp
for (const auto& a : container) {
  if (a.type() == typeid(int)) {
    const auto& value = std::any_cast<int>(a);
    std::cout << value;
  }
  else if (a.type() == typeid(const char*)) {
    const auto& value = std::any_cast<const char*>(a);
    std::cout << value;
  }
  else if (a.type() == typeid(bool)) {
    const auto& value = std::any_cast<bool>(a);
    std::cout << value;
  }
}
```

We simply cannot print it with a regular stream operator since the std::any object has no idea of how to access its stored value. Therefore, the following code does not compile; the compiler does not know what's stored in std::any:

```
for (const auto& a : container) {
  std::cout << a;                  // Does not compile
}
```

We usually don't need the full flexibility of types that std::any offers, and in many cases, we are better off using the std::variant, which we will cover next.

The std::variant

If we don't need the ability to store *any* type in the container, but instead we want to concentrate on a fixed set of types declared at container initialization, then std::variant is a better choice.

The std::variant has two main advantages over std::any:

- It does not store its contained type on the heap (unlike std::any)
- It can be invoked with a generic lambda, meaning you don't explicitly have to know its currently contained type (more about this in the later sections of this chapter)

The std::variant works in a somewhat similar manner to a tuple, except that it only stores one object at a time. The contained type and value are the type and value we assigned it last. The following image illustrates the difference between a std::tuple and a std::variant when they've been instantiated with the same types:

Figure 9.2: Tuple of types versus variant of types

Here's an example of using a std::variant:

```
using VariantType = std::variant<int, std::string, bool>;
VariantType v{};
std::holds_alternative<int>(v);  // true, int is first alternative
```

```
v = 7;
std::holds_alternative<int>(v);   // true
v = std::string{"Anne"};
std::holds_alternative<int>(v);   // false, int was overwritten
v = false;
std::holds_alternative<bool>(v); // true, v is now bool
```

We are using `std::holds_alternative<T>()` to check whether the variant currently holds a given type. You can see that the type changes when we assign the variant new values.

Apart from storing the actual value, a `std::variant` also keeps track of the currently held alternative by using an index that's usually of size `std::size_t`. This means that the total size of a `std::variant` is typically the size of the biggest alternative, plus the size of the index. We can verify this by using the `sizeof` operator for our types:

```
std::cout << "VariantType: "<< sizeof(VariantType) << '\n';
std::cout << "std::string: "<< sizeof(std::string) << '\n';
std::cout << "std::size_t: "<< sizeof(std::size_t) << '\n';
```

Compiling and running this code using Clang 10.0 with libc++ generates the following output:

```
VariantType: 32
std::string: 24
std::size_t: 8
```

As you can see, the size of the `VariantType` is the sum of `std::string` and `std::size_t`.

Exception safety of std::variant

When a new value is assigned to a `std::variant` object, it is placed in the same location as the currently held value of the variant. If, for some reason, the construction or assignment of the new value fails and throws an exception, the old value may not be restored. Instead, the variant can become **valueless**. You can check whether a variant object is valueless by using the member function `valueless_by_ exception()`. This can be demonstrated when trying to construct an object using the `emplace()` member function:

```
struct Widget {
  explicit Widget(int) {     // Throwing constructor
    throw std::exception{};
  }
};
```

```
auto var = std::variant<double, Widget>{1.0};
try {
  var.emplace<1>(42); // Try to construct a Widget instance
} catch (...) {
  std::cout << "exception caught\n";
  if (var.valueless_by_exception()) {  // var may or may not
    std::cout << "valueless\n";        // be valueless
  } else {
    std::cout << std::get<0>(var) << '\n';
  }
}
```

The initial `double` value 1.0 may or may not be gone after the exception has been thrown and caught. The operation is not guaranteed to be rolled back, which we usually can expect from standard library containers. In other words, `std::variant` doesn't provide a strong exception safety guarantee, and the reason for this is performance overhead since it would require `std::variant` to use heap allocations. This behavior of `std::variant` is a useful feature rather than a shortcoming, because it means that you can safely use `std::variant` in code with real-time requirements.

If you instead want a heap allocating version but with a strong exception safety guarantee and a "never-empty" guarantee, `boost::variant` offers this functionality. If you are interested in the challenges of implementing such a type, `https://www.boost.org/doc/libs/1_74_0/doc/html/variant/design.html` offers an interesting read.

Visiting variants

When accessing variables in the `std::variant`, we use the global function `std::visit()`. As you might have guessed, we have to use our main companion when dealing with heterogeneous types: the generic lambda:

```
auto var = std::variant<int, bool, float>{};
std::visit([](auto&& val) { std::cout << val; }, var);
```

When invoking `std::visit()` with the generic lambda and the variant var in the example, the compiler will conceptually transform the lambda into a regular class with `operator()` overloads for every type in the variant. This will look something similar to this:

```
struct GeneratedFunctorImpl {
  auto operator()(int&& v)   { std::cout << v; }
  auto operator()(bool&& v)  { std::cout << v; }
  auto operator()(float&& v) { std::cout << v; }
};
```

The `std::visit()` function is then expanded to an `if...else` chain using
`std::holds_alternative<T>()`, or a jump table using the index of the `std::variant`,
to generate the correct call to `std::get<T>()`.

In the previous example, we passed the value in our generic lambda directly to
`std::cout`, regardless of the currently held alternative. But what if we want to do
different things, depending on what type we are visiting? A pattern that may be
used for this situation is to define a variadic class template that will inherit from
a set of lambdas. We then need to define this for each type that we are visiting.
Sounds complicated, doesn't it? This may seem a bit magic at first and also puts our
metaprogramming skills to the test, but once we have the variadic class template in
place, it's easy to use.

We will begin with the variadic class template. Here is how it looks:

```
template<class... Lambdas>
struct Overloaded : Lambdas... {
  using Lambdas::operator()...;
};
```

If you are on a C++17 compiler you also need to add an explicit deduction guide, but
it's not needed as of C++20:

```
template<class... Lambdas>
Overloaded(Lambdas...) -> Overloaded<Lambdas...>;
```

That's it. The template class `Overloaded` will inherit from all lambdas that we will
instantiate the template with, and the function call operator, `operator()()`, will be
overloaded once by each lambda. It's now possible to create a stateless object that
only contains multiple overloads of the call operator:

```
auto overloaded_lambdas = Overloaded{
  [](int v)   { std::cout << "Int: " << v; },
  [](bool v)  { std::cout << "Bool: " << v; },
  [](float v) { std::cout << "Float: " << v; }
};
```

We can test it using different arguments and verify that the correct overload is being called:

```
overloaded_lambdas(30031);    // Prints "Int: 30031"
overloaded_lambdas(2.71828f); // Prints "Float: 2.71828"
```

Now, we can use this with `std::visit()` and without the need of having the `Overloaded` object stored in an lvalue. Here is how it finally looks:

```
auto var = std::variant<int, bool, float>{42};

std::visit(Overloaded{
  [](int v)   { std::cout << "Int: " << v; },
  [](bool v)  { std::cout << "Bool: " << v; },
  [](float v) { std::cout << "Float: " << v; }
}, var);
// Outputs: "Int: 42"
```

So, once we have the `Overloaded` template in place, we can use this convenient way of specifying a set of lambdas for different types of arguments. In the next section, we will start using `std::variant` together with standard containers.

Heterogenous collections using variant

Now that we have a variant that can store any type of a provided list, we can expand upon this to a heterogeneous collection. We do this by simply creating a `std::vector` of our variant:

```
using VariantType = std::variant<int, std::string, bool>;
auto container = std::vector<VariantType>{};
```

We can now push elements of different types to our vector:

```
container.push_back(false);
container.push_back("I am a string"s);
container.push_back("I am also a string"s);
container.push_back(13);
```

The vector will now look like this in memory, where every element in the vector contains the size of the variant, which in this case is `sizeof(std::size_t) + sizeof(std::string)`:

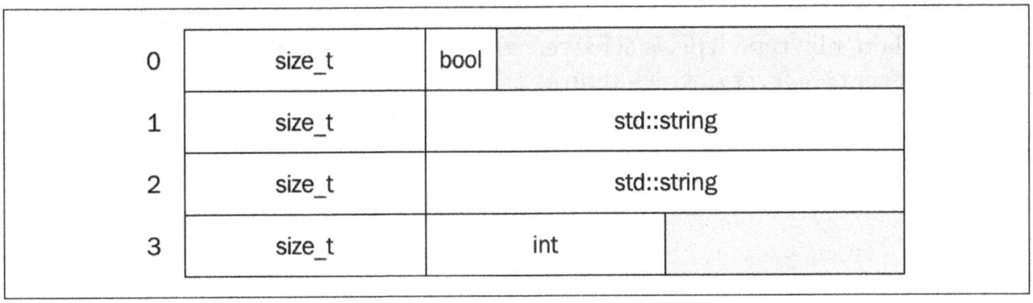

0	size_t	bool	
1	size_t	std::string	
2	size_t	std::string	
3	size_t	int	

Figure 9.3: Vector of variants

Of course, we can also pop_back() or modify the container in any other way the container allows:

```
container.pop_back();
std::reverse(container.begin(), container.end());
// etc...
```

Accessing the values in our variant container

Now that we have the boilerplate for a heterogeneous collection that's dynamic in size, let's see how we can use it like a regular std::vector:

1. **Construct a heterogeneous container of variants**: Here, we construct a std::vector with different types. Note that the initializer list contains different types:
   ```
   using VariantType = std::variant<int, std::string, bool>;
   auto v = std::vector<VariantType>{ 42, "needle"s, true };
   ```

2. **Print the content by iterating with a regular for-loop**: To iterate the container with a regular for-loop, we utilize std::visit() and a generic lambda. The global function std::visit() takes care of the type conversion. The example prints each value to std::cout, independent of the type:
   ```
   for (const auto& item : v) {
     std::visit([](const auto& x) { std::cout << x << '\n';}, item);
   }
   ```

3. **Inspect what types are in the container**: Here, we inspect each element of the container by type. This is achieved by using the global function `std::holds_alternative<type>`, which returns `true` if the variant currently holds the type asked for. The following example counts the number of Booleans currently contained in the container:

```
auto num_bools = std::count_if(v.begin(), v.end(),
                              [](auto&& item) {
   return std::holds_alternative<bool>(item);
});
```

4. **Find content by both contained type and value**: In this example, we're inspecting the container both for type and value by combining `std::holds_alternative()` and `std::get()`. This example checks whether the container contains a `std::string` with the value `"needle"`:

```
auto contains = std::any_of(v.begin(), v.end(),
                           [](auto&& item) {
   return std::holds_alternative<std::string>(item) &&
     std::get<std::string>(item) == "needle";
});
```

Global function std::get()

The global function template `std::get()` can be used for `std::tuple`, `std::pair`, `std::variant`, and `std::array`. There are two ways to instantiate `std::get()`, with an index or with a type:

- **`std::get<Index>()`**: When `std::get()` is used with an index, as in `std::get<1>(v)`, it returns the value at the corresponding index in a `std::tuple`, `std::pair`, or `std::array`.

- **`std::get<Type>()`**: When `std::get()` is used with a type, as in `std::get<int>(v)`, the corresponding value in a `std::tuple`, `std::pair` or `std::variant` is returned. In the case of `std::variant`, a `std::bad_variant_access` exception is thrown if the variant doesn't currently hold that type. Note that if v is a `std::tuple` and `Type` is contained more than once, you have to use the index to access the type.

Having discussed the essential templates from the Utility library, let's look at some real-world applications of what we have covered in this chapter.

Some real-world examples

We will end this chapter by examining two examples where `std::tuple`, `std::tie()`, and some template metaprogramming can help us to write clean and efficient code in practice.

Example 1: projections and comparison operators

The need to implement comparison operators for classes dramatically decreased with C++20, but there are still cases where we need to provide a custom comparison function when we want to sort objects in some custom order for a specific scenario. Consider the following class:

```cpp
struct Player {
  std::string name_{};
  int level_{};
  int score_{};
  // etc...
};

auto players = std::vector<Player>{};
// Add players here...
```

Say that we want to sort the players by their attributes: the primary sort order `level_` and the secondary sort order `score_`. It's not uncommon to see code like this when implementing comparison and sorting:

```cpp
auto cmp = [](const Player& lhs, const Player& rhs) {
  if (lhs.level_ == rhs.level_) {
    return lhs.score_ < rhs.score_;
  }
  else {
    return lhs.level_ < rhs.level_;
  }
};

std::sort(players.begin(), players.end(), cmp);
```

Writing comparison operators in this style using nested `if-else` blocks quickly becomes error-prone when the number of attributes increases. What we really want to express is that we are comparing a *projection* of `Player` attributes (in this case, a strict subset). The `std::tuple` can help us rewrite this code in a cleaner way without the need for `if-else` statements.

Let's use `std::tie()`, which creates a `std::tuple` holding references to the lvalues we pass to it. The following code creates two projections, `p1` and `p2`, and compares them using the `<` operator:

```
auto cmp = [](const Player& lhs, const Player& rhs) {
   auto p1 = std::tie(lhs.level_, lhs.score_); // Projection
   auto p2 = std::tie(lhs.level_, lhs.score_); // Projection
   return p1 < p2;
};
std::sort(players.begin(), players.end(), cmp);
```

This is very clean and easy to read compared to the initial version using `if-else` statements. But is this really efficient? It seems like we need to create temporary objects just to compare two players. When running this in a microbenchmark and also inspecting the generated code, there is really no overhead at all to using `std::tie()`; in fact, the version using `std::tie()` was, in this example, slightly faster than the version using `if-else` statements.

Using the ranges algorithms, we can do the sorting by providing the projection as an argument to `std::ranges::sort()`, which makes the code even cleaner:

```
std::ranges::sort(players, std::less{}, [](const Player& p) {
   return std::tie(p.level_, p.score_);
});
```

This is an example of how `std::tuple` can be used in contexts where a full struct with named members is not needed, without sacrificing any clarity in the code.

Example 2: reflection

The term **reflection** refers to the ability to inspect a class without knowing anything about its contents. In contrast to many other programming languages, C++ does not have built-in reflection, which means we have to write the reflection functionality ourselves. Reflection is planned to be included in future versions of the C++ standard; hopefully, we will see this feature in C++23.

In this example, we are going to limit the reflection to give classes the ability to iterate their members, just like we can iterate the members of a tuple. By using reflection, we can create generic functions for serialization or logging that automatically work with any class. This reduces large amounts of boilerplate code, which is traditionally required for classes in C++.

Making a class reflect its members

Since we need to implement all the reflection functionality ourselves, we will start by exposing the member variables via a function called `reflect()`. We will continue to use the `Player` class that was introduced in the previous section. Here is how it looks when we add the `reflect()` member function and a constructor:

```cpp
class Player {
public:
  Player(std::string name, int level, int score)
      : name_{std::move(name)}, level_{level}, score_{score} {}

  auto reflect() const {
    return std::tie(name_, level_, score_);
  }
private:
  std::string name_;
  int level_{};
  int score_{};
};
```

The `reflect()` member function returns a tuple of references to the member variables by invoking `std::tie()`. We can now start using the `reflect()` function, but first, a note about alternatives to using handcrafted reflection.

C++ libraries that simplify reflection

There have been quite a few attempts in the C++ library world to simplify the creation of reflection. One example is the metaprogramming library *Boost Hana* by Louis Dionne, which gives classes reflection capabilities via a simple macro. Recently, *Boost* has also added *Precise and Flat Reflection* by Anthony Polukhin, which *automatically* reflects public content of classes, as long as all members are simple types.

However, for clarity, in this example, we will only use our own `reflect()` member function.

Using reflection

Now that the `Player` class has the ability to reflect its member variables, we can automate the creation of bulk functionality, which would otherwise require us to retype every member variable. As you may already know, C++ automatically can generate constructors, destructors, and comparison operators, but other operators must be implemented by the programmer. One such function is the `operator<<()`, which outputs its contents to a stream in order to store them in a file, or more commonly, log them in an application log.

By overloading `operator<<()` and using the `tuple_for_each()` function template we implemented earlier in this chapter, we can simplify the creation of `std::ostream` output for a class, like this:

```cpp
auto& operator<<(std::ostream& ostr, const Player& p) {
  tuple_for_each(p.reflect(), [&ostr](const auto& m) {
    ostr << m << " ";
  });
  return ostr;
}
```

Now, the class can be used with any `std::ostream` type, like this:

```cpp
auto v = Player{"Kai", 4, 2568};
std::cout << v;                    // Prints: "Kai 4 2568 "
```

By reflecting our class members via a tuple, we only have to update our reflect function when members are added/removed from our class, instead of updating every function and iterating all member variables.

Conditionally overloading global functions

Now that we have a mechanism to write bulk functions using reflection rather than manually typing each variable, we still need to type the simplified bulk functions for every type. What if we wanted these functions to be generated for every type that can be reflected?

We can conditionally enable `operator<<()` for all classes that have a `reflect()` member function by using a constraint.

First, we need to create a new concept that refers to the `reflect()` member function:

```
template <typename T>
concept Reflectable = requires (T& t) {
  t.reflect();
};
```

Of course, this concept only checks whether a class has a member function named `reflect()`; it doesn't always return a tuple. In general, we should be skeptical about weak concepts that only use a single member function like this, but it serves the purpose of the example. Anyway, we can now overload `operator<<()` in the global namespace, giving all reflectable classes the ability to be compared and printed to a `std::ostream`:

```
auto& operator<<(std::ostream& os, const Reflectable auto& v) {
  tuple_for_each(v.reflect(), [&os](const auto& m) {
    os << m << " ";
  });
  return os;
}
```

The preceding function template will only be instantiated for types that contain the `reflect()` member function, and will therefore not collide with any other overload.

Testing reflection capabilities

Now, we have everything in place:

- The `Player` class we will test has a `reflect()` member function returning a tuple of references to its members
- The global `std::ostream& operator<<()` is overloaded for reflectable types

Here is a simple test that verifies this functionality:

```
int main() {
  auto kai = Player{"Kai", 4, 2568};
  auto ari = Player{"Ari", 2, 1068};

  std::cout << kai; // Prints "Kai 4 2568"
  std::cout << ari; // Prints "Ari 2 1068"
}
```

These examples have demonstrated the usefulness of small but essential utilities such as `std::tie()` and `std::tuple` when combined with a little bit of metaprogramming.

Summary

In this chapter you have learned how to use `std::optional` to represent optional values in your code. You have also seen how to combine `std::pair`, `std::tuple`, `std::any`, and `std::variant` together with standard containers and metaprogramming to store and iterate over elements of different types. You also learned that `std::tie()` is a conceptually simple yet powerful tool that can be used for projection and reflection.

In the next chapter, you will find out how to further expand your C++ toolbox to create libraries by learning how to construct hidden proxy objects.

10

Proxy Objects and Lazy Evaluation

In this chapter, you will learn how to use proxy objects and lazy evaluation in order to postpone the execution of certain code until required. Using proxy objects enables optimizations to occur under the hood, thereby leaving the exposed interfaces intact.

This chapter covers:

- Lazy and eager evaluation
- Using proxy objects to avoid superfluous computations
- Overloading operators when working with proxy objects

Introducing lazy evaluation and proxy objects

First and foremost, the techniques used in this chapter are used to hide optimizations in a library from the user of that library. This is useful because exposing every single optimization technique as a separate function requires a lot of attention and education from the user of the library. It also bloats the code base with a multitude of specific functions, making it hard to read and understand. By using proxy objects, we can achieve optimizations under the hood; the resultant code is both optimized and readable.

Lazy versus eager evaluation

Lazy evaluation is a technique used to postpone an operation until its result is really needed. The opposite, where operations are performed right away, is called **eager evaluation**. In some situations, eager evaluation is undesirable as we might end up constructing a value that is never used.

To demonstrate the difference between eager and lazy evaluation, let's assume we are writing some sort of game with multiple levels. Whenever a level has been completed, we need to display the current score. Here we will focus on a few components of our game:

- A ScoreView class responsible for displaying the user's score with an optional bonus image if a bonus was achieved
- An Image class that represents an image loaded into memory
- A load() function that loads images from disk

The implementation of the classes and functions is not important in this example, but the declarations look like this:

```cpp
class Image { /* ... */ };                // Buffer with JPG data
auto load(std::string_view path) -> Image;   // Load image at path

class ScoreView {
public:
  // Eager, requires loaded bonus image
  void display(const Image& bonus);

  // Lazy, only load bonus image if necessary
  void display(std::function<Image()> bonus);

  // ...
};
```

Two versions of display() are provided: the first one requires a fully loaded bonus image, whereas the second one accepts a function that will be called only if a bonus image is needed. Using the first *eager* version would look like this:

```cpp
// Always load bonus image eagerly
const auto eager = load("/images/stars.jpg");
score.display(eager);
```

Using the second *lazy* version would look like this:

```
// Load default image lazily if needed
auto lazy = [] { return load("/images/stars.jpg"); };
score.display(lazy);
```

The eager version will always load the default image into memory even if it's never displayed. However, the lazy loading of the bonus image will guarantee that the image is only loaded if the ScoreView really needs to show the bonus image.

This is a very simple example, but the idea is that your code gets expressed almost in the same way as if it were declared eagerly. A technique for hiding the fact that the code evaluates lazily is to use proxy objects.

Proxy objects

Proxy objects are internal library objects that aren't intended to be visible to the user of the library. Their task is to postpone operations until required and to collect the data of an expression until it can be evaluated and optimized. However, proxy objects act in the dark; the user of the library should be able to handle the expressions as if the proxy objects were not there. In other words, using proxy objects, you can encapsulate optimizations in your libraries while leaving the interfaces intact. You will now learn how to use proxy objects in order to evaluate more advanced expressions lazily.

Avoiding constructing objects using proxy objects

Eager evaluation can have the undesirable effect that objects are unnecessarily constructed. Often this is not a problem, but if the objects are expensive to construct (because of heap allocations, for example), there might be legitimate reasons to optimize away the unnecessary construction of short-lived objects that serve no purpose.

Comparing concatenated strings using a proxy

We will now walk through a minimal example of using proxy objects to give you an idea of what they are and can be used for. It's not meant to provide you with a general production-ready solution to optimizing string comparisons.

With that said, take a look at this code snippet that concatenates two strings and compares the result:

```cpp
auto a = std::string{"Cole"};
auto b = std::string{"Porter"};
auto c = std::string{"ColePorter"};
auto is_equal = (a + b) == c;        // true
```

Here is a visual representation of the preceding code snippet:

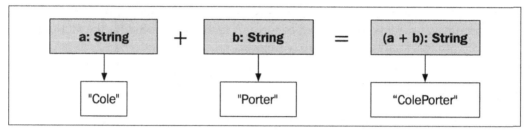

Figure 10.1: Concatenating two strings into a new string

The problem here is that (a + b) constructs a new temporary string in order to compare it with c. Instead of constructing a new string, we can just compare the concatenation right away, like this:

```cpp
auto is_concat_equal(const std::string& a, const std::string& b,
                     const std::string& c) {
  return
    a.size() + b.size() == c.size() &&
    std::equal(a.begin(), a.end(), c.begin()) &&
    std::equal(b.begin(), b.end(), c.begin() + a.size());
}
```

We can then use it like this:

```cpp
auto is_equal = is_concat_equal(a, b, c);
```

Performance-wise, we've achieved a win, but syntactically, a code base littered with special-case convenience functions like this is hard to maintain. So, let's see how this optimization can be achieved with the original syntax still intact.

Implementing the proxy

First, we'll create a proxy class representing the concatenation of two strings:

```
struct ConcatProxy {
  const std::string& a;
  const std::string& b;
};
```

Then, we'll construct our own String class that contains a std::string and an overloaded operator+() function. Note that this is an example of how to make and use proxy objects; creating your own String class is not something I recommend:

```
class String {
public:
  String() = default;
  String(std::string str) : str_{std::move(str)} {}
  std::string str_{};
};

auto operator+(const String& a, const String& b) {
    return ConcatProxy{a.str_, b.str_};
}
```

Here's a visual representation of the preceding code snippet:

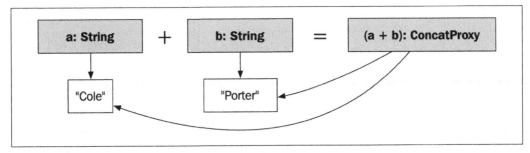

Figure 10.2: A proxy object representing the concatenation of two strings

Lastly, we'll create a global operator==() function, which in turn will use the optimized is_concat_equal() function, as follows:

```
auto operator==(ConcatProxy&& concat, const String& str) {
    return is_concat_equal(concat.a, concat.b, str.str_);
}
```

Now that we have everything in place, we can get the best of both worlds:

```
auto a = String{"Cole"};
auto b = String{"Porter"};
auto c = String{"ColePorter"};
auto is_equal = (a + b) == c;      // true
```

In other words, we gained the performance of is_concat_equal() while preserving the expressive syntax of using operator==().

The rvalue modifier

In the preceding code, the global operator==() function only accepts ConcatProxy rvalues:

```
auto operator==(ConcatProxy&& concat, const String& str) { // ...
```

If we were to accept a ConcatProxy lvalue, we could end up accidentally misusing the proxy, like this:

```
auto concat = String{"Cole"} + String{"Porter"};
auto is_cole_porter = concat == String{"ColePorter"};
```

The problem here is that both the temporary String objects holding "Cole" and "Porter" have been destructed by the time the comparison is executed, leading to a failure. (Remember that the ConcatProxy class only holds references to the strings.) But since we forced the concat object to be an rvalue, the preceding code will not compile and thereby saves us from a likely runtime crash. Of course, you could force it to compile by casting it to an rvalue using std::move(concat) == String("ColePorter"), but that wouldn't be a realistic case.

Assigning a concatenated proxy

Now, you might be thinking, what if we actually want to store the concatenated string as a new string rather than just compare it? What we do is simply overload an operator String() function, as follows:

```
struct ConcatProxy {
  const std::string& a;
  const std::string& b;
  operator String() const && { return String{a + b}; }
};
```

The concatenation of two strings can now implicitly convert itself to a string:

```
String c = String{"Marc"} + String{"Chagall"};
```

There is one little snag, though: we cannot initialize the new String object with the auto keyword, as this would result in ConcatProxy:

```
auto c = String{"Marc"} + String{"Chagall"};
// c is a ConcatProxy due to the auto keyword here
```

Unfortunately, we have no way to get around this; the result must be explicitly cast to String.

It's time to see how much faster our optimized version is compared to the normal case.

Performance evaluation

To evaluate the performance benefits, we'll use the following benchmark, which concatenates and compares 10'000 strings of size 50:

```
template <typename T>
auto create_strings(int n, size_t length) -> std::vector<T> {
  // Create n random strings of the specified length
  // ...
}

template <typename T>
void bm_string_compare(benchmark::State& state) {
  const auto n = 10'000, length = 50;
  const auto a = create_strings<T>(n, length);
  const auto b = create_strings<T>(n, length);
  const auto c = create_strings<T>(n, length * 2);
  for (auto _ : state) {
    for (auto i = 0; i < n; ++i) {
      auto is_equal = a[i] + b[i] == c[i];
      benchmark::DoNotOptimize(is_equal);
```

```
      }
    }
  }
  BENCHMARK_TEMPLATE(bm_string_compare, std::string);
  BENCHMARK_TEMPLATE(bm_string_compare, String);
  BENCHMARK_MAIN();
```

I achieved a 40x speedup using gcc when executing on an Intel Core i7 CPU. The version using std::string directly completed in 1.6 ms, whereas the proxy version using String completed in only 0.04 ms. When running the same test using short strings of length 10, the speedup was around 20x. One reason for the big variation is that small strings will avoid heap allocations by utilizing the small string optimization discussed in *Chapter 7, Memory Management*. The benchmark shows us that the speedup with a proxy object is considerable when we get rid of the temporary string and the possible heap allocation that comes with it.

The ConcatProxy class helped us to hide an optimization when comparing strings. Hopefully this simple example has inspired you to start thinking about ways to keep your API design clean while implementing performance optimizations.

Next, you will see another useful optimization that can be hidden behind a proxy class.

Postponing sqrt computations

This section will show you how to use a proxy object in order to postpone, or even avoid, using the computationally heavy std::sqrt() function when comparing the length of two-dimensional vectors.

A simple two-dimensional vector class

Let's start with a simple two-dimensional vector class. It has *x* and *y* coordinates and a member function called length() that calculates the distance from the origin to the location *(x, y)*. We will call the class Vec2D. Here follows the definition:

```
class Vec2D {
public:
  Vec2D(float x, float y) : x_{x}, y_{y} {}
  auto length() const {
    auto squared = x_*x_ + y_*y_;
    return std::sqrt(squared);
  }
```

```
private:
  float x_{};
  float y_{};
};
```

Here is an example of how clients can use Vec2D:

```
auto a = Vec2D{3, 4};
auto b = Vec2D{4, 4};
auto shortest = a.length() < b.length() ? a : b;
auto length = shortest.length();

std::cout << length; // Prints 5
```

The example creates two vectors and compares their lengths. The length of the shortest vector is then printed to standard out. *Figure 10.3* illustrates the vector and the calculated length to the origin:

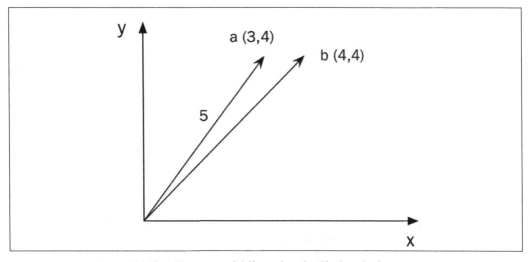

Figure 10.3: Two 2D vectors of different lengths. The length of vector a is 5.

The underlying mathematics

Looking into the mathematics of the calculation, you may notice something interesting. The formula used for length is as follows:

$$length = \sqrt{x^2 + y^2}$$

However, if we only need to compare the distance between two vectors, the squared length is all we need, as the following formula shows:

$$length^2 = x^2 + y^2$$

The square root can be computed using the function `std::sqrt()`. But, as mentioned, as the square root operation is not required if we just want to compare lengths between two vectors, we can omit it. The nice thing is that `std::sqrt()` is a relatively slow operation, meaning that if we compare a lot of vectors by their length, we can gain some performance. The question is, how can we do this while preserving a clean syntax? Let's see how we can use a proxy object to make a simple library perform this optimization under the hood when comparing lengths.

For clarity, we start with the original `Vec2D` class but we split the `length()` function into two parts – `length_squared()` and `length()`, as follows:

```
class Vec2D {
public:
  Vec2D(float x, float y) : x_{x}, y_{y} {}
  auto length_squared() const {
    return x_*x_ + y_*y_;
  }
  auto length() const {
    return std::sqrt(length_squared());
  }
private:
  float x_{};
  float y_{};
};
```

Now clients to our `Vec2D` class can use `length_squared()` if they want to gain some performance when only comparing the lengths of different vectors.

Let's say that we want to implement a convenient utility function that returns the minimum length of a range of `Vec2D` objects. We now have two options: either use the `length()` function or the `length_squared()` function when doing the comparison. Their corresponding implementations are shown in the following examples:

```
// Simple version using length()
auto min_length(const auto& r) -> float {
  assert(!r.empty());
  auto cmp = [](auto&& a, auto&& b) {
    return a.length () < b.length();
  };
```

```
    auto it = std::ranges::min_element(r, cmp);
    return it->length();
}
```

The second optimized version using `length_squared()` for comparison would look like this:

```
// Fast version using length_squared()
auto min_length(const auto& r) -> float {
  assert(!r.empty());
  auto cmp = [](auto&& a, auto&& b) {
    return a.length_squared() < b.length_squared(); // Faster
  };
  auto it = std::ranges::min_element(r, cmp);
  return it->length(); // But remember to use length() here!
}
```

The first version using `length()` inside `cmp` has the advantage of being more readable and easier to get right, whereas the second version has the advantage of being faster. To remind you, the speedup of the second version is because we can avoid the call to `std::sqrt()` inside the `cmp` lambda.

The optimal solution would be to have the syntax of the first version using `length()` and the performance of the second version using `length_squared()`.

Depending on the context this class will be used in, there might be good reasons to expose a function such as `length_squared()`. But let's assume that other developers on our team don't understand the reason for having the `length_squared()` function and find the class confusing. So, we decide to come up with something better to avoid having two versions of a function that exposes a length property of the vector. As you might have guessed, it's time for a proxy class that hides this complexity.

In order to achieve this, instead of returning a `float` value from the `length()` member function, we return an intermediate object hidden from the user. Depending on how the user uses the hidden proxy object, it should avoid the `std::sqrt()` operation until it is really required. In sections to come, we will implement a class called `LengthProxy`, which will be the type of proxy object we will return from `Vec2D::length()`.

Implementing the LengthProxy object

It's time to implement the `LengthProxy` class containing a `float` data member that represents the squared length. The actual squared length is never exposed in order to prevent users of the class from mixing the squared length with the regular length.

Instead, `LengthProxy` has a hidden `friend` function that compares its squared length with a regular length, as follows:

```cpp
class LengthProxy {
public:
  LengthProxy(float x, float y) : squared_{x * x + y * y} {}
  bool operator==(const LengthProxy& other) const = default;
  auto operator<=>(const LengthProxy& other) const = default;
  friend auto operator<=>(const LengthProxy& proxy, float len) {
    return proxy.squared_ <=> len*len;    // C++20
  }
  operator float() const {       // Allow implicit cast to float
    return std::sqrt(squared_);
  }
private:
  float squared_{};
};
```

We have defined `operator float()` to allow implicit casts from `LengthProxy` to `float`. `LengthProxy` objects can also be compared with each other. By using the new C++20 comparisons, we simply `default` the equality operator and three-way comparison operator to have the compiler generate all the necessary comparison operators for us.

Next, we rewrite the `Vec2D` class to return objects of the class `LengthProxy` instead of the actual `float` length:

```cpp
class Vec2D {
public:
  Vec2D(float x, float y) : x_{x}, y_{y} {}
  auto length() const {
    return LengthProxy{x_, y_};    // Return proxy object
  }
  float x_{};
  float y_{};
};
```

With these additions in place, it's time to use our new proxy class.

Comparing lengths with LengthProxy

In this example, we'll compare two vectors, a and b, and determine whether a is shorter than b. Note how the code syntactically looks exactly the same as if we had not utilized a proxy class:

```
auto a = Vec2D{23, 42};
auto b = Vec2D{33, 40};
bool a_is_shortest = a.length() < b.length();
```

Under the hood, the final statement is expanded to something similar to this:

```
// These LengthProxy objects are never visible from the outside
LengthProxy a_length = a.length();
LengthProxy b_length = b.length();
// Member operator< on LengthProxy is invoked,
// which compares member squared_
auto a_is_shortest = a_length < b_length;
```

Nice! The std::sqrt() operation is omitted while the interface of the Vec2D class is still intact. The simple version of min_length() we implemented earlier now performs its comparison more efficiently, as the std::sqrt() operation is omitted. What follows is the simple implementation, which now has become efficient as well:

```
// Simple and efficient
auto min_length(const auto& r) -> float {
  assert(!r.empty());
  auto cmp = [](auto&& a, auto&& b) {
    return a.length () < b.length();
  };
  auto it = std::ranges::min_element(r, cmp);
  return it->length();
}
```

The optimized length comparisons between Vec2D objects now happen under the hood. The programmer implementing the min_length() function doesn't need to know about this optimization in order to benefit from it. Let's see what it looks like if we need the actual length.

Calculating length with LengthProxy

When requesting the actual length, the calling code changes a little bit. To trig the implicit cast to float, we have to commit to a float when declaring the len variable below; that is, we can't just use auto as we usually do:

```
auto a = Vec2D{23, 42};
float len = a.length(); // Note, we cannot use auto here
```

If we were to just write auto, the len object would be of type LengthProxy rather than float. We do not want the users of our code base to explicitly handle LengthProxy objects; proxy objects should operate in the dark and only their results should be utilized (in this case, the comparison result or the actual distance value is float). Even though we cannot hide proxy objects completely, let's see how we can tighten them to prevent misuse.

Preventing the misuse of LengthProxy

You may have noted that there can be a case where using the LengthProxy class might lead to worse performance. In the example that follows, the std::sqrt() function is invoked multiple times according to the programmer's request for the length value:

```
auto a = Vec2D{23, 42};
auto len = a.length();
float f0 = len;        // Assignment invoked std::sqrt()
float f1 = len;        // std::sqrt() of len is invoked again
```

Although this is an artificial example, there can be real-world cases where this might happen, and we want to force users of Vec2d to only invoke operator float() once per LengthProxy object. In order to prevent misuse we make the operator float() member function invocable only on rvalues; that is, the LengthProxy object can only be converted to a floating point if it is not tied to a variable.

We force this behavior by using && as a modifier on the operator float() member function. The && modifier works just like a const modifier, but where a const modifier forces the member function to not modify the object the && modifier forces the function to operate on temporary objects.

The modification looks like this:

```
operator float() const && { return std::sqrt(squared_); }
```

If we were to invoke operator float() on a LengthProxy object tied to a variable, such as the dist object in the following example, the compiler would refuse to compile:

```
auto a = Vec2D{23, 42};
auto len = a.length(); // Len is of type LenghtProxy
float f = len;         // Doesn't compile: len is not an rvalue
```

However, we can still invoke operator float() directly on the rvalue returned from length(), like this:

```
auto a = Vec2D{23, 42};
float f = a.length();    // OK: call operator float() on rvalue
```

A temporary LengthProxy instance will still be created in the background, but since it is not tied to a variable, we are allowed to implicitly convert it to float. This will prevent misuse such as invoking operator float() several times on a LengthProxy object.

Performance evaluation

For the sake of it, let's see how much performance we've actually gained. We will benchmark the following version of min_element():

```
auto min_length(const auto& r) -> float {
  assert(!r.empty());
  auto it = std::ranges::min_element(r, [](auto&& a, auto&& b) {
    return a.length () < b.length(); });
  return it->length();
}
```

In order to compare the proxy object optimization with something, we will define an alternative version, Vec2DSlow, which always computes the actual length using std::sqrt():

```
struct Vec2DSlow {
  float length() const {               // Always compute
    auto squared = x_ * x_ + y_ * y_;   // actual length
    return std::sqrt(squared);          // using sqrt()
  }
  float x_, y_;
};
```

Using Google Benchmark with a function template, we can see how much performance we gain when finding the minimum length of 1,000 vectors:

```
template <typename T>
void bm_min_length(benchmark::State& state) {
  auto v = std::vector<T>{};
  std::generate_n(std::back_inserter(v), 1000, [] {
    auto x = static_cast<float>(std::rand());
    auto y = static_cast<float>(std::rand());
    return T{x, y};
  });
  for (auto _ : state) {
    auto res = min_length(v);
    benchmark::DoNotOptimize(res);
  }
}

BENCHMARK_TEMPLATE(bm_min_length, Vec2DSlow);
BENCHMARK_TEMPLATE(bm_min_length, Vec2D);
BENCHMARK_MAIN();
```

Running this benchmark on an Intel i7 CPU generated the following results:

- Using unoptimized Vec2DSlow with std::sqrt() took 7,900 ns
- Using Vec2D with LengthProxy took 1,800 ns

This performance win corresponds to a speedup of more than 4x.

This was one example of how we can avoid computations that are not necessary in some situations. But instead of making the interface of Vec2D more complicated, we managed to encapsulate the optimization inside the proxy object so that all clients could benefit from the optimization, without sacrificing clarity.

A related technique for optimizing expressions in C++ is **expression templates**. This uses template metaprogramming to generate expression trees at compile time. The technique can be used for avoiding temporaries and to enable lazy evaluation. Expression templates is one of the techniques that makes linear algebra algorithms and matrix operations fast in Boost **Basic Linear Algebra Library (uBLAS)** and **Eigen**, http://eigen.tuxfamily.org. You can read more about how expression templates and fused operations can be used when designing a matrix class in *The C++ Programming Language, 4th Edition*, by Bjarne Stroustrup.

We will end this chapter by looking at other ways to benefit from proxy objects when they are combined with overloaded operators.

Creative operator overloading and proxy objects

As you might already know, C++ has the ability to overload several operators, including the standard math operators such as plus and minus. Overloaded math operators can be utilized to create custom math classes that behave as numeric built-in types to make the code more readable. Another example is the stream operator, which in the standard library is overloaded in order to convert the objects to streams, as shown here:

```
std::cout << "iostream " << "uses " << "overloaded " << "operators.";
```

Some libraries, however, use overloading in other contexts. The Ranges library, as discussed earlier, uses overloading to compose views like this:

```
const auto r = {-5, -4, -3, -2, -1, 0, 1, 2, 3, 4, 5};
auto odd_positive_numbers = r
  | std::views::filter([](auto v) { return v > 0; })
  | std::views::filter([](auto v) { return (v % 2) == 1; });
```

Next, we will explore how to use the pipe operator with proxy classes.

The pipe operator as an extension method

Compared to other languages, for example, C#, Swift, and JavaScript, C++ does not support extension methods; that is, you cannot extend a class locally with a new member function.

For example, you cannot extend std::vector with a contains(T val) function to be used like this:

```
auto numbers = std::vector{1, 2, 3, 4};
auto has_two = numbers.contains(2);
```

However, you can overload the pipe operator to achieve this, almost equivalent, syntax:

```
auto has_two = numbers | contains(2);
```

By using a proxy class, it's possible to accomplish this without much trouble.

The pipe operator

Our goal here is to implement a simple pipe operator so that we can write the following:

```
auto numbers = std::vector{1, 3, 5, 7, 9};
auto seven = 7;
bool has_seven = numbers | contains(seven);
```

The contains() function used with a pipeable syntax has two arguments: numbers and seven. Since the left argument, numbers, could be anything, we need the overload to contain something unique on the right-hand side. So, we create a struct template named ContainsProxy, which holds onto the argument on the right-hand side; this way, the overloaded pipe operator can recognize the overload:

```
template <typename T>
struct ContainsProxy { const T& value_; };

template <typename Range, typename T>
auto operator|(const Range& r, const ContainsProxy<T>& proxy) {
  const auto& v = proxy.value_;
  return std::find(r.begin(), r.end(), v) != r.end();
}
```

Now we can use ContainsProxy like this:

```
auto numbers = std::vector{1, 3, 5, 7, 9};
auto seven = 7;
auto proxy = ContainsProxy<decltype(seven)>{seven};
bool has_seven = numbers | proxy;
```

The pipe operator works, although the syntax is still ugly as we need to specify the type. In order to make the syntax neater, we can simply make a convenience function that takes the value and creates a proxy containing the type:

```
template <typename T>
auto contains(const T& v) { return ContainsProxy<T>{v}; }
```

That's all we need; we can now use it for any type or container:

```
auto penguins = std::vector<std::string>{"Ping","Roy","Silo"};
bool has_silo = penguins | contains("Silo");
```

The example covered in this section show a rudimentary approach to implementing the pipe operator. Libraries such as the Ranges library and the Fit library by Paul Fultz, available at `https://github.com/pfultz2/Fit`, implement adaptors that take a regular function and give it the ability to be invoked using the pipe syntax.

Summary

In this chapter, you learned the difference between lazy evaluation and eager evaluation. You also learned how to use hidden proxy objects to implement lazy evaluation behind the scenes, meaning that you now understand how to implement lazy evaluation optimizations while preserving the easy-to-use interface of your classes. Hiding complex optimizations inside library classes instead of having them exposed in the application code makes the application code more readable and less error-prone.

In the next chapter, we will shift focus and move on to concurrent and parallel programming using C++.

11
Concurrency

After covering lazy evaluation and proxy objects in the last chapter, we will now explore how to write concurrent programs in C++ using threads with shared memory. We will look at ways to make concurrent programs correct by writing programs that are free from data races and deadlocks. This chapter will also contain advice on how to make concurrent programs run with low latency and high throughput.

Before we go any further, you should know that this chapter is not a complete introduction to concurrent programming, nor will it cover all the details of concurrency in C++. Instead, this chapter is an introduction to the core building blocks of writing concurrent programs in C++, mixed with some performance-related guidelines. If you haven't written concurrent programs before, it is wise to go through some introductory material to cover the theoretical aspects of concurrent programming. Concepts such as deadlocks, critical sections, condition variables, and mutexes will be very briefly discussed, but this will serve more as a refresher than a thorough introduction to the concepts.

The chapter covers the following:

- The fundamentals of concurrent programming, including parallel execution, shared memory, data races, and deadlocks
- An introduction to the C++ thread support library, the atomic library, and the C++ memory model
- A short example of lock-free programming
- Performance guidelines

Understanding the basics of concurrency

A concurrent program can execute multiple tasks at the same time. Concurrent programming is, in general, a lot harder than sequential programming, but there are several reasons why a program may benefit from being concurrent:

- **Efficiency**: The smartphones and desktop computers of today have multiple CPU cores that can execute multiple tasks in parallel. If you manage to split a big task into subtasks that can be run in parallel, it is theoretically possible to divide the running time of the big task by the number of CPU cores. For programs that run on machines with one single core, there can still be a gain in performance if a task is I/O bound. While one subtask is waiting for I/O, other subtasks can still perform useful work on the CPU.

- **Responsiveness and low latency contexts**: For applications with a graphical user interface, it is important to never block the UI so that the application becomes unresponsive. To prevent unresponsiveness, it is common to let long-running tasks (like loading a file from disk or fetching some data from the network) execute in separate background threads so that the thread responsible for the UI is never blocked by long-running tasks. Another example where low latency matters is real-time audio. The function responsible for producing buffers of audio data is executed in a separate high-priority thread, while the rest of the program can run in lower-priority threads to handle the UI and so on.

- **Simulation**: Concurrency can make it easier to simulate systems that are concurrent in the real world. After all, most things around us happen concurrently, and sometimes it is very hard to model concurrent flows with a sequential programming model. We will not focus on simulation in this book, but will instead focus on performance-related aspects of concurrency.

Concurrency solves many problems for us, but introduces new ones, as we will discuss next.

What makes concurrent programming hard?

There are a number of reasons why concurrent programming is hard, and, if you have written concurrent programs before, you have most likely already encountered the ones listed here:

- Sharing state between multiple threads in a safe manner is hard. Whenever we have data that can be read and written to at the same time, we need some way of protecting that data from data races. You will see many examples of this later on.

- Concurrent programs are usually more complicated to reason about because of the multiple parallel execution flows.

- Concurrency complicates debugging. Bugs that occur because of data races can be very hard to debug since they are dependent on how threads are scheduled. These kinds of bugs can be hard to reproduce and, in the worst-case scenario, they may even cease to exist when running the program using a debugger. Sometimes an innocent debug trace to the console can change the way a multithreaded program behaves and make the bug temporarily disappear. You have been warned!

Before we start looking at concurrent programming using C++, a few general concepts related to concurrent and parallel programming will be introduced.

Concurrency and parallelism

Concurrency and **parallelism** are two terms that are sometimes used interchangeably. However, they are not the same and it is important to understand the differences between them. A program is said to run concurrently if it has multiple individual control flows running during overlapping time periods. In C++, each individual control flow is represented by a thread. The threads may or may not execute at the exact same time, though. If they do, they are said to execute in parallel. For a concurrent program to run in parallel, it needs to be executed on a machine that has support for parallel execution of instructions; that is, a machine with multiple CPU cores.

At first glance, it might seem obvious that we always want concurrent programs to run in parallel if possible, for efficiency reasons. However, that is not necessarily always true. A lot of synchronization primitives (such as mutex locks) covered in this chapter are required only to support the parallel execution of threads. Concurrent tasks that are not run in parallel do not require the same locking mechanisms and can be a lot easier to reason about.

Time slicing

You might ask, "How are concurrent threads executed on machines with only a single CPU core?" The answer is **time slicing**. It is the same mechanism that is used by the operating system to support the concurrent execution of processes. In order to understand time slicing, let's assume we have two separate sequences of instructions that should be executed concurrently, as shown in the following figure:

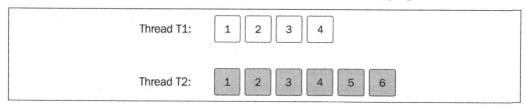

Figure 11.1: Two separate sequences of instructions

The numbered boxes represent the instructions. Each sequence of instructions is executed in a separate thread, labeled **T1** and **T2**. The operating system will schedule each thread to have some limited time on the CPU and then perform a context switch. The context switch will store the current state of the running thread and load the state of the thread that should be executed. This is done often enough so that it appears as if the threads are running at the same time. A context switch is time-consuming, though, and most likely will generate a lot of cache misses each time a new thread gets to execute on a CPU core. Therefore, we don't want context switches to happen too often.

The following figure shows a possible execution sequence of two threads that are being scheduled on a single CPU:

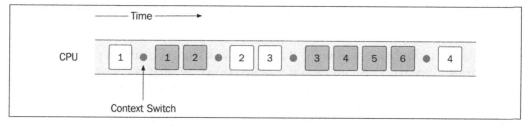

Figure 11.2: A possible execution of two threads. The dots indicate context switches

The first instruction of thread T1 starts, and is then followed by a context switch to let thread T2 execute the first two instructions. As programmers, we must make sure that the program can run as expected, regardless of how the operating system scheduler is scheduling the tasks. If a sequence, for some reason, is invalid, there are ways to control the order in which the instructions get executed by using locks, which will be covered later on.

If a machine has multiple CPU cores, it is possible to execute the two threads in parallel. However, there is no guarantee (it's even unlikely) that the two threads will execute on one core each throughout the lifetime of the program. The entire system shares time on the CPU, so the scheduler will let other processes execute as well. This is one of the reasons why the threads are not scheduled on dedicated cores.

Figure 11.3 shows the execution of the same two threads, but now they are running on a machine with two CPU cores. As you can see, the second and third instructions of the first thread (white boxes) are executing at the exact same time as the other thread is executing — the two threads are executing in parallel:

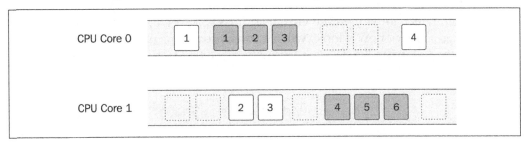

Figure 11.3: Two threads executing on a multicore machine. This makes it possible to execute the two threads in parallel.

Let's discuss shared memory next.

Shared memory

Threads created in the same process share the same virtual memory. This means that a thread can access any data that is addressable within the process. The operating system, which protects memory between processes using virtual memory, does nothing to protect us from accidentally accessing memory inside a process that was not intended to be shared among different threads. Virtual memory only protects us from accessing memory allocated in different processes to our own.

Sharing memory between multiple threads can be a very efficient way to handle communication between threads. However, sharing memory in a safe way between threads is one of the major challenges when writing concurrent programs in C++. We should always strive to minimize the number of shared resources between threads.

Fortunately, not all memory is shared by default. Each thread has its own stack for storing local variables and other data necessary for handling function calls. Unless a thread passes references or pointers to local variables to other threads, no other thread will be able to access the stack from that thread. This is one more reason to use the stack as much as possible (if you are not already convinced that the stack is a good place for your data after reading *Chapter 7, Memory Management*).

There is also **thread local storage**, sometimes abbreviated to **TLS**, which can be used to store variables that are global in the context of a thread but which are not shared between threads. A thread local variable can be thought of as a global variable where each thread has its own copy.

Everything else is shared by default; that is, dynamic memory allocated on the heap, global variables, and static local variables. Whenever you have shared data that is mutated by some thread, you need to ensure that no other thread is accessing that data at the same time or you will have a data race.

Remember the figure from the *Process memory* section of *Chapter 7, Memory Management*, which illustrated the virtual address space of a process? Here it is again, but modified to show how it looks when a process contains multiple threads. As you can see in the following figure, each thread has its own stack memory, but there is only one heap for all threads:

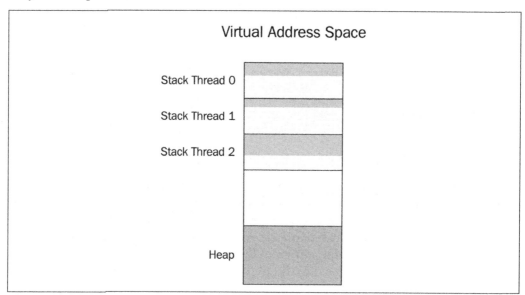

Figure 11.4: A possible layout of the virtual address space for a process

The process contains three threads in this example. The heap memory is by default shared by all threads.

Data races

A **data race** happens when two threads are accessing the same memory at the same time and at least one of the threads is mutating the data. If your program has a data race, it means that your program has undefined behavior. The compiler and optimizer will *assume* that there are no data races in your code and optimize it under that assumption. This may result in crashes or other completely surprising behavior. In other words, you can under no circumstances allow data races in your program. The compiler usually doesn't warn you about data races since they are hard to detect at compile time.

 Debugging data races can be a real challenge and sometimes requires tools such as **ThreadSanitizer** (from Clang) or **Concurrency Visualizer** (a Visual Studio extension). These tools typically instrument the code so that a runtime library can detect, warn about, or visualize potential data races while running the program you are debugging.

Example: A data race

Figure 11.5 shows two threads that are going to update an integer called counter. Imagine that these threads are both incrementing a global counter variable with the instruction ++counter. It turns out that incrementing an int might involve multiple CPU instructions. This can be done in different ways on different CPUs, but let's pretend that ++counter generates the following made-up machine instructions:

- **R**: Read counter from memory
- **+1**: Increment counter
- **W**: Write new counter value to memory

Now, if we have two threads that are going to update the `counter` value that initially is 42, we would expect it to become 44 after both threads have run. However, as you can see in the following figure, there is no guarantee that the instructions will be executed sequentially to guarantee a correct increment of the `counter` variable.

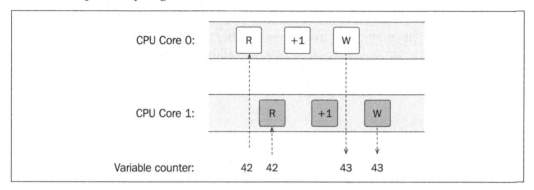

Figure 11.5: The two threads are both incrementing the same shared variable

Without a data race, the counter would have reached the value 44, but instead, it only reaches 43.

In this example, both threads read the value 42 and increment that value to 43. Then, they both write the new value, 43, which means that we never reach the correct answer of 44. Had the first thread been able to write the value 43 before the next thread started to read, we would have ended up with 44 instead. Note also that this would have been possible even if there was only one CPU core. The scheduler could have scheduled the two threads in a similar way so that both read instructions were executed before any writes.

Again, this is one possible scenario, but the important thing is that the behavior is undefined. Anything could happen when your program has a data race. One such example is **tearing**, which is the common term for **torn reads** and **torn writes**. This happens when a thread writes parts of a value to memory while another thread reads the value at the same time and therefore ends up with a corrupt value.

Avoiding data races

How can we avoid data races? There are two main options:

- Use an atomic data type instead of the int. This will tell the compiler to execute the read, increment, and write atomically. We will spend more time discussing atomic data types later in this chapter.

- Use a mutually exclusive lock (mutex) that guarantees that multiple threads never execute a critical section at the same time. A **critical section** is a place in the code that must not be executed simultaneously since it updates or reads shared memory that potentially could generate data races.

It is also worth emphasizing that immutable data structures — data structures that are never changed — can be accessed by multiple threads without any risk of data races. Minimizing the use of mutable objects is good for many reasons, but it becomes even more important when writing concurrent programs. A common pattern is to always create new immutable objects instead of mutating existing objects. When the new object is fully constructed and represents the new state, it can be swapped with the old object. In that way, we can minimize the critical sections of our code. Only the swap is a critical section, and hence needs to be protected by an atomic operation or a mutex.

Mutex

A **mutex**, short for **mutual exclusion lock**, is a synchronization primitive for avoiding data races. A thread that needs to enter a critical section first needs to lock the mutex (locking is sometimes also called acquiring a mutex lock). This means that no other thread can lock the same mutex until the first thread that holds the lock has unlocked the mutex. In that way, the mutex guarantees that only one thread at a time is inside a critical section.

In *Figure 11.6*, you can see how the race condition demonstrated in the section *A data race example* can be avoided by using a mutex. The instruction labeled **L** is a lock instruction and the instruction labeled **U** is an unlock instruction. The first thread executing on Core 0 reaches the critical section first and locks the mutex before reading the value of the counter. It then adds 1 to the counter and writes it back to memory. After that, it releases the lock.

The second thread, executing on Core 1, reaches the critical section just after the first thread has acquired the mutex lock. Since the mutex is already locked, the thread is blocked until the first thread has updated the counter undisturbed and released the mutex:

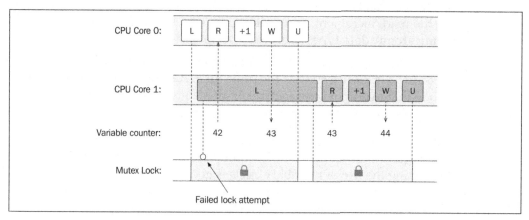

Figure 11.6: The mutex lock is protecting the critical section and avoids data races on the counter variable

The net result is that the two threads can update the mutable shared variable in a safe and correct way. However, it also means that the two threads can no longer be run in parallel. If most of the work a thread does cannot be done without serializing the work, there is, from a performance perspective, no point in using threads.

The state where the second thread is blocked by the first thread is called **contention**. This is something we strive to minimize, because it hurts the scalability of a concurrent program. Adding more CPU cores will not improve performance if the degree of contention is high.

Deadlock

When using mutex locks to protect shared resources, there is a risk of getting stuck in a state called **deadlock**. A deadlock can happen when two threads are waiting for each other to release their locks. Neither of the threads can proceed and they are stuck in a deadlock state. One condition that needs to be fulfilled for a deadlock to occur is that one thread that already holds a lock tries to acquire an additional lock. When a system grows and gets larger, it becomes more and more difficult to track all locks that might be used by all threads running in a system. This is one reason for always trying to minimize the use of shared resources, and this demonstrates the need for exclusive locking.

Figure 11.7 shows two threads in a waiting state, trying to acquire the lock held by the other thread:

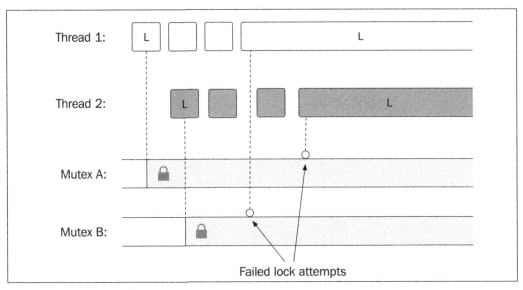

Figure 11.7: An example of a deadlock state

Let's discuss synchronous and asynchronous tasks next.

Synchronous and asynchronous tasks

I will refer to **synchronous tasks** and **asynchronous tasks** in this chapter. Synchronous tasks are like ordinary C++ functions. When a synchronous task is finished doing whatever it is supposed to do, it will return the control to the caller of the task. The caller of the task is waiting or blocked until the synchronous task has finished.

An asynchronous task, on the other hand, will return the control back to the caller immediately and instead perform its work concurrently.

The sequence in *Figure 11.8* shows the difference between calling a synchronous and asynchronous task, respectively:

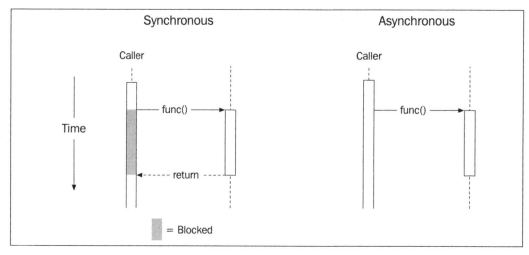

Figure 11.8: Synchronous versus asynchronous calls. The asynchronous task returns immediately but continues to work after the caller has regained control.

If you haven't seen asynchronous tasks before, they might look strange at first, since ordinary functions in C++ always stop executing when they encounter a return statement or reach the end of the function body. Asynchronous APIs are getting more and more common, though, and it is likely that you have encountered them before, for example, when working with asynchronous JavaScript.

Sometimes, we use the term **blocking** for operations that block the caller; that is, make the caller wait until the operation has finished.

With a general introduction to concurrency behind us, it's time to explore the support for threaded programming in C++.

Concurrent programming in C++

The concurrency support in C++ makes it possible for a program to execute multiple tasks concurrently. As mentioned earlier, writing a correct concurrent C++ program is, in general, a lot harder than writing a program that executes all tasks sequentially in one thread. This section will also demonstrate some common pitfalls to make you aware of all the difficulties involved in writing concurrent programs.

Concurrency support was first introduced in C++11 and has since been extended into C++14, C++17, and C++20. Before concurrency was part of the language, it was implemented with native concurrency support from the operating system, **POSIX Threads (pthreads)**, or some other library.

With concurrency support directly in the C++ language, we can write cross-platform concurrent programs, which is great! Sometimes, however, you have to reach for platform-specific functionality when dealing with concurrency on your platform. For example, there is no support in the C++ standard library for setting thread priorities, configuring CPU affinity (CPU pinning), or setting the stack size of new threads.

It should also be said that the thread support library has been extended quite a bit with the release of C++20, and more features are likely to be added in future versions of the language. The need for good concurrency support is increasing because of the way hardware is being developed, and there is a lot yet to be discovered when it comes to the efficiency, scalability, and correctness of highly concurrent programs.

The thread support library

We will now take a tour through the C++ thread support library and cover its most important components.

Threads

A running program contains at least one thread. When your main function is called, it is executed on a thread usually referred to as the **main thread**. Each thread has an identifier, which can be useful when debugging a concurrent program. The following program prints the thread identifier of the main thread:

```
int main() {
  std::cout << "Thread ID: " <<  std::this_thread::get_id() << '\n';
}
```

Running the preceding program might produce something like this:

```
Thread ID: 0x1001553c0
```

It is possible to make a thread sleep. Sleep is rarely used in production code but can be very useful during debugging. For example, if you have a data race that only occurs under rare circumstances, adding sleep to your code might make it appear more often. This is how to make the currently running thread sleep for a second:

```
std::this_thread::sleep_for(std::chrono::seconds{1});
```

Your program should never expose any data races after inserting random sleeps in your code. Your program may not work satisfactorily after adding sleeps; buffers may become full, the UI may lag, and so on, but it should always behave in a predictable and defined way. We don't have control over the scheduling of the threads, and random sleeps simulate unlikely but possible scheduling scenarios.

Now, let's create an additional thread using the std::thread class from the <thread> header. It represents a single thread of execution and is usually a wrapper around an operating system thread. The print() function will be invoked from a thread created by us explicitly:

```
void print() {
  std::this_thread::sleep_for(std::chrono::seconds{1});
  std::cout << "Thread ID: "<<  std::this_thread::get_id() << '\n';
}

int main() {
  auto t1 = std::thread{print};
  t1.join();
  std::cout << "Thread ID: "<<  std::this_thread::get_id() << '\n';
}
```

When creating the thread, we pass in a callable object (a function, lambda, or a function object) that the thread will begin to execute whenever it gets scheduled time on the CPU. I have added a call to sleep to make it obvious why we need to call join() on the thread. When a std::thread object is destructed, it must have been *joined* or *detached* or it will cause the program to call std::terminate(), which by default will call std::abort() if we haven't installed a custom std::terminate_handler.

In the preceding example, the join() function is blocking — it waits until the thread has finished running. So, in the preceding example, the main() function will not return until thread t1 has finished running. Consider the following line:

```
t1.join();
```

Suppose we detach the thread `t1` by replacing the preceding line with the following line:

```
t1.detach();
```

In such a case, our main function will end before thread `t1` wakes up to print the message, and, as a result, the program will (most likely) only output the thread ID of the main thread. Remember, we have no control of the scheduling of the threads and it is possible, but very unlikely, that the main thread will output its message *after* the `print()` function has had time to sleep, wake up, and print its thread ID.

Using `detach()` instead of `join()` in this example also introduces another problem. We are using `std::cout` from both threads without any synchronization, and since `main()` is no longer waiting for thread `t1` to finish, they both could theoretically use `std::cout` in parallel. Fortunately, `std::cout` is thread-safe and can be used from multiple threads without introducing data races, so there is no undefined behavior. However, it is still possible that the output generated by the threads is interleaved, resulting in something like the following:

```
Thread ID: Thread ID: 0x1003a93400x700004fd4000
```

If we want to avoid the interleaved output, we need to treat the outputting of characters as a critical section and synchronize access to `std::cout`. We will talk more about critical sections and race conditions in a while, but first, let's cover some details about `std::thread`.

Thread states

Before we go any further, you should have a good understanding of what a `std::thread` object really represents and in what states it can be. We haven't yet talked about what sort of threads there normally are in a system executing a C++ program.

In the following figure, you can see a snapshot of a hypothetical running system.

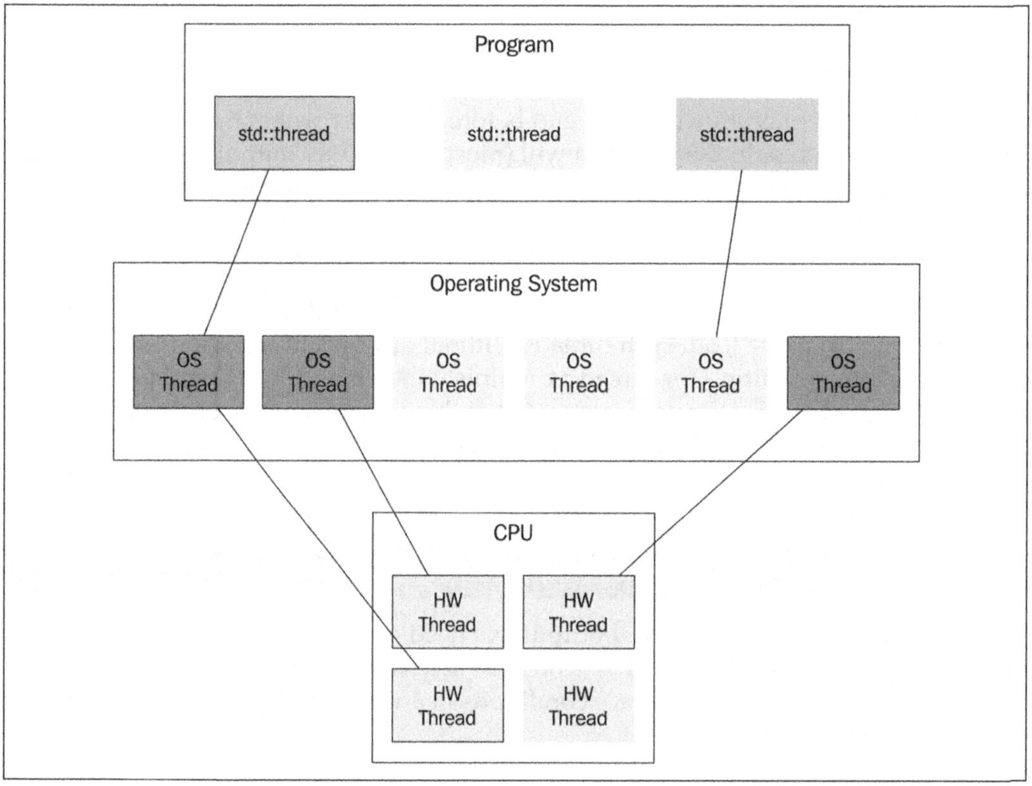

Figure 11.9: Snapshot of a hypothetical running system

Starting from the bottom, the figure shows the CPU and its **hardware threads**. Those are the execution units on the CPU. In this example, the CPU provides four hardware threads. Usually that means it has four cores, but it could be some other configuration; for example, some cores can execute two hardware threads. This is usually called **hyperthreading**. The total number of hardware threads can be printed at runtime with this:

```
std::cout << std::thread::hardware_concurrency() << '\n';
// Possible output: 4
```

The preceding code might also output 0 if the number of hardware threads cannot be determined on the running platform.

The layer above the hardware threads contains the **operating system threads**. These are the actual software threads. The operating system scheduler determines when and for how long an operating system thread is executed by a hardware thread. In *Figure 11.9*, there are currently three out of six software threads executing.

The topmost layer in the figure contains the std::thread objects. A std::thread object is nothing more than an ordinary C++ object that may or may not be associated with an underlying operating system thread. Two instances of std::thread cannot be associated with the same underlying thread. In the figure, you can see that the program currently has three instances of std::thread; two are associated with threads and one is not. It's possible to use the std::thread::joinable property to find out what state a std::thread object is in. A thread is *not* joinable if it has been:

- Default constructed; that is, if it has nothing to execute
- Moved from (its associated running thread has been transferred to another std::thread object)
- Detached by a call to detach()
- Already joined by a call to join()

Otherwise, the std::thread object is in the joinable state. Remember, when a std::thread object is destructed, it must no longer be in the joinable state or the program will terminate.

Joinable thread

C++20 introduced a new thread class named std::jthread. It is very similar to std::thread, but with a couple of important additions:

- std::jthread has support for stopping a thread using a stop token. This is something that we had to implement manually before C++20 when using std::thread.
- Instead of terminating the app when it is being destructed in a non-joinable state, the destructor of std::jthread will send a stop request and join the thread on destruction.

I will illustrate the latter point next. First, we will use the print() function, which is defined like this:

```
void print() {
  std::this_thread::sleep_for(std::chrono::seconds{1});
  std::cout << "Thread ID: "<<  std::this_thread::get_id() << '\n';
}
```

It sleeps for a second, and then prints the current thread identifier:

```cpp
int main() {
    std::cout << "main begin\n";
    auto joinable_thread = std::jthread{print};
    std::cout << "main end\n";
} // OK: jthread will join automatically
```

The following output was produced when running the code on my machine:

```
main begin
main end
Thread ID: 0x1004553c0
```

Now let's change our `print()` function so that it output messages continuously in a loop. We then need some way to communicate to the `print()` function when to stop. The `std::jthread` (as opposed to `std::thread`) has built-in support for this by using a stop token. When `std::jthread` invokes the `print()` function, it can pass an instance of a `std::stop_token` if the `print()` function accepts such an argument. Here is an example of how we could implement this new `print()` function using a stop token:

```cpp
void print(std::stop_token stoken) {
    while (!stoken.stop_requested()) {
        std::cout << std::this_thread::get_id() << '\n';
        std::this_thread::sleep_for(std::chrono::seconds{1});
    }
    std::cout << "Stop requested\n";
}
```

The `while`-loop checks at each iteration whether the function has been requested to stop by calling `stop_requested()`. From our `main()` function, it's now possible to request a stop by calling `request_stop()` on our `std::jthread` instance:

```cpp
int main() {
    auto joinable_thread = std::jthread(print);
    std::cout << "main: goes to sleep\n";
    std::this_thread::sleep_for(std::chrono::seconds{3});
    std::cout << "main: request jthread to stop\n";
    joinable_thread.request_stop();
}
```

When I run this program, it generates the following output:

```
main: goes to sleep
Thread ID: 0x70000f7e1000
```

```
Thread ID: 0x70000f7e1000
Thread ID: 0x70000f7e1000
main: request jthread to stop
Stop requested
```

In this example, we could have omitted the explicit call to request_stop() because jthread will call request_stop() automatically on destruction.

The new jthread class is a welcome addition to the C++ thread library and it should be the first choice when reaching for a thread class in C++.

Protecting critical sections

As I already mentioned, our code must not contain any data races. Unfortunately, writing code with data races is very easy. Finding the critical sections and protecting them with locks is something we constantly need to think about when writing concurrent programs in this style using threads.

C++ provides us with a std::mutex class that can be used for protecting critical sections and avoiding data races. I will demonstrate how to use a mutex with a classic example using a shared mutable counter variable updated by multiple threads.

First, we define a global mutable variable and the function incrementing the counter:

```
auto counter = 0; // Warning! Global mutable variable

void increment_counter(int n) {
  for (int i = 0; i < n; ++i)
    ++counter;
}
```

The main() function that follows creates two threads that will both execute the increment_counter() function. Note also in this example how we can pass arguments to the function invoked by the thread. We can pass an arbitrary number of arguments to the thread constructor in order to match the parameters in the signature of the function to be called. Finally, we assert that the counter has the value we would expect it to have if the program was free from race conditions:

```
int main() {
  constexpr auto n = int{100'000'000};
  {
    auto t1 = std::jthread{increment_counter, n};
    auto t2 = std::jthread{increment_counter, n};
```

```
    }
    std::cout << counter << '\n';
    // If we don't have a data race, this assert should hold:
    assert(counter == (n * 2));
}
```

This program will most likely fail. The `assert()` function doesn't hold since the program currently contains a race condition. When I repeatedly run the program, I end up with different values of the counter. Instead of reaching the value 200000000, I once ended up with no more than 137182234. This example is very similar to the data race example that was illustrated earlier in this chapter.

The line with the expression ++counter is a critical section — it uses a shared mutable variable and is executed by multiple threads. In order to protect the critical section, we will now use the `std::mutex` included in the `<mutex>` header. Later on, you will see how we can avoid data races in this example by using atomics, but, for now, we will use a lock.

First, we add the global `std::mutex` object next to the `counter`:

```
auto counter = 0; // Counter will be protected by counter_mutex
auto counter_mutex = std::mutex{};
```

But isn't the `std::mutex` object itself a mutable shared variable that can generate data races if used by multiple threads? Yes, it is a mutable shared variable, but no, it will not generate data races. The synchronization primitives from the C++ thread library, such as `std::mutex`, are designed for this particular purpose. In that respect, they are very special and use hardware instructions, or whatever is necessary on our platform, to guarantee that they don't generate data races themselves.

Now we need to use the mutex in our critical section that reads and updates the counter variable. We could use the `lock()` and `unlock()` member functions on the counter_mutex, but the preferred and safer method is to always use RAII for handling the mutex. Think of the mutex as a resource that always needs to be unlocked when we have finished using it. The thread library provides us with some useful RAII class templates for handling locking. Here, we will use the `std::scoped_lock<Mutex>` template to ensure that we release the mutex safely. Below is the updated `increment_counter()` function, which is now protected with a mutex lock:

```
void increment_counter(int n) {
  for (int i = 0; i < n; ++i) {
    auto lock = std::scoped_lock{counter_mutex};
    ++counter;
  }
}
```

The program is now free from data races and works as expected. If we run it again, the condition in the `assert()` function will now hold true.

Avoiding deadlocks

As long as a thread never acquires more than one lock at a time, there is no risk of deadlocks. Sometimes, though, it is necessary to acquire another lock while already holding onto a previously acquired lock. The risk of deadlocks in these situations can be avoided by grabbing both locks at the exact same time. C++ has a way to do this by using the `std::lock()` function, which takes an arbitrary number of locks and blocks until all locks have been acquired.

The following is an example of transferring money between accounts. Both accounts need to be protected during the transaction, and therefore we need to acquire two locks at the same time. Here is how it works:

```cpp
struct Account {
  Account() {}
  int balance_{0};
  std::mutex m_{};
};

void transfer_money(Account& from, Account& to, int amount) {
    auto lock1 = std::unique_lock<std::mutex>{from.m_, std::defer_lock};
    auto lock2 = std::unique_lock<std::mutex>{to.m_, std::defer_lock};

    // Lock both unique_locks at the same time
    std::lock(lock1, lock2);

    from.balance_ -= amount;
    to.balance_ += amount;
}
```

We again use a RAII class template to ensure that we release the lock whenever this function returns. In this case, we use `std::unique_lock`, which provides us with the possibility to defer the locking of the mutex. Then, we explicitly lock both mutexes at the same time by using the `std::lock()` function.

Condition variables

A **condition variable** makes it possible for threads to wait until some specific condition has been met. Threads can also use a condition variable to signal to other threads that the condition has changed.

A common pattern in a concurrent program is to have one or many threads that are waiting for data to be consumed somehow. These threads are usually called **consumers**. Another group of threads is then responsible for producing data that is ready to be consumed. These threads producing data are called **producers**, or a **producer** if it is only one thread.

The producer and consumer pattern can be implemented using a condition variable. We can use a combination of `std::condition_variable` and `std::unique_lock` for this purpose. Let's have a look at an example of a producer and consumer to make them less abstract:

```cpp
auto cv = std::condition_variable{};
auto q = std::queue<int>{};
auto mtx = std::mutex{};      // Protects the shared queue
constexpr int sentinel = -1; // Value to signal that we are done

void print_ints() {
  auto i = 0;
  while (i != sentinel) {
    {
      auto lock = std::unique_lock<std::mutex>{mtx};
      while (q.empty()) {
        cv.wait(lock); // The lock is released while waiting
      }
      i = q.front();
      q.pop();
    }
    if (i != sentinel) {
      std::cout << "Got: " << i << '\n';
    }
  }
}

auto generate_ints() {
  for (auto i : {1, 2, 3, sentinel}) {
    std::this_thread::sleep_for(std::chrono::seconds(1));
    {
```

```
        auto lock = std::scoped_lock{mtx};
        q.push(i);
    }
    cv.notify_one();
  }
}

int main() {
    auto producer = std::jthread{generate_ints};
    auto consumer = std::jthread{print_ints};
}
```

We are creating two threads: one `consumer` thread and one `producer` thread. The producer thread generates a sequence of integers and pushes them to a global `std::queue<int>` once every second. Whenever an element is added to the queue, the producer signals that the condition has changed using `notify_one()`.

The program checks whether there is data in the queue that is available for consumption by the consumer thread. Note also that it is not required to hold the lock while notifying the condition variable.

The consumer thread is responsible for printing the data (that is, the integers) to the console. It uses the condition variable to wait for the empty queue to change. When the consumer calls `cv.wait(lock)`, the thread goes to sleep and leaves the CPU for other threads to execute. It is important to understand why we need to pass the variable `lock` when calling `wait()`. Apart from putting the thread to sleep, `wait()` also unlocks the mutex while sleeping and then acquires the mutex before it returns. If `wait()` didn't release the mutex, the producer would not be able to add elements to the queue.

Why is the consumer waiting on the condition variable with a `while`-loop around it and not an `if` statement? This is a common pattern, and sometimes we need to do that since there might be other consumers that were also woken up and emptied the queue before us. In our program, we only have one consumer thread, though, so that cannot happen. However, it is possible for the consumer to be awoken from its wait even though the producer thread did not signal. This phenomenon is called **spurious wakeup**, and the reasons that this can happen are beyond the scope of this book.

As an alternative to using a `while`-loop, we can use an overloaded version of `wait()` that accepts a predicate. This version of `wait()` check if the predicate is satisfied and will do the looping for us. In our example it would look like this:

```
// ...
auto lock = std::unique_lock<std::mutex>{mtx};
cv.wait(lock, [] { return !q.empty(); });
// ...
```

You can find more information about spurious wakeups in *C++ Concurrency in Action, Second Edition*, by Anthony Williams. You now at least know how to handle situations where spurious wakeups can happen: always check the condition in a while loop or use the overloaded version of `wait()` that accepts a predicate.

Condition variables and mutexes are synchronization primitives that have been available in C++ since the introduction of threads in C++. C++20 comes with additional useful class templates for synchronizing threads, namely `std::counting_semaphore`, `std::barrier`, and `std::latch`. We will cover these new primitives later on. First we are going to spend some time on return values and error handling.

Returning data and handling errors

The examples presented so far in this chapter have used shared variables to communicate state between threads. We have used mutex locks to ensure that we avoid data races. Using shared data with mutexes, as we have been doing, can be very hard to do correctly when the size of a program increases. There is also a lot of work in maintaining code that uses explicit locking spread out over a code base. Keeping track of shared memory and explicit locking moves us further away from what we really want to accomplish and spend time on when writing a program.

In addition, we haven't dealt with error handling at all yet. What if a thread needs to report an error to some other thread? How do we do that using exceptions, as we are used to doing when a function needs to report a runtime error?

In the standard library `<future>` header, we can find some class templates that help us with writing concurrent code without global variables and locks, and, in addition, can communicate exceptions between threads for handling errors. I will now present **futures** and **promises**, which represent two sides of a value. The future is the receiving side of the value and the promise is the returning side of the value.

The following is an example of using `std::promise` to return the result to the caller:

```
auto divide(int a, int b, std::promise<int>& p) {
  if (b == 0) {
```

```
      auto e = std::runtime_error{"Divide by zero exception"};
      p.set_exception(std::make_exception_ptr(e));
    }
    else {
      const auto result = a / b;
      p.set_value(result);
    }
  }

  int main() {
      auto p = std::promise<int>{};
      std::thread(divide, 45, 5, std::ref(p)).detach();

      auto f = p.get_future();
      try {
        const auto& result = f.get(); // Blocks until ready
        std::cout << "Result: " << result << '\n';
      }
      catch (const std::exception& e) {
        std::cout << "Caught exception: " << e.what() << '\n';
      }
  }
```

The caller (the main() function) creates the std::promise object and passes it to the divide() function. We need to use std::ref from <functional> so that a reference can be correctly forwarded through the std::thread to compute().

When the divide() function has computed the result, it passes the return value through the promise by calling the set_value() function. If an error occurs in the divide() function, it calls the set_exception() function on the promise instead.

The future represents the value of the computation that may or may not be computed yet. Since the future is an ordinary object, we can, for example, pass it around to other objects that need the computed value. Finally, when the value is needed by some client, it calls get() to get hold of the actual value. If it is not computed at that point in time, the call to get() will block until it is finished.

Note also how we managed to pass data back and forth with proper error handling, without using any shared global data and with no explicit locking. The promise takes care of that for us, and we can focus on implementing the essential logic of the program instead.

Tasks

With futures and promises, we managed to get away from explicit locks and shared global data. Our code will benefit from using higher-level abstractions when possible, especially when the code base grows. Here, we will go further and explore classes that automatically set up the futures and promises for us. You will also see how we can get rid of the manual administration of threads and leave that to the library.

In many cases, we don't have any need for managing threads; instead, what we really need is to be able to execute a **task** asynchronously and have that task execute on its own concurrently with the rest of the program, and then eventually get the result or error communicated to the parts of the program that need it. The task should be carried out in isolation to minimize contention and the risk of data races.

We will begin by rewriting our previous example that divided two numbers. This time, we will use the `std::packaged_task` from `<future>`, which makes all the work of setting up the promise correct for us:

```cpp
int divide(int a, int b) { // No need to pass a promise ref here!
  if (b == 0) {
    throw std::runtime_error{"Divide by zero exception"};
  }
  return a / b;
}

int main() {
  auto task = std::packaged_task<decltype(divide)>{divide};
  auto f = task.get_future();
  std::thread{std::move(task), 45, 5}.detach();

  // The code below is unchanged from the previous example
  try {
    const auto& result = f.get(); // Blocks until ready
    std::cout << "Result: " << result << '\n';
  }
  catch (const std::exception& e) {
    std::cout << "Caught exception: " << e.what() << '\n';
  }
  return 0;
}
```

`std::packaged_task` is itself a callable object that can be moved to the `std::thread` object we are creating. As you can see, `std::packaged_task` now does most of the work for us: we don't have to create the promise ourselves. But, more importantly, we can write our `divide()` function just like a normal function, without the need for explicitly returning values or exceptions through the promise; the `std::packaged_task` will do that for us.

As a last step in this section, we would also like to get rid of the manual thread management. Creating threads is not free, and you will see later on that the number of threads in a program can affect performance. It seems like the question of whether we should create a new thread for our `divide()` function is not necessarily up to the caller of `divide()`. The library again helps us here by providing another useful function template called `std::async()`. The only thing we need to do in our `divide()` example is replace the code creating the `std::packaged_task` and the `std::thread` object with a simple call to `std::async()`:

```
auto f = std::async(divide, 45, 5);
```

We have now switched from a thread-based programming model to a task-based model. The complete task-based example now looks like this:

```cpp
int divide(int a, int b) {
  if (b == 0) {
    throw std::runtime_error{"Divide by zero exception"};
  }
  return a / b;
}

int main() {
  auto future = std::async(divide, 45, 5);
  try {
    const auto& result = future.get();
    std::cout << "Result: " << result << '\n';
  }
  catch (const std::exception& e) {
    std::cout << "Caught exception: " << e.what() << '\n';
  }
}
```

There is really a minimal amount of code left here for handling concurrency. The recommended way to call functions asynchronously is to use `std::async()`. For a deeper discussion about why and when `std::async()` is preferred, I highly recommend the *Concurrency* chapter in *Effective Modern C++* by Scott Meyers.

Additional synchronization primitives in C++20

C++20 comes with a few additional synchronization primitives, namely `std::latch`, `std::barrier`, and `std::counting_semaphore` (and the template specialization `std::binary_semaphore`). This section will be an overview of these new types and some typical scenarios where they can be useful. We'll begin with `std::latch`.

Using latches

A latch is a synchronization primitive that can be used for synchronizing multiple threads. It creates a synchronization point where all threads must arrive at. You can think of a latch as a decrementing counter. Typically, all threads decrement the counter once and then wait for the latch to reach zero before moving on.

A latch is constructed by passing an initial value of the internal counter:

```cpp
auto lat = std::latch{8}; // Construct a latch initialized with 8
```

Threads can then decrement the counter using `count_down()`:

```cpp
lat.count_down(); // Decrement but don't wait
```

A thread can wait on the latch to reach zero:

```cpp
lat.wait(); // Block until zero
```

It's also possible to check (without blocking) to see whether the counter has reached zero:

```cpp
if (lat.try_wait()) {
  // All threads have arrived ...
}
```

It's common to wait for the latch to reach zero right after decrementing the counter, as follows:

```cpp
lat.count_down();
lat.wait();
```

In fact, this use case is common enough to deserve a tailor-made member function; `arrive_and_wait()` decrements the latch and then waits for the latch to reach zero:

```cpp
lat.arrive_and_wait(); // Decrement and block while not zero
```

Joining a set of forked tasks is a common scenario when working with concurrency. If the tasks only need to be joined at the end, we can use an array of future objects (to wait on) or just wait for all the threads to complete. But in other cases, we want a set of asynchronous tasks to arrive at a common synchronization point, and then have the tasks continue running. These situations typically occur when some sort of initialization is needed before multiple worker threads start their actual work.

Example: Initializing threads using std::latch

The following example demonstrates how `std::latch` can be used when multiple worker threads need to run some initialization code before they start working.

When a thread is created, a contiguous block of memory is allocated for the stack. Typically, this memory does not yet reside in physical memory when it is first allocated in the virtual address space. Instead, when the stack is being used, *page faults* will be generated in order to map the virtual memory to physical memory. The operating system handles the mapping for us, and it is an efficient way to lazily map memory when needed. Usually, this is just what we want: we pay for the cost of mapping memory as late as possible and only if needed. However, in circumstances where low latency is important, for example in real-time code, it might be necessary to completely avoid page faults. The stack memory is unlikely to be paged out by the operating system, so it is usually enough to run some code that will generate page faults and thereby map the virtual stack memory to physical memory. This process is called **prefaulting**.

There is no portable way to set or get the stack size of a C++ thread, so here we will just assume that the stack is at least 500 KB. The following code is an attempt to prefault the first 500 KB of the stack:

```
void prefault_stack() {
  // We don't know the size of the stack
  constexpr auto stack_size = 500u * 1024u;
  // Make volatile to avoid optimization
  volatile unsigned char mem[stack_size];
  std::fill(std::begin(mem), std::end(mem), 0);
}
```

The idea here is to allocate an array on the stack that will occupy a significant chunk of stack memory. Then, in order to generate page faults, we write to every element in the array using `std::fill()`. The volatile keyword was not mentioned earlier and is a somewhat confusing keyword in C++. It has nothing to do with concurrency; it's only added here to prevent the compiler from optimizing away this code. By declaring the `mem` array `volatile`, the compiler is not allowed to ignore the writes to the array.

Now, let's focus on the actual `std::latch`. Let's say we want to create a number of worker threads that should only start their work once all thread stacks have been prefaulted. We can achieve this synchronization using a `std::latch`, as follows:

```
auto do_work() { /* ... */ }

int main() {
  constexpr auto n_threads = 2;
  auto initialized = std::latch{n_threads};
  auto threads = std::vector<std::thread>{};
  for (auto i = 0; i < n_threads; ++i) {
    threads.emplace_back([&] {
      prefault_stack();
      initialized.arrive_and_wait();
      do_work();
    });
  }
  initialized.wait();
  std::cout << "Initialized, starting to work\n";
  for (auto&& t : threads) {
    t.join();
  }
}
```

After all threads have arrived, the main thread can start to submit work to the worker threads. In this example, all threads are waiting for the other threads to arrive by calling `arrive_and_wait()` on the latch. Once the latch has reached zero, it can no longer be reused. There is no function for resetting the latch. If we have a scenario that requires multiple synchronization points, we can instead use a `std::barrier`.

Using barriers

Barriers are similar to latches but with two major additions: a barrier can be *reused*, and it can run a *completion function* whenever all threads have reached the barrier.

A barrier is constructed by passing an initial value of the internal counter and a completion function:

```
auto bar = std::barrier{8, [] {
  // Completion function
  std::cout "All threads arrived at barrier\n";
}};
```

Threads can arrive and wait in the same way we use a latch:

```
bar.arrive_and_wait(); // Decrement but don't wait
```

Whenever all threads have arrived (that is, when the internal counter of the barrier reaches zero) two things happens:

- The completion function provided to the constructor is called by the barrier.
- The internal counter is reset to its initial value after the completion function has returned.

Barriers are useful in parallel programming algorithms that are based on the **fork-join model**. Typically, an iterative algorithm contains a part that can be run in parallel and another part that needs to run sequentially. Multiple tasks are forked and run in parallel. Then, when all tasks have finished and joined, some single-threaded code is executed to determine whether the algorithm should continue or finish.

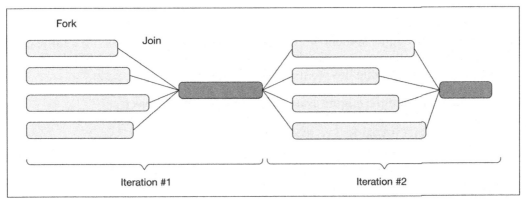

Figure 11.10: An example of the fork-join model

Concurrent algorithms that follow the fork-join model will benefit from using barriers and can avoid other explicit locking mechanisms in an elegant and efficient way. Let's see how we can use a barrier but with two major for a simple problem.

Example: Fork-join using std::barrier

Our next example is a toy problem that will demonstrate the fork-join model. We will create a small program that will simulate a set of dice being rolled and count the number of rolls it takes before getting all 6s. Rolling a set of dice is something we can do concurrently (forked). The join step, executing in a single thread, checks the result and determines whether to roll the dice again or to finish.

First, we need to implement the code for rolling a dice with six faces. For generating a number between 1 and 6 we can use a combination of classes found in the `<random>` header, as follows:

```
auto engine =
  std::default_random_engine{std::random_device{}()};
auto dist = std::uniform_int_distribution<>{1, 6};
auto result = dist(engine);
```

Here the `std::random_device` is responsible for generating a seed to the engine that will produce pseudo-random numbers. To pick an integer between 1 and 6 with equal probability, we are using `std::uniform_int_distribution`. The variable `result` is the result of rolling a dice.

Now we want to encapsulate this code into a function that will generate a random integer. Generating the seed and creating the engine is typically slow and something we want to avoid doing at every call. A common way to do this is to declare the random engine with `static` duration so that it lives during the entire lifetime of the program. However, the classes in `<random>` are not thread-safe so we need to protect the `static` engine somehow. Instead of synchronizing access with a mutex, which would make the random number generator run sequentially, I will take the opportunity to demonstrate how to use thread-local storage.

Here is how to declare the engine as a `static thread_local` object:

```
auto random_int(int min, int max) {
  // One engine instance per thread
  static thread_local auto engine =
    std::default_random_engine{std::random_device{}()};

  auto dist = std::uniform_int_distribution<>{min, max};
  return dist(engine);
}
```

A static variable with `thread_local` storage duration will be created once per thread; it's therefore safe to call `random_int()` from multiple threads concurrently without using any synchronization primitives. With this small helper function in place, we can move on to implement the rest of our program using a `std::barrier`:

```
int main() {

  constexpr auto n = 5; // Number of dice

  auto done = false;
```

```
auto dice = std::array<int, n>{};
auto threads = std::vector<std::thread>{};
auto n_turns = 0;

auto check_result = [&] { // Completion function
  ++n_turns;
  auto is_six = [](auto i) { return i == 6; };
  done = std::all_of(dice.begin(), dice.end(), is_six);
};
auto bar = std::barrier{n, check_result};
for (int i = 0; i < n; ++i) {
  threads.emplace_back([&, i] {
    while (!done) {
      dice [i] = random_int(1, 6); // Roll dice
      bar.arrive_and_wait();       // Join
    }});
}
for (auto&& t : threads) {
  t.join();
}
std::cout << n_turns << '\n';
}
```

The lambda check_result() is the completion function that will be called every time all the threads have arrived at the barrier. The completion function checks the values of each dice and determines whether a new round should be played or if we are done.

The lambda passed to the std::thread objects captures the index i by value so that all threads have a unique index. The other variables, done, dice, and bar, are captured by reference.

Note also how we can mutate and read the variables captured by reference from different threads without introducing any data races thanks to the coordination performed by the barrier.

Signalling and resource counting using semaphores

The word **semaphore** means something that can be used for signaling, such as a flag or a light. In the example that follows, you will see how we can use semaphores for signaling different states that other threads can be waiting for.

A semaphore can also be used to control access to a resource, similarly to how a `std::mutex` restricts access to a critical section:

```cpp
class Server {
public:
  void handle(const Request& req) {
    sem_.acquire();
    // Restricted section begins here.
    // Handle at most 4 requests concurrently.
    do_handle(req);
    sem_.release();
  }
private:
  void do_handle(const Request& req) { /* ... */ }
  std::counting_semaphore<4> sem_{4};
};
```

In this case, the semaphore is initialized with a value of 4, which means that at most four concurrent requests can be handled at the same time. Instead of mutually exclusive access to a section in the code, multiple threads can have access to the same section but with restrictions concerning the number of threads currently in that section.

The member function `acquire()` decrements the semaphore if the semaphore is greater than zero. Otherwise `acquire()` blocks until the semaphore allows it to decrement and enter the restricted section. `release()` increments the counter without blocking. If the semaphore was zero before it was incremented by `release()`, waiting threads will be signaled.

In addition to the `acquire()` function, it's also possible to try to decrement the counter *without blocking* using the `try_acquire()` function. It returns `true` if it managed to decrement the counter, or `false` otherwise. The functions `try_acquire_for()` and `try_acquire_until()` can be used in a similar way. But instead of immediately returning `false` when the counter is already zero, they automatically try to decrement the counter within a specified time before returning to the caller.

This trio of functions follows the same pattern as other types in the standard library, for example, `std::timed_mutex` and its `try_lock()`, `try_lock_for()`, and `try_lock_until()` member functions.

The `std::counting_semaphore` is a template with one template parameter accepting the maximum value of the semaphore. It is considered a programming error to increment (release) a semaphore above its maximum value.

A `std::counting_semaphore` with a maximum size of 1 is called a **binary semaphore**. The `<semaphore>` header includes an alias-declaration for binary semaphores:

```
std::binary_semaphore = std::counting_semaphore<1>;
```

A binary semaphore is guaranteed to be implemented more efficiently than a counting semaphore with a higher maximum value.

Another important property of semaphores is that the thread that releases a semaphore may not be the thread that acquired it. This is in contrast with `std::mutex`, which requires that the thread that acquired the mutex is also the thread that must release it. However, with semaphores it's common to have one type of task to do the waiting (acquire) and another type of task to do the signaling (release). This will be demonstrated in our next example.

Example: A bounded buffer using semaphores

The following example demonstrates a bounded buffer. It's a fixed-size buffer that can have multiple threads reading and writing from it. Again, this example demonstrates the kind of producer-consumer pattern that you have already seen using condition variables. The producer threads are the ones writing to the buffer and the reader threads are the ones reading (and popping elements) from the buffer.

The following figure shows the buffer (a fixed-size array) and the two variables that keep track of the read and write positions:

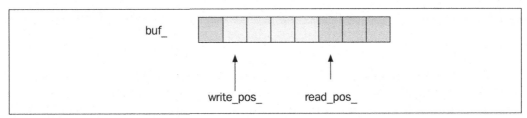

Figure 11.11: A bounded buffer has a fixed size

We will take one step at a time and start with a version that focuses on the internal logic of the bounded buffer. The signaling using semaphores will be added in the next version. Here, the initial attempt demonstrates how the read and write positions are used:

```cpp
template <class T, int N>
class BoundedBuffer {
  std::array<T, N> buf_;
  std::size_t read_pos_{};
  std::size_t write_pos_{};
  std::mutex m_;

  void do_push(auto&& item) {
    /* Missing: Should block if buffer is full */
    auto lock = std::unique_lock{m_};
    buf_[write_pos_] = std::forward<decltype(item)>(item);
    write_pos_ = (write_pos_ + 1) % N;
  }

public:
  void push(const T& item) { do_push(item); }
  void push(T&& item) { do_push(std::move(item)); }

  auto pop() {
    /* Missing: Should block if buffer is empty */
    auto item = std::optional<T>{};
    {
      auto lock = std::unique_lock{m_};
      item = std::move(buf_[read_pos_]);
      read_pos_ = (read_pos_ + 1) % N;
    }
    return std::move(*item);
  }
};
```

This first attempt contains the fixed-sized buffer, the read and write positions, and a mutex for protecting the data members from data races. This implementation should be able to have an arbitrary number of threads calling push() and pop() concurrently.

The push() function overloads on const T& and T&&. This is an optimization technique used by the standard library containers. The T&& version avoids copying the argument when the caller passes an rvalue.

To avoid duplicating the logic of the push operation, a helper function, do_push(), contains the actual logic. By using a forwarding reference (auto&& item) together with std::forward, the item parameter will be move assigned or copy assigned, depending on whether the client called push() with an rvalue or lvalue.

This version of the bounded buffer is not complete, though, because it doesn't protect us from having the write_pos point at (or beyond) the read_pos. Similarly, the read_pos must never point at the write_pos (or beyond). What we want is a buffer where producer threads block when the buffer is full and consumer threads block when the buffer is empty.

This is a perfect application for using counting semaphores. A semaphore *blocks* a thread that tries to decrease the semaphore when it is already zero. A semaphore *signals* the blocked threads whenever a semaphore that has the value zero increments.

For the bounded buffer we need two semaphores:

- The first semaphore, n_empty_slots, keeps track of the number of empty slots in the buffer. It will start with a value of the size of the buffer.

- The second semaphore, n_full_slots, keeps track of the number of full slots in the buffer.

Make sure you understand why two counting semaphores are needed (rather than one). The reason is that there are two distinct *states* that need to be signaled: when the buffer is *full* and when the buffer is *empty*.

After adding signal handling using two counting semaphores, the bounded buffer now looks like this (lines added in this version are marked with "new"):

```cpp
template <class T, int N>
class BoundedBuffer {
  std::array<T, N> buf_;
  std::size_t read_pos_{};
  std::size_t write_pos_{};
  std::mutex m_;
  std::counting_semaphore<N> n_empty_slots_{N}; // New
  std::counting_semaphore<N> n_full_slots_{0};  // New

  void do_push(auto&& item) {
    // Take one of the empty slots (might block)
    n_empty_slots_.acquire();                    // New
    try {
      auto lock = std::unique_lock{m_};
```

```
        buf_[write_pos_] = std::forward<decltype(item)>(item);
        write_pos_ = (write_pos_ + 1) % N;
      } catch (...) {
        n_empty_slots_.release();                    // New
        throw;
      }
      // Increment and signal that there is one more full slot
      n_full_slots_.release();                        // New
    }

  public:
    void push(const T& item) { do_push(item); }
    void push(T&& item) { do_push(std::move(item)); }

    auto pop() {
      // Take one of the full slots (might block)
      n_full_slots_.acquire();                        // New
      auto item = std::optional<T>{};
      try {
        auto lock = std::unique_lock{m_};
        item = std::move(buf_[read_pos_]);
        read_pos_ = (read_pos_ + 1) % N;
      } catch (...) {
        n_full_slots_.release();                      // New
        throw;
      }
      // Increment and signal that there is one more empty slot
      n_empty_slots_.release();                        // New
      return std::move(*item);
    }
};
```

This version supports multiple producers and consumers. The use of both semaphores guarantees that neither of the semaphores will reach a value greater than the maximum number of elements in the buffer. For example, there is no way a producer thread can add a value and increment the n_full_slots semaphore without first checking that there is at least one empty slot.

Note also that acquire() and release() are called from different threads. For example, the consumer threads are waiting (acquire()) on the n_full_slots semaphore and the producer threads are signaling (release()) on the very same semaphore.

The new synchronization primitives added to C++20 are well known constructs that are commonly found in threading libraries. They offer convenient and often more efficient alternatives to synchronize access to shared resources compared to `std::mutex` and `std::condition_variable`.

Atomic support in C++

The standard library contains support for **atomic variables**, sometimes called **atomics**. An atomic variable is a variable that can safely be used and mutated from multiple threads without introducing data races.

Do you remember the data race example we looked at earlier where two threads updated a global counter? We solved it by adding a mutex lock together with the counter. Instead of using an explicit lock, we could have used a `std::atomic<int>` instead:

```
std::atomic<int> counter;

auto increment_counter(int n) {
  for (int i = 0; i < n; ++i)
    ++counter; // Safe, counter is now an atomic<int>
}
```

The `++counter` is a convenient way of saying `counter.fetch_add(1)`. All member functions that can be invoked on an atomic are safe to call from multiple threads concurrently.

The atomic types are from the `<atomic>` header. There are typedefs for all the scalar data types named on the `std::atomic_int` form. This is identical to saying `std::atomic<int>`. It is possible to wrap a custom type in a `std::atomic` template, as long as the custom type is trivially copyable. Basically, this means that an object of a class is fully described by the bits of its data members. In that way, an object can be copied with, for example, `std::memcpy()`, by only copying the raw bytes. So, if a class contains virtual functions, pointers to dynamic memory, and so on, it's no longer possible to just copy the raw bits of the object and expect it to work, and hence it is not trivially copyable. This can be checked at compile time, so you will get a compilation error if you try to create an atomic of a type that is not trivially copyable:

```
struct Point {
  int x_{};
  int y_{};
};
```

```
auto p = std::atomic<Point>{};        // OK: Point is trivially copyable
auto s = std::atomic<std::string>{}; // Error: Not trivially copyable
```

It's also possible to create atomic pointers. This makes the pointer itself atomic, but not the object it points at. We will talk more about atomic pointers and references in a while.

The lock-free property

A reason for using atomics rather than protecting access to a variable with a mutex is to avoid the performance overhead introduced by using `std::mutex`. Also, the fact that a mutex can block the thread for a non-deterministic duration of time and introduce priority inversion (see the section *Thread priorities*) rules out mutexes in low latency contexts. In other words, there might be parts of your code with latency requirements that completely forbid the use of mutexes. In those cases, it's important to know whether an atomic variable is using a mutex.

An atomic variable may or may not use a lock to protect the data; this depends on the type of the variable and the platform. If the atomic does not use a lock, it is said to be **lock-free**. You can query the variable in runtime if it's lock-free:

```
auto variable = std::atomic<int>{1};
assert(variable.is_lock_free());          // Runtime assert
```

This is good, because now we at least assert when running the program that using the `variable` object is lock-free. Typically, all atomic objects of the same type will be either lock-free or not, but on some exotic platforms there is a possibility that two atomic objects might generate different answers.

It's generally more interesting to know whether an atomic type (`std::atomic<T>`) is guaranteed to be lock-free on a certain platform, and preferably we would like to know that at compile time rather than runtime. Since C++17, it's also possible to verify that an atomic specialization is lock-free at compile time by using `is_always_lock_free()`, like this:

```
static_assert(std::atomic<int>::is_always_lock_free);
```

This code will generate a compilation error if `atomic<int>` is not lock-free on the platform we are targeting. Now, if we compile a program that assumes that `std::atomic<int>` doesn't use locks, it will fail to compile, which is exactly want we want.

On modern platforms, any `std::atomic<T>` where T fits into the native word size will typically be *always lock-free*. And on modern x64 chips, you even get double that amount. For example, on libc++ compiled on a modern Intel CPU, `std::atomic<std::complex<double>>` is always lock-free.

Atomic flags

An atomic type that is guaranteed to always be lock-free is `std::atomic_flag` (regardless of the target platform). As a consequence, `std::atomic_flag` does not provide us with the `is_always_lock_free()`/`is_lock_free()` functions since they would always return `true`.

Atomic flags can be used to protect critical sections as an alternative to using `std::mutex`. Since a lock is conceptually easy to understand, I will use that as an example here. It should be noted, though, that the implementations of locks that I demonstrate in this book are not production-ready code, but rather conceptual implementation. The following example demonstrates how to conceptually implement a simple spinlock:

```
class SimpleMutex {
  std::atomic_flag is_locked_{};          // Cleared by default
public:
  auto lock() noexcept {
    while (is_locked_.test_and_set()) {
      while (is_locked_.test());          // Spin here
    }
  }
  auto unlock() noexcept {
    is_locked_.clear();
  }
};
```

The `lock()` function calls `test_and_set()` to set the flag and at the same time obtain the previous value of the flag. If `test_and_set()` returns `false`, it means that the caller managed to acquire the lock (setting the flag when it was previously cleared). Otherwise, the inner while-loop will constantly poll the state of the flag using `test()` in a spinning loop. The reason we use `test()` in an extra inner loop is performance: `test()` doesn't invalidate the cache line, whereas `test_and_set()` does. This locking protocol is called **test and test-and-set**.

This spinlock works but is not very resource-friendly; when the thread is executing, it constantly uses the CPU to check the same condition over and over again. We could add a short sleep with an exponential backoff in each iteration, but finetuning this for various platforms and scenarios is hard.

Fortunately, C++20 added a wait and notify API to std::atomic, which makes it possible for threads to wait (in a resource-friendly manner) on an atomic variable to change its value.

Atomic wait and notify

Since C++20, std::atomic and std::atomic_flag provide the functionality for waiting and notifying. The function wait() blocks the current thread until the value of the atomic variable changes and some other thread notifies the waiting thread about it. A thread can notify that a change has occurred by calling either notify_one() or notify_all().

With this new functionality, we can avoid continuously polling the state of the atomic and instead wait in a more resource-friendly way until the value changes; this is similar to how a std::condition_variable allows us to wait and notify state changes.

By using wait and notify, the SimpleMutex implemented in the previous section can be rewritten like this:

```
class SimpleMutex {
  std::atomic_flag is_locked_{};
public:
  auto lock() noexcept {
    while (is_locked_.test_and_set())
      is_locked_.wait(true);     // Don't spin, wait
  }

  auto unlock() noexcept {
    is_locked_.clear();
    is_locked_.notify_one();    // Notify blocked thread
  }
};
```

We pass the old value (true) to wait(). By the time wait() returns, the atomic variable is guaranteed to have changed so that it is no longer true. However, there is no guarantee that we will catch *all* the changes to the variable. The variable might have changed from state A to state B and then back to state A without notifying the waiting thread. This is a phenomenon in lock-free programming called the **ABA problem**.

This example demonstrated the wait and notify functions using `std::atomic_flag`. The same wait and notify API is also available on the `std::atomic` class template.

 Please note that the spinlocks presented in this chapter are not production-ready code. Implementing a highly efficient lock typically involves the correct use of memory orderings (discussed later) and non-portable code for yielding, which is beyond the scope of this book. A detailed discussion can be found at `https://timur.audio/ using-locks-in-real-time-audio-processing-safely`.

Now, we will continue talking about atomic pointers and atomic references.

Using shared_ptr in a multithreaded environment

What about the `std::shared_ptr`? Can it be used in a multithreaded environment, and how is reference counting handled when multiple threads are accessing an object referenced by multiple shared pointers?

To understand shared pointers and thread safety, we need to recall how `std::shared_ptr` is typically implemented (see also *Chapter 7, Memory Management*). Consider the following code:

```
// Thread 1
auto p1 = std::make_shared<int>(42);
```

The code creates an `int` on the heap and a reference-counted smart pointer pointing at the `int` object. When creating the shared pointer with `std::make_shared()`, a `control block` is created next to the `int`. The control block contains, among other things, a variable for the reference count, which is incremented whenever a new pointer to the `int` is created and decremented whenever a pointer to the `int` is destroyed. To summarize, when the preceding code line is executed, three separate entities are created:

- The actual `std::shared_ptr` object p1 (local variable on the stack)
- A control block (heap object)
- An int (heap object)

The following figure shows the three objects:

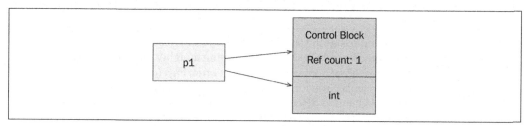

Figure 11.12: A shared_ptr instance, p1, that points to the integer object and a control block that contains the reference counting. In this case, there is only one shared pointer using the int, and hence the ref count is 1.

Now, consider what would happen if the following code was executed by a second thread:

```
// Thread 2
auto p2 = p1;
```

We are creating a new pointer pointing at the `int` (and the control block). When creating the p2 pointer, we read p1, but we also need to mutate the control block when updating the reference counter. The control block lives on the heap and is shared among the two threads, so it needs synchronization to avoid data races. Since the control block is an implementation detail hidden behind the `std::shared_ptr` interface, there is no way for us to know how to protect it, and it turns out that it has already been taken care of by the implementation.

Typically, it would use a mutable atomic counter. In other words, the ref counter update is thread-safe so that we can use multiple shared pointers from different threads without worrying about synchronizing the ref counter. This is a good practice and something to think about when designing classes. If you are mutating variables in methods that appear to be semantically read-only (`const`) from the client's perspective, you should make the mutating variables thread-safe. On the other hand, everything that can be detected by the client as mutating functions should be left to the client of the class to synchronize.

The following figure shows two `std::shared_ptrs`, p1 and p2, that have access to the same object. The `int` is the shared object and the control block is an internally shared object between the `std::shared_ptr` instances. The control block is thread-safe by default:

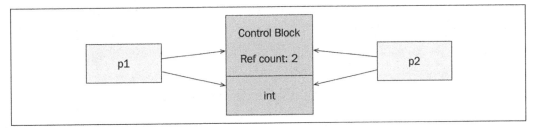

Figure 11.13: Two shared_ptrs accessing the same object

To summarize:

- The shared object, the int in this example, is not thread-safe and needs explicit locking if it is accessed from multiple threads.
- The control block is already thread-safe, so the reference counting mechanism works in multi-threaded environments.

Let's move on to protecting the shared_ptr instance.

Protecting the shared_ptr instance

Now there is only one part remaining: what about the actual std::shared_ptr objects, p1 and p2, in the previous example? To understand this, let's turn to an example using only one global std::shared_ptr object called p:

```
// Global, how to protect?
auto p = std::shared_ptr<int>{};
```

How can we mutate p from multiple threads without introducing a data race? One option is to protect p with an explicit mutex whenever we use p. Or, we could use a template specialization of std::atomic for std::shared_ptr (introduced in C++20). In other words, it's possible to declare p as an atomic shared pointer like this:

```
// Global, protect using atomic
auto p = std::atomic<std::shared_ptr<int>>{};
```

This template specialization may or may not be lock-free. You can verify this with the is_lock_free() member function. Another thing to note is that the specialization std::atomic<std::shared_ptr<T>> is an exception to the rule that std::atomic can only be specialized with types that are trivially copyable. Regardless, we are glad to finally have this useful type in the standard library.

The following example demonstrates how to load and store a shared pointer object atomically from multiple threads:

```
// Thread T1 calls this function
auto f1() {
  auto new_p = std::make_shared<int>(std::rand());
  // ...
  p.store(new_p);
}

// Thread T2 calls this function
auto f2() {
  auto local_p = p.load();
  // Use local_p...
}
```

In the preceding example, we assume that there are two threads, T1 and T2, that call functions f1() and f2(), respectively. New heap-allocated int objects are created from the thread T1 with the call to std::make_shared<int>().

There is one subtle detail to consider in this example: in which thread is the heap-allocated int deleted? When local_p goes out of scope in the f2() function, it might be the last reference to the int (the reference count reaches zero). In that case, the deletion of the heap-allocated int will happen from thread T2. Otherwise, the deletion will happen from thread T1 when std::atomic_store() is called. So, the answer is that the deletion of the int can happen from both threads.

Atomic references

So far you have seen std::atomc_flag and std::atomic<> with numerous useful specializations. std::atomic can be specialized with pointers such as std::atomic<T*>, but you haven't seen how to use atomics with reference types. It's not possible to write std::atomic<T&>; instead, the standard library provides us with a template called std::atomic_ref.

The template std::atomic_ref was introduced in C++20. Its interface is identical to std::atomic and the reason for having a separate name is to avoid the risk of impacting existing generic code that uses std::atomic<T>.

An atomic reference allows us to perform atomic operations on a non-atomic object that we have a reference to. This can be convenient when we reference objects provided by a client or some third-party code that doesn't provide internally synchronized objects. We will look at an example to demonstrate the usefulness of atomic references.

Example: Using atomic references

Assume that we are writing a function that flips a coin a specified number of times:

```
void flip_coin(std::size_t n, Stats& outcomes);
```

The outcomes are accumulated in the outcomes object of type Stats, which looks like this:

```
struct Stats {
  int heads_{};
  int tails_{};
};

std::ostream& operator<<(std::ostream& os, const Stats &s) {
  os << "heads: " << s.heads_ << ", tails: " << s.tails_;
  return os;
}
```

A client can call flip_coins() multiple times using the same Stats instance, and the outcomes of the flipping are added to the Stats:

```
auto outcomes = Stats{};
flip_coin(30, outcomes);
flip_coin(10, outcomes);
```

Let's say we want to parallelize the implementation of flip_coin() and have multiple threads mutate the Stats object. In addition, we can assume the following:

- The Stats struct cannot be changed (maybe it's from a third-party library).
- We want the client to be unaware of the fact that our utility function flip_coin() is concurrent; that is, the concurrency of the flip_coin() function should be completely *transparent to the caller*.

For this example, we will reuse our previously defined function for generating random numbers:

```
int random_int(int min, int max); // See implementation above
```

Now we are ready to define our flip_coin() function, which will use two threads to flip a coin n number of times:

```
void flip_coin(std::size_t n, Stats &outcomes) {
  auto flip = [&outcomes](auto n) {
    auto heads = std::atomic_ref<int>{outcomes.heads_};
```

```
      auto tails = std::atomic_ref<int>{outcomes.tails_};
      for (auto i = 0u; i < n; ++i) {
        random_int(0, 1) == 0 ? ++heads : ++tails;
      }
    };
    auto t1 = std::jthread{flip, n / 2};        // First half
    auto t2 = std::jthread{flip, n - (n / 2)}; // The rest
  }
```

Both threads will update the non-atomic outcome object whenever they have tossed a coin. Instead of using a `std::mutex`, we will create two `std::atomic_ref<int>` variables that atomically update the members of the outcome object. It is important to remember that in order to protect the heads and tails counters from data races, all concurrent accesses to the counters need to be protected using `std::atomic_ref`.

The following small program demonstrates that the `flip_coin()` function can be called without any knowledge about the concurrent implementation of `flip_coin()`:

```
int main() {
  auto stats = Stats{};
  flip_coin(5000, stats);       // Flip 5000 times
  std::cout << stats << '\n';
  assert((stats.tails_ + stats.heads_) == 5000);
}
```

Running this program on my machine produced the following output:

```
heads: 2592, tails: 2408
```

This example concludes our section about the various atomic class templates in C++. Atomics have been part of the standard library since C++11 and have continued to evolve. C++20 introduced:

- The specialization `std::atomic<std::shared_ptr<T>>`
- Atomic references; that is, the `std::atomic_ref<T>` template
- The wait and notify API, which is a lightweight alternative to using condition variables

We will now move on to discuss the C++ memory model and how it relates to atomics and concurrent programming.

The C++ memory model

Why are we talking about the memory model of C++ in a chapter about concurrency? The memory model is closely related to concurrency since it defines how the reads and writes to the memory should be visible among threads. This is a rather complicated subject that touches on both compiler optimizations and multicore computer architecture. The good news, though, is that if your program is free from data races and you use the memory order that the atomics library provides by default, your concurrent program will behave according to an intuitive memory model that is easy to understand. Still, it is important to at least have an understanding of what the memory model is and what the default memory order guarantees.

The concepts covered in this section are thoroughly explained by Herb Sutter in his talks *Atomic Weapons: The C++ Memory Model and Modern Hardware 1 & 2*. The talks are freely available at https://herbsutter.com/2013/02/11/atomic-weapons-the-c-memory-model-and-modern-hardware/ and are highly recommended if you need more depth on this subject.

Instruction reordering

To understand the importance of the memory model, you first need some background about how the programs we write are actually executed.

When we write and run a program, it would be reasonable to assume that the instructions in the source code will be executed in the same order as they appear in the source code. This is not true. The code we write will be optimized in multiple stages before it is finally executed. Both the compiler and the hardware will reorder instructions with the goal of executing the program more efficiently. This is not new technology: compilers have done this for a long time, and this is one reason why an optimized build runs faster than a non-optimized build. The compiler (and hardware) are free to reorder instructions as long as the reordering is not observable when running the program. The program runs *as if* everything happens in program order.

Let's look at an example code snippet:

```
int a = 10;        // 1
std::cout << a;    // 2
int b = a;         // 3
std::cout << b;    // 4
// Observed output: 1010
```

Here, it is obvious that line number two and line number three could be swapped without introducing any observable effect:

```
int a = 10;        // 1
int b = a;         // 3 This line moved up
std::cout << a;    // 2 This line moved down
std::cout << b;    // 4
// Observed output: 1010
```

Here is another example, which is similar, but not identical, to the example from *Chapter 4*, *Data Structures*, where the compiler can optimize a cache-unfriendly version when iterating over a two-dimensional matrix:

```
constexpr auto ksize = size_t{100};
using MatrixType = std::array<std::array<int, ksize>, ksize>;

auto cache_thrashing(MatrixType& matrix, int v) { // 1
  for (size_t i = 0; i < ksize; ++i)              // 2
    for (size_t j = 0; j < ksize; ++j)            // 3
      matrix[j][i] = v;                           // 4
}
```

You saw in *Chapter 4*, *Data Structures*, that code similar to this produces a lot of cache misses, which hurts performance. A compiler is free to optimize this by reordering the for statements, like this:

```
auto cache_thrashing(MatrixType& matrix, int v) { // 1
  for (size_t j = 0; j < ksize; ++j)              // 3 Line moved up
    for (size_t i = 0; i < ksize; ++i)            // 2 Line moved down
      matrix[j][i] = v;                           // 4
}
```

There is no way to observe the difference between the two versions when executing the program, but the latter will run faster.

Optimizations performed by the compiler and the hardware (including instruction pipelining, branch prediction, and cache hierarchies) are very complicated and constantly evolving technologies. Fortunately, all these transformations of the original program can be seen as re-orderings of reads and writes in the source code. This also means that it doesn't matter whether it is the compiler or some part of the hardware that performs the transformations. The important thing for C++ programmers to know is that the instructions can be re-ordered but without any observable effect.

If you have been trying to debug an optimized build of your program, you have probably noticed that it can be hard to step through it because of the re-orderings. So, by using a debugger, the re-orderings are in some sense observable, but they are not observable when running the program in a normal way.

Atomics and memory orders

When writing single-threaded programs in C++, there is no risk of data races occurring. We can write our programs happily without being aware of instruction re-orderings. However, when it comes to shared variables in multi-threaded programs, it is a completely different story. The compiler (and hardware) does all its optimizations based on what is true and observable for *one* thread only. The compiler cannot know what other threads are able to observe through shared variables, so it is our job as programmers to inform the compiler of what re-orderings are allowed. In fact, that is exactly what we are doing when we are using an atomic variable or a mutex to protect us from data races.

When protecting a critical section with a mutex, it is guaranteed that only the thread that currently owns the lock can execute the critical section. But, the mutex is also creating memory fences around the critical section to inform the system that certain re-orderings are not allowed at the critical section boundaries. When acquiring the lock, an `acquire` fence is added, and when releasing the lock, a `release` fence is added.

I will demonstrate this with an example. Imagine that we have four instructions: **i1**, **i2**, **i3**, and **i4**. There is no dependency between each one, so the system could reorder the instructions arbitrarily without any observable effect. The instructions i2 and i3 are using shared data and are, therefore, critical sections that needs to be protected by a mutex. After adding the `acquire` and `release` of the mutex lock, there are now some re-orderings that are no longer valid. Obviously, we cannot move the instructions that are part of the critical section outside of the critical section, or they will no longer be protected by the mutex. The one-way fences ensure that no instructions can be moved out from the critical section. The i1 instruction could be moved inside the critical section by passing the acquire fence, but not beyond the release fence. The i4 instruction could also be moved inside the critical section by passing the release fence, but not beyond the acquire fence.

The following figure shows how one-way fences limit the reordering of instructions. No read or write instructions can pass above the acquire fence, and nothing can pass below the release fence:

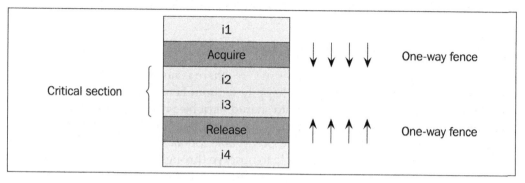

Figure 11.14: One-way fences limit the reordering of the instructions

When acquiring a mutex, we are creating an acquire memory fence. It tells the system that no memory accesses (reads or writes) can be moved above the line where the acquire fence is located. It is possible for the system to move the i4 instruction above the release fence beyond the i3 and i2 instructions, but no further than that because of the acquire fence.

Now, let's have a look at atomic variables instead of mutexes. When we use a shared atomic variable in our program, it gives us two things:

- **Protection against torn writes**: The atomic variable is always updated atomically so there is no way a reader can read a partially written value.

- **Synchronization of memory by adding sufficient memory fences**: This prevents certain instruction re-orderings to guarantee a certain memory order specified by the atomic operations.

The C++ memory model guarantees **sequential consistency** if our program is free from data races and we use the default memory order when using atomics. So, what is sequential consistency? Sequential consistency guarantees that the result of the execution is the same as if the operations were executed in the order specified by the original program. The interleaving of instructions among threads is arbitrary; that is, we have no control over the scheduling of the threads. This may sound complicated at first, but it is probably the way you already think about how a concurrent program is executed.

The downside with sequential consistency is that it can hurt performance. It is, therefore, possible to use atomics with a relaxed memory model instead. This means that you only get the protection against torn writes, but not the memory order guarantees provided by sequential consistency.

I strongly advise you against using anything else except the default sequential consistency memory order, unless you have a very thorough understanding of the effects a weaker memory model can introduce.

We will not discuss relaxed memory order any further here because it is beyond the scope of this book. But as a side note, you may be interested to know that the reference counter in a `std::shared_ptr` uses a relaxed model when incrementing the counter (but not when decrementing the counter). This is the reason why the `std::shared_ptr` member function `use_count()` only reports the approximate number of actual references when it is used in a multi-threaded environment.

One area where the memory model and atomics are highly relevant is lock-free programming. The following section will give you a taste of what lock-free programming is and some of its applications.

Lock-free programming

Lock-free programming is hard. We will not spend a lot of time discussing lock-free programming in this book, but instead I will provide you with an example of how a very simple lock-free data structure could be implemented. There is a great wealth of resources — on the web and in books (such as the Anthony Williams book mentioned earlier) — dedicated to lock-free programming that will explain the concepts you need to understand before writing your own lock-free data structures. Some concepts you might have heard of, such as **compare-and-swap** (**CAS**) and the ABA problem, will not be further discussed in this book.

Example: A lock-free queue

Here, you are going to see an example of a lock-free queue, which is a relatively simple but useful lock-free data structure. Lock-free queues can be used for one-way communication with threads that cannot use locks to synchronize access to shared data.

Its implementation is straightforward because of the limited requirements: it only supports *one reader* thread and *one writer* thread. The capacity of the queue is also fixed and cannot change during runtime.

A lock-free queue is an example of a component that might be used in environments where exceptions are typically abandoned. The queue that follows is therefore designed without exceptions, which makes the API differ from other examples in this book.

The class template `LockFreeQueue<T>` has the following public interface:

- `push()`: Adds an element to the queue and returns `true` on success. This function must only be called by the (one and only) *writer thread*. To avoid unnecessary copying when the client provides an rvalue, `push()` overloads on `const T&` and `T&&`. This technique was also used in the `BoundedBuffer` class presented earlier in this chapter.

- `pop()`: Returns an `std::optional<T>` with the front element of the queue unless the queue is empty. This function must only be called by the (one and only) *reader thread*.

- `size()`: Returns the current size of the queue. This function can be called by *both threads* concurrently.

The following is the complete implementation of the queue:

```
template <class T, size_t N>
class LockFreeQueue {
  std::array<T, N> buffer_{};   // Used by both threads
  std::atomic<size_t> size_{0}; // Used by both threads
  size_t read_pos_{0};          // Used by reader thread
  size_t write_pos_{0};         // Used by writer thread
  static_assert(std::atomic<size_t>::is_always_lock_free);

  bool do_push(auto&& t) {        // Helper function
    if (size_.load() == N) {
      return false;
    }
    buffer_[write_pos_] = std::forward<decltype(t)>(t);
    write_pos_ = (write_pos_ + 1) % N;
    size_.fetch_add(1);
    return true;
  }

public:
  // Writer thread
  bool push(T&& t) { return do_push(std::move(t)); }
  bool push(const T& t) { return do_push(t); }

  // Reader thread
  auto pop() -> std::optional<T> {
    auto val = std::optional<T>{};
    if (size_.load() > 0) {
```

```
      val = std::move(buffer_[read_pos_]);
      read_pos_ = (read_pos_ + 1) % N;
      size_.fetch_sub(1);
    }
    return val;
  }
  // Both threads can call size()
  auto size() const noexcept { return size_.load(); }
};
```

The only data member that needs atomic access is the `size_` variable. The `read_pos_` member is only used by the reader thread, and the `write_pos_` is only used by the writer thread. So what about the buffer of type `std::array`? It is mutable and accessed by both threads? Doesn't that require synchronization? Since the algorithm ensures that the two threads are never accessing the same element in the array concurrently, C++ guarantees that individual elements in an array can be accessed without data races. It doesn't matter how small the elements are; even a `char` array holds this guarantee.

When can a non-blocking queue like this be useful? One example is in audio programming, when there is a UI running on the main thread that needs to send or receive data from a real-time audio thread, which cannot block under any circumstances. The real-time thread cannot use mutex locks, allocate/free memory, or do anything else that may cause the thread to wait on threads with lower priority. Lock-free data structures are required for scenarios like these.

Both the reader and the writer are lock-free in `LockFreeQueue`, so we could have two instances of the queue to communicate in both directions between the main thread and the audio thread, as the following figure demonstrates:

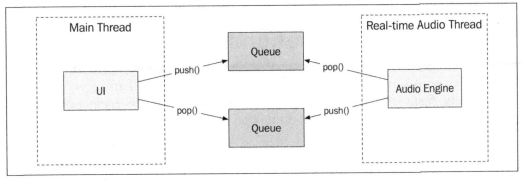

Figure 11.15: Using two lock-free queues to pass state between the main thread and a real-time audio thread

As already mentioned, this book only scratches the surface of lock-free programming. It's time to end this chapter now with a few guidelines on performance when writing concurrent programs.

Performance guidelines

I cannot stress enough the importance of having a concurrent program running *correctly* before trying to improve the performance. Also, before applying any of these guidelines related to performance, you first need to set up a reliable way of measuring what you are trying to improve.

Avoid contention

Whenever multiple threads are using shared data, there will be contention. Contention hurts performance and sometimes the overhead caused by contention can make a parallel algorithm work slower than a single-threaded alternative.

Using a lock that causes a wait and a context switch is an obvious performance penalty, but what is not equally obvious is that both locks and atomics disable optimizations in the code generated by the compiler, and they do so at runtime when the CPU executes the code. This is necessary in order to guarantee sequential consistency. But remember, the solution to such problems is never to ignore synchronization and therefore introduce data races. Data races mean undefined behavior, and having a fast but incorrect program makes nobody happy.

Instead, we need to minimize the time spent in critical sections. We can do that by entering a critical section less often, and by minimizing the critical section itself so that once we are in it, we leave it as soon as possible.

Avoid blocking operations

To write a modern responsive UI application that always runs smoothly, it is absolutely necessary to never block the main thread for more than a few milliseconds. A smoothly running app updates its interface 60 times per second. This means that if you are doing something that blocks the UI thread for more than 16 ms, the FPS will drop.

You can design your internal APIs in an application with this in mind. Whenever you write a function that performs I/O or something else that might take more than a few milliseconds, it needs to be implemented as an asynchronous function. This pattern has become very common in iOS and Windows, where, for example, all network APIs have become asynchronous.

Number of threads/CPU cores

The more CPU cores a machine has, the more active running threads you can have. If you manage to split a sequential CPU-bound task into a parallel version, you can gain performance by having multiple cores working on the task in parallel.

Going from a single-threaded algorithm to an algorithm that can be run by two threads can, in the best-case scenario, double the performance. But, after adding more and more threads, you will eventually reach a limit when there is no more performance gain. Adding more threads beyond that limit will actually degrade performance since the overhead caused by context switching becomes more significant the more threads you add.

I/O-intensive tasks, for example, a web crawler that will spend a lot of time waiting for network data, require a lot of threads before reaching the limit where the CPU is oversubscribed. A thread that is waiting for I/O will most likely be switched out from the CPU to make room for other threads that are ready to execute. For CPU-bound tasks, there is usually no point in using more threads than there are cores on the machine.

Controlling the total number of threads in a big program can be hard. A good way of controlling the number of threads is to use a thread pool that can be sized to match the current hardware.

In *Chapter 14, Parallel Algorithms*, you will see examples of how to parallelize algorithms and how to tweak the amount of concurrency based on the number of CPU cores.

Thread priorities

The priority of a thread affects how the thread is scheduled. A thread with high priority is likely to be scheduled more often than threads with lower priorities. Thread priorities are important for lowering the latency of tasks.

Threads provided by the operating system usually have priorities. There is currently no way of setting the priority on a thread with the current C++ thread APIs. However, by using `std::thread::native_handle`, you can get a handle to the underlying operating system thread and use native APIs to set priorities.

One phenomenon related to thread priorities that can hurt the performance, and should be avoided, is called **priority inversion**. It happens when a thread with high priority is waiting to acquire a lock that is currently held by a low-priority thread. Such dependencies hurt the high-priority thread, which is blocked until the next time the low-priority thread gets scheduled so that it can release the lock.

For real-time applications, this is a big problem. In practice, it means that you cannot use locks to protect any shared resources that need to be accessed by real-time threads. A thread that produces real-time audio, for example, runs with the highest possible priority, and in order to avoid priority inversion, it is not possible for the audio thread to call any functions (including `std::malloc()`) that might block and cause a context switch.

Thread affinity

Thread affinity makes it possible to give the scheduler hints about which threads could benefit from sharing the same CPU caches. In other words, this is a request to the scheduler that some threads should be executed on a particular core if possible, to minimize cache misses.

Why would you want one thread to be executed on a particular core? The answer is (again) caching. Threads that operate on the same memory could benefit from running on the same core, and hence take advantage of warm caches. For the scheduler, this is just one of many parameters to take into account when assigning a thread to a core, so this is hardly any guarantee, but again, the behavior is very different among operating systems. Thread priorities, and even utilization of all cores (to avoid overheating), are one of the requirements that need to be taken into account by a modern scheduler.

It is not possible to set thread affinity in a portable way with the current C++ APIs, but most platforms support some way of setting an affinity mask on a thread. In order to access platform-specific functionality, you need to get a handle on the native thread. The example that follows demonstrates how to set the thread affinity mask on Linux:

```
#include <pthreads> // Non-portable header

auto set_affinity(const std::thread& t, int cpu) {
  cpu_set_t cpuset;
  CPU_ZERO(&cpuset);
  CPU_SET(cpu, &cpuset);
  pthread_t native_thread = t.native_handle();
  pthread_set_affinity(native_thread, sizeof(cpu_set_t), &cpuset);
}
```

 Note, this is not portable C++, but it is likely that you need to do some non-portable configuration of threads if you are doing performance-critical concurrency programming.

False sharing

False sharing, or destructive interference, can degrade performance very significantly. It occurs when two threads use some data (that is not logically shared between the threads) but happen to be located in the same cache line. Imagine what will happen if the two threads are executing on different cores and constantly updating the variable residing on the shared cache line. The threads will invalidate the cache line for each other, although there is no true sharing of data between the threads.

False sharing will most likely occur when using global data or dynamically allocated data that is shared between threads. An example where false sharing is likely to occur is when allocating an array that is shared between threads, but each thread is only using a single element of the array.

The solution to this problem is to pad each element in the array so that two adjacent elements cannot reside on the same cache line. Since C++17, there is a portable way of doing this using the `std::hardware_destructive_interference_size` constant defined in `<new>` in combination with the `alignas` specifier. The following example demonstrates how to create an element that prevents false sharing:

```
struct alignas(std::hardware_destructive_interference_size) Element {
    int counter_{};
};

auto elements = std::vector<Element>(num_threads);
```

The elements in the vector are now guaranteed to reside on separate cache lines.

Summary

In this chapter, you have seen how to create programs that can execute multiple threads concurrently. We also covered how to avoid data races by protecting critical sections with locks or by using atomics. You learned that C++20 comes with some useful synchronization primitives: latches, barriers, and semaphores. We then looked into execution order and the C++ memory model, which becomes important to understand when writing lock-free programs. You also discovered that immutable data structures are thread-safe. The chapter ended with some guidelines for improving performance in concurrent applications.

The next two chapters are dedicated to a completely new C++20 feature called coroutines, which allows us to write asynchronous code in a sequential style.

12
Coroutines and Lazy Generators

Computing has become a world of waiting, and we need support in our programming languages to be able to express *wait*. The general idea is to suspend (temporarily pause) the current flow and hand execution over to some other flow, whenever it reaches a point where we know that we might have to wait for something. This *something* that we need to wait for could be a network request, a click from a user, a database operation, or even a memory access that is taking too long for us to block at. Instead, we say in our code that we will wait, continue some other flow, and then come back when ready. Coroutines allow us to do that.

In this chapter, we're mainly going to focus on coroutines added to C++20. You will learn what they are, how to use them, and their performance characteristics. But we will also spend some time looking at coroutines in a broader sense, since the concept is apparent in many other languages.

C++ coroutines come with very little support from the standard library. Adding standard library support for coroutines is a high-priority feature for the C++23 release. In order to use coroutines effectively in our day-to-day code, we need to implement some general abstractions. This book will show you how to implement these abstractions for the purpose of learning C++ coroutines rather than providing you with production-ready code.

It's also important to understand the various types of coroutines that exist, what coroutines can be used for, and what motivated C++ to add new language features to support coroutines.

This chapter covers a lot of ground. The next chapter is also about coroutines but with a focus on asynchronous applications. In summary, this chapter will guide you through:

- General theory about coroutines, including the difference between stackful and stackless coroutines, and how they are transformed by the compiler and executed on a computer.

- An introduction to stackless coroutines in C++. The new language support for coroutines in C++20 using co_await, co_yield, and co_return will be discussed and demonstrated.

- The abstractions that are needed for using C++20 coroutines as generators.

- A few real-world examples that show the benefits in terms of readability and simplicity of using coroutines and how we can write composable components that will evaluate lazily by using coroutines.

If you have been working with coroutines in other languages, you need to be prepared for two things before reading the rest of this chapter:

- Some content may feel basic to you. Although the details about how C++ coroutines work are far from trivial, the usage examples might feel trivial to you.

- Some terms we will use in this chapter (coroutines, generators, tasks, and so forth) might not align with your current view of what these are.

On the other hand, if you are completely new to coroutines, parts of this chapter may very well look like magic and take some time to grasp. I will therefore begin by showing you a few examples of how C++ code can look when using coroutines.

A few motivating examples

Coroutines are one of those features, similar to lambda expressions, that offer a way to completely change the way we write and think about C++ code. The concept is very general and can be applied in many different ways. To give you a taste of how C++ can look when using coroutines, we will here look briefly at two examples.

Yield-expressions can be used for implementing generators—objects that produce sequences of values lazily. In this example, we will use the keywords co_yield and co_return to control the flow:

```
auto iota(int start) -> Generator<int> {
  for (int i = start; i < std::numeric_limits<int>::max(); ++i) {
    co_yield i;
  }
}
```

```
}

auto take_until(Generator<int>& gen, int value) -> Generator<int> {
  for (auto v : gen) {
    if (v == value) {
      co_return;
    }
    co_yield v;
  }
}

int main() {
  auto i = iota(2);
  auto t = take_until(i, 5);
  for (auto v : t) {              // Pull values
    std::cout << v << ", ";
  }
  return 0;
}
// Prints: 2, 3, 4
```

In the preceding example, iota() and take_until() are coroutines. iota() generates a sequence of integers and take_until() yields values until it finds the specified value. The Generator template is a custom type that I will show you how to design and implement later on in this chapter.

Building generators is one common use case for coroutines, another one is implementing asynchronous tasks. The next example will demonstrate how we can use the operator co_await to wait for something without blocking the currently executing thread:

```
auto tcp_echo_server() -> Task<> {
  char data[1024];
  for (;;) {
    size_t n = co_await async_read(socket, buffer(data));
    co_await async_write(socket, buffer(data, n));
  }
}
```

Instead of blocking, co_await suspends the execution until it gets resumed and the asynchronous read and write functions have completed. The example presented here is incomplete because we don't know what Task, socket, buffer, and the asynchronous I/O functions are. But we will get there in the next chapter when focusing on asynchronous tasks.

Don't worry if it is not clear how these examples work at this point—we will spend a lot of time delving into the details later on in this chapter. The examples are here to give you a hint about what coroutines allow us to do if you have never encountered them before.

Before digging into C++20 coroutines, we need to discuss some terminology and common foundational ground to better understand the design and motivation for adding a rather complicated language feature to C++ in 2020.

The coroutine abstraction

We will now take a step back and talk about coroutines in general and not just focus on the coroutines added to C++20. This will give you a better understanding of why coroutines are useful but also what types of coroutines there are and how they differ. If you are already familiar with stackful and stackless coroutines and how they are executed, you can skip this section and jump right to the next section, *Coroutines in C++*.

The coroutine abstraction has been around for more than 60 years and many languages have adopted some sort of coroutines into their syntax or standard libraries. This means that coroutines can denote slightly different things in different languages and environments. Since this is a book about C++, I will use the terminology used in the C++ standard.

Coroutines are very similar to subroutines. In C++, we don't have anything explicitly called subroutines; instead, we write functions (free functions or member functions, for example) to create subroutines. I will use the terms **ordinary functions** and **subroutines** interchangeably.

Subroutines and coroutines

To understand the difference between coroutines and subroutines (ordinary functions), we will here focus on the most basic properties of subroutines and coroutines, namely, how to start, stop, pause, and resume them. A subroutine is started when some other part of our program calls it. When the subroutine returns back to the caller, the subroutine stops:

```
auto subroutine() {
  // Sequence of statements ...

  return;      // Stop and return control to caller
}
```

```
subroutine(); // Call subroutine to start it
// subroutine has finished
```

The call chain of subroutines is strictly nested. In the diagram that follows, subroutine f() cannot return to main() until subroutine g() has returned:

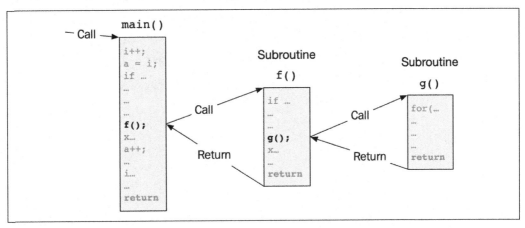

Figure 12.1: A chain of subroutine calls and returns

Coroutines can also be started and stopped just like subroutines, but they can also be **suspended** (paused) and **resumed**. If you haven't worked with coroutines before, this may seem very strange at first. The point where a coroutine is suspended and resumed is called a **suspend/resume point**. Some suspend points are implicit whereas others are explicitly marked in the code in one way or another. The following pseudo code shows three explicit suspend/resume points marked using await and yield:

```
// Pseudo code
auto coroutine() {
  value = 10;
  await something;       // Suspend/Resume point
  // ...
  yield value++;         // Suspend/Resume point
  yield value++;         // Suspend/Resume point
  // ...
  return;
}

auto res = coroutine();  // Call
res.resume();            // Resume
```

In C++, the explicit suspend points are marked using the keywords co_await and co_yield. The diagram that follows shows how a coroutine is invoked (called) from one subroutine and then later resumed from different parts of the code:

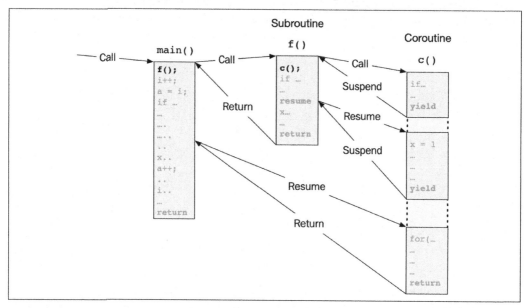

Figure 12.2: An invocation of a coroutine can suspend and resume. The coroutine invocation maintains its internal state while being suspended.

The states of local variables inside a coroutine are preserved while the coroutine is suspended. The states belong to a certain invocation of a coroutine. That is, they are not like static local variables, which are globally shared among all invocations of a function.

To summarize, coroutines are subroutines that also can be suspended and resumed. Another way to look at it is to say that subroutines are a specialization of coroutines that cannot be suspended or resumed.

From now on, I will be very strict when distinguishing between *call* and *resume*, and *suspend* and *return*. They mean completely different things. Calling a coroutine creates a new instance of a coroutine that can be suspended and resumed. Returning from a coroutine destroys the coroutine instance and it can no longer be resumed.

To really understand how coroutines can help us write efficient programs, you need to be aware of some low-level details about how functions in C++ are usually transformed to machine code and then executed.

Executing subroutines and coroutines on the CPU

We have talked about memory hierarchies, caches, virtual memory, scheduling of threads, and other hardware and operating system concepts in this book. But we haven't really talked about how instructions are being executed on the CPU using CPU registers and the stack. These concepts are important to understand when comparing subroutines with various flavors of coroutines.

CPU registers, instructions, and the stack

This section will provide a very simplified model of a CPU for the purpose of understanding context switching, function calls, and a few more details regarding the call stack. When I say CPUs in this context, I refer to some CPUs that are similar to the x86 family of CPUs equipped with multiple general-purpose registers.

A program contains a sequence of instructions that the CPU executes. The sequence of instructions is stored somewhere in the memory of the computer. The CPU keeps track of the address of the currently executing instruction in a register called a **program counter**. In that way, the CPU knows what instruction to execute next.

The CPU contains a fixed number of registers. A register is similar to a variable with a predefined name that can store a value or a memory address. Registers are the fastest data storage available on a computer and sit closest to the CPU. When the CPU manipulates data, it uses the registers. Some of the registers have a special meaning to the CPU, whereas other registers can be used more freely by the currently executing program.

Two very important registers that have a special meaning to the CPU are:

- **Program counter** (PC): The register that stores the memory address of the currently executing instruction. This value is automatically incremented whenever an instruction is executed. Sometimes it is also called an *instruction pointer*.

- **Stack pointer** (SP): It stores the address of the top of the currently used call stack. Allocating and deallocating stack memory is a matter of changing the value stored in this single register.

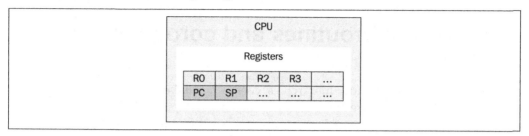

Figure 12.3: A CPU with registers

Assume that the registers are called **R0**, **R1**, **R2**, and **R3** as in the preceding diagram. A typical arithmetic instruction could then look like this:

```
add 73, R1    // Add 73 to the value stored in R1
```

Data can also be copied between registers and memory:

```
mov SP, R2    // Copy the stack pointer address to R2
mov R2, [R1]  // Copy value of R2 to memory address stored in R1
```

A set of instructions refers implicitly to the call stack. The CPU knows where the top of the call stack is through the stack pointer. Allocating memory on the stack is only a matter of updating the stack pointer. The value increases or decreases depending on whether the stack grows towards higher or lower addresses.

The following instruction uses the stack:

```
push R1      // Push value of R1 to the top of the stack
```

The push instruction copies the value in the register to the place in memory pointed at by the stack pointer *and* increments (or decrements) the stack pointer.

We can also pop values from the stack by using the pop instruction, which also reads and updates the stack pointer:

```
pop R2       // Pop value from the stack into R2
```

Whenever an instruction is executed, the CPU automatically increments the program counter. But the program counter can also be explicitly updated through instructions, for example, the jump instruction:

```
jump R3      // Set the program counter to the address in R3
```

The CPU can operate in two modes: user mode or kernel mode. The CPU registers are used differently when running in user mode and kernel mode. When the CPU is executing in user mode, it runs with restricted privileges that cannot access hardware. The operating system provides system calls that run in kernel mode. A C++ library function such as std::puts(), which prints values to stdout, must therefore make a system call to complete its task, forcing the CPU to switch between user mode and kernel mode.

Transitioning between user and kernel mode is expensive. To understand why, let's think about our schematic CPU again. The CPU operates efficiently by using its registers and therefore avoids spilling values onto the stack unnecessarily. But the CPU is a shared resource among all user processes and the operating system, and whenever we need to switch between tasks (for example, when entering kernel mode), the state of the processor, including all of its registers, needs to be saved in memory so that it can be resumed later on.

Call and return

Now that you have a basic understanding of how the CPU uses registers and the stack, we can discuss subroutine invocations. There are a lot of mechanisms involved when calling and returning from a subroutine that we might take for granted. Our compilers are doing an excellent job when they transform a C++ function to highly optimized machine code.

The following list shows the aspects that need to be considered when calling, executing, and returning from a subroutine:

- Calling and returning (jumping between points in the code).
- Passing parameters — parameters can be passed through registers or on the stack, or both.
- Allocating storage for local variables on the stack.
- Returning a value — the value returned from a subroutine needs to be stored in a place where the caller can find it. Typically, this is a dedicated CPU register.
- Using registers without interfering with other functions — the registers that a subroutine uses need to be restored to the state they were in before the subroutine was called.

The exact details about how function calls are carried out are specified by something called **calling conventions**. They provide a protocol for the caller/callee to agree on who is responsible for which parts. Calling conventions differ among CPU architectures and compilers and are one of the major parts that constitutes an **application binary interface (ABI)**.

When a function is being called, a **call frame** (or activation frame) for that function is being created. The call frame contains:

- The *parameters* passed to the function.

- The *local variables* of the function.

- A *snapshot of the registers* that we intend to use and therefore need to restore before returning.

- A *return address* that links back to the place in memory where the caller invoked the function from.

- An optional *frame pointer* that points back to the top of the caller's call frame. Frame pointers are useful for debuggers when inspecting the stack. We will not discuss frame pointers further in this book.

Thanks to the strictly nested nature of subroutines, we can save the call frames of the subroutines on the stack to support nested calls very efficiently. A call frame stored on the stack is usually called a **stack frame**.

The following diagram shows multiple call frames on a call stack and highlights the contents of a single call frame:

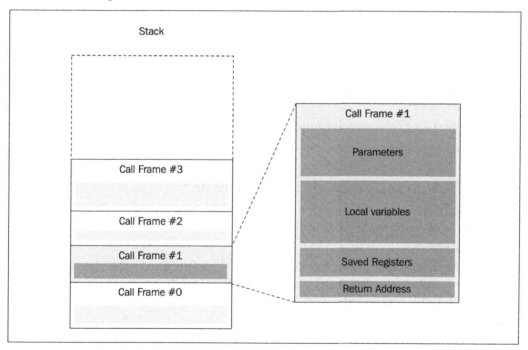

Figure 12.4: A call stack with multiple call frames. The call frame on the right-hand side is a zoomed-in version of a single call frame.

When a subroutine returns back to its caller, it uses the return address to know where to jump, restores the registers it has mutated, and pops (deallocates) the entire call frame off the stack. In this way, both the stack and the registers are restored to the states they were in before the call of the subroutine was invoked. However, there are two exceptions. Firstly, the program counter (PC) has moved to the instruction after the call. Secondly, a subroutine that returns a value back to its caller usually stores that value in a dedicated register where the caller knows where to find it.

After understanding how a subroutine is executed by temporarily using the stack and then restoring the CPU registers before returning control back to its caller, we can now start to look at how it's possible to suspend and resume coroutines.

Suspend and resume

Consider the following pseudo code that defines a coroutine with multiple suspend/resume points:

```
// Pseudo code
auto coroutine() {
  auto x = 0;
  yield x++;        // Suspend
  g();              // Call some other function
  yield x++;        // Suspend
  return;           // Return
}

auto co = coroutine(); // Call subroutine to start it
// ...                 // Coroutine is suspended
auto a = resume(co);   // Resume coroutine to get
auto b = resume(co);   // next value
```

When `coroutine()` suspends, we can no longer remove the call frame as we do when a subroutine returns back to its caller. Why? Because we need to keep the current value of the variable, x, and also remember *where* in the coroutine we should continue executing the next time the coroutine is resumed. This information is placed into something called a **coroutine frame**. The coroutine frame contains all the information that is needed in order to resume a paused coroutine. This raises several new questions, though:

- Where is the coroutine frame stored?
- How big is the coroutine frame?

- When a coroutine calls a subroutine, it needs a stack to manage the nested call frames. What happens if we try to resume from within a nested call frame? Then we would need to restore the entire stack when the coroutine resumes.

- What is the runtime overhead of calling and returning from a coroutine?

- What is the runtime overhead of suspending and resuming a coroutine?

The short answer to these questions is that it depends on what type of coroutine we are discussing: stackless or stackful coroutines.

Stackful coroutines have a separate side stack (similar to a thread) that contains the coroutine frame and the nested call frames. This makes it possible to suspend from nested call frames:

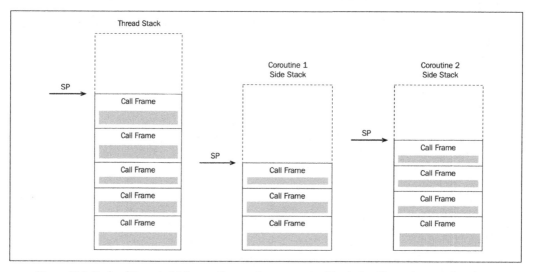

Figure 12.5: Each call to a stackful coroutine creates a separate side stack with a unique stack pointer

Suspending and resuming stackless coroutines

Stackless coroutines need to store the coroutine frame somewhere else (typically on the heap) and then use the stack of the currently executing thread to store nested call frames.

But this is not the entire truth. The caller is the one responsible for creating the call frame, saving the return address (current value of the program counter), and the parameters on the stack. The caller doesn't know that it is calling a coroutine that will suspend and resume. Therefore, the coroutine itself needs to create the coroutine frame and copy the parameters and registers from the call frame to the coroutine frame when it is called:

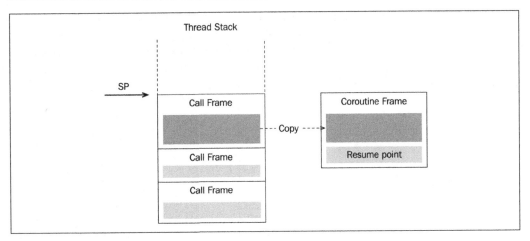

Figure 12.6: A stackless coroutine has a separate coroutine frame (usually on the heap) that contains the state necessary for resuming the coroutine

When a coroutine initially suspends, the stack frame for the coroutine is popped from the stack, but the coroutine frame continues to live on. A memory address (handle/pointer) to the coroutine frame is returned back to the caller:

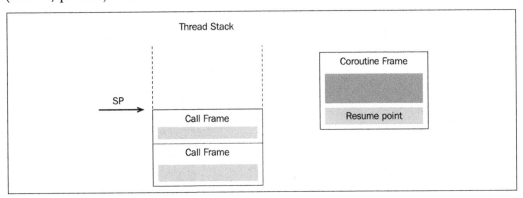

Figure 12.7: A suspended coroutine. The coroutine frame contains all the information required for resuming the coroutine.

To resume a coroutine, the caller uses the handle it received earlier and calls a resume function and passes the coroutine handle as a parameter. The resume function uses the suspend/resume point stored in the coroutine frame to continue executing the coroutine. The call to the resume function is also an ordinary function call that will generate a stack frame as illustrated in the following diagram:

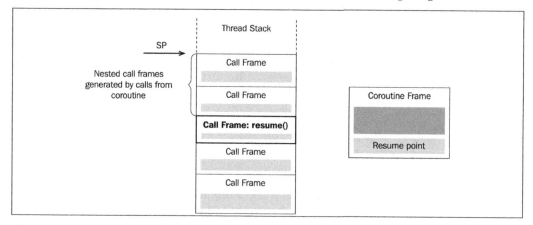

Figure 12.8: Resuming a coroutine creates a new call frame for the resume call. The resume function uses the handle to the coroutine state to resume from the right suspend point.

Finally, when a coroutine returns, it is usually suspended and eventually deallocated. The state of the stack is shown in the following diagram:

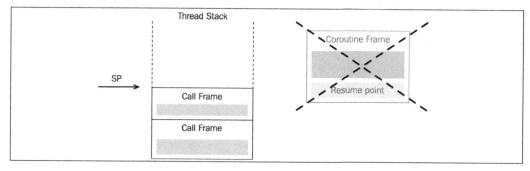

Figure 12.9: The coroutine frame is deallocated when it returns

An important consequence of not having a separate side stack per coroutine invocation is that when a stackless coroutine is suspended, it cannot have any nested call frames left on the stack. Remember, when the control is transferred back to the caller, the caller's call frame must be on the top of the stack.

As a final note, it should also be mentioned that the memory needed for the coroutine frame could be allocated *within* the call frame of the caller under some circumstances. We will discuss that in more detail when looking at C++20 coroutines.

Stackless versus stackful coroutines

As stated in the previous section, stackless coroutines use the stack of the currently running thread to handle nested function calls. The effect of this is that a stackless coroutine can never suspend from a nested call frame.

Stackful coroutines are sometimes called **fibers**, and in the programming language Go, they are called **goroutines**. Stackful coroutines remind us of threads, where each thread manages its own stack. There are two big differences between stackful coroutines (or fibers) and OS threads, though:

- OS threads are scheduled by the kernel and switching between two threads is a kernel mode operation.

- Most OSes switch OS threads **preemptively** (the thread is interrupted by the scheduler), whereas a switch between two fibers happens **cooperatively**. A running fiber keeps running until it passes control over to some manager that can then schedule another fiber.

There is also a category of threads called **user-level threads** or **green threads**. These are lightweight threads that don't involve kernel mode switching (because they run in user mode and are therefore unknown to the kernel). Fibers are one example of user-level threads. But it is also possible for user-level threads to be scheduled preemptively by a user library or by a virtual machine. Java threads are one example of preemptive user-level threads.

Stackless coroutines also allow us to write and compose multiple concurrently running tasks but without the need for an individual side stack per flow. Stackless coroutines and state machines are tightly related. It's possible to transform a state machine into a coroutine and vice versa. Why is this useful to know? Firstly, it gives you a better understanding of what stackless coroutines are. Secondly, if you are already good at identifying problems that can be solved using state machines, you can more easily see where coroutines might fit in as an appropriate solution. State machines are very general abstractions and can be applied to a great variety of problems. However, some areas where state machines are usually applied are parsing, gesture recognition, and I/O multiplexing, to mention a few. These are all areas where stackless coroutine can really shine both in terms of expressiveness and performance.

Performance cost

Coroutines are an abstraction that allow us to write lazy evaluated code and asynchronous programs in a clear and concise way. But there is a performance cost related to creating and destroying coroutines as well as suspending and resuming coroutines. When comparing the performance cost of stackless and stackful coroutines, two main aspects need to be addressed: *memory footprint* and *context switching*.

Memory footprint

Stackful coroutines need a separate call stack in order to handle suspension from within nested call frames. When calling a coroutine, we therefore need to dynamically allocate a chunk of memory for this new side stack. This immediately raises the question: how big a stack do we need to allocate? Unless we have some policy regarding how much stack a coroutine and its nested call frames can consume, we probably need to have a stack of approximately the same size as a normal call stack of a thread.

Some implementations have experimented with a segmented stack, which would allow the stack to grow if necessary. Another alternative is to start with a small contiguous stack and then copy the stack to a bigger newly allocated memory region when needed (similar to how std::vector grows). The coroutine implementation in Go (goroutines) has switched from using a segmented stack to a dynamically growing contiguous stack.

Stackless coroutines do not need to allocate memory for a separate side stack. Instead, they need a single allocation for storing each coroutine frame in order to support suspend and resume. This allocation happens when the coroutine is called (but not on suspend/resume). The call frame is deallocated when the coroutine returns.

In summary, stackful coroutines demand a big initial memory allocation for the coroutine frame and the side stack, or need to support a growing stack. Stackless coroutines only need to allocate memory for the coroutine frame. The memory footprint of calling a coroutine can be summarized as follows:

*   Stackless: Coroutine frame
*   Stackful: Coroutine frame + call stack

The next aspect of performance cost relates to suspending and resuming coroutines.

Context switching

Context switching can occur at different levels. In general, a context switch happens when we need the CPU to switch between two or many ongoing tasks. The task that is about to be paused needs to save the entire state of the CPU so that it can be restored at a later stage.

Switching between different processes and OS threads are fairly expensive operations that involve system calls, requiring the CPU to enter kernel mode. Memory caches are invalidated and, for process switching, the tables that contain the mappings between the virtual memory and physical memory need to be replaced.

Suspending and resuming coroutines is also a kind of context switch because we are switching between multiple concurrent flows. Switching between coroutines is substantially faster than switching between processes and OS threads, partly because it doesn't involve any system calls that require the CPU to run in kernel mode.

However, there is still a difference when switching between stackful coroutines and switching between stackless coroutines. The relative runtime performance of the context switches of stackful versus stackless coroutines can depend on the call patterns. But, in general, a stackful coroutine has a more expensive context switch operation since it has more information to save and restore during suspend and resume compared to a stackless coroutine. Resuming a stackless coroutine is comparable to a normal function call.

The stackless versus stackful debate has been going on in the C++ community for quite a few years now and I will do my best to stay away from the debate by concluding that they both have valid use cases—some use cases will favor stackful coroutines and other use cases will favor stackless coroutines.

This section took a little detour for the purpose of you having a better understanding of how coroutines execute and perform. Let's have a short recap of what you have learned.

What you have learned so far

Coroutines are functions that can be suspended and resumed. An ordinary function does not have this ability, which makes it possible to remove the call frame of a function that returns. However, a coroutine that is suspended needs to keep the call frame alive to be able to restore the state of the coroutine once it gets resumed. Coroutines are more powerful than subroutines and involve more bookkeeping in the generated machine code. However, thanks to the close relationship between coroutines and ordinary functions, the compilers of today are very good at optimizing stackless coroutines.

Stackful coroutines can be seen as non-preemptive user-level threads, whereas stackless coroutines offer a way to write state machines in a direct imperative fashion using the keywords `await` and `yield` to specify the suspend points.

After this introduction to the general coroutine abstraction, it's now time to understand how stackless coroutines are implemented in C++.

Coroutines in C++

The coroutines added to C++20 are stackless coroutines. There are options to use stackful coroutines in C++ as well by using third-party libraries. The most well-known cross-platform library is Boost.Fiber. C++20 stackless coroutines introduce new language constructs, while Boost.Fiber is a library that can be used with C++11 and onward. We will not discuss stackful coroutines any further in this book but will instead focus on the stackless coroutines that have been standardized in C++20.

The stackless coroutines in C++20 were designed with the following goals:

- Scalable in the sense that they add very little memory overhead. This makes it possible to have many more coroutines alive compared to the possible number of threads or stackful coroutines alive.

- Efficient context switching, which means that suspending and resuming a coroutine should be about as cheap as an ordinary function call.

- Highly flexible. C++ coroutines have more than 15 customization points, which gives application developers and library writers a lot of freedom to configure and shape coroutines as they like. Decisions about how coroutines are supposed to work can be determined by us developers rather than being hardcoded in a language specification. One example is whether a coroutine should be suspended directly after being called or continue executing to the first explicit suspend point. Such questions are usually hard-coded in other languages, but in C++ we can customize this behavior using customization points.

- Do not require C++ exceptions to handle errors. This means that you can use coroutines in environments where exceptions are turned off. Remember that coroutines are a low-level feature comparable to ordinary functions, which can be highly useful in embedded environments and systems with real-time requirements.

With these goals in mind, it's probably not a surprise that C++ coroutines can be a bit complicated to grasp at first.

What's included in standard C++ (and what's not)?

Some C++ features are pure library features (such as the Ranges library) whereas other features are pure language features (such as type inference with the help of the auto keyword). However, some features require additions to both the core language and the standard library. C++ coroutines are one of those features; they introduce new keywords to the language, but also add new types to the standard library.

On the language side, to recap, we have the following keywords related to coroutines:

- co_await: An operator that suspends the current coroutine
- co_yield: Returns a value to the caller and suspends the coroutine
- co_return: Completes the execution of a coroutine and can, optionally, return a value

On the library side, there is a new <coroutine> header including the following:

- std::coroutine_handle: A template class that refers to the coroutine state, enabling the suspending and resuming of the coroutine
- std::suspend_never: A trivial awaitable type that never suspends
- std::suspend_always: A trivial awaitable type that always suspends
- std::coroutine_traits: Used to define the promise type of a coroutine

The library types that comes with C++20 are the absolute minimum. For example, the infrastructure for communicating between the coroutine and the caller is not part of the C++ standard. Some of the types and functions that we need in order to use coroutines effectively in our application code have already been suggested in new C++ proposals, for example the template classes task and generator and the functions sync_wait() and when_all(). The library part of C++ coroutines will most likely be complemented in C++23.

In this book, I will provide some simplified types for filling this gap instead of using a third-party library. By implementing those types, you will get a deep understanding of how C++ coroutines work. However, designing robust library components that can be used with coroutines is hard to get right without introducing lifetime issues. So, if you are planning to use coroutines in your current project, using a third-party library may be a better alternative to implementing them from scratch. At the time of writing, the **CppCoro** library is the de facto standard for these general-purpose primitives. The library was created by Lewis Baker and is available at https://github.com/lewissbaker/cppcoro.

What makes a C++ function a coroutine?

A C++ function is a coroutine if it contains any of the keywords co_await, co_yield, or co_return. In addition, the compiler puts special requirements on the return type of a coroutine. But, nevertheless, we need to inspect the definition (the body) and not only the declaration to know whether we are facing a coroutine or an ordinary function. This means that the caller of a coroutine doesn't need to know whether it calls a coroutine or an ordinary function.

Compared to ordinary functions, a coroutine also has the following restrictions:

- A coroutine cannot use variadic arguments like f(const char*...)
- A coroutine cannot return auto or a concept type: auto f()
- A coroutine cannot be declared constexpr
- Constructors and destructors cannot be coroutines
- The main() function cannot be a coroutine

Once the compiler has decided that a function is a coroutine, it associates the coroutine with a number of types for making the coroutine machinery work. The following diagram highlights the different components that are involved when a *caller* uses a *coroutine*:

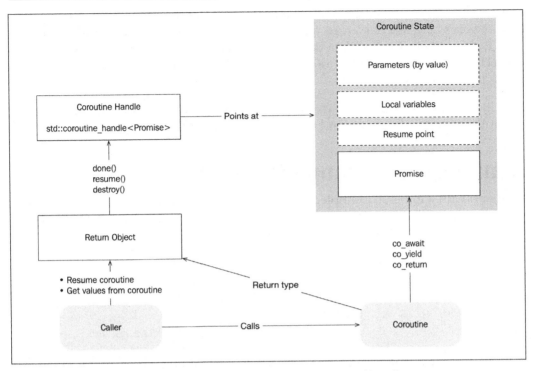

Figure 12.10: Relationship between a coroutine and its caller

The caller and the coroutine are the actual functions we will normally implement in our application code.

The **Return Object** is the type that the coroutine returns and is typically a general class template designed for some specific use case, for example, *generators* or *asynchronous tasks*. The *caller* interacts with the return object to resume the coroutine and to get values emitted from the coroutine. The return object usually delegates all its calls to the coroutine handle.

The **Coroutine Handle** is a non-owning handle to the **Coroutine State**. Through the coroutine handle we can resume and destroy the coroutine state.

The *coroutine state* is what I have previously referred to as the coroutine frame. It's an opaque object, which means that we don't know its size and we cannot access it in any other way than through the handle. The coroutine state stores everything necessary in order to resume the coroutine where it was last suspended. The coroutine state also contains the **Promise**.

The promise object is what the coroutine itself communicates with indirectly through the keywords co_await, co_yield, and co_return. If values or errors are submitted from the coroutine, they will first reach the promise object. The promise object acts like a channel between the coroutine and the caller, but neither of them have direct access to the promise.

Admittedly, this can look pretty dense at first sight. A complete but minimal example will help you understand the different parts a little better.

A minimal but complete example

Let's start with a minimal example for the purpose of understanding how coroutines work. Firstly, we implement a small *coroutine* that is suspended and resumed before it returns:

```
auto coroutine() -> Resumable {      // Initial suspend
  std::cout << "3 ";
  co_await std::suspend_always{};   // Suspend (explicit)
  std::cout << "5 ";
}                                    // Final suspend then return
```

Secondly, we create the *caller* of the coroutine. Pay attention to the output and the control flow of this program. Here it is:

```
int main() {
  std::cout << "1 ";
  auto resumable = coroutine(); // Create coroutine state
  std::cout << "2 ";
  resumable.resume();           // Resume
  std::cout << "4 ";
  resumable.resume();           // Resume
  std::cout << "6 ";
}                               // Destroy coroutine state
// Outputs: 1 2 3 4 5 6
```

Thirdly, the return object of the coroutine, Resumable, needs to be defined:

```
class Resumable {                    // The return object

  struct Promise { /*...*/ };     // Nested class, see below
  std::coroutine_handle<Promise> h_;
  explicit Resumable(std::coroutine_handle<Promise> h) : h_{h} {}
```

```
public:
  using promise_type = Promise;
  Resumable(Resumable&& r) : h_{std::exchange(r.h_, {})} {}
  ~Resumable() { if (h_) { h_.destroy(); } }
  bool resume() {
    if (!h_.done()) { h_.resume(); }
    return !h_.done();
  }
};
```

Finally, the promise type is implemented as a nested class inside the `Resumable`, like this:

```
struct Promise {
  Resumable get_return_object() {
    using Handle = std::coroutine_handle<Promise>;
    return Resumable{Handle::from_promise(*this)};
  }
  auto initial_suspend() { return std::suspend_always{}; }
  auto final_suspend() noexcept { return std::suspend_always{}; }
  void return_void() {}
  void unhandled_exception() { std::terminate(); }
};
```

This example is minimal, but walks through a lot of things that are worth paying attention to and need to be understood:

- The function `coroutine()` is a coroutine because it contains the explicit suspend/resume point using `co_await`
- The coroutine doesn't yield any values but still needs to return a type (the `Resumable`) with certain constraints so that the caller can resume the coroutine
- We are using an *awaitable type* called `std::suspend_always`
- The `resume()` function of the `resumable` object resumes the coroutine from the point it was suspended
- The `Resumable` is the owner of the coroutine state. When the `Resumable` object is destructed, it destroys the coroutine using the `coroutine_handle`

The relationship between the caller, the coroutine, the coroutine handle, the promise, and the resumable is illustrated in the following diagram:

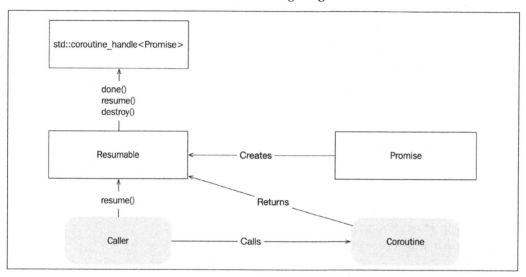

Figure 12.11: Relationship between the functions/coroutines and objects involved in the resumable example

Now it's time to look a little closer at each part. We'll begin with the Resumable type.

The coroutine return object

Our coroutine returns an object of type Resumable. This Resumable class is very simple. This is the object that the coroutine returns and which the caller can use in order to resume and destroy the coroutine. Here is the complete definition again for your convenience:

```cpp
class Resumable {                    // The return object
  struct Promise { /*...*/ };   // Nested class
  std::coroutine_handle<Promise> h_;
  explicit Resumable(std::coroutine_handle<Promise> h) : h_{h} {}
public:
  using promise_type = Promise;
  Resumable(Resumable&& r) : h_{std::exchange(r.h_, {})} {}
  ~Resumable() { if (h_) { h_.destroy(); } }
  bool resume() {
    if (!h_.done()) { h_.resume(); }
    return !h_.done();
  }
};
```

`Resumable` is a move-only type that is the owner of the coroutine handle (and therefore controls the lifetime of the coroutine). The move constructor ensures that the coroutine handle is cleared in the source object by using `std::exchange()`. When a `Resumable` object is destructed, it destroys the coroutine if it still owns it.

The `resume()` member function delegates the resume call to the coroutine handle if the coroutine is still alive.

Why do we need the member type alias `promise_type = Promise` inside `Resumable`? With each coroutine there is also an associated promise object. When the compiler sees a coroutine (by inspecting the body of a function), it needs to figure out the associated promise type. For that, the compiler uses the `std::coroutine_traits<T>` template, where `T` is the return type of your coroutine. You can provide a template specialization of `std::coroutine_traits<T>` or exploit the fact that the default implementation of `std::coroutine_traits` will look for a `public` member type or alias named `promise_type` in the return type `T` of the coroutine. In our case, the `Resumable::promise_type` is an alias for `Promise`.

The promise type

The promise type controls the behavior of the coroutine. Again, here is the full definition reproduced for convenience:

```
struct Promise {
  auto get_return_object() { return Resumable{*this}; }
  auto initial_suspend() { return std::suspend_always{}; }
  auto final_suspend() noexcept { return std::suspend_always{}; }
  void return_void() {}
  void unhandled_exception() { std::terminate(); }
};
```

We should not call these functions directly; instead, the compiler inserts calls to the promise objects when it transforms a coroutine into machine code. If we don't provide these member functions, the compiler doesn't know how to generate code for us. You can think about the promise as a coroutine controller object that is responsible for:

- Producing the value returned from the invocation of the coroutine. This is handled by the function `get_return_object()`.

- Defining the behavior when the coroutine is created and before it gets destroyed by implementing the functions `initial_suspend()` and `final_supsend()`. In our `Promise` type, we say that the coroutine should be suspended at these points by returning `std::suspend_always` (see the next section).

- Customizing the behavior when the coroutine finally returns. If a coroutine uses a co_return with an expression that evaluates to a value of type T, the promise must define a member function named return_value(T). Our coroutine returns no value, but the C++ standard requires us to provide the customization point called return_void(), which we leave empty here.

- Handling exceptions that are not handled inside the coroutine body. In the function unhandled_exception(), we simply call std::terminate(), but we will handle it more gracefully in later examples.

There are some final pieces of the code that require some more attention, namely the co_await expression and awaitable types.

Awaitable types

We added one explicit suspend point in our code using co_await and passed it an instance of the awaitable type, std::suspend_always. The implementation of std::suspend_always looks something like this:

```
struct std::suspend_always {
  constexpr bool await_ready() const noexcept { return false; }
  constexpr void await_suspend(coroutine_handle<>) const noexcept {}
  constexpr void await_resume() const noexcept {}
};
```

std::suspend_always is called a trivial awaitable type because it will always make a coroutine suspend by saying that it is never ready. There is another trivial awaitable type that always reports that it is ready, called std::suspend_never:

```
struct std::suspend_never {
  constexpr bool await_ready() const noexcept { return true; }
  constexpr void await_suspend(coroutine_handle<>) const noexcept {}
  constexpr void await_resume() const noexcept {}
};
```

We could create our own awaitable types, which we will cover in the next chapter, but for now we can manage with those two trivial standard types.

This completes the example. But we can do some more experimenting when we have the Promise and the Resumable types in place. Let's see what we can do with a started coroutine.

Passing our coroutine around

Once the `Resumable` object is created, we can pass it to other function and resume it from there. We can even pass the coroutine to another thread. The following example shows some of this flexibility:

```
auto coroutine() -> Resumable {
  std::cout << "c1 ";
  co_await std::suspend_always{};
  std::cout << "c2 ";
}

auto coro_factory() {                  // Create and return a coroutine
  auto res = coroutine();
  return res;
}

int main() {
  auto r = coro_factory();
  r.resume();                          // Resume from main

  auto t = std::jthread{[r = std::move(r)]() mutable {
    using namespace std::chrono_literals;
    std::this_thread::sleep_for(2s);
    r.resume();                        // Resume from thread
  }};
}
```

The preceding example demonstrates that once we have called our coroutine and have got a handle to it, we can move it around just like any other moveable type. This ability to pass it to other threads is actually very useful in situations where we need to avoid the possible heap allocation of the coroutine state on a specific thread.

Allocating the coroutine state

The coroutine state, or the coroutine frame, is where the coroutine stores its state while it is suspended. The lifetime of the coroutine state starts when the coroutine is invoked by a call, and is destroyed when the coroutine executes a `co_return` statement (or the control flows off the end of the coroutine body), unless it was destroyed earlier through the coroutine handle.

The coroutine state is normally allocated on the heap. A separate heap allocation is inserted by the compiler. In some cases, though, this separate heap allocation can be elided by inlining the coroutine state into the frame of the caller (which could be an ordinary stack frame or another coroutine frame). Unfortunately, there is never any guarantee of this elision of the heap allocation.

For the compiler to be able to elide the heap allocation, the complete lifetime of the coroutine state must be strictly nested within the lifetime of the caller. In addition, the compiler needs to figure out the total size of the coroutine state and generally needs to have visibility of the body of the called coroutine so that parts of it can be inlined. Situations like virtual function calls, and calls to functions in other translation units or shared libraries, typically make this impossible. If the compiler is missing the information it needs, it will insert a heap allocation.

The heap allocation of the coroutine state is performed using operator new. It is possible to provide a custom class-level operator new on the promise type, which will then be used instead of global operator new. It's therefore possible to check whether the heap allocation was elided or not. And if it wasn't, we can find out how much memory is needed for the coroutine state. Here is an example using the Promise type we defined earlier:

```cpp
struct Promise {

  /* Same as before ... */

  static void* operator new(std::size_t sz) {
    std::cout << "custom new for size " << sz << '\n';
    return ::operator new(sz);
  }
  static void operator delete(void* ptr) {
    std::cout << "custom delete called\n";
    ::operator delete(ptr);
  }
}
```

Another trick to verify that the heap allocations are completely elided for all coroutines using some specific promise type would be to declare operator new and operator delete but leave out their definitions. If the compiler then inserts calls to these operators, the program will fail to link due to unresolved symbols.

Avoiding dangling references

The fact that a coroutine can be passed around in our code means that we need to be very careful about the lifetime of parameters we pass to a coroutine to avoid dangling references. The coroutine frame contains copies of the objects that normally live on the stack, such as local variables and parameters passed to the coroutine. If a coroutine accepts an argument by reference, the *reference* is copied, not the object. This means that we can easily end up with dangling references when following the usual guidelines for function parameters; that is, pass objects that are expensive to copy by reference to const.

Passing parameters to coroutines

The following coroutine uses a reference to a const std::string:

```
auto coroutine(const std::string& str) -> Resumable {
  std::cout << str;
  co_return;
}
```

Suppose we have a factory function that creates and returns the coroutine, like this:

```
auto coro_factory() {
  auto str = std::string{"ABC"};
  auto res = coroutine(str);
  return res;
}
```

And finally, a main() function that uses the coroutine:

```
int main() {
  auto coro = coro_factory();
  coro.resume();
}
```

This code exhibits undefined behavior as the std::string object containing the string "ABC" is no longer alive when the coroutine tries to access it. Hopefully, this doesn't come as a surprise to you. This problem is similar to having a lambda capture a variable by reference, and then passing the lambda to some other code without keeping the referenced object alive. A similar example can be achieved when passing around a lambda capturing variables by reference:

```cpp
auto lambda_factory() {
  auto str = std::string{"ABC"};
  auto lambda = [&str]() {          // Capture str by reference
    std::cout << str;
  };
  return lambda;                     // Ops! str in lambda becomes
}                                     // a dangling reference

int main() {
  auto f = lambda_factory();
  f();                               // Undefined behavior
}
```

As you can see, the same problem can happen with lambdas. In *Chapter 2, Essential C++ Techniques*, I warned you about capturing references with lambdas, and it is usually better to avoid this by capturing by value instead.

The solution to avoid dangling references with coroutines is similar: avoid passing parameters by reference when using coroutines. Instead, use pass by value, and the entire parameter object will be placed safely in the coroutine frame:

```cpp
auto coroutine(std::string str) -> Resumable {  // OK, by value!
  std::cout << str;
  co_return;
}
auto coro_factory() {
  auto str = std::string{"ABC"};
  auto res = coroutine(str);
  return res;
}
int main() {
  auto coro = coro_factory();
  coro.resume();                                // OK!
}
```

Parameters are an important and common source of lifetime issues when using coroutines, but they are not the only source. Now we will explore some other pitfalls related to coroutines and dangling references.

Member functions that are coroutines

A member function can also be a coroutine. For example, there is nothing that stops us from using co_await inside a member function, as in the following example:

```
struct Widget {
auto coroutine() -> Resumable {        // A member function
    std::cout << i_++ << " ";          // Access data member
    co_await std::suspend_always{};
    std::cout << i_ ++ << " ";
  }
  int i_{};
};

int main() {
  auto w = Widget{99};
  auto coro = w.coroutine();
  coro.resume();
  coro.resume();
}
// Prints: 99 100
```

It's important to understand that it's the responsibility of the caller of coroutine() (in this case, main()) to ensure that the Widget object, w, is kept alive during the entire lifetime of the coroutine. The coroutine is accessing data members from the object it belongs to, but the Widget object itself is *not* kept alive by the coroutine. This can easily become a problem if we pass the coroutine to some other part of the program.

Let's say we are using some coroutine factory function as demonstrated earlier, but instead return a member function coroutine:

```
auto widget_coro_factory() {        // Create and return a coroutine
  auto w = Widget{};
  auto coro = w.coroutine();
  return coro;
}                                   // Object w destructs here

int main() {
  auto r = widget_coro_factory();
```

```
    r.resume();                     // Undefined behavior
    r.resume();
}
```

This code exhibits undefined behavior because we now have a dangling reference from the coroutine to the `Widget` object created and destructed in the `widget_coro_factory()` function. In other words, we end up with two objects with distinct lifetimes, whereas one of the objects references the other but without any explicit ownership.

Lambdas that are coroutines

Not only member functions can become coroutines. It's also possible to create coroutines using lambda expressions by inserting `co_await`, `co_return`, and/or `co_yield` in the body of a lambda.

Coroutine lambdas can be a little extra tricky to deal with. One way to understand the most common lifetime issue with coroutine lambdas is to think about function objects. Recall from *Chapter 2, Essential C++ Techniques,* that a lambda expression is transformed into a function object by the compiler. The type of this object is a class with the call operator implemented. Now, let's say we use `co_return` inside the body of a lambda; it means that the call operator `operator()()` becomes a coroutine.

Consider the following code using a lambda:

```
auto lambda = [](int i) -> Resumable {
  std::cout << i;
  co_return;                // Make it a coroutine
};
auto coro = lambda(42);     // Call, creates the coroutine frame
coro.resume();              // Outputs: 42
```

The type that the lambda corresponds to looks something like this:

```
struct LambdaType {
  auto operator()(int i) -> Resumable {  // Member function
    std::cout << i;                       // Body
    co_return;
  }
};
auto lambda = LambdaType{};
auto coro = lambda(42);
coro.resume();
```

The important thing to note here is that the actual coroutine is a *member function*, namely the call operator `operator()()`. The previous section already demonstrated the pitfalls of having coroutine member functions: we need to keep the object alive during the lifetime of the coroutine. In the preceding example, it means we need to keep the function object named `lambda` alive as long as the coroutine frame is alive.

Some usages of lambdas make it really easy to accidentally destruct the function object before the coroutine frame is destroyed. For example, by using an *immediately invoked lambda*, we can easily get into trouble:

```
auto coro = [i = 0]() mutable -> Resumable {
  std::cout << i++;
  co_await std::suspend_always{};
  std::cout << i++;
}();                   // Invoke Lambda immediately
coro.resume();         // Undefined behavior! Function object
coro.resume();         // already destructed
```

This code looks innocent; the lambda is not capturing anything by reference. However, the function object created by the lambda expression is a temporary object that will be destructed once it has been invoked and the coroutine captures a reference to it. When the coroutine is resumed, the program will likely crash or produce garbage.

Again, a way to understand this better is to transform the lambda to an ordinary class with `operator()` defined:

```
struct LambdaType {
  int i{0};
  auto operator()() -> Resumable {
    std::cout << i++;
    co_await std::suspend_always{};
    std::cout << i++;
  }
};
auto coro = LambdaType{}(); // Invoke operator() on temporary object
coro.resume();              // Ops! Undefined behavior
```

Now you can see that this is very similar to the case where we had a member function that was a coroutine. The function object is not kept alive by the coroutine frame.

Guidelines to prevent dangling references

Unless you have good reasons for accepting arguments by reference, choose to accept arguments by value if you are writing a coroutine. The coroutine frame will then keep a full copy of the object you pass to it, and the object is guaranteed to live as long as the coroutine frame.

If you are using lambdas or member functions that are coroutines, pay special attention to the lifetime of the object that the coroutine belongs to. Remember that the object (or function object) is *not* stored in the coroutine frame. It's the responsibility of the caller of the coroutine to keep it alive.

Handling errors

There are different ways to transfer errors from a coroutine back to the part of the code that called it or resumed it. We are not forced to use exceptions for signaling errors. Instead, we can customize error handling as we want.

A coroutine can pass an error back to the client using the coroutine by either throwing an exception or returning an error code when the client gets a value back from the coroutine (when the coroutine yields or returns).

If we are using exceptions and an exception is propagated out of the body of the coroutine, the function `unhandled_exception()` of the promise object is called. This call happens inside a catch block inserted by the compiler, so that it is possible to use `std::current_exception()` to get hold of the exception that was thrown. The result from `std::current_exception()` can then be stored in the coroutine as a `std::exception_ptr` and rethrown later on. You will see examples of this in the next chapter when using asynchronous coroutines.

Customization points

You have already seen many customization points, and I think a valid question is: why so many customization points?

- **Generality**: The customization points make it possible to use coroutines in various ways. There are very few assumptions about how to use the C++ coroutines. Library writers can customize the behavior of `co_await`, `co_yield`, and `co_return`.

- **Efficiency**: Some of the customization points are there for enabling possible optimizations depending on use cases. One example is `await_ready()`, which can return `true` to avoid an unnecessary suspension if a value is already computed.

It should also be said that we are exposed to these customization points because the C++ standard doesn't provide any types (except for the `std::coroutine_handle`) to communicate with a coroutine. Once they are in place, we can reuse those types and not worry too much about some of those customization points. Nevertheless, knowing the customization points is valuable in order to fully understand how to use C++ coroutines efficiently.

Generators

A generator is a type of coroutine that yields values back to its caller. For example, at the beginning of this chapter, I demonstrated how the generator `iota()` yielded increasing integer values. By implementing a general-purpose generator type that can act as an iterator, we can simplify the work of implementing iterators that are compatible with range-based for-loops, standard library algorithms, and ranges. Once we have a generator template class in place, we can reuse it.

So far in this book, you have mostly seen iterators in the context of accessing container elements and when using standard library algorithms. However, an iterator does not have to be tied to a container. It's possible to write iterators that produce values.

Implementing a generator

The generator we are about to implement is based on the generator from the CppCoro library. The generator template is intended to be used as a return type for coroutines that produces a sequence of values. It should be possible to use objects of this type together with a range-based for - loop and standard algorithms that accept iterators and ranges. To make this possible, we will implement three components:

- The `Generator`, which is the return object
- The `Promise`, which acts as the coroutine controller
- The `Iterator`, which is the interface between the client and the `Promise`

These three types are tightly coupled and the relationships between them and the coroutine state are presented in the following diagram:

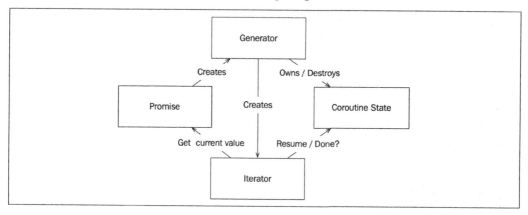

Figure 12.12: The relationships between the Iterator, Generator, Promise, and the coroutine state

The return object, in this case the Generator class, is tightly coupled with the Promise type; the Promise type is responsible for creating the Generator object, and the Generator type is responsible for exposing the correct promise_type to the compiler. Here is the implementation of Generator:

```cpp
template <typename T>
class Generator {
  struct Promise { /* ... */ };    // See below
  struct Sentinel {};
  struct Iterator { /* ... */ };   // See below

  std::coroutine_handle<Promise> h_;
  explicit Generator(std::coroutine_handle<Promise> h) : h_{h} {}

public:
  using promise_type = Promise;

  Generator(Generator&& g) : h_(std::exchange(g.h_, {})) {}
  ~Generator() { if (h_) { h_.destroy(); } }

  auto begin() {
    h_.resume();
    return Iterator{h_};
  }
  auto end() { return Sentinel{}; }
};
```

The implementation of `Promise` and `Iterator` will follow soon. The `Generator` is not that different from the `Resumable` class we defined earlier. The `Generator` is the return object of the coroutine and the owner of the `std::coroutine_handle`. The generator is a moveable type. When being moved, the coroutine handle is transferred to the newly constructed `Generator` object. When a generator that owns a coroutine handle is destructed, it destroys the coroutine state by calling `destroy` on the coroutine handle.

The `begin()` and `end()` functions make it possible to use this generator in range-based for-loops and algorithms that accept ranges. The `Sentinel` type is empty—it's a dummy type—and the `Sentinel` instance is there to be able to pass something to the comparison operators of the `Iterator` class. The implementation of the `Iterator` looks like this:

```cpp
struct Iterator {

  using iterator_category = std::input_iterator_tag;
  using value_type = T;
  using difference_type = ptrdiff_t;
  using pointer = T*;
  using reference = T&;

  std::coroutine_handle<Promise> h_;   // Data member

  Iterator& operator++() {
    h_.resume();
    return *this;
  }
  void operator++(int) { (void)operator++(); }
  T operator*() const { return h_.promise().value_; }
  T* operator->() const { return std::addressof(operator*()); }
  bool operator==(Sentinel) const { return h_.done(); }
};
```

The iterator needs to store the coroutine handle in a data member so that it can delegate the calls to the coroutine handle and the promise object:

- When the iterator is dereferenced, it returns the current value held by the promise

- When the iterator is incremented, it resumes the coroutine
- When the iterator is compared with the sentinel value, the iterator ignores the sentinel and delegates the call to the coroutine handle, which knows whether there are more elements to be generated

Now there is only the `Promise` type left for us to implement. The complete definition of `Promise` looks like this:

```cpp
struct Promise {
  T value_;
  auto get_return_object() -> Generator {
    using Handle = std::coroutine_handle<Promise>;
    return Generator{Handle::from_promise(*this)};
  }
  auto initial_suspend() { return std::suspend_always{}; }
  auto final_suspend() noexcept { return std::suspend_always{}; }
  void return_void() {}
  void unhandled_exception() { throw; }
  auto yield_value(T&& value) {
    value_ = std::move(value);
    return std::suspend_always{};
  }
  auto yield_value(const T& value) {
    value_ = value;
    return std::suspend_always{};
  }
};
```

The promise object for our generator is responsible for:

- Creating the `Generator` object
- Defining the behavior when the initial and final suspend points are reached
- Keeping track of the last value that was yielded from the coroutine
- Handling exceptions thrown by the coroutine body

That's it! We now have all the pieces in place. A coroutine that returns some `Generator<T>` type can now yield values lazily using `co_yield`. The caller of the coroutine interacts with the `Generator` and `Iterator` objects to retrieve values. The interaction between the objects is illustrated next:

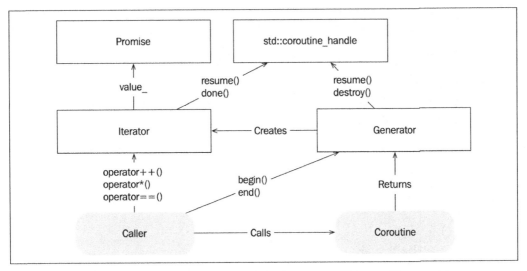

Figure 12.13: The caller communicates with the Generator and Iterator objects to retrieve values from the coroutine

Now, let's see how we can use the new `Generator` template and how it can simplify the implementation of various iterators.

Using the Generator class

This example is inspired from the talk *C++ Coroutines: Under the covers*, by Gor Nishanov at CppCon 2016 (`https://sched.co/7nKt`). It clearly demonstrates how we can benefit from the generator types we just implemented. Small composable generators can now be implemented like this:

```
template <typename T>
auto seq() -> Generator<T> {
  for (T i = {};; ++i) {
    co_yield i;
  }
}

template <typename T>
auto take_until(Generator<T>& gen, T value) -> Generator<T> {
  for (auto&& v : gen) {
    if (v == value) {
      co_return;
    }
    co_yield v;
```

```
    }
  }

  template <typename T>
  auto add(Generator<T>& gen, T adder) -> Generator<T> {
    for (auto&& v : gen) {
      co_yield v + adder;
    }
  }
```

A small usage example demonstrates that we can pass our generators to range-based for-loops:

```
int main() {
  auto s = seq<int>();
  auto t = take_until<int>(s, 10);
  auto a = add<int>(t, 3);

  int sum = 0;
  for (auto&& v : a) {
    sum += v;
  }
  return sum; // returns 75
}
```

The generators are lazily evaluated. No values are produced until the program reaches the for-loop, which pulls the values out from the chain of generators.

Another interesting aspect of this program is that when I compile it using Clang 10 with optimizations turned on, the assembly code for the *entire* program looks like this:

```
main:   # @main
mov   eax, 75
ret
```

Amazing! The program simply defines a main function that returns the value 75. In other words, the compiler optimizer has been able to completely evaluate the chain of generators at compile time and come up with the single value 75.

Our Generator class can also be used with range algorithms. In the following example we use the algorithm includes() to see if the sequence {5,6,7} is a subrange of the numbers produced by the generator:

```
int main() {
  auto s = seq<int>();                         // Same as before
  auto t = take_until<int>(s, 10);
  auto a = add<int>(t, 3);

  const auto v = std::vector{5, 6, 7};
  auto is_subrange = std::ranges::includes(a, v); // True
}
```

With the Generator template implemented, we can reuse it for all sorts of generator functions. We have implemented a general and highly useful library component that application code can benefit from in a great many places when building lazy generators.

Solving generator problems

I will now present a small problem and we will try to solve it using different techniques for the purpose of understanding which programming idioms we can potentially replace with generators. We are about to write a small utility for generating linearly spaced sequences between a start value and a stop value.

If you have been using MATLAB/Octave or Python NumPy, you might recognize this way of generating evenly (linearly) spaced numbers using a function called linspace(). It's a handy utility that can be used in various contexts with arbitrary ranges.

We will call our generator lin_space(). Here is a usage example of generating five equally spaced values between 2.0 and 3.0:

```
for (auto v: lin_space(2.0f, 3.0f, 5)) {
  std::cout << v << ", ";
}
// Prints: 2.0, 2.25, 2.5, 2.75, 3.0,
```

When generating floating-point values, we have to be a little bit cautious because we cannot simply compute the size of each step (0.25 in the preceding example) and accumulate it, since the step size might not be possible to represent exactly using a floating-point data type. The possible rounding error will add up at each iteration and eventually we may end up with completely nonsensical values. What we instead need to do is to calculate a number between the start and stop value at a specific increment using linear interpolation.

C++20 added a handy utility to `<cmath>` called `std::lerp()`, which computes the linear interpolation between two values with a specified amount. In our case, the amount will be a value between 0.0 and 1.0; an amount of 0 returns the `start` value and a value of 1.0 returns the `stop` value. Here are a few examples of using `std::lerp()`:

```
auto start = -1.0;
auto stop = 1.0;
std::lerp(start, stop, 0.0);    // -1.0
std::lerp(start, stop, 0.5);    //  0.0
std::lerp(start, stop, 1.0);    //  1.0
```

The `lin_space()` functions we are about to write will all use the following small utility function template:

```
template <typename T>
auto lin_value(T start, T stop, size_t index, size_t n) {
  assert(n > 1 && index < n);
  const auto amount = static_cast<T>(index) / (n - 1);
  const auto v = std::lerp(start, stop, amount);    // C++20
  return v;
}
```

The function returns a value in the linear sequence in the range [`start`, `stop`]. The `index` parameter is the current number in the sequence of the n total numbers we are about to generate.

With the `lin_value()` helper in place, we can now easily implement the `lin_space()` generator. Before seeing a solution using a coroutine, we will examine other common techniques. The sections to follow will explore the following different approaches when implementing `lin_space()`:

- Eagerly generate and return all values
- Using a callback (lazy)
- Using a custom iterator (lazy)
- Using the Ranges library (lazy)
- Using coroutines with our `Generator` class (lazy)

For each example, there will be a short reflection of the strengths and weaknesses of each approach.

An eager linear range

We'll begin by implementing a simple eager version that computes all the values in the range and returns a vector with all values:

```
template <typename T>
auto lin_space(T start, T stop, size_t n) {
  auto v = std::vector<T>{};
  for (auto i = 0u; i < n; ++i)
    v.push_back(lin_value(start, stop, i, n));
  return v;
}
```

Since this version returns a standard container, it's possible to use the return value with range-based for-loops and other standard algorithms:

```
for (auto v : lin_space(2.0, 3.0, 5)) {
  std::cout << v << ", ";
}
// Prints: 2, 2.25, 2.5, 2.75, 3,
```

This version is straightforward, and fairly easy to read. The downside is that we need to allocate a vector and fill it with *all* values, although the caller is not necessarily interested in all values. This version also lacks composability as there is no way to filter out elements in the middle without first generating all values.

Now let's try to implement a lazy version of the `lin_space()` generator.

A lazy version using a callback

In *Chapter 10, Proxy Objects and Lazy Evaluation*, we concluded that lazy evaluation can be accomplished by using callback functions. The lazy version we will implement will be based on passing a callback to `lin_space()` and invoking the callback function when emitting values:

```
template <typename T, typename F>
requires std::invocable<F&, const T&>            // C++20
void lin_space(T start, T stop, std::size_t n, F&& f) {
  for (auto i = 0u; i < n; ++i) {
    const auto y = lin_value(start, stop, i, n);
    f(y);
  }
}
```

If we want to print the values produced by the generator, we can call this function like this:

```
auto print = [](auto v) { std::cout << v << ", "; };
lin_space(-1.f, 1.f, 5, print);
// Prints: -1, -0.5, 0, 0.5, 1,
```

The iteration now take places within the lin_space() function. There is no way to cancel the generator, but with some changes we could have the callback function return a bool to indicate whether it wants more elements to be generated.

This approach works but is not very elegant. The problem with this design becomes more apparent when trying to compose generators. If we wanted to add a filter that would select some special values, we would end up having nested callback functions.

We will now move on to see how we can implement an iterator-based solution to our problem.

An iterator implementation

Another alternative is to implement a type that conforms to the range concept by exposing the begin() and end() iterators. The class template LinSpace, defined here, makes it possible to iterate over the linear range of values:

```
template <typename T>
struct LinSpace {
  LinSpace(T start, T stop, std::size_t n)
      : begin_{start, stop, 0, n}, end_{n} {}

  struct Iterator {
    using difference_type = void;
    using value_type = T;
    using reference = T;
    using pointer = T*;
    using iterator_category = std::forward_iterator_tag;
    void operator++() { ++i_; }
    T operator*() { return lin_value(start_, stop_, i_, n_);}
    bool operator==(std::size_t i) const { return i_ == i; }
    T start_{};
    T stop_{};
    std::size_t i_{};
    std::size_t n_{};
```

```
  };
  auto begin() { return begin_; }
  auto end() { return end_; }

 private:
  Iterator begin_{};
  std::size_t end_{};
};

template <typename T>
auto lin_space(T start, T stop, std::size_t n) {
  return LinSpace{start, stop, n};
}
```

This implementation is very efficient. However, it is afflicted with a lot of boilerplate code and the small algorithm we are trying to encapsulate is now spread out into different parts: the LinSpace constructor implements the initial work of setting up the start and stop values, whereas the work needed for computing the values ends up in the member functions of the Iterator class. This makes the implementation of the algorithm harder to understand compared with the other versions we have looked at.

A solution using the Ranges library

Yet another alternative is to compose our algorithm using building blocks from the Ranges library (C++20), as shown here:

```
template <typename T>
auto lin_space(T start, T stop, std::size_t n) {
  return std::views::iota(std::size_t{0}, n) |
    std::views::transform([=](auto i) {
      return lin_value(start, stop, i, n);
    });
}
```

Here we have the entire algorithm encapsulated inside a small function. We are using std::views::iota to generate the indexes for us. Converting an index to a linear value is a simple transformation that can be chained after the iota view.

This version is efficient and composable. The object returned from lin_space() is a random-access range of type std::ranges::view, which can be iterated over using range-based for-loops or passed to other algorithms.

Finally, it's time to use our `Generator` class to implement our algorithm as a coroutine.

A solution using a coroutine

After looking at no less than four versions of this very same problem, we have now reached the last solution. Here I will present a version that uses the general `Generator` class template implemented earlier:

```
template <typename T>
auto lin_space(T start, T stop, std::size_t n) -> Generator<T> {
    for (auto i = 0u; i < n; ++i) {
        co_yield lin_value(start, stop, i, n);
    }
}
```

It's compact, straightforward, and easy to understand. By using `co_yield`, we can write the code in such a way that it looks similar to the simple eager version, but without the need for collecting all the values in a container. It's possible to chain multiple generators based on coroutines, as you will see at the end of this chapter.

This version is also compatible with range-based `for`-loops and standard algorithms. However, this version exposes an input range, so it's not possible to skip ahead arbitrary number of elements, which is possible with the version using the Ranges library.

Conclusion

Obviously, there is more than one way to do it. But why did I show all these approaches?

Firstly, if you are new to coroutines, you will hopefully start to see the patterns where it can be advantageous to use coroutines.

Secondly, the `Generator` template and the use of `co_yield` allows us to implement lazy generators in a very clear and concise way. This becomes obvious when we compare the solution with other versions.

Lastly, some approaches might look very contrived for this example problem but are frequently being used in other contexts. C++ is by default an eager language, and many (myself included) have become accustomed to creating code similar to the eager version. The version using a callback might look very strange but is a commonly used pattern in asynchronous code, where coroutines can wrap or replace those callback-based APIs.

The generator type we implemented is partly based on the synchronous generator template from the CppCoro library. CppCoro also provides an `async_generator` template, which makes it possible to use the `co_await` operator within the generator coroutine. I provided the `Generator` template in this chapter for the purpose of demonstrating how a generator can be implemented and how we can interact with coroutines. But if you plan to start using generators in your code, consider using a third-party library.

A real-world example using generators

Using coroutines for simplifying iterators really shines when the examples are a little bit more advanced. Using `co_yield` with the `Generator` class allows us to implement and combine small algorithms efficiently and without the need for boilerplate code to glue it all together. This next example will try to prove that.

The problem

We will here go through an example of how we can use our `Generator` class to implement a compression algorithm that can be used in search engines to compress the search index typically stored on disk. The example is thoroughly described in the book *Introduction to Information Retrieval* by Manning et al, which is freely available at https://nlp.stanford.edu/IR-book/. Here follows a brief background and a short description of the problem.

Search engines use some variant of a data structure called an **inverted index**. It is like an index at the end of a book. Using the index, we can find all pages that contain the terms we are searching for.

Now imagine that we have a database full of recipes and that we build an inverted index for this database. Parts of this index might look something like this:

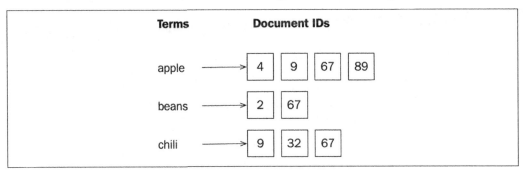

Figure 12.14: An inverted index with three terms and their corresponding lists of document references

Each term is associated with a sorted list of document identifiers. (For example, the term **apple** is included in the recipes with IDs **4, 9, 67,** and **89.**) If we want to find recipes that contain both **beans** *and* **chili**, we can run a merge-like algorithm to find the intersection of the lists for **beans** and **chili**:

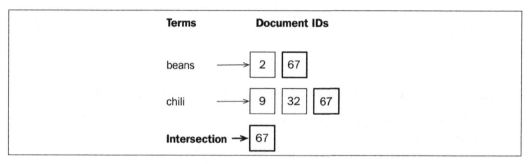

Figure 12.15 Intersection of the document lists for the terms "beans" and "chili"

Now imagine that we have a big database and we choose to represent the document identifier with a 32-bit integer. The lists of document identifiers can become very long for terms that appear in many documents and therefore we need to compress those lists. One possible way to do that is to use delta encoding combined with a variable byte encoding scheme.

Delta encoding

Since the lists are sorted, we could, instead of saving the document identifiers, store the **gap** between two adjacent elements. This technique is called **delta encoding** or **gap encoding**. The following diagram shows an example using document IDs and gaps:

	Encoding	Document Identifiers			
tomato	DocID	...	7234510	7234522	723425 ...
	Gap	...	32	12	3 ...
salt	DocID	...	7234510	7234511	7234512 ...
	Gap	...	1	1	1 ...
saffron	DocID	1027	4234510		
	Gap	1027	4233483		

Figure 12.16: Gap encoding stores the gap between two adjacent elements in a list

Gap encoding is well-suited for this type of data; frequently used terms will consequently have many small gaps. The really long lists will only contain very small gaps. After the lists have been gap encoded, we can use a variable byte encoding scheme to actually compress the lists by using fewer bytes for smaller gaps.

But first, let's start implementing the gap encoding functionality. We will begin by writing two small coroutines that will do the gap encoding/decoding. The encoder transforms a sorted sequence of integers to a sequence of gaps:

```
template <typename Range>
auto gap_encode(Range& ids) -> Generator<int> {
  auto last_id = 0;
  for (auto id : ids) {
    const auto gap = id - last_id;
    last_id = id;
    co_yield gap;
  }
}
```

By using co_yield, there is no need to eagerly pass a complete list of numbers and allocate a big output list of gaps. Instead, the coroutine lazily handles one number at a time. Note how the function gap_encode() contains everything that there is to know about how to convert document IDs to gaps. Implementing this as a traditional iterator would be possible, but this would have logic spread out in constructors and operators on iterators.

We can build a small program to test our gap encoder:

```
int main() {
  auto ids = std::vector{10, 11, 12, 14};
  auto gaps = gap_encode();
  for (auto&& gap : gaps) {
    std::cout << gap << ", ";
  }
} // Prints: 10, 1, 1, 2,
```

The decoder does the opposite; it takes as input a range of gaps and transforms it to the list of ordered numbers:

```
template <typename Range>
auto gap_decode(Range& gaps) -> Generator<int> {
  auto last_id = 0;
  for (auto gap : gaps) {
    const auto id = gap + last_id;
```

```
    co_yield id;
    last_id = id;
  }
}
```

By using gap encoding, we will on average, store much smaller numbers. But since we are still using int values for storing the small gaps, we haven't really gained anything if we save these gaps to disk. Unfortunately, we cannot just use a smaller fixed-size data type, because there is still a possibility that we will encounter a really big gap that would require a full 32-bit int. What we want is a way to store small gaps using fewer bits, as illustrated in the following diagram:

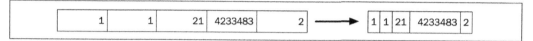

Figure 12.17: Small numbers should use fewer bytes

In order to make this list physically smaller, we can use **variable byte encoding** so that small gaps are encoded with fewer bytes than bigger gaps, as illustrated in the preceding diagram.

Variable byte encoding

Variable byte encoding is a very common compression technique. UTF-8 and MIDI message are some of the well-known encodings that uses this technique. In order to use a variable number of bytes when encoding, we use 7-bits of each byte for the actual payload. The first bit of each byte represents a **continuation bit**. It is set to 0 if there are more bytes to read, or 1 for the last byte of the encoded number. The encoding scheme is exemplified in the following diagram:

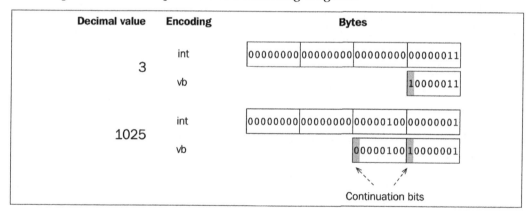

Figure 12.18: Using variable byte encoding, only one byte is required to store the decimal value 3 and two bytes for encoding the decimal value 1025

Now we are ready to implement the variable byte encoding and decoding scheme. This is a little bit more complicated than delta encoding. The encoder should transform a number into a sequence of one or multiple bytes:

```cpp
auto vb_encode_num(int n) -> Generator<std::uint8_t> {
  for (auto cont = std::uint8_t{0}; cont == 0;) {
    auto b = static_cast<std::uint8_t>(n % 128);
    n = n / 128;
    cont = (n == 0) ? 128 : 0;
    co_yield (b + cont);
  }
}
```

The continuation bit, named cont in the code, is either 0 or 128, which corresponds to the bit sequence 10000000. The details in this example are not that important to understand, but to make the encoding easier, the bytes are generated in reverse order so that the least significant byte comes first. This is not a problem since we can handle that easily during the decoding.

With the number encoder in place, it's easy to encode a sequence of numbers and transform them into a sequence of bytes:

```cpp
template <typename Range>
auto vb_encode(Range& r) -> Generator<std::uint8_t> {
  for (auto n : r) {
    auto bytes = vb_encode_num(n);
    for (auto b : bytes) {
      co_yield b;
    }
  }
}
```

The decoder is probably the most complicated part. But again, it is fully encapsulated into one single function with a clean interface:

```cpp
template <typename Range>
auto vb_decode(Range& bytes) -> Generator<int> {
  auto n = 0;
  auto weight = 1;
  for (auto b : bytes) {
    if (b < 128) {  // Check continuation bit
      n += b * weight;
      weight *= 128;
    }
```

```
    else {
      // Process last byte and yield
      n += (b - 128) * weight;
      co_yield n;
      n = 0;        // Reset
      weight = 1;   // Reset
    }
  }
}
```

As you can see, there is very little boilerplate code needed in this code. Each coroutine encapsulates all states and describes clearly how to process one piece at a time.

The last piece we need is to combine the gap encoder with the variable byte encoder in order to compress our sorted list of document identifiers:

```
template <typename Range>
auto compress(Range& ids) -> Generator<int> {
  auto gaps = gap_encode(ids);
  auto bytes = vb_encode(gaps);
  for (auto b : bytes) {
    co_yield b;
  }
}
```

Decompress is a simple chaining of vb_decode() followed by gap_decode():

```
template <typename Range>
auto decompress(Range& bytes) -> Generator<int> {
  auto gaps = vb_decode(bytes);
  auto ids = gap_decode(gaps);
  for (auto id : ids) {
    co_yield id;
  }
}
```

Since the Generator class exposes iterators, we can take this example even further and easily stream the values to and from disk using iostreams. (Although, a more realistic approach would be to use memory-mapped I/O for better performance.) Here are two small functions that writes and reads the compressed data to and from disk:

```cpp
template <typename Range>
void write(const std::string& path, Range& bytes) {
  auto out = std::ofstream{path, std::ios::out | std::ofstream::binary};
  std::ranges::copy(bytes.begin(), bytes.end(),
                    std::ostreambuf_iterator<char>(out));
}

auto read(std::string path) -> Generator<std::uint8_t> {
  auto in = std::ifstream {path, std::ios::in | std::ofstream::binary};
  auto it = std::istreambuf_iterator<char>{in};
  const auto end = std::istreambuf_iterator<char>{};
  for (; it != end; ++it) {
    co_yield *it;
  }
}
```

A small test program will wrap this example up:

```cpp
int main() {
  {
    auto documents = std::vector{367, 438, 439, 440};
    auto bytes = compress(documents);
    write("values.bin", bytes);
  }
  {
    auto bytes = read("values.bin");
    auto documents = decompress(bytes);
    for (auto doc : documents) {
      std::cout << doc << ", ";
    }
  }
}
// Prints: 367, 438, 439, 440,
```

This example aims to show that we can divide lazy programs into small encapsulated coroutines. The low overhead of C++ coroutines makes them suitable for building efficient generators. The Generator we implemented initially is a fully reusable class that helps us with minimizing the amount of boilerplate code in examples like this.

This ends the section about generators. We will now move on to discuss some general performance considerations when using coroutines.

Performance

Each time a coroutine is created (when it is first called) a coroutine frame is allocated to hold the coroutine state. The frame can be allocated on the heap, or on the stack in some circumstances. However, there are no guarantees to completely avoid the heap allocation. If you are in a situation where heap allocations are forbidden (for example, in a real-time context) the coroutine can be created and immediately suspended in a different thread, and then passed to the part of the program that needs to actually use the coroutine. Suspend and resume are guaranteed to not allocate any memory and have a cost comparable with an ordinary function call.

At the time of writing this book, compilers have experimental support for coroutines. Small experiments have shown promising results related to performance, showing that coroutines are friendly to the optimizer. However, I will not provide you with any benchmarks of coroutines in this book. Instead, I have shown you how stackless coroutines are evaluated and how it's possible for coroutines to be implemented with minimal overheads.

The generator example demonstrated that coroutines can potentially be very friendly to the compiler. The chain of generators we wrote in that example was completely evaluated at runtime. In practice, this is a very good property of C++ coroutines. They allow us to write code that is easy for both compilers and human beings to understand. C++ coroutines usually produce clean code that is easy to optimize.

Coroutines that execute on the same thread can share state without using any locking primitives and can therefore avoid the performance overhead incurred by synchronizing multiple threads. This will be demonstrated in the next chapter.

Summary

In this chapter, you have seen how to use C++ coroutines for building generators using the keywords co_yield and co_return. To better understand how C++ stackless coroutines differ from stackful coroutines, we compared the two and also looked at the customization points that C++ coroutines offer. This gave you a deep understanding of how flexible C++ coroutines are, as well as how they can be used to achieve efficiency. Stackless coroutines are closely related to state machines. By rewriting a traditionally implemented state machine into code that uses coroutines, we explored this relationship and you saw how well compilers can transform and optimize our coroutines to machine language.

In the next chapter, we will continue to discuss coroutines by focusing on asynchronous programming and will deepen your understanding of the co_await keyword.

13

Asynchronous Programming with Coroutines

The generator class implemented in the previous chapter helped us to use coroutines for building lazily evaluated sequences. C++ coroutines can also be used for asynchronous programming by having a coroutine represent an asynchronous computation or an **asynchronous task**. Although asynchronous programming is the most important driver for having coroutines in C++, there is no support for asynchronous tasks based on coroutines in the standard library. If you want to use coroutines for asynchronous programming, I recommend you find and use a library that complements C++20 coroutines. I've already recommended CppCoro (https://github.com/lewissbaker/cppcoro), which at the time of writing seems like the most promising alternative. It's also possible to use asynchronous coroutines with the well-established library Boost.Asio, as you will see later on in this chapter.

This chapter will show that asynchronous programming is possible using coroutines and that there are libraries available to complement C++20 coroutines. More specifically, we will focus on:

- The co_await keyword and awaitable types
- The implementation of a rudimentary task type—a type that can be returned from coroutines that perform some asynchronous work
- Boost.Asio to exemplify asynchronous programming using coroutines

Before moving on, it should also be said that there are no performance-related topics in this chapter and very few guidelines and best practices are presented. Instead, this chapter serves more as an introduction to the novel feature of asynchronous coroutines in C++. We'll begin this introduction by exploring awaitable types and co_await statements.

Awaitable types revisited

We already talked a bit about awaitable types in the previous chapter. But now we need to get a little bit more specific about what co_await does and what an awaitable type is. The keyword co_await is a unary operator, meaning that it takes a single argument. The argument we pass to co_await needs to fulfill some requirements that we will explore in this section.

When we say co_await in our code, we express that we are *waiting* for something that may or may not be ready for us. If it's not ready, co_await suspends the currently executing coroutine and returns control back to its caller. When the asynchronous task has completed, it should transfer the control back to the coroutine originally waiting for the task to finish. From here on, I will typically refer to the awaiting function as the **continuation**.

Now consider the following expression:

```
co_await X{};
```

For this code to compile, X needs to be an awaitable type. So far we have only used the trivial awaitable types: std::suspend_always and std::suspend_never. Any type that directly implements the three member functions listed next, or alternatively defines operator co_wait() to produce an object with these member functions, is an awaitable type:

- **await_ready()** returns a bool that indicates whether the result is ready (true) or whether it is necessary to suspend the current coroutine and wait for the result to become ready.

- **await_suspend(coroutine_handle)** – If await_ready() returned false, this function will be called with a handle to the coroutine that executed co_await. This function gives us an opportunity to start asynchronous work and subscribe for a notification that will trigger when the task has finished and thereafter resume the coroutine.

- **await_resume()** is the function responsible for unpacking the result (or error) back to the coroutine. If an error has occurred during the work initiated by await_suspend(), this function could rethrow the caught error or return an error code. The result of the entire co_await expression is whatever await_resume() returns.

To demonstrate the use of operator co_await(), here is a snippet inspired by a section from the C++20 standard that defines operator co_await for a time interval:

```
using namespace std::chrono;
template <class Rep, class Period>
auto operator co_await(duration<Rep, Period> d) {
  struct Awaitable {
    system_clock::duration d_;
    Awaitable(system_clock::duration d) : d_(d) {}
    bool await_ready() const { return d_.count() <= 0; }
    void await_suspend(std::coroutine_handle<> h) { /* ... */ }
    void await_resume() {}
  };
  return Awaitable{d};
}
```

With this overload in place, we can now pass a time interval to the co_await operator, as follows:

```
std::cout << "just about to go to sleep...\n";
co_await 10ms;                     // Calls operator co_await()
std::cout << "resumed\n";
```

The example is not complete but gives you a hint about how to use the unary operator co_await. As you may have noticed, the three await_*() functions are not called directly by us; instead, they are invoked by code inserted by the compiler. Another example will clarify the transformations made by the compiler. Assume that the compiler stumbles upon the following statement in our code:

```
auto result = co_await expr;
```

Then the compiler will (very) roughly transform the code into something like this:

```
// Pseudo code
auto&& a = expr;          // Evaluate expr, a is the awaitable
if (!a.await_ready()) {   // Not ready, wait for result
  a.await_suspend(h);     // Handle to current coroutine
                          // Suspend/resume happens here
}
auto result = a.await_resume();
```

The `await_ready()` function is first called to check whether a suspension is needed. If so, `await_suspend()` is called with a handle to the coroutine that will be suspended (the coroutine with the `co_await` statement). Finally, the result of the awaitable is requested and assigned to the `result` variable.

The implicit suspend points

As you have seen in numerous examples, a coroutine defines *explicit* suspend points by using `co_await` and `co_yield`. Each coroutine also has two *implicit* suspend points:

- The **initial suspend point**, which occurs at the initial invocation of a coroutine before the coroutine body is executed
- The **final suspend point**, which occurs after the coroutine body has been executed and before the coroutine is destroyed

The promise type defines the behavior of these two points by implementing `initial_suspend()` and `final_suspend()`. Both functions return awaitable objects. Typically, we pass `std::suspend_always` from the `initial_suspend()` function so that the coroutine is started lazily rather than eagerly.

The final suspend point plays an important role for asynchronous tasks, because it makes it possible for us to tweak the behavior of `co_await`. Normally, a coroutine that has been `co_await`:ed should resume the awaiting coroutine at the final suspend point.

Next, let's get a better understanding of how the three awaitable functions are meant to be used and how they cooperate with the `co_await` operator.

Implementing a rudimentary task type

The task type we are about to implement is a type that can be returned from coroutines that represent asynchronous tasks. The task is something that a caller can wait for using `co_await`. The goal is to be able to write asynchronous application code that looks like this:

```
auto image = co_await load("image.jpg");
auto thumbnail = co_await resize(image, 100, 100);
co_await save(thumbnail, "thumbnail.jpg");
```

The standard library already provides a type that allows a function to return an object that a caller can use for waiting on a result to be computed, namely `std::future`. We could potentially wrap `std::future` into something that would conform to the awaitable interface. However, `std::future` does not support continuations, which means that whenever we try to get the value from a `std::future`, we block the current thread. In other words, there is no way to compose asynchronous operations without blocking when using `std::future`.

Another alternative would be to use `std::experimental::future` or a future type from the Boost library, which supports continuations. But these future types allocate heap memory and include synchronization primitives that are not needed in the use cases set out for our tasks. Instead, we will create a new type with minimum overhead with the responsibilities to:

- Forward return values and exceptions to the caller
- Resume the caller waiting for the result

A coroutine task type has been proposed (see P1056R0 at `http://www7.open-std.org/JTC1/SC22/WG21/docs/papers/2018/p1056r0.html`), and the proposal gives us a good hint about what components we need. The implementation that follows is based on work presented by Gor Nishanov and source code shared by Lewis Baker, which is available in the CppCoro library.

Here is the implementation of the class template for representing an asynchronous task:

```cpp
template <typename T>
class [[nodiscard]] Task {
  struct Promise { /* ... */ };          // See below
  std::coroutine_handle<Promise> h_;
  explicit Task(Promise & p) noexcept
      : h_{std::coroutine_handle<Promise>::from_promise(p)} {}

public:
  using promise_type = Promise;
  Task(Task&& t) noexcept : h_{std::exchange(t.h_, {})} {}
  ~Task() { if (h_) h_.destroy(); }

  // Awaitable interface
  bool await_ready() { return false; }
```

```cpp
    auto await_suspend(std::coroutine_handle<> c) {
      h_.promise().continuation_ = c;
      return h_;
    }
    auto await_resume() -> T {
      auto& result = h_.promise().result_;
      if (result.index() == 1) {
        return std::get<1>(std::move(result));
      } else {
        std::rethrow_exception(std::get<2>(std::move(result)));
      }
    }
  }
};
```

An explanation of each part will follow in the subsequent sections, but first we need the implementation of the promise type that uses a std::variant to hold a value or an error. The promise also keeps a reference to the coroutine waiting for the task to complete using the continuation_ data member:

```cpp
struct Promise {
  std::variant<std::monostate, T, std::exception_ptr> result_;
  std::coroutine_handle<> continuation_;  // A waiting coroutine

  auto get_return_object() noexcept { return Task{*this}; }
  void return_value(T value) {
    result_.template emplace<1>(std::move(value));
  }
  void unhandled_exception() noexcept {
    result_.template emplace<2>(std::current_exception());
  }
  auto initial_suspend() { return std::suspend_always{}; }
  auto final_suspend() noexcept {
    struct Awaitable {
      bool await_ready() noexcept { return false; }
      auto await_suspend(std::coroutine_handle<Promise> h) noexcept {
        return h.promise().continuation_;
      }
      void await_resume() noexcept {}
    };
    return Awaitable{};
  }
};
```

It's important to distinguish between the two coroutine handles we are using: the handle identifying the *current coroutine* and the handle identifying the *continuation*.

Note that this implementation doesn't support Task<void> due to limitations of std::variant, and also the limitation that we can't have both return_value() and return_void() on the same promise type. Not supporting Task<void> is unfortunate since not all asynchronous tasks necessarily return values. We will overcome this limitation in a while by providing a template specialization for Task<void>.

Since we implemented a few coroutine return types in the previous chapter (Resumable and Generator), you will already be familiar with the requirements of a type that can be returned from a coroutine. Here, we will focus on the things that are new to you, such as exception handling and the ability to resume the caller currently waiting for us. Let's start looking at how Task and Promise handle return values and exceptions.

Handling return values and exceptions

An asynchronous task can complete by returning (a value or void) or by throwing an exception. The value and the error need to be handed over to the caller, which has been waiting for the task to complete. As usual, this is the responsibility of the promise object.

The Promise class uses a std::variant to store the result of three possible outcomes:

- No value at all (the std::monostate). We use this in our variant to make it default-constructible, but without requiring the other two types to be default-constructible.

- A return value of type T, where T is the template argument of Task.

- A std::exception_ptr, which is a handle to an exception that was thrown earlier.

The exception is captured by using the std::current_exception() function inside the function Promise::unhandled_exception(). By storing a std::exception_ptr, we can later rethrow this exception in another context. This is also the mechanism used when exceptions are passed between threads.

A coroutine that uses co_return value; must have a promise type that implements return_value(). However, coroutines that use co_return;, or run off the body without returning a value, must have a promise type that implements return_void(). Implementing a promise type that contains both return_void() and return_value() generates a compilation error.

Resuming an awaiting coroutine

When the asynchronous task has completed, it should transfer the control back to the coroutine waiting for the task to finish. To be able to resume this continuation, the Task object needs the coroutine_handle to the continuation coroutine. This handle was passed to the Task object's await_suspend() function, and conveniently we made sure to save that handle into the promise object:

```
class Task {
  // ...
  auto await_suspend(std::coroutine_handle<> c) {
    h_.promise().continuation_ = c;       // Save handle
    return h_;
  }
  // ...
```

The final_suspend() function is responsible for suspending at the final suspend point of this coroutine and transferring execution to the awaiting coroutine. This is the relevant part of the Promise reproduced for your convenience:

```
auto Promise::final_suspend() noexcept {
  struct Awaitable {
    bool await_ready() noexcept { return false; } // Suspend
    auto await_suspend(std::coroutine_handle<Promise> h) noexcept{
      return h.promise().continuation_;  // Transfer control to
    }                                    // the waiting coroutine
    void await_resume() noexcept {}
  };
  return Awaitable{};
}
```

To begin with, returning false from await_ready() will leave the coroutine suspended at the final suspend point. The reason we do this is so that the promise is still alive and available for the continuation to have a chance to pull the result out from this promise.

Next, let's have a look at the await_suspend() function. This is the place where we want to resume the continuation. We could potentially call resume() directly on the continuation_ handle and wait for it to finish, like this:

```
// ...
auto await_suspend(std::coroutine_handle<Promise> h) noexcept {
  h.promise().resume();              // Not recommended
}
// ...
```

However, that would run the risk of creating a long chain of nested call frames on the stack, which eventually could result in a stack overflow. Let's see how this could happen with a short example using two coroutines, a() and b():

```
auto a() -> Task<int> {  co_return 42; }
auto b() -> Task<int> {             // The continuation
  auto sum = 0;
  for (auto i = 0; i < 1'000'000; ++i) {
    sum += co_await a();
  }
  co_return sum;
}
```

If the Promise object associated with coroutine a() directly called resume() on the handle to coroutine b(), a new call frame to resume b() would be created on the stack on top of the call frame for a(). This process would be repeated over and over again in the loop, creating new nested call frames on the stack for each iteration. This call sequence when two functions call each other is a form of recursion, sometimes called mutual recursion:

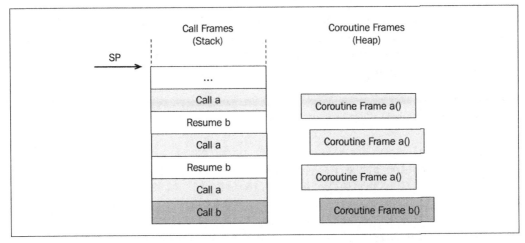

Figure 13.1: Coroutine b() calls coroutine a(), which resumes b(), which calls a(), which resumes b(), and so on

Even though there is only one coroutine frame created for b(), each call to resume() that resumes coroutine b() creates a new frame on the stack. The solution to avoid this problem is called **symmetric transfer**. Instead of resuming the continuation directly from the coroutine that is about to finish, the task object instead returns the coroutine_handle identifying the continuation from await_suspend():

```
// ...
auto await_suspend(std::coroutine_handle<Promise> h) noexcept {
  return h.promise().continuation_;      // Symmetric transfer
}
// ...
```

An optimization called *tail call optimization* is then guaranteed to happen by the compiler. In our case, this means that the compiler will be able to transfer control directly to the continuation without creating a new nested call frame.

We will not spend more time on the details of symmetric transfer and tail calls, but an excellent and more in-depth explanation of these topics can be found in the article C++ *Coroutines: Understanding Symmetric Transfer* by Lewis Baker, available at https://lewissbaker.github.io/2020/05/11/understanding_symmetric_transfer.

As mentioned earlier, our Task template has the limitation of not handling a template parameter of type void. Now it's time to fix that.

Supporting void tasks

To overcome the limitations addressed earlier regarding the inability to handle tasks that do not produce any values, we need a template specialization for Task<void>. It is spelled out here for completeness, but it does not add many new insights beyond the general Task template defined earlier:

```
template <>
class [[nodiscard]] Task<void> {

  struct Promise {
    std::exception_ptr e_;    // No std::variant, only exception
    std::coroutine_handle<> continuation_;

    auto get_return_object() noexcept { return Task{*this}; }
    void return_void() {}   // Instead of return_value()
    void unhandled_exception() noexcept {
      e_ = std::current_exception();
    }
```

```
      auto initial_suspend() { return std::suspend_always{}; }
      auto final_suspend() noexcept {
        struct Awaitable {
          bool await_ready() noexcept { return false; }
          auto await_suspend(std::coroutine_handle<Promise> h) noexcept {
            return h.promise().continuation_;
          }
          void await_resume() noexcept {}
        };
        return Awaitable{};
      }
    };
    std::coroutine_handle<Promise> h_;
    explicit Task(Promise& p) noexcept
        : h_{std::coroutine_handle<Promise>::from_promise(p)} {}

  public:
    using promise_type = Promise;

    Task(Task&& t) noexcept : h_{std::exchange(t.h_, {})} {}
    ~Task() { if (h_) h_.destroy(); }

    // Awaitable interface
    bool await_ready() { return false; }
    auto await_suspend(std::coroutine_handle<> c) {
      h_.promise().continuation_ = c;
      return h_;
    }
    void await_resume() {
      if (h_.promise().e_)
        std::rethrow_exception(h_.promise().e_);
    }
};
```

The promise type in this template specialization only keeps a reference to a potentially unhandled exception. And instead of having return_value() defined, the promise contains the member function return_void().

We can now represent tasks that return values or void. But there is still some work to be done before we can actually build a standalone program to test our Task type.

Synchronously waiting for a task to complete

An important aspect of the Task type is that whatever invokes a coroutine that returns a Task must co_await on it, and is therefore also a coroutine. This creates a chain of coroutines (continuations). For example, assume we have a coroutine like this:

```
Task<void> async_func() {        // A coroutine
  co_await some_func();
}
```

Then, it's not possible to use it in the following way:

```
void f() {
  co_await async_func(); // Error: A coroutine can't return void
}
```

Once we call an asynchronous function that returns a Task, we need to co_await on it, or nothing will happen. This is also the reason why we declare Task to be nodiscard: so that it generates a compilation warning if the return value is ignored, like this:

```
void g() {
  async_func();           // Warning: Does nothing
}
```

The forced chaining of coroutines has the interesting effect that we finally get to the main() function of the program, which the C++ standard says is not allowed to be a coroutine. This needs to be addressed somehow, and the proposed solution is to provide at least one function that synchronously waits on the asynchronous chains to complete. For example, the CppCoro library includes the function sync_wait(), which has this effect of breaking the chain of coroutines, which makes it possible for an ordinary function to use coroutines.

Unfortunately, implementing sync_wait() is rather complicated, but in order to at least make it possible to compile and test our Task type, I will here provide a simplified version based on the Standard C++ Proposal P1171R0, https://wg21.link/P1171R0. Our goal here is to be able to write a test program like this:

```
auto some_async_func() -> Task<int> { /* ... */ }

int main() {
  auto result = sync_wait(some_async_func());
  return result;
}
```

With the aim of testing and running asynchronous tasks, let's continue with the implementation of sync_wait().

Implementing sync_wait()

sync_wait() internally uses a custom task class specifically designed for our purpose, called SyncWaitTask. Its definition will be revealed in a while, but first let's have a look at the definition of the function template sync_wait():

```cpp
template<typename T>
using Result = decltype(std::declval<T&>().await_resume());

template <typename T>
Result<T> sync_wait(T&& task) {
  if constexpr (std::is_void_v<Result<T>>) {
    struct Empty {};
    auto coro = [&]() -> detail::SyncWaitTask<Empty> {
      co_await std::forward<T>(task);
      co_yield Empty{};
      assert(false);
    };
    coro().get();
  } else {
    auto coro = [&]() -> detail::SyncWaitTask<Result<T>> {
      co_yield co_await std::forward<T>(task);
      // This coroutine will be destroyed before it
      // has a chance to return.
      assert(false);
    };
    return coro().get();
  }
}
```

First, in order to specify the type that the task is returning, we use a combination of decltype and declval. The rather cumbersome using-expression gives us the type returned by T::await_resume(), where T is the type of the task passed to sync_wait().

Inside sync_wait() we distinguish between tasks that return values and tasks that return void. We make a distinction here to avoid the need for implementing a template specialization of SyncWaitTask to handle both void and non-void types. Both cases are handled similarly by introducing an empty struct, which can be provided as the template argument to SyncWaitTask for handling void tasks.

In the case where an actual value is returned, a lambda expression is used to define a coroutine that will co_await on the result and then finally yield its value. It's important to note that the coroutine might resume from co_await on another thread, which requires us to use a synchronization primitive in the implementation of SyncWaitTask.

Calling get() on the coroutine lambda resumes the coroutine until it yields a value. The implementation of SyncWaitTask guarantees that the coroutine lambda will never have a chance to resume again after the co_yield statement.

We used co_yield extensively in the previous chapter, but without mentioning its relationship to co_await; namely that the following co_yield expression:

```
co_yield some_value;
```

is transformed by the compiler into:

```
co_await promise.yield_value(some_value);
```

where promise is the promise object associated with the currently executing coroutine. Knowing this is helpful when trying to understand the control flow between sync_wait() and the SyncWaitTask class.

Implementing SyncWaitTask

Now we are ready to inspect the SyncWaitTask, which is a type intended only to be used as a helper for sync_wait(). For that reason, we add it under a namespace called detail to make it clear that this class is an implementation detail:

```
namespace detail { // Implementation detail

template <typename T>
class SyncWaitTask {  // A helper class only used by sync_wait()
  struct Promise { /* ... */ }; // See below
  std::coroutine_handle<Promise> h_;
  explicit SyncWaitTask(Promise& p) noexcept
      : h_{std::coroutine_handle<Promise>::from_promise(p)} {}

public:
  using promise_type = Promise;

  SyncWaitTask(SyncWaitTask&& t) noexcept
      : h_{std::exchange(t.h_, {})} {}
  ~SyncWaitTask() { if (h_) h_.destroy();}
```

```
  // Called from sync_wait(). Will block and retrieve the
  // value or error from the task passed to sync_wait()
  T&& get() {
    auto& p = h_.promise();
    h_.resume();
    p.semaphore_.acquire();                // Block until signal
    if (p.error_)
      std::rethrow_exception(p.error_);
    return static_cast<T&&>(*p.value_);
  }
  // No awaitable interface, this class will not be co_await:ed
};
} // namespace detail
```

The most interesting part to pay attention to is the function get() and its blocking
call to acquire() on a semaphore owned by the promise object. This is what makes
this task type synchronously wait for a result to be ready for us. The promise type
that owns the binary semaphore looks like this:

```
struct Promise {

  T* value_{nullptr};
  std::exception_ptr error_;
  std::binary_semaphore semaphore_;

  SyncWaitTask get_return_object() noexcept {
    return SyncWaitTask{*this};
  }
  void unhandled_exception() noexcept {
    error_ = std::current_exception();
  }
  auto yield_value(T&& x) noexcept {       // Result has arrived
    value_ = std::addressof(x);
    return final_suspend();
  }
  auto initial_suspend() noexcept {
    return std::suspend_always{};
  }
  auto final_suspend() noexcept {
  struct Awaitable {
      bool await_ready() noexcept { return false; }
```

```
        void await_suspend(std::coroutine_handle<Promise> h) noexcept {
          h.promise().semaphore_.release();                // Signal!
        }
        void await_resume() noexcept {}
      };
      return Awaitable{};
    }
    void return_void() noexcept { assert(false); }
  };
```

There's a lot of boilerplate code here that we have already talked about. But pay special attention to `yield_value()` and `final_suspend()`, which is the interesting part of this class. Recall that the coroutine lambda inside `sync_wait()` yielded the return value like this:

```
  // ...
  auto coro = [&]() -> detail::SyncWaitTask<Result<T>> {
    co_yield co_await std::forward<T>(task);
    // ...
```

So, once the value is yielded, we end up in `yield_value()` of the promise object. And the fact that `yield_value()` can return an awaitable type gives us the opportunity to customize the behavior of the `co_yield` keyword. In this case, `yield_value()` returns an awaitable that will signal through the binary semaphore that a value from the original `Task` object has been produced.

The semaphore is signaled inside `await_suspend()`. We cannot signal earlier than that because the other end of the code waiting for the signal will eventually destroy the coroutine. Destroying a coroutine must only happen if the coroutine is in a suspended state.

The blocking call to `semaphore_.acquire()` from within `SyncWaitTask::get()` will return on the signal, and finally the computed value will be handed over to the client that called `sync_wait()`.

Testing asynchronous tasks with sync_wait()

Finally, a small asynchronous test program using `Task` and `sync_wait()` can be constructed like this:

```
auto height() -> Task<int> { co_return 20; }      // Dummy coroutines
auto width() -> Task<int> { co_return 30; }
auto area() -> Task<int> {
  co_return co_await height() * co_await width();
}

int main() {
  auto a = area();
  int value = sync_wait(a);
  std::cout << value;          // Outputs: 600
}
```

We have implemented the absolute minimum infrastructure for using asynchronous tasks with C++ coroutines. More infrastructure is needed, though, in order to use coroutines for asynchronous programming effectively. This is a big difference from the generator (presented in the previous chapter), which required a fairly small amount of groundwork before we could really benefit from it. To get a little bit closer to the real world, we will, in the following sections, explore some examples using Boost.Asio. The first thing we will do is to try to wrap a callback-based API inside an API compatible with C++ coroutines.

Wrapping a callback-based API

There are many asynchronous APIs based on callbacks. Typically, an asynchronous function takes a callback function provided by the caller. The asynchronous function returns immediately and then eventually invokes the callback (completion handler) when the asynchronous function has a computed value or is done waiting for something.

To show you what an asynchronous callback-based API can look like, we will take a peek at a Boost library for asynchronous I/O named **Boost.Asio**. There is a lot to learn about Boost.Asio that won't be covered here; I will only describe the absolute minimum of the Boost code and instead focus on the parts directly related to C++ coroutines.

To make the code fit the pages of the book, the examples assume that the following namespace alias has been defined whenever we use code from Boost.Asio:

```
namespace asio = boost::asio;
```

Here is a complete example of using Boost.Asio for delaying a function call but without blocking the current thread. This asynchronous example runs in a single thread:

```cpp
#include <boost/asio.hpp>
#include <chrono>
#include <iostream>

using namespace std::chrono;
namespace asio = boost::asio;

int main() {
  auto ctx = asio::io_context{};
  auto timer = asio::system_timer{ctx};
  timer.expires_from_now(1000ms);
  timer.async_wait([](auto error) {        // Callback
    // Ignore errors..
    std::cout << "Hello from delayed callback\n";
  });
  std::cout << "Hello from main\n";
  ctx.run();
}
```

Compiling and running this program will generate the following output:

```
Hello from main
Hello from delayed callback
```

When using Boost.Asio, we always need to create an `io_context` object that runs an event processing loop. The call to `async_wait()` is asynchronous; it returns immediately back to `main()` and invokes the callback (the lambda) when the timer expires.

The timer example does not use coroutines but instead a callback API to provide asynchronicity. Boost.Asio is also compatible with C++20 coroutines, which I will demonstrate later on. But on our path to explore awaitable types, we will take a detour and instead assume that we need to provide a coroutine-based API that returns awaitable types on top of the callback-based API of Boost.Asio. In that way, we can use a `co_await` expression to call and wait (but without blocking the current thread) for the asynchronous task to complete. Instead of using a callback, we would like to be able to write something like this:

```cpp
std::cout << "Hello! ";
co_await async_sleep(ctx, 100ms);
```

```
  std::cout << "Delayed output\n";
```

Let's see how we can implement the function `async_sleep()` so that it can be used with co_await. The pattern we will follow is to have `async_sleep()` return an awaitable object that will implement the three required functions: `await_ready()`, `await_suspend()`, and `await_resume()`. An explanation of the code will follow after it:

```
template <typename R, typename P>
auto async_sleep(asio::io_context& ctx,
                 std::chrono::duration<R, P> d) {
  struct Awaitable {
    asio::system_timer t_;
    std::chrono::duration<R, P> d_;
    boost::system::error_code ec_{};

    bool await_ready() { return d_.count() <= 0; }
    void await_suspend(std::coroutine_handle<> h) {
      t_.expires_from_now(d_);
      t_.async_wait([this, h](auto ec) mutable {
        this->ec_ = ec;
        h.resume();
      });
    }
    void await_resume() {
      if (ec_) throw boost::system::system_error(ec_);
    }
  };
  return Awaitable{asio::system_timer{ctx}, d};
}
```

Once again, we are creating a custom awaitable type that does all the necessary work:

- `await_ready()` will return `false` unless the timer has already reached zero.

- `await_suspend()` starts the asynchronous operation and passes a callback that will be called when the timer has expired or produced an error. The callback saves the error code (if any) and resumes the suspended coroutine.

- `await_resume()` has no result to unpack because the asynchronous function we are wrapping, `boost::asio::timer::async_wait()`, does not return any value except an optional error code.

Before we can actually test `async_sleep()` in a standalone program, we need some way to start the `io_context` run loop and break the chain of coroutines, as we did when testing the `Task` type previously. We will do that in a rather hacky way here by implementing two functions, `run_task()` and `run_task_impl()`, and a naive coroutine return type called `Detached` that ignores error handling and can be discarded by the caller:

```cpp
// This code is here just to get our example up and running
struct Detached {
  struct promise_type {
    auto get_return_object() { return Detached{}; }
    auto initial_suspend() { return std::suspend_never{}; }
    auto final_suspend() noexcept { return std::suspend_never{};}
    void unhandled_exception() { std::terminate(); } // Ignore
    void return_void() {}
  };
};

Detached run_task_impl(asio::io_context& ctx, Task<void>&& t) {
  auto wg = asio::executor_work_guard{ctx.get_executor()};
  co_await t;
}

void run_task(asio::io_context& ctx, Task<void>&& t) {
  run_task_impl(ctx, std::move(t));
  ctx.run();
}
```

The `Detached` type makes the coroutine start immediately and runs the coroutine detached from the caller. The `executor_work_guard` prevents the `run()` call from returning until the coroutine `run_task_impl()` has completed.

Starting operations and detaching them should typically be avoided. It's similar to detached threads or allocated memory without any references. However, the purpose of this example is to demonstrate what we can use awaitable types for and how we can write asynchronous programs and run them single-threaded.

Everything is in place; the wrapper called `async_sleep()` returns a `Task` and a function `run_task()`, which can be used to execute a task. It's time to write a small coroutine to test the new code we implemented:

```cpp
auto test_sleep(asio::io_context& ctx) -> Task<void> {
  std::cout << "Hello!  ";
  co_await async_sleep(ctx, 100ms);
  std::cout << "Delayed output\n";
}

int main() {
  auto ctx = asio::io_context{};
  auto task = test_sleep(ctx);
  run_task(ctx, std::move(task));
};
```

Executing this program will generate the following output:

```
Hello! Delayed output
```

You have seen how a callback-based API can be wrapped in a function that can be used by co_await and therefore allows us to use coroutines instead of callbacks for asynchronous programming. This program also provided a typical example of how the functions in the awaitable type can be used. However, as mentioned earlier, it turns out that recent versions of Boost, starting with 1.70, already provide an interface that is compatible with C++20 coroutines. In the next section, we will use this new coroutine API when building a tiny TCP server.

A concurrent server using Boost.Asio

This section will demonstrate how to write concurrent programs that have multiple threads of execution but only use a single OS thread. We are about to implement a rudimentary concurrent single-threaded TCP server that can handle multiple clients. There are no networking capabilities in the C++ standard library, but fortunately Boost.Asio provides us with a platform-agnostic interface for handling socket communication.

Instead of wrapping the callback-based Boost.Asio API, I will demonstrate how to use the boost::asio::awaitable class for the purpose of showing a more realistic example of how asynchronous application programming using coroutines can look. The class template boost::asio::awaitable corresponds to the Task template we created earlier; it's used as a return type for coroutines that represent asynchronous computations.

Implementing the server

The server is very simple; once a client connects, it starts updating a numeric counter and writes back the value whenever it is updated. This time we will follow the code from top to bottom, starting with the `main()` function:

```cpp
#include <boost/asio.hpp>
#include <boost/asio/awaitable.hpp>
#include <boost/asio/use_awaitable.hpp>

using namespace std::chrono;
namespace asio = boost::asio;
using boost::asio::ip::tcp;

int main() {
  auto server = [] {
    auto endpoint = tcp::endpoint{tcp::v4(), 37259};
    auto awaitable = listen(endpoint);
    return awaitable;
  };
  auto ctx = asio::io_context{};
  asio::co_spawn(ctx, server, asio::detached);
  ctx.run(); // Run event loop from main thread
}
```

The mandatory `io_context` runs the event processing loop. It's possible to invoke `run()` from multiple threads as well, if we want our server to execute multiple OS threads. In our case we only use one thread but with multiple concurrent flows. The function `boost::asio::co_spawn()` starts a detached concurrent flow. The server is implemented using a lambda; it defines a TCP endpoint (with port 37259) and starts listening for incoming client connections on the endpoint.

The coroutine `listen()` is fairly simple and looks like this:

```cpp
auto listen(tcp::endpoint endpoint) -> asio::awaitable<void> {
  auto ex = co_await asio::this_coro::executor;
  auto a = tcp::acceptor{ex, endpoint};
  while (true) {
    auto socket = co_await a.async_accept(asio::use_awaitable);
    auto session = [s = std::move(socket)]() mutable {
      auto awaitable = serve_client(std::move(s));
      return awaitable;
    };
```

```
        asio::co_spawn(ex, std::move(session), asio::detached);
    }
}
```

The executor is the object responsible for actually executing our asynchronous functions. An executor may represent a thread pool or a single system thread, for example. We will most likely see some form of executors in upcoming versions of C++ to give us programmers more control and flexibility over when and where our code executes (including GPUs).

Next, the coroutine runs an infinite loop and waits for TCP clients to connect. The first co_await expression returns a socket when a new client successfully connects to our server. The socket object is then moved to the coroutine serve_client(), which will serve the newly connected client until the client disconnects.

The main application logic of the server happens in the coroutine that handles each client. Here is how it looks:

```
auto serve_client(tcp::socket socket) -> asio::awaitable<void> {
  std::cout << "New client connected\n";
  auto ex = co_await asio::this_coro::executor;
  auto timer = asio::system_timer{ex};
  auto counter = 0;
  while (true) {
    try {
      auto s = std::to_string(counter) + "\n";
      auto buf = asio::buffer(s.data(), s.size());
      auto n = co_await async_write(socket, buf, asio::use_awaitable);
      std::cout << "Wrote " << n << " byte(s)\n";
      ++counter;
      timer.expires_from_now(100ms);
      co_await timer.async_wait(asio::use_awaitable);
    } catch (...) {
      // Error or client disconnected
      break;
    }
  }
}
```

Each coroutine invocation serves one unique client during the entire client session; it runs until the client disconnects from the server. The coroutine updates a counter at regular intervals (every 100 ms) and writes the value asynchronously back to the client using `async_write()`. Note how we can write the function `serve_client()` in a linear fashion although it invokes two asynchronous operations: `async_write()` and `async_wait()`.

Running and connecting to the server

Once we have started this server, we can connect clients on port 37259. To try this out, I'm using a tool called nc (netcat), which can be used for communicating over TCP and UDP. Here is an example of a short session where a client connects to the server running on localhost:

```
[client] $ nc localhost 37259
0
1
2
3
```

We can start multiple clients and they will all be served by a dedicated `serve_client()` coroutine invocation and have their own copy of the incrementing counter variable, as shown in the screenshot below:

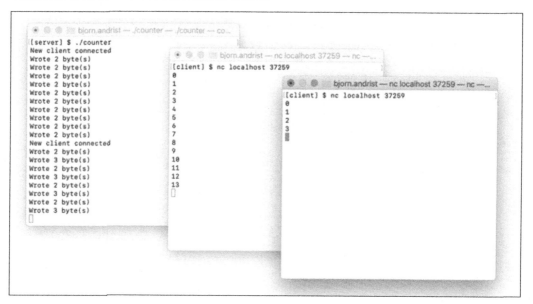

Figure 13.2: A running server with two connected clients

Another way to create an application serving multiple sessions concurrently would be to create one thread for each new client that connects. However, the memory overhead of threads would set the limit of the number of sessions substantially lower compared to this model using coroutines.

The coroutines in this example are all executed on the same thread, which makes the locking of shared resources unnecessary. Imagine we had a global counter that each session updated. If we used multiple threads, the access to the global counter would need some kind of synchronization (using a mutex or an atomic data type). This is not necessary for coroutines that execute on the same thread. In other words, coroutines that execute on the same thread can share state without using any locking primitives.

What we have achieved with the server (and what we haven't)

The example application using Boost.Asio demonstrates that coroutines can be used for asynchronous programming. Instead of implementing continuations with nested callbacks, we can write code in a linear fashion using co_await statements. However, this example is minimal and avoids some really important aspects of asynchronous programming, such as:

- Asynchronous read and write operations. The server only writes data to its clients and ignores the challenge of synchronizing read and write operations.

- Canceling asynchronous tasks and graceful shutdown. The server runs in an infinite loop, completely ignoring the challenge of a clean shutdown.

- Error handling and exception safety when using multiple co_await statements.

These topics are immensely important but are out of scope for this book. I already mentioned that detached operations are best avoided. Creating detached tasks using boost::asio::co_spawn(), as shown in the example, should be done with utmost caution. A fairly new programming paradigm for avoiding detached work is called **structured concurrency**. It aims to solve exception safety and the cancellation of multiple asynchronous tasks by encapsulating concurrency into general and reusable algorithms such as when_all() and stop_when(). The key idea is to never allow some child task to exceed the lifetime of its parent. This makes it possible to pass local variables by reference to asynchronous child operations safely and with better performance. Strictly nested lifetimes of concurrent tasks also make the code easier to reason about.

Another important aspect is that asynchronous tasks should always be lazy (immediately suspended), so that continuations can be attached before any exceptions can be thrown. This is also a requirement if you want to be able to cancel a task in a safe manner.

There will most likely be a lot of talks, libraries, and articles related to this important subject in the years to come. Two talks from CppCon 2019 addressed this topic:

- *A Unifying Abstraction for Async in C++*, Eric Neibler and D. S. Hollman, `https://sched.co/SfrC`
- *Structured Concurrency: Writing Safer Concurrent Code with Coroutines and Algorithms*, Lewis Baker, `https://sched.co/SfsU`

Summary

In this chapter, you've seen how to use C++ coroutines for writing asynchronous tasks. To be able to implement the infrastructure in the form of a `Task` type and a `sync_wait()` function, you needed to fully understand the concept of awaitable types and how they can be used to customize the behavior of coroutines in C++.

By using Boost.Asio, we could build a truly minimal but fully functional concurrent server application executing on a single thread while handling multiple client sessions.

Lastly, I briefly introduced a methodology called structured concurrency and gave some directions for where you can find more information about this topic.

In the next chapter, we will move on to explore parallel algorithms, which are a way to speed up concurrent programs by utilizing multiple cores.

14

Parallel Algorithms

The previous chapters have focused on how to introduce concurrency and asynchrony in our programs by using threads and coroutines. This chapter focuses on parallel execution of independent tasks, which is related to but distinct from concurrency.

In earlier chapters, I stressed that I prefer standard library algorithms over handcrafted for-loops. In this chapter, you will see some great advantages of using standard library algorithms with the execution policies introduced with C++17.

This chapter is not going to go in depth into theories of parallelizing algorithms or parallel programming in general, as these subjects are far too complex to cover in a single chapter. Also, there are a multitude of books on this subject. Instead, this chapter is going to take a more practical approach and demonstrate how to extend a current C++ code base to utilize parallelism while preserving the readability of the code base. In other words, we do not want the parallelism to get in the way of readability; rather, we want the parallelism to be abstracted away so that parallelizing the code is only a matter of changing a parameter to an algorithm.

In this chapter, you will learn:

- Various techniques for implementing parallel algorithms
- How to evaluate the performance of parallel algorithms
- How to adapt a code base to use the parallel extensions of the standard library algorithms

Parallel programming is a complicated topic, so before starting, you need to understand the motivation for introducing parallelism in the first place.

The importance of parallelism

From a programmer's perspective, it would be very convenient if the computer hardware of today was a 100 GHz single core CPU rather than a 3 GHz multi-core CPU; we wouldn't need to care about parallelism. Unfortunately, making single-core CPUs faster and faster has hit a physical limit. So, as the evolution of computer hardware is going in the direction of multi-core CPUs and programmable GPUs, programmers have to use efficient parallel patterns in order to make the most of the hardware.

Parallel algorithms allow us to optimize our programs by executing multiple individual tasks or subtasks at the exact same time on a multi-core CPU or GPU.

Parallel algorithms

As mentioned in *Chapter 11, Concurrency*, the terms *concurrency* and *parallelism* can be a little hard to distinguish from each other. As a reminder, a program is said to run concurrently if it has multiple individual control flows running during overlapping time periods. On the other hand, a parallel program executes multiple tasks or subtasks simultaneously (at the exact same time), which requires hardware with multiple cores. We use parallel algorithms to optimize latency or throughput. It makes no sense to parallelize algorithms if we don't have hardware that can execute multiple tasks simultaneously to achieve better performance. A few simple formulas will now follow to help you understand what factors need to be considered when evaluating parallel algorithms.

Evaluating parallel algorithms

In this chapter, **speedup** is defined as the ratio between a sequential and a parallel version of an algorithm, as follows:

$$Speedup = \frac{T_1}{T_n}$$

T_1 is the time it takes to solve a problem using a sequential algorithm executing at one core, and T_n is the time it takes to solve the same problem using n cores. *Time* refers to wall-clock time (not CPU time).

A parallel algorithm is usually more complicated and requires more computational resources (CPU time, for example) compared to its sequential equivalent. The benefits of the parallel version come from the ability to spread the algorithm onto several processing units.

With that in mind, it's also notable that not all algorithms gain the same performance boost when run in parallel. The **efficiency** of a parallel algorithm can be computed by the following formula:

$$Efficiency = \frac{T_1}{T_n * n}$$

In this formula, *n* is the number of cores executing the algorithm. Since T_1/T_n denote the speedup, the efficiency can also be expressed as *Speedup/n*.

If the efficiency is *1.0*, the algorithm parallelizes perfectly. For example, it means that we achieve an 8x speedup when executing a parallel algorithm on a computer with eight cores. In practice, though, there are a multitude of parameters that limit parallel execution, such as creating threads, memory bandwidth, and context switches, as mentioned in *Chapter 11, Concurrency*. So, typically, the efficiency is well below 1.0.

The efficiency of a parallel algorithm depends on how independently each chunk of work can be processed. For example, `std::transform()` is trivial to parallelize in the sense that each element is processed completely independently of every other. This will be demonstrated later in this chapter.

The efficiency also depends on the problem size and the number of cores. For example, a parallel algorithm may perform very poorly on small data sets due to the overhead incurred by the added complexity of a parallel algorithm. Likewise, executing a program on a great many cores might hit other bottlenecks in the computer such as memory bandwidth. We say that a parallel algorithm scales if the efficiency stays constant when we change the number of cores and/or the size of the input.

It's also important to keep in mind that not all parts of a program can be parallelized. This fact limits the theoretical maximum speedup of a program even if we had an unlimited number of cores. We can compute the maximum possible speedup by using **Amdahl's law**, which was introduced in *Chapter 3, Analyzing and Measuring Performance*.

Amdahl's law revisited

Here, we will apply Amdahl's law to parallel programs. It works like this: the total running time of a program can be split into two distinct parts or *fractions*:

- F_{seq} is the fraction of the program that can only be executed *sequentially*
- F_{par} is the fraction of the program that can be executed in *parallel*

Since these two fractions together make up the entire program, it means that $F_{seq} = 1 - F_{par}$. Now, Amdahl's law tells us that the **maximum speedup** of a program executing on n cores is:

$$Maximum\ speedup = \frac{1}{\dfrac{F_{par}}{n} + F_{seq}} = \frac{1}{\dfrac{F_{par}}{n} + (1 - F_{par})}$$

To visualize the effect of this law, the following image shows the execution time of a program with the sequential fraction at the bottom and the parallel fraction on the top. Increasing the number of cores only affects the parallel fraction, which sets a limit on the maximum speedup:

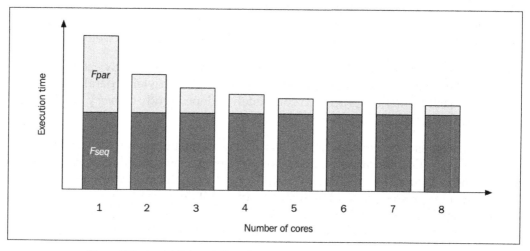

Figure 14.1: Amdahl's law defines the maximum speedup; in this case it is 2x

In the figure above, the sequential part accounts for 50% of the execution time when running on a single CPU. Therefore, the maximum speedup we can achieve by adding more cores when executing such a program is 2x.

To give you some idea of how parallel algorithms can be implemented, we will now go through a few examples. We will begin with std::transform() because it is relatively easy to split into multiple independent parts.

Implementing parallel std::transform()

Although algorithmically std::transform() is easy to implement, in practice, implementing even a rudimentary parallel version is more complex than it might appear at first sight.

The algorithm `std::transform()` calls a function for each element in a sequence, and stores the result in another sequence. A possible implementation of a sequential version of `std::transform()` may look something like this:

```
template<class SrcIt, class DstIt, class Func>
auto transform(SrcIt first, SrcIt last, DstIt dst, Func func) {
  while (first != last) {
      *dst++ = func(*first++);
  }
}
```

The standard library version also returns the `dst` iterator, but we will ignore that in our examples. To understand the challenges with a parallel version of `std::transform()`, let's begin with a naive approach.

Naive implementation

A naive parallel implementation of `std::transform()` would probably look something like this:

- Divide the elements into chunks corresponding to the number of cores in the computer
- Process each chunk in a separate task
- Wait for all tasks to finish

Using `std::thread::hardware_concurrency()` to determine the number of supported hardware threads, a possible implementation could look like this:

```
template <typename SrcIt, typename DstIt, typename Func>
auto par_transform_naive(SrcIt first, SrcIt last, DstIt dst, Func f) {
  auto n = static_cast<size_t>(std::distance(first, last));
  auto n_cores = size_t{std::thread::hardware_concurrency()};
  auto n_tasks = std::max(n_cores, size_t{1});
  auto chunk_sz = (n + n_tasks - 1) / n_tasks;
  auto futures = std::vector<std::future<void>>{};
  // Process each chunk on a separate
  for (auto i = 0ul; i < n_tasks; ++i) {
    auto start = chunk_sz * i;
    if (start < n) {
      auto stop = std::min(chunk_sz * (i + 1), n);
      auto fut = std::async(std::launch::async,
        [first, dst, start, stop, f]() {
            std::transform(first + start, first + stop, dst + start, f);
```

```
      });
        futures.emplace_back(std::move(fut));
    }
  }
  // Wait for each task to finish
  for (auto&& fut : futures) {
    fut.wait();
  }
}
```

Note that `hardware_concurrency()` might return 0 if it, for some reason, is undetermined, and therefore is clamped to be at least one.

A subtle difference between `std::transform()` and our parallel version is that they put different requirements on the iterators. `std::transform()` can operate on input and output iterators such as `std::istream_iterator<>` bound to `std::cin`. This is not possible with `par_transform_naive()` since the iterators are copied and used from multiple tasks. As you will see, there are no parallel algorithms presented in this chapter that can operate on input and output iterators. Instead, the parallel algorithms at least require forward iterators that allow multi-pass traversal.

Performance evaluation

Continuing the naive implementation, let's measure its performance with a simple performance evaluation compared to the sequential version of `std::transform()` executing at a single CPU core.

In this test we will measure the time (clock on the wall) and the total time spent on the CPUs when varying the input size of the data.

We will set up this benchmark using Google Benchmark, which was introduced in *Chapter 3, Analyzing and Measuring Performance*. To avoid duplicating code, we'll implement a function that will set up a test fixture for our benchmark. The fixture needs a source range with some example values, a destination range for the result, and a transform function:

```
auto setup_fixture(int n) {
  auto src = std::vector<float>(n);
  std::iota(src.begin(), src.end(), 1.0f); // Values from 1.0 to n
  auto dst = std::vector<float>(src.size());
  auto transform_function = [](float v) {
    auto sum = v;
    for (auto i = 0; i < 500; ++i) {
      sum += (i * i * i * sum);
```

```
      }
      return sum;
   };
   return std::tuple{src, dst, transform_function};
}
```

Now we have our fixture set up, it's time to implement the actual benchmark. There will be two versions: one for the sequential `std::transform()` and one for our parallel version, `par_transform_naive()`:

```
void bm_sequential(benchmark::State& state) {
  auto [src, dst, f] = setup_fixture(state.range(0));
  for (auto _ : state) {
    std::transform(src.begin(), src.end(), dst.begin(), f);
  }
}
```

```
void bm_parallel(benchmark::State& state) {
  auto [src, dst, f] = setup_fixture(state.range(0));
  for (auto _ : state) {
    par_transform_naive(src.begin(), src.end(), dst.begin(), f);
  }
}
```

Only the code within the `for`-loops will be measured. By using `state.range(0)` for input size, we can generate different values by appending a range of values to each benchmark. In fact, we need to specify a couple of arguments for each benchmark, so we create a helper function that applies all the settings we need:

```
void CustomArguments(benchmark::internal::Benchmark* b) {
  b->Arg(50)->Arg(10'000)->Arg(1'000'000)   // Input size
    ->MeasureProcessCPUTime()                // Measure all threads
    ->UseRealTime()                          // Clock on the wall
    ->Unit(benchmark::kMillisecond);         // Use ms
}
```

A few things to note about the custom arguments:

- We pass the values 50, 10,000, and 1,000,000 as arguments to the benchmark. They are used as the input size when creating the vectors in the `setup_fixture()` function. These values are accessed using `state.range(0)` in the test functions.

- By default, Google Benchmark only measures CPU time on the main thread. But since we are interested in the total amount of CPU time on all threads, we use `MeasureProcessCPUTime()`.

- Google Benchmark decides how many times each test needs to be repeated until a statistically stable result has been achieved. We want the library to use the clock-on-the-wall time for this rather than CPU time, and therefore we apply the setting `UseRealTime()`.

That's almost it. Finally, register the benchmarks and call main:

```
BENCHMARK(bm_sequential)->Apply(CustomArguments);
BENCHMARK(bm_parallel)->Apply(CustomArguments);
BENCHMARK_MAIN();
```

After compiling this code with optimizations turned on (using gcc with -O3), I executed this benchmark on a laptop using eight cores. The following table shows the results when using 50 elements:

Algorithm	CPU	Time	Speedup
`std::transform()`	0.02 ms	0.02 ms	0.25x
`par_transform_naive()`	0.17 ms	0.08 ms	

CPU is the total time spent on the CPU. *Time* is the wall-clock time, which is what we are most interested in. *Speedup* is the relative speedup when comparing the elapsed time of the sequential version with the parallel version (0.02/0.08 in this case).

Clearly, the sequential version outperforms the parallel algorithm for this small data set with only 50 elements. With 10,000 elements we really start to see the benefits of parallelization though:

Algorithm	CPU	Time	Speedup
`std::transform()`	0.89 ms	0.89 ms	4.5x
`par_transform_naive()`	1.95 ms	0.20 ms	

Finally, using 1,000,000 elements gives us even higher efficiency, as can be seen in the following table:

Algorithm	CPU	Time	Speedup
`std::transform()`	9071 ms	9092 ms	7.3x
`par_transform_naive()`	9782 ms	1245 ms	

The efficiency of the parallel algorithm in this last run is really high. It was executed on eight cores, so the efficiency is 7.3x/8 = 0.925. The results presented here (both the absolute execution time and the relative speedup) should not be relied upon too much. Among other things, the results depend on the computer architecture, the OS scheduler, and how much other work is currently running on the machine when performing the test. Nevertheless, the benchmarking results confirm a few important points discussed earlier:

- For small data sets, the sequential version `std::transform()` is much faster than the parallel version because of the overhead incurred by creating threads etc.

- The parallel version always uses more computational resources (CPU time) compared to `std::transform()`.

- For large data sets, the parallel version outperforms the sequential version when measuring wall-clock time. The speedup is over 7x when running on a machine with eight cores.

One reason for the high efficiency of our algorithm (at least on large data sets) is that the computational cost is evenly distributed, and each subtask is highly independent. This is not always the case, though.

Shortcomings of the naive implementation

The naive implementation might do a good job if each chunk of work has the same computational cost and the algorithm executes in an environment where no other application utilizes the hardware. However, this is rarely the case; rather, we want a good general-purpose parallel implementation that is both efficient and scalable.

The following illustrations show the problems we want to avoid. If the computational cost is not equivalent for each chunk, the implementation is limited to the chunk that takes the most time:

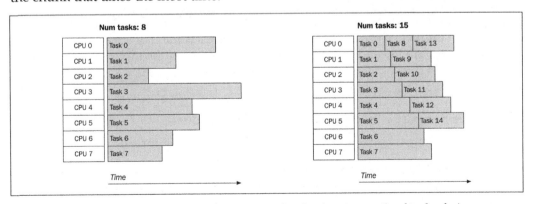

Figure 14.2: Possible scenarios where computation time is not proportional to chunk size

If the application and/or the operating system has other processes to handle, the operation will not process all chunks in parallel:

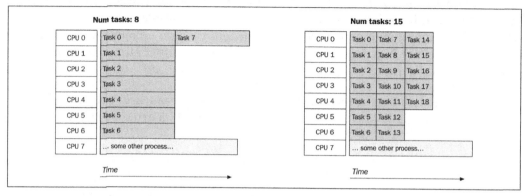

Figure 14.3: Possible scenarios where computation time is proportional to chunk size

As you can see in *Figure 14.3*, splitting the operation into smaller chunks makes the parallelization adjust to the current condition, avoiding single tasks that stall the whole operation.

Also note that the naive implementation was unsuccessful for small data sets. There are many ways to adjust the naive implementation to perform better. For instance, we could create more tasks and smaller tasks by multiplying the number of cores by some factor greater than 1. Or, to avoid significant overhead on small data sets, we could let the chunk size decide the number of tasks to create etc.

You now have the knowledge of how to implement and evaluate a simple parallel algorithm. We will not do any fine-tuning of the naive implementation; instead, I will show a different useful technique to use when implementing parallel algorithms.

Divide and conquer

An algorithm technique for dividing a problem into smaller subproblems is called **divide and conquer**. We will here implement another version of a parallel transform algorithm using divide and conquer. It works as follows: if the input range is smaller than a specified threshold, the range is processed; otherwise, the range is split into two parts:

- The first part is processed on a newly branched task
- The other part is recursively processed at the calling thread

The following illustration shows how the divide and conquer algorithm would recursively transform a range using the following data and parameters:

- Range size: 16
- Source range contains floats from 1.0 to 16.0
- Chunk size: 4
- Transformation function: [](auto x) { return x*x; }

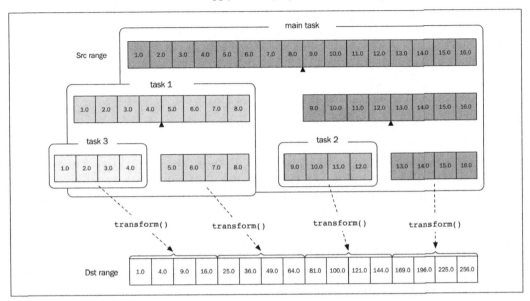

Figure 14.4: A range is divided recursively for parallel processing. The source array contains float values from 1.0 to 8.0. The destination array contains the transformed values.

In *Figure 14.4*, you can see that the main task spawns two asynchronous tasks (**task 1** and **task 2**) and finally transforms the last chunk in the range. **Task 1** spawns **task 3** and then transforms the remaining elements containing values 5.0, 6.0, 7.0, and 8.0. Let's head over to the implementation.

Implementation

Implementation-wise, it's quite a small bit of code. The incoming range is recursively split into two chunks; the first chunk is invoked as a new task, and the second chunk is recursively processed on the same task:

```
template <typename SrcIt, typename DstIt, typename Func>
auto par_transform(SrcIt first, SrcIt last, DstIt dst,
                   Func func, size_t chunk_sz) {
  const auto n = static_cast<size_t>(std::distance(first, last));
  if (n <= chunk_sz) {
    std::transform(first, last, dst, func);
    return;
```

```
  }
  const auto src_middle = std::next(first, n / 2);

  // Branch of first part to another task
  auto future = std::async(std::launch::async, [=, &func] {
    par_transform(first, src_middle, dst, func, chunk_sz);
  });

  // Recursively handle the second part
  const auto dst_middle = std::next(dst, n / 2);
  par_transform(src_middle, last, dst_middle, func, chunk_sz);
  future.wait();
}
```

Combining recursion with multithreading like this can take a while to get your head around. In the following examples, you will see that this pattern can be used when implementing more complicated algorithms as well. But first, let's see how it performs.

Performance evaluation

To evaluate our new version, we will modify the benchmark fixture by updating the transform function with a version that takes more time depending on the input value. The range of input values will be increased by filling the range using std::iota(). Doing this means the algorithms need to process jobs of different sizes. Here is the new setup_fixture() function:

```
auto setup_fixture(int n) {
  auto src = std::vector<float>(n);
  std::iota(src.begin(), src.end(), 1.0f);  // From 1.0 to n
  auto dst = std::vector<float>(src.size());
  auto transform_function = [](float v) {
    auto sum = v;
    auto n = v / 20'000;                    // The larger v is,
    for (auto i = 0; i < n; ++i) {          // the more to compute
      sum += (i * i * i * sum);
    }
    return sum;
  };
  return std::tuple{src, dst, transform_function};
}
```

We can now try to find an optimal chunk size to be used by the divide-and-conquer algorithm by using an increasing parameter for the chunk size. It would also be interesting to see how our divide-and-conquer algorithm performs compared to the naive version on this new fixture, which needs to process jobs of different sizes. Here is the full code:

```cpp
// Divide and conquer version
void bm_parallel(benchmark::State& state) {
  auto [src, dst, f] = setup_fixture(10'000'000);
  auto n = state.range(0);          // Chunk size is parameterized
  for (auto _ : state) {
    par_transform(src.begin(), src.end(), dst.begin(), f, n);
  }
}


// Naive version
void bm_parallel_naive(benchmark::State& state) {
  auto [src, dst, f] = setup_fixture(10'000'000);
  for (auto _ : state) {
    par_transform_naive(src.begin(), src.end(), dst.begin(), f);
  }
}

void CustomArguments(benchmark::internal::Benchmark* b) {
  b->MeasureProcessCPUTime()
    ->UseRealTime()
    ->Unit(benchmark::kMillisecond);
}

BENCHMARK(bm_parallel)->Apply(CustomArguments)
  ->RangeMultiplier(10)             // Chunk size goes from
  ->Range(1000, 10'000'000);        // 1k to 10M
BENCHMARK(bm_parallel_naive)->Apply(CustomArguments);
BENCHMARK_MAIN();
```

The following diagram reveals the results I achieved when running the tests on macOS using an Intel Core i7 CPU with eight cores:

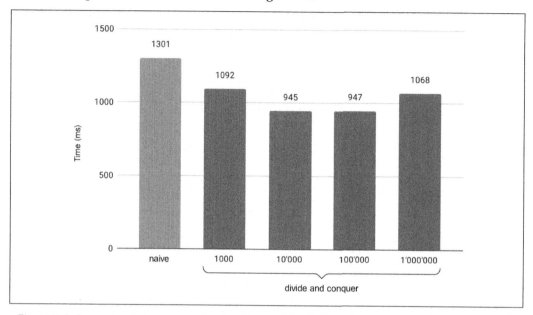

Figure 14.5: Comparison between our naive algorithm and the divide-and-conquer algorithm using different chunk sizes

The best efficiency was achieved when using chunk sizes of around 10,000 elements, which creates 1,000 tasks. With larger chunks, the performance is bottlenecked in the time it takes to process the final chunks, whereas too small chunks result in too much overhead in creating and invoking tasks compared to the computation.

A takeaway from this example is that the performance penalty of scheduling 1,000 smaller tasks rather than a few big ones isn't a problem here. It would be possible to restrict the number of threads using a thread pool, but `std::async()` seems to work fairly well in this scenario. A generic implementation would opt for using a fairly large number of tasks rather than trying to match the exact number of cores.

Finding optimal values for chunk size and the number of tasks is a real problem when implementing parallel algorithms. As you can see, it depends on many variables and also whether you optimize for latency or throughput. The best way to gain insights is to measure in the environment that your algorithms are supposed to run.

Now that you have learned how to implement a parallel transform algorithm using divide and conquer, let's see how the same technique can be applied to other problems.

Implementing parallel std::count_if()

A nice thing with divide and conquer is that it can be applied to many problems. We can easily use the same technique to implement a parallel version of std::count_if(), with the difference being that we need to accumulate the returned value, like this:

```cpp
template <typename It, typename Pred>
auto par_count_if(It first, It last, Pred pred, size_t chunk_sz) {
  auto n = static_cast<size_t>(std::distance(first, last));
  if (n <= chunk_sz)
    return std::count_if(first, last, pred);
  auto middle = std::next(first, n/2);
  auto fut = std::async(std::launch::async, [=, &pred] {
    return par_count_if(first, middle, pred, chunk_sz);
  });
  auto num = par_count_if(middle, last, pred, chunk_sz);
  return num + fut.get();
}
```

As you can see, the only difference here is that we need to sum the result at the end of the function. If you want to have the chunk size depend on the number of cores, you can easily wrap the par_count_if() in an outer function:

```cpp
template <typename It, typename Pred>
auto par_count_if(It first, It last, Pred pred) {
  auto n = static_cast<size_t>(std::distance(first, last));
  auto n_cores = size_t{std::thread::hardware_concurrency()};
  auto chunk_sz = std::max(n / n_cores * 32, size_t{1000});

  return par_count_if(first, last, pred, chunk_sz);
}
```

The magic number 32 here is a somewhat arbitrary factor that will give us more chunks and smaller chunks if we are given a large input range. As usual, we would need to measure the performance to come up with a good constant here. Let's now move on and try to tackle a more complicated parallel algorithm.

Implementing parallel std::copy_if()

We've had a look at `std::transform()` and `std::count_if()`, which are quite easy to implement both sequentially and in parallel. If we take another algorithm that is easily implemented sequentially, `std::copy_if()`, things get a lot harder to perform in parallel.

Sequentially, implementing `std::copy_if()` is as easy as this:

```
template <typename SrcIt, typename DstIt, typename Pred>
auto copy_if(SrcIt first, SrcIt last, DstIt dst, Pred pred) {
  for (auto it = first; it != last; ++it) {
    if (pred(*it)) {
      *dst = *it;
      ++dst;
    }
  }
  return dst;
}
```

To demonstrate how it can be used, consider the following example where we have a range that contains a sequence of integers and we want to copy only the odd integers into another range:

```
const auto src = {1, 2, 3, 4};
auto dst = std::vector<int>(src.size(), -1);
auto new_end = std::copy_if(src.begin(), src.end(), dst.begin(),
                            [](int v) { return (v % 2) == 1; });
// dst is {1, 3, -1, -1}
dst.erase(new_end, dst.end()); // dst is now {1, 3}
```

Now, if we want to make a parallel version of `copy_if()`, we immediately run into problems as we cannot write to the destination iterator concurrently. Here is a failed attempt with undefined behavior, since both tasks will write to the same position in the destination range:

```
// Warning: Undefined behavior
template <typename SrcIt, typename DstIt, typename Func>
auto par_copy_if(SrcIt first, SrcIt last, DstIt dst, Func func) {
  auto n = std::distance(first, last);
  auto middle = std::next(first, n / 2);
  auto fut0 = std::async([=]() {
    return std::copy_if(first, middle, dst, func); });
  auto fut1 = std::async([=]() {
```

```
        return std::copy_if(middle, last, dst, func); });
  auto dst0 = fut0.get();
  auto dst1 = fut1.get();
  return *std::max(dst0, dst1); // Just to return something...
}
```

We now have two simple approaches: either we synchronize the index we write to (by using an atomic/lock-free variable), or we split the algorithm into two parts. We will explore both approaches next.

Approach 1: Use a synchronized write position

The first approach we might consider is to synchronize the write position by using an atomic `size_t` and the `fetch_add()` member function, as you learned about in *Chapter 11, Concurrency*. Whenever a thread tries to write a new element, it fetches the current index and adds one atomically; thus, each value is written to a unique index.

In our code, we will split the algorithm into two functions: an inner function and an outer function. The atomic write index will be defined in the outer function, whereas the main part of the algorithm will be implemented in the inner function.

Inner function

The inner function requires an atomic `size_t` that synchronizes the write positions. As the algorithm is recursive, it cannot store the atomic `size_t` itself; it requires an outer function to invoke the algorithm:

```
template <typename SrcIt, typename DstIt, typename Pred>
void inner_par_copy_if_sync(SrcIt first, SrcIt last, DstIt dst,
                            std::atomic_size_t& dst_idx,
                            Pred pred, size_t chunk_sz) {
  const auto n = static_cast<size_t>(std::distance(first, last));
  if (n <= chunk_sz) {
    std::for_each(first, last, [&](const auto& v) {
      if (pred(v)) {
        auto write_idx = dst_idx.fetch_add(1);
        *std::next(dst, write_idx) = v;
      }
    });
    return;
  }
  auto middle = std::next(first, n / 2);
```

```
  auto future = std::async([first, middle, dst, chunk_sz, &pred, &dst_idx] {
    inner_par_copy_if_sync(first, middle, dst, dst_idx, pred, chunk_sz);
  });
  inner_par_copy_if_sync(middle, last, dst, dst_idx, pred, chunk_sz);
  future.wait();
}
```

This is still a divide-and-conquer algorithm and hopefully you will start to see the pattern we are using. The atomic update of the write index `dst_idx` ensures that multiple threads never write to the same index in the destination sequence.

Outer function

The outer function, called from the client code, is simply a placeholder for the atomic `size_t`, which is initialized to zero. The function then initializes the inner function, which parallelizes the code further:

```
template <typename SrcIt, typename DstIt, typename Pred>
auto par_copy_if_sync(SrcIt first,SrcIt last,DstIt dst,
                      Pred p, size_t chunk_sz) {
  auto dst_write_idx = std::atomic_size_t{0};
  inner_par_copy_if_sync(first, last, dst, dst_write_idx, p, chunk_sz);
  return std::next(dst, dst_write_idx);
}
```

Once the inner function returns, we can use `dst_write_idx` to compute the end iterator of the destination range. Let's now have a look at the other approach to solve the same problem.

Approach 2: Split the algorithm into two parts

The second approach is to split the algorithm into two parts. First, the conditional copying is performed in parallel chunks, and then the resulting sparse range is squeezed to a continuous range.

Part one – Copy elements in parallel into the destination range

The first part copies the elements in chunks, resulting in the sparse destination array illustrated in *Figure 14.6*. Each chunk is conditionally copied in parallel, and the resulting range iterators are stored in std::future objects for later retrieval:

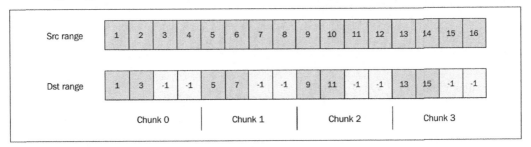

Figure 14.6: The sparse destination range after the first step of the conditional copying

The following code implements the first half of the algorithm:

```
template <typename SrcIt, typename DstIt, typename Pred>
auto par_copy_if_split(SrcIt first, SrcIt last, DstIt dst,
                       Pred pred, size_t chunk_sz) -> DstIt {
  auto n = static_cast<size_t>(std::distance(first, last));
  auto futures = std::vector<std::future<std::pair<DstIt, DstIt>>>{};
  futures.reserve(n / chunk_sz);

  for (auto i = size_t{0}; i < n; i += chunk_sz) {
    const auto stop_idx = std::min(i + chunk_sz, n);
    auto future = std::async([=, &pred] {
      auto dst_first = dst + i;
      auto dst_last = std::copy_if(first+i, first+stop_idx,
                                   dst_first, pred);
      return std::make_pair(dst_first, dst_last);
    });
    futures.emplace_back(std::move(future));
  }
  // To be continued ...
```

We have now copied the elements (that should be copied) into the sparse destination range. It's time to fill the gaps by moving the elements to the left in the range.

Part two – Move the sparse range sequentially into a continuous range

When the sparse range is created, it is merged using the resulting value from each `std::future`. The merge is performed sequentially as the parts overlap:

```
// ...continued from above...
// Part #2: Perform merge of resulting sparse range sequentially
auto new_end = futures.front().get().second;
for (auto it = std::next(futures.begin()); it != futures.end(); ++it)
{
  auto chunk_rng = it->get();
  new_end = std::move(chunk_rng.first, chunk_rng.second, new_end);
}
return new_end;
} // end of par_copy_if_split
```

This second part of the algorithm that moves all the subranges to the beginning of the range is illustrated in the following image:

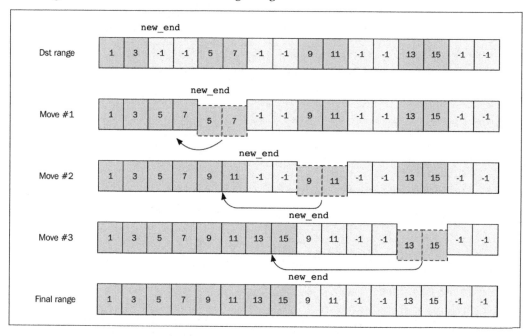

Figure 14.7: Merging a sparse range into a continuous range

With two algorithms solving the same problem, it's time to see how they measure up.

Performance evaluation

The performance boost from using this parallelized version of copy_if() is heavily dependent on how expensive the predicate is. Therefore, we use two different predicates in our benchmark with different computational costs. Here is the *inexpensive* predicate:

```
auto is_odd = [](unsigned v) {
  return (v % 2) == 1;
};
```

The more *expensive* predicate checks whether its argument is a prime number:

```
auto is_prime = [](unsigned v) {
  if (v < 2) return false;
  if (v == 2) return true;
  if (v % 2 == 0) return false;
  for (auto i = 3u; (i * i) <= v; i+=2) {
    if ((v % i) == 0) {
      return false;
    }
  }
  return true;
};
```

Note, this is not a particularly optimal way to implement is_prime(), and is only used here for the purposes of the benchmark.

The benchmarking code is not spelled out here but is included in the accompanying source code. Three algorithms are compared: std::copy_if(), par_copy_if_split(), and par_copy_if_sync(). The following graph shows the results as measured using an Intel Core i7 CPU. The parallel algorithms use a chunk size of 100,000 in this benchmark.

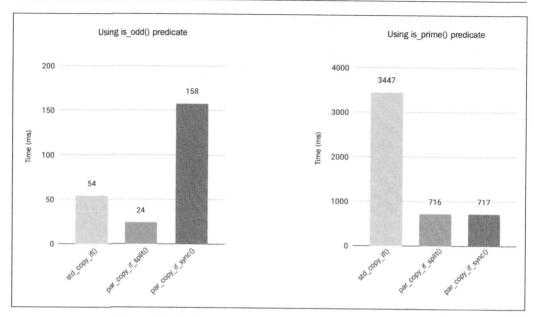

Figure 14.8: Conditional copy strategies versus computation time

The most obvious observation when measuring the performance is how ridiculously slow the synchronized version `par_copy_if_sync()` is when using the inexpensive `is_odd()` predicate. The disastrous performance is actually not due to the atomic write index; rather, it is because the cache mechanism of the hardware is trashed due to several threads writing to the same cache line (as you learned about in *Chapter 7, Memory Management*).

So, with this knowledge, we understand now why `par_copy_if_split()` performs better. On the inexpensive predicate, `is_odd()`, `par_copy_if_split()` is about 2x faster than `std::copy_if()`, but with the expensive `is_prime()`, the efficiency increases to almost 5x. The increased efficiency is a result of spending most of the computations in the first part of the algorithm, which executes in parallel.

You should now have a grasp of some techniques that can be used for parallelizing an algorithm. These new insights will help you understand the requirements and expectations when using parallel algorithms from the standard library.

Parallel standard library algorithms

As of C++17, the standard library has been extended with parallel versions of most, but not all, algorithms. Changing your algorithms to allow for parallel execution is simply a matter of adding a parameter that tells the algorithm which parallel execution policy to use.

As stressed earlier in this book, if your code base is based upon standard library algorithms, or at least if you have the habit of writing C++ by using algorithms, you will get an instant performance boost almost for free by adding an execution policy where suitable:

```
auto v = std::vector<std::string>{
  "woody", "steely", "loopy", "upside_down"
};
// Parallel sort
std::sort(std::execution::par, v.begin(), v.end());
```

Once you specify an execution policy, you are in the realm of parallel algorithms, which have some notable differences compared to their original sequential versions. Firstly, the minimum iterator category requirements change from input iterators to forward iterators. Secondly, exceptions thrown by your code (from copy constructors or function objects passed to the algorithm) never reach you. Instead, the algorithm is required to call `std::terminate()`. Thirdly, the complexity guarantees (both time and memory) of the algorithm might be relaxed because of the added complexity of parallel implementations.

When using a parallel version of the standard library algorithms, you specify an execution policy that states how an algorithm is allowed to parallelize the execution. An implementation may decide to execute the algorithm sequentially, though. If you compare the efficiency and scalability of parallel algorithms in different standard library implementations, you can expect to see big differences.

Execution policies

An **execution policy** informs an algorithm if and how the execution can be parallelized. There are four default execution policies included in the parallel extensions of the standard library. Compilers and third-party libraries can extend these policies for certain hardware and conditions. For example, it's already possible to use the parallel power of the modern graphics card from standard library algorithms using vendor-specific policies.

The execution policies are defined in the header `<execution>` and reside in the namespace `std::execution`. There are currently four distinct tag types, one for each execution policy. The types cannot be instantiated by you; instead, there is one predefined object per type. For instance, the parallel execution policy has a type called `std::execution::parallel_policy` and the predefined instance of this type is named `std::execution::par`. The reason there is one *type* per policy (rather than one type with multiple predefined instances) is so that the policies you provide can be distinguished at compile time by the library.

Sequenced policy

The sequenced execution policy, std::execution::seq, makes the algorithm execute sequentially with no parallelism, similar to how the algorithms without the extra execution policy argument would run. However, whenever you specify an execution policy, it means that you are using a version of the algorithm with relaxed complexity guarantees and stricter iterator requirements; it also assumes that the code you provide doesn't throw exceptions, or the algorithm will call std::terminate().

Parallel policy

The parallel execution policy, std::execution::par, can be considered the standard execution policy for parallel algorithms. The code you provide to the algorithm needs to be thread safe. A way to understand this requirement is to think about the loop body in the sequential version of the algorithm you are about to use. For example, think about the sequential version of copy_if(), which we spelled out like this earlier in the chapter:

```
template <typename SrcIt, typename DstIt, typename Pred>
auto copy_if(SrcIt first, SrcIt last, DstIt dst, Pred pred) {
  for (auto it = first; it != last; ++it)
  {                                 // Start of loop body
    if (pred(*it)) {                // Call predicate
      *dst = *it;                   // Copy construct
      ++dst;
    }
  }                                 // End of loop body
  return dst;
}
```

In this algorithm, the code inside the loop body will call the predicate you provided and invoke the copy assignment operator on the elements in the range. If you pass std::execution::par to copy_if(), it is your responsibility to guarantee that these parts are thread safe and can safely be executed in parallel.

Let's look at an example where we provide unsafe code and then see what we can do about it. Assume we have a vector of strings:

```
auto v = std::vector<std::string>{"Ada", "APL" /* ... */ };
```

If we want to compute the total size of all strings in the vector using a parallel algorithm, an inadequate way to do this would be to use std::for_each(), like this:

```
auto tot_size = size_t{0};
std::for_each(std::execution::par, v.begin(), v.end(),
              [&](const auto& s) {
  tot_size += s.size(); // Undefined behavior, data race!
});
```

Since the body of the function object is not thread safe (as it updates a shared variable from multiple threads), this code exhibits undefined behavior. We could, of course, protect the `tot_size` variable with a `std::mutex`, but that would defeat the whole purpose of executing this code in parallel, since the mutex would only allow one thread at a time to enter the body. Using an `std::atomic` data type would be another option, but that could also degrade the efficiency.

The solution here is to *not* use `std::for_each()` for this problem at all. Instead, we can use `std::transform_reduce()` or `std::reduce()`, which are tailor-made for this kind of job. Here is how you would do it using `std::reduce()`:

```
auto tot_size = std::reduce(std::execution::par, v.begin(), v.end(),
                            size_t{0}, [](auto i, const auto& s) {
  return i + s.size();   // OK! Thread safe
});
```

By getting rid of the mutable reference inside the lambda, the body of the lambda is now thread safe. The `const` reference to the `std::string` objects is fine, because it never mutates any string objects and therefore doesn't introduce any data races.

Normally, the code you pass to an algorithm is thread safe unless your function objects capture objects by reference or have other side effects such as writing to files.

Unsequenced policy

The unsequenced policy was added in C++20. It tells the algorithm that the loop is allowed to be vectorized using, for example, SIMD instructions. In practice, this means that you cannot use any synchronization primitives in the code you pass to the algorithm, since this could result in deadlocks.

To understand how a deadlock can occur, we will get back to the previous inadequate example when counting the total size of all strings in a vector. Assume that, instead of using `std::reduce()`, we protect the `tot_size` variable by adding a mutex, like this:

```
auto v = std::vector<std::string>{"Ada", "APL" /* ... */ };
auto tot_size = size_t{0};
```

```
auto mut = std::mutex{};
std::for_each(std::execution::par, v.begin(), v.end(),
              [&](const auto& s) {
    auto lock = std::scoped_lock{mut}; // Lock
    tot_size += s.size();
  }                                     // Unlock
);
```

This code is now safe to execute using std::execution::par, but it is very inefficient. If we were to change the execution policy to std::execution::unseq, the result would not only be an inefficient program but also a program that runs the risk of deadlocking!

The unsequenced execution policy tells the algorithm that it may reorder the instruction of our code in a way that is normally not allowed by the optimizing compiler.

For the algorithm to benefit from vectorization, it needs to read multiple values from the input range, and then apply SIMD instructions to multiple values at once. Let's analyze what two iterations in the loop of for_each() could look like, with and without reorderings. Here are two loop iterations without any reorderings:

```
{ // Iteration 1
  const auto& s = *it++;
  mut.lock();
  tot_size += s.size();
  mut.unlock();
}
{ // Iteration 2
  const auto& s = *it++;
  mut.lock();
  tot_size += s.size();
  mut.unlock();
}
```

The algorithm is allowed to merge these two iterations in the following way:

```
{ // Iteration 1 & 2 merged
  const auto& s1 = *it++;
  const auto& s2 = *it++;
  mut.lock();
  mut.lock();                  // Deadlock!
  tot_size += s1.size();       // Replace these operations
```

```
    tot_size += s2.size();      // with vectorized instructions
    mut.unlock();
    mut.unlock();
}
```

Trying to execute this code on the same thread will deadlock because we are trying to lock the very same mutex twice consecutively. In other words, when using the `std::execution::unseq` policy, you must make sure that the code you provide to the algorithm doesn't acquire any locks.

Note that the optimizing compiler is free to vectorize your code anytime. However, in those cases, it's up to the compiler to guarantee that the vectorization doesn't change the meaning of the program, just like any other optimizations that the compiler and hardware are allowed to perform. The difference here, when explicitly providing the `std::execute::unseq` policy to an algorithm, is that *you* guarantee that the code you provide is safe to vectorize.

Parallel unsequenced policy

The parallel unsequenced policy, `std::execution::par_unseq`, executes the algorithm in parallel like the parallel policy, with the addition that it may also vectorize the loop.

Apart from the four standard execution policies, standard library vendors can provide you with additional policies with custom behavior and put other constraints on the input. For example, the Intel Parallel STL library defines four custom execution policies that only accept random access iterators.

Exception handling

If you provide one of the four standard execution policies to an algorithm, your code must not throw exceptions, or the algorithm will call `std::terminate()`. This is a big difference from the normal single-threaded algorithms, which always propagate exceptions back to the caller:

```
auto v = {1, 2, 3, 4};
auto f = [](auto) { throw std::exception{}; };
try {
  std::for_each(v.begin(), v.end(), f);
} catch (...) {
  std::cout << "Exception caught\n";
}
```

Running the same code with an execution policy results in a call to
`std::terminate()`:

```
try {
  std::for_each(std::execution::seq, v.begin(), v.end(), f);
} catch (...) {
  // The thrown std:::exception never reaches us.
  // Instead, std::terminate() has been called
}
```

You might think that this means the parallel algorithms are declared `noexcept`, but that's not the case. Many parallel algorithms need to allocate memory, and therefore the standard parallel algorithms themselves are allowed to throw `std::bad_alloc`.

It should also be said that execution policies provided by other libraries may handle exceptions in a different way.

Now, we will move on to discuss some of the algorithms that were added and modified when the parallel algorithms were first introduced in C++17.

Additions and changes to parallel algorithms

Most algorithms in the standard library are available as parallel versions straight out the box. However, there are some noteworthy exceptions, including `std::accumulate()` and `std::for_each()`, as their original specifications required in-order execution.

std::accumulate() and std::reduce()

The `std::accumulate()` algorithm cannot be parallelized as it must be executed in the order of the elements, which is not possible to parallelize. Instead, a new algorithm called `std::reduce()` has been added, which works just like `std::accumulate()` with the exception that it is executed unordered.

With commutative operations, their results are the same, as the order of accumulation doesn't matter. In other words, given a range of integers:

```
const auto r = {1, 2, 3, 4};
```

accumulating them by addition or multiplication:

```
auto sum =
  std::accumulate(r.begin(), r.end(), 0, std::plus<int>{});
```

```
auto product =
  std::accumulate(r.begin(), r.end(), 1, std::multiplies<int>{});
```

would yield the same result as invoking `std::reduce()` instead of `std::accumulate()`, as both the addition and multiplication of integers are commutative. For example:

$$(1 + 2 + 3 + 4) = (3 + 1 + 4 + 2) \; and \; (1 \cdot 2 \cdot 3 \cdot 4) = (3 \cdot 2 \cdot 1 \cdot 4)$$

But, if the operation is not commutative, the result is *non-deterministic* since it depends on the order of the arguments. For example, if we were to accumulate a list of strings as follows:

```
auto v = std::vector<std::string>{"A", "B", "C"};
auto acc = std::accumulate(v.begin(), v.end(), std::string{});
std::cout << acc << '\n'; // Prints "ABC"
```

this code will always produce the string `"ABC"`. But, by using `std::reduce()`, the characters in the resulting string could be in any order because string concatenation is not commutative. In other words, the string `"A"` + `"B"` is not equal to `"B"` + `"A"`. Therefore, the following code using `std::reduce()` might produce different results:

```
auto red = std::reduce(v.begin(), v.end(), std::string{});
std::cout << red << '\n';
// Possible output: "CBA" or "ACB" etc
```

An interesting point related to performance is that floating-point math is not commutative. By using `std::reduce()` on floating-point values, the results may vary, but it also means that `std::reduce()` is potentially much faster than `std::accumulate()`. This is because `std::reduce()` is allowed to reorder operations and utilize SIMD instructions in a way that `std::accumulate()` isn't allowed to do when using strict floating-point math.

std::transform_reduce()

As an addition to the standard library algorithms, `std::transform_reduce()` has also been added to the `<numeric>` header. It does exactly what it says: it transforms a range of elements as `std::transform()` and then applies a function object. This accumulates them out of order, like `std::reduce()`:

```
auto v = std::vector<std::string>{"Ada","Bash","C++"};
auto num_chars = std::transform_reduce(
  v.begin(), v.end(), size_t{0},
  [](size_t a, size_t b) { return a + b; },      // Reduce
```

```
  [](const std::string& s) { return s.size(); } // Transform
);
// num_chars is 10
```

Both `std::reduce()` and `std::transform_reduce()` were added to C++17 when parallel algorithms were introduced. Another necessary change was to adjust the return type of `std::for_each()`.

std::for_each()

A somewhat rarely used property of `std::for_each()` is that it returns the function object passed into it. This makes it possible to use `std::for_each()` to accumulate values inside a stateful function object. The following examples demonstrate a possible use case:

```
struct Func {
  void operator()(const std::string& s) {
    res_ += s;
  };
  std::string res_{};    // State
};
auto v = std::vector<std::string>{"A", "B", "C"};
auto s = std::for_each(v.begin(), v.end(), Func{}).res_;
// s is "ABC"
```

This usage is similar to what we can achieve using `std::accumulate()` and therefore also exhibits the same problem when trying to parallelize it: executing the function object out of order would yield non-deterministic results as the invocation order is undefined. Consequently, the parallel version of `std::for_each()` simply returns void.

Parallelizing an index-based for-loop

Even though I recommend using algorithms, sometimes a raw, index-based for-loop is required for a specific task. The standard library algorithms provide an equivalent of a range-based for-loop by including the algorithm `std::for_each()` in the library.

However, there is no algorithm equivalent of an index-based for-loop. In other words, we cannot easily parallelize code like this by simply adding a parallel policy to it:

```
auto v = std::vector<std::string>{"A", "B", "C"};
for (auto i = 0u; i < v.size(); ++i) {
```

```
    v[i] += std::to_string(i+1);
  }
  // v is now { "A1", "B2", "C3" }
```

But let's see how we can build one by combining algorithms. As you will have already concluded, implementing parallel algorithms is complicated. But in this case, we will build a `parallel_for()` algorithm using `std::for_each()` as a building block, thus leaving the complex parallelism to `std::for_each()`.

Combining std::for_each() with std::views::iota()

An index-based for-loop based on a standard library algorithm can be created by combining `std::for_each()` with `std::views::iota()` from the ranges library (see *Chapter 6, Ranges and Views*). This is how it would look:

```
auto v = std::vector<std::string>{"A", "B", "C"};
auto r = std::views::iota(size_t{0}, v.size());
std::for_each(r.begin(), r.end(), [&v](size_t i) {
  v[i] += std::to_string(i + 1);
});
// v is now { "A1", "B2", "C3" }
```

This can then be further parallelized by using the parallel execution policy:

```
std::for_each(std::execution::par, r.begin(), r.end(), [&v](size_t i) {
  v[i] += std::to_string(i + 1);
});
```

As stated earlier, we have to be very careful when passing references to a lambda that will be invoked from multiple threads like this. By only accessing vector elements via the unique index i, we avoid introducing data races when mutating the strings in the vector.

Simplifying construction via a wrapper

In order to iterate the indices with a neat syntax, the previous code is wrapped into a utility function named `parallel_for()`, as shown here:

```
template <typename Policy, typename Index, typename F>
auto parallel_for(Policy&& p, Index first, Index last, F f) {
  auto r = std::views::iota(first, last);
```

```
    std::for_each(p, r.begin(), r.end(), std::move(f));
}
```

The `parallel_for()` function template can then be used directly like this:

```
auto v = std::vector<std::string>{"A", "B", "C"};
parallel_for(std::execution::par, size_t{0}, v.size(),
             [&](size_t i) { v[i] += std::to_string(i + 1); });
```

As the `parallel_for()` is built upon `std::for_each()`, it accepts any policy that `std::for_each()` accepts.

We will wrap this chapter up with a short introductory overview of GPUs and how they can be used for parallel programming, now and in the future.

Executing algorithms on the GPU

Graphics processing units (GPUs) were originally designed and used for processing points and pixels for computer graphics rendering. Briefly, what the GPUs did was retrieve buffers of pixel data or vertex data, perform a simple operation on each buffer individually, and store the result in a new buffer (to eventually be displayed).

Here are some examples of simple, independent operations that could be executed on the GPU at an early stage:

- Transform a point from world coordinates to screen coordinates
- Perform a lighting calculation at a specific point (by lighting calculation, I am referring to calculating the color of a specific pixel in an image)

As these operations could be performed in parallel, the GPUs were designed for executing small operations in parallel. Later on, these graphics operations became programmable, although the programs were written in terms of computer graphics (that is, the memory reads were done in terms of reading colors from a texture, and the result was always written as a color to a texture). These programs are called **shaders**.

Over time, more shader-type programs were introduced, and shaders gained more and more low-level options, such as reading and writing raw values from buffers instead of color values from textures.

Technically, a CPU commonly consists of a few general-purpose cached cores, whereas a GPU consists of a huge number of highly specialized cores. This means that parallel algorithms that scale well are highly suitable to execute on a GPU.

GPUs have their own memory and before an algorithm can execute on the GPU, the CPU needs to allocate memory in the GPU memory and copy data from main memory to GPU memory. The next thing that happens is that the CPU launches a routine (also called a kernel) on the GPU. Finally, the CPU copies data back from the GPU memory into the main memory, making it accessible for "normal" code executing on the CPU. The overhead incurred by copying data back and forth between the CPU and the GPU is one of the reasons why GPUs are more suitable for batch processing tasks where throughput is more important than latency.

There are several libraries and abstraction layers available today that make GPU programming accessible from C++, but standard C++ offers nearly nothing in this area. However, the parallel execution policies `std::execution::par` and `std::execution::par_unseq` allow compilers to move the execution of standard algorithms from the CPU to the GPU. One example of this is NVC++, the NVIDIA HPC compiler. It can be configured to compile standard C++ algorithms for execution on NVIDIA GPUs.

If you want to learn more about the current status of C++ and GPU programming, I highly recommend the talk *GPU Programming with modern C++* by Michael Wong (`https://accu.org/video/spring-2019-day-3/wong/`) from the ACCU 2019 conference.

Summary

In this chapter, you have learned about the complexity of handcrafting an algorithm to execute in parallel. You also now know how to analyze, measure, and tune the efficiency of parallel algorithms. The insights you gained while learning about parallel algorithms will have deepened your understanding of the requirements and the behaviors of the parallel algorithms found in the C++ standard library. C++ comes with four standard execution policies, which can be extended by compiler vendors. This opens up the door for utilizing the GPU for standard algorithms. The next C++ standard, C++23, will most likely add increased support for parallel programming on the GPU.

You have now reached the end of the book. Congratulations! Performance is an important aspect of code quality. But too often, performance comes at the expense of other quality aspects, such as readability, maintainability, and correctness. Mastering the art of writing efficient and clean code requires practical training. My hope is that you have learned things from this book that you can incorporate into your day-to-day life while creating stunning software.

Solving performance problems usually comes down to a willingness to investigate things further. More often than not, it requires understanding the hardware and underlying OS well enough to be able to draw conclusions from measurement data. This book has scratched the surface in these areas when I've felt it necessary. After writing about C++20 features in this second edition, I'm now looking forward to starting to use these features in my profession as a software developer. As I've mentioned previously, a lot of the code presented in this book is only partially supported by the compilers today. I will keep updating the GitHub repository and adding information about compiler support. Best of luck!

Share your experience

Thank you for taking the time to read this book. If you enjoyed this book, help others to find it. Leave a review at https://www.amazon.com/dp/1839216549.

Other Books
You May Enjoy

If you enjoyed this book, you may be interested in these other books by Packt:

Modern C++ Programming Cookbook - Second Edition

Marius Bancila

ISBN: 978-1-80020-898-8

- Understand the new C++20 language and library features and the problems they solve

- Become skilled at using the standard support for threading and concurrency for daily tasks

- Leverage the standard library and work with containers, algorithms, and iterators

- Solve text searching and replacement problems using regular expressions

- Work with different types of strings and learn the various aspects of compilation
- Take advantage of the file system library to work with files and directories
- Implement various useful patterns and idioms
- Explore the widely used testing frameworks for C++

Extreme C

Kamran Amini

ISBN: 978-1-78934-362-5

- Build advanced C knowledge on strong foundations, rooted in first principles
- Understand memory structures and compilation pipeline and how they work, and how to make most out of them
- Apply object-oriented design principles to your procedural C code
- Write low-level code that's close to the hardware and squeezes maximum performance out of a computer system
- Master concurrency, multithreading, multi-processing, and integration with other languages
- Unit Testing and debugging, build systems, and inter-process communication for C programming

Index

Symbols

&& modifier
applying, to class member functions 36

A

ABA problem 366
abstractions
in programming languages 2-4
algorithm library
limitations 174, 176
sorting algorithms 160
algorithms, from the standard library
binary search, using 138, 139
certain conditions, testing for 139
clamp function 141, 142
elements, counting 140, 141
elements, generating 136, 137
elements, searching 137, 138
elements, sorting 137
maximum function 141, 142
minimum function 141, 142
sequence, iterating over 135, 136
Amdahl's law 467, 468
using 89, 90
amortized time complexity 74-76
arena 221
building 221-225
fixed-size allocations 221
limited lifetime 222
single-threaded 221
associative containers 109, 110
asymptotic computational complexity 68-73
asynchronous tasks 335, 336
testing, with sync_wait() 454

atomic references
using 371, 372
atomic variables 363
auto keyword
using, for automatic type deduction 17
using, for variables 19
using, in function signatures 18
automatic type deduction
auto keyword, using 17
awaitable types 440, 441
awaiting coroutine
resuming 446-448

B

barriers
using 354, 355
Basic Linear Algebra Library (uBLAS) 320
best practices, constrained algorithms 160
container copies, avoiding 170, 171
data, sorting 160, 161
data sorting, performance evaluation 162
data sorting, use cases 162
big O notation 68-73
growth rate 73
binary_search() 70
binary semaphore 359
blocks 101
Boost.Fiber 402
Boost.Asio
using, for concurrent server 459
Boost library 15
bounded buffer
demonstrating, with semaphores 359-362
bugs 40

C

C++ 5
deterministic destruction 13
drawbacks 15
need for 1
object ownership 12
versus, programming languages 5
C++ atomic support,
    concurrent programming 363
atomic flags 365
atomic wait and notify 366
lock-free property 364
C++ code
optimizations 76
workflow 77, 78
C++, features
portability 5
robustness 5
zero-cost abstractions 2
C++ performance
versus, programming languages
    performance 6-8
C++ references
used, for avoiding null objects 13, 14
cache thrashing 102
callback-based API
wrapping 455-459
call frame 394
calling conventions 393
capture block 53
capture by reference, versus capture by
    value 54
used, for capturing all variables 58, 59
variables, initializing 55, 56
C function pointers
assigning, to lambda expressions 60
class invariant 41-43
class template argument deduction
    (CTAD) 241
code and hot spots 82, 83
code and hot spots, profilers
instrumentation profilers 83-85
sampling profilers 85-87
comparison operators
implementing 299, 300
compile-time hash function

implementing 270
compile-time hash sum calculation
advantages 269
compressed pair 232
reference link 232
computer memory
properties 99-103
concatenated proxy
assigning 310, 311
concatenated strings
comparing, proxy objects used 307, 308
concatenated strings, of size 50
comparing, for performance
    evaluation 311, 312
concepts 255, 256
defining 259
constraining types, using with 260
in standard library 264
concurrency 326, 327
benefits 326
concurrent programming 336, 337
atomic references 370
difficulties 326, 327
shared_ptr, using in multithreaded
    environment 367, 368
shared_ptr instance, protecting 369, 370
concurrent programming, performance
    guidelines 380
blocking operations, avoiding 380
contention, avoiding 380
false sharing 383
number, of threads/CPU cores 381
thread affinity 382
thread priorities 381
concurrent server
with Boost.Asio 459
concurrent server, Boost.Asio
connecting 462, 463
implementing 460, 461, 462
running 462, 463
constant expressions
constexpr function, evaluating in
    runtime context 248
if constexpr statement 249, 250
immediate function, declaring
    with consteval 249
programming errors, checking at

compile time 253
    programming with 247, 248
const auto
    using 22
const reference 20
consteval
    used, for declaring immediate function 249
constexpr function
    evaluating, in runtime context 248
constrained algorithms 134
    complexity guarantees 154, 155
    features 148-155
    projections, using 152, 153
    using, best practices 160
constraints 255, 256
    adding, to code 263, 264
    Point2D template, constrained
        version 261-263
    Point2D template, unconstrained
        version 256, 257
    syntactic overview 259
constructing objects
    avoiding, with proxy objects 307
constructor parameters
    moving 39
consumers 346
container adaptors 114
    priority queue 115, 116
containers 213
contention 334
continuation bit 434
contracts 41
    asserts, disabling 44
    asserts, enabling 44
    maintaining 43, 44
copy-and-swap 49
copy elision 36
    reference link 37
coroutine
    abstraction 388-390
    examples 386-388
    executing, on CPU 391
    performance, measuring 438
    resuming 395-398
    suspending 395-398
    using 430
coroutine frame 395, 405

Coroutine Handle 405
Coroutine State 405
CppCoro library
    URL 404
CPU registers
    using 391-393
creative operator overloading 321
custom comparator functions
    using 152
customization points
    efficiency 419
    generality 418
custom memory allocator 225-229
custom memory management 220, 221
    debugging and diagnostics 220
    performance 221
    sandboxing 220
custom memory resource
    implementing 234, 235

D

data races 331
    avoiding 333
    example 331, 332
data structures
    using, in generic algorithms 157-159
deadlock 334
decltype(auto)
    used, for forwarding return type deduction 19
default-created move-assignments
    using, pitfall 34, 35
delete operators 201-203
delta encoding 432-434
    variable byte encoding 434-437
Design by Contract 40, 44
divide-and-conquer algorithm 477
dynamic sized heterogenous collections 291
    std::variant 292, 293

E

eager evaluation 306
    versus lazy evaluation 306, 307
Eigen
    URL 320
equal_range() 138, 139

error handling 44
  programming errors 45
  recoverable runtime errors 47
  runtime errors 45
error messages 257, 258
exceptions
  handling 445
execution time
  speedup 79, 80
explicit suspend points 442

F

features, constrained algorithms 148
fibers 399
final suspend point 442
first in, first out (FIFO) 114
fork-join model
  demonstrating, with std::barrier 355-357
for-loop
  using 166
forwarding reference 21
function objects
  used, for creating lambda expressions 52
functions
  executing, on CPU 391
function signatures
  auto keyword, using 18

G

gap encoding 432
Generator class
  used, for solving generator problems 426
  using 423, 424
  using, for iterator implementation 428, 429
generator problems
  eager linear range, implementing 427
  lazy version, implementing with
    callback 427, 428
  solving, with Generator class 426
generators 419
  implementing 419-423
  using, real-world example 431, 432
generic algorithms
  data structures, using 157, 159
  non-generic algorithms, transforming to 156
  using 156

  writing 156
generic interfaces 257, 258
generic lambdas 65
generic modulus function
  example 252, 253
get_bitmap_resource()
  evaluating, with PrehashedString 273, 274
global functions
  overloading 302, 303
goroutines 399
GPU
  parallel algorithms, executing on 496, 497
green threads 399

H

handcrafted for loop
  using 166
hash 111
heap memory 198, 199
heterogenous collections 279
  std::pair, using 281
  std::tuple 281
hyperthreading 340

I

if constexpr statement 249, 251
  comparing, with runtime
    polymorphism 251, 252
  generic modulus function, example 252, 253
immediate function 249
  declaring, with consteval 249
implicit suspend points 442
index-based for-loop
  construction, simplifying via
    wrapper 495, 496
  parallelizing 494, 495
  std::for_each() library, combining with
    std::views::iota() library 495
initial suspend point 442
instruction pointer 391
instructions
  using 391-393
instrumentation profilers 83-85
interfaces
  designing, with error handling 40
invariant 41

inverted index 431
Iterator library 134
iterators 142
   categories 145-147
   past-the-end iterator 143, 144
   responsibilities 142
   sentinel value 143

L

lambda expressions
   and class, similarity between 54, 55
   and std::function 61
   C function pointers, assigning to 60
   syntax 52, 53
   types 60
   used, for creating function objects 52
lambda member variables
   mutating 57
   mutating, from compiler's perspective 58
last in, first out (LIFO) 114
latches
   using 352, 353
lazy evaluation 305
   versus eager evaluation 306, 307
LengthProxy object
   implementing 315, 316
   lengths, calculating with 318
   lengths, comparing with 317
   misuse, preventing 318, 319
libc++
   reference link 219
linear_search() 68
lock-free programming 377
   example 377-380
lock-free queue 377-380
loop invariant 41
lower_bound() 138

M

mathematics 313-315
memcpy() 155
memory
   objects 199
   physical memory 192
memory alignment 203-206
memory management unit (MMU) 192

memory model 373
   atomics and memory orders 375-377
   instruction reordering 373, 374
memory ownership 210, 211
   containers 213
   resources, handling 211-213
   smart pointers 213, 214
memory pages 192, 193
memory pool 221
metaprogramming
   examples 264
   generic safe cast function, creating 265-268
   hash strings, at compile time 268, 269
microbenchmarking 87, 88
   Amdahl's law, using 89, 90
   example 91-96
   limitations 92
move semantics 24
   default move semantics 31, 32
   named variables 29, 31
   resource acquisition 26-29
   rule of five 26-29
   rule of zero 33
   rvalue 29, 31
mutable reference 21
mutex 333, 334

N

named variable 30
new operators 201, 202, 203
non-generic algorithms
   transforming, to generic algorithms 156
non-performance-related C++ language
     features 8
   const correctness 11
   value semantics 9
non-standard containers
   reference link 228
null objects
   avoiding, with C++ references 13, 14

O

objects
   copy-constructing 24, 25
   creating 199
   delete operators 201-203

deleting 199
in memory 199
move-constructing 25
new operators 201-203
placement new 200, 201
resources, swapping 25
operator< 151
operator== 151
ordered associative containers 110
ordinary functions 388

P

padding 208-210
page fault 192
pagefile 192
paging 193
parallel algorithms 466
additions 492
changes 492
evaluating 466, 467
executing, on GPU 496, 497
parallel arrays 123-130
parallelism 327
need for 466
parallel standard library algorithms 486, 487
exception handling 491, 492
parallel standard library algorithms,
execution policies 487
parallel policy 488, 489
parallel unsequenced policy 491
sequenced policy 488
unsequenced policy 489, 490, 491
parallel std::copy_if() algorithm
elements in parallel, coping into destination
range 483
implementing 480, 481
implementing, in inner function 481
implementing, in outer function 482
performance evaluation 485, 486
sparse range, moving sequentially into
continuous range 484
synchronized write position, using 481
parallel std::count_if() algorithm
implementing 479
parallel std::transform() algorithm
divide and conquer 474, 475

implementing 468
parallel std::transform() algorithm, divide and
conquer implementation 475
performance evaluation 476-478
parallel std::transform() algorithm, naive
implementation 469, 470
performance evaluation 470-473
shortcomings 473, 474
pass-by-value
applicability 37, 38
non-applicability scenarios 38
using 39
past-the-end iterator 143, 144
performance considerations 120
API functions, using 121-123
complexity guarantees and overhead,
balancing between 120, 121
performance consideration, std::function 63
dynamically allocated memory, for captured
variables 63
prevented inline optimizations 63
run-time computation 64
performance counters 80, 81
Performance Monitoring Counters (PMC) 80
performance properties 78
concepts 78, 79
performance testing
best practices 81, 82
pipe operator 322, 323
using, as extension method 321
placement new 200, 201
Point2D template
constrained version 261-263
unconstrained version 256, 257
pointers
const-propagation 22, 23
polymorphic memory allocators
using 230-233
postcondition 41
precondition 41
prefaulting 353
prefetcher 103
PrehashedString class
constructing 270, 272
evaluating 272
used, for evaluating
get_bitmap_resource() 273

priority inversion **381**
process memory **194, 195**
  heap memory 198, 199
  stack memory 195-197
profilers **82, 83**
  instrumentation profilers 83-85
  sampling profilers 85-87
producers **346**
program counter (PC) **391**
programming errors **40, 45**
  bugs, finding with asserts 46
  checking, at compile time 253
  performance impact 46, 47
  problem space, narrowing by assumptions 45
  triggering, with static_assert() at compile
      time 254, 255
  triggering, with static_assert() at runtime 254
programming languages
  abstractions 2, 3, 4
  versus, C++ 5
programming languages performance
  versus, C++ performance 6-8
projections **152**
  implementing 299, 300
promise object **405**
proxy
  implementing 309, 310
proxy objects **305, 307, 321**
  constructing objects, avoiding with 307
  used, for comparing concatenated
      strings 307, 308

R

ranges **142, 144**
Ranges library **134**
  features 173, 174
  future 189
  using 429
  views 176, 177
range views **184**
recoverable runtime errors **47**
  exceptions 47, 48
  performance 51
  resource acquisition 50
  valid state, preserving 48-50
reflect() function

creating 301
reflection **300**
  C++ libraries, simplifying 301
  using 302
reflection capabilities
  testing 303
Resource Acquisition Is Initialization
    (RAII) **212**
Return Object **405**
return type deduction
  forwarding, with decltype(auto) 19
return value optimization (RVO) **36**
return values
  handling 445
rudimentary task type
  implementing 442-445
rule of five **26**
rule of three **28**
rule of zero **33**
  empty destructors 33, 34
runtime error **40, 45**
  recoverable runtime errors 40, 47
  unrecoverable runtime errors 40
runtime polymorphism
  comparison 251, 252
Runtime Type Information (RTTI) **4**
rvalue **29, 31**
rvalue modifier **310**

S

safe_cast()
  cases 265
sampling profilers **85-87**
sampling views **186**
semaphores
  used, for counting resource 358, 359
  used, for demonstrating bounded
      buffer 359-362
  used, for signalling 358, 359
sentinel values **143**
separate chaining **111**
sequence containers **104**
  basic_string 109
  deque 107
  forward_list 108
  list 108, 109

selecting, considerations 104
vectors and arrays 105, 107
sequential consistency 376, 377
shaders 496
shared memory 329, 330
shared pointer 214, 215
simple two-dimensional vector
    class 312, 313
small object optimization 217-220
small-size optimization 109
smart pointers 213, 214
shared pointer 214, 215
unique pointer 214
weak pointer 216
spatial locality 101
spurious wakeup 347
sqrt computations
performance evaluation 319, 320
postponing 312
stack
using 391-393
stack frame 394
stackful coroutines 399
context switching 401
memory footprint 400
performance cost 400
stackless coroutines 399
as member functions 415, 416
context switching 401
creating, with lambda expressions 416, 417
customization points 418
dangling references, avoiding 413
dangling references, preventing 418
errors, handling 418
guidelines, for preventing dangling
    references 418
in C++ 402
memory footprint 400
parameters, passing 413-415
passing around 411
performance cost 400
promise type 409, 410
return object 408, 409
state, allocating 411, 412
working 406-408
stack memory 195-197
properties 195

Stack Pointer (SP) 392
standard library
views 184
standard library algorithms 134
evolution 134, 135
used, for solving issues 135
standard algorithms, using over raw for-loops
comparing, with zero optimization 169
exceptions and performance problems 165
optimizations, exploiting 168, 169
real-world code base example 164, 165
standard library containers 104
associative containers 109
container adaptors 114
sequence containers 104
Standard Template Library (STL) 134
stateless lambdas 53
static_assert()
using, at compile time 254, 255
std::abort 338
std::accumulate() algorithm 492, 493
std::advance 145
std::align 205
std::align_val_t 207
std::all_of 357
std::allocator 226-227
std::allocator_traits 227
std::any 291, 292
std::any_cast 291
std::any_of 285
std::array 104, 107
std::async 351
std::atomc_flag 370
std::atomic 372
std::atomic_flag 365
std::atomic_int 363
std::atomic_ref 370
std::atomic_store 370
std::back_inserter 150, 151
std::bad_optional_access 277
std::bad_variant 298
std::barrier 355-357
std::basic_string 109
std::binary_semaphore 359
std::bitset 130
std::chrono::steady_clock 84
std::clamp 141

std::condition_variable 346
std::construct_at 201
std::copy 33, 155
std::copy_if 480
std::coroutine_handle 403
std::coroutine_traits 403
std::count 126, 147
std::count_if 479
std::counting_semaphore 359
std::current_exception 418, 445
std::decay 246
std::defer_lock 345
std::deque 104, 107
std::destroy_at 201
std::distance 139
std::equal 264
std::erase 106
std::erase_if 106
std::exception_ptr 418, 445
std::execute::unseq 491
std::execution 487
std::execution::par 487, 488
std::execution::par_unseq 491, 497
std::execution::parallel_policy 487
std::execution::seq 488
std::execution::unseq 490, 491
std::experimental::propagate_const 23
std::fill 155, 353
std::find 151, 164, 168
std::find_if 152
std::floating_point 259
std::fmod 252
std::for_each() 494
std::forward_list 104, 108
std::free 202
std::function
    and lambda expressions 61
    performance consideration 63
    simple Button class, implementing
        with 62, 63
std::future 443
std::generate 158
std::get 282
std::hardware_destructive_interference_size
    383
std::has_single_bit 205
std::hash 271

std::holds_alternative 293
std::integral 260
std::ios::ate 109
std::iota 137, 476
std::jthread 341
std::latch
    used, for initializing threads 353, 354
std::lerp 426
std::less 152
std::list 104, 108
std::lock 345
std::make_shared 214
std::make_tuple 281
std::make_unique 214
std::malloc 200
std::map 110
std::max 141
std::max_align_t 205
std::max_element 151
std::memcpy 363
std::min 141
std::minmax 280
std::move()
    avoiding 36
std::move_if_noexcept 106
std::multimap 110
std::multiset 110
std::mutex 343, 344
std::next 154
std::nth_element 161
std::optional 276
std::packaged_task 350
std::pair
    using 280, 281
std::partial_sort 161
std::pmr::memory_resource 233, 234
std::pmr::monotonic_buffer_resource 233
std::pmr::new_delete_resource 233
std::pmr::polymorphic_allocator 232
std::pmr::set 234
std::pmr::vector 235
std::prev 145
std::priority_queue 114
std::promise 348
std::queue 114
std::ranges::any_of 140
std::ranges::binary_search 138

std::ranges::common_view 188
std::ranges::copy 177
std::ranges::filter_view 178
std::ranges::istream_view 187
std::ranges::max_element 171, 174
std::ranges::ref_view 178
std::ranges::subrange 159
std::rangers::transform 150
std::ranges::transform_view 180
std::ranges::view 184
std::reduce() 492, 493
std::remove_cvref 244
std::rotate()
  advantages 167
std::scoped_lock 213, 344
std::set 110
std::shared_ptr 12, 213
std::span 119, 187
  used, for eliminating array decay 119, 120
std::sqrt 312, 314
std::stack 114
std::stop_token 342
std::string 109
std::string_view 117, 187
std::suspend_always 403, 440
std::suspend_never 403, 440
std::swap 25
std::vector 105
std::this_thread::get_id 337, 338
std::this_thread::sleep_for 337, 338
std::thread 339
std::thread::hardware_concurrency 340
std::thread::joinable 341
std::thread::native_handle 381
std::tie()
  using 300
std::transform 150, 164, 177, 467
std::transform_reduce() 493
std::tuple 281
  algorithms, implementing 285, 286
  elements, accessing 286
  examples 299
  members, accessing 282, 283
  members, iterating 283
  structured bindings 287
  unrolling 283, 285
  variadic template parameter pack 288

std::uniform_int_distribution 356
std::uninitialized_fill_n 201
std::unique 148
std::unique_lock 345
std::unique_ptr 213
std::unitialized_fill_n 201
std::unordered_map 110
std::unordered_multimap 110
std::unordered_multiset 110
std::unordered_set 110
std::valarray 147
std::variant 292, 293
  advantages 292
  container values, accessing 297, 298
  global function std::get() 298
  exception safety 293, 294
  used, for heterogenous collections 296
  visiting 294-296
std::vector 104
std::views::common 145
std::views::counted 159
std::views::drop 186
std::views::drop_while 186
std::views::filter 186
std::views::iota 185
std::views::join 185
std::views::split 185
std::views::take 184
std::views::transform 185
std::visit 294
std::weak_ptr 213
string_view
  used, for avoiding copies 117, 118
structured bindings 287
structured concurrency 463
subroutine 388
  calling from 393-395
  returning from 393-395
suspend/resume point 389
swap file 192
swap space 192
symmetric transfer 448
synchronization primitives, in C++20 352
  barriers 354, 355
  latches 352, 353
  resource, counting with
    semaphores 358, 359

signalling, with semaphores 358, 359
synchronous tasks 335, 336
sync_wait()
    asynchronous tasks, testing 454
    implementing 451, 452
SyncWaitTask
    implementing 452-454
syntactic overview
    constraining types, with concepts 260, 261
    function overloading 261
    new concepts, defining 259
    of constraints and concepts 259

T

tail call optimization 448
task
    waiting to complete, synchronously 450
tearing 332
template metaprogramming 238, 239
    abbreviated function template 243
    advantages 238
    compiler, handling template
        function 242, 243
    creating 239, 240
    integers, using as template
        parameters 241, 242
    specializations, providing 242
    variable type, receiving with
        decltype 244, 245
temporal locality 101
test and test-and-set 365
thrashing 194
**thread support library, concurrent
      programming 337**
    condition variable 346-348
    critical sections, protecting 343-345
    data, running 348, 349
    deadlocks, avoiding 345
    errors, handling 348, 349
    joinable thread 341-343
    tasks 350, 351
    threads 337-339
    thread states 339-341
time slicing 328, 329
to_vector() 182
torn reads 332
torn writes 332

type traits 245
    categories 245, 246
    using 246

U

unique pointer 214
universal reference 21
unordered associative containers 110
unordered sets and maps 111
    equal value 112-114
    hash policy 114
    hash value 112-114
upper_bound() 138, 139
user-level threads 399
utility views 186

V

variable byte encoding 434
variadic template parameter pack 288
    constructing 289
    function, example with variadic number
        of arguments 288
views 117
    generating views 185
    sampling views 186
    transforming views 185
    utility views 186
views, Ranges library 176, 177
    composable 178, 179
    lazy evaluated 183, 184
    materialized, into containers 181, 182
    non-owning ranges, with complexity
        guarantees 180
    range adaptors 179, 180
views, Standard Library 184
virtual address space 192
void tasks
    supporting 448, 449

W

weak pointer 216

Z

zero-overhead principle 4

Made in the USA
Middletown, DE
19 September 2021

48556940R00303